ASSESSMENT IN APPLIED SPORT PSYCHOLOGY

ASSESSMENT IN APPLIED SPORT PSYCHOLOGY

Jim Taylor, PhD, CC-AASP

Taylor Prime Performance

Editor

Human Kinetics

Library of Congress Cataloging-in-Publication Data

Names: Taylor, Jim, 1958- editor.
Title: Assessment in applied sport psychology / Jim Taylor, editor.
Description: Champaign, IL : Human Kinetics, [2018] | Includes
  bibliographical references and index.
Identifiers: LCCN 2016044769 (print) | LCCN 2016045547 (ebook) | ISBN
  9781492526346 (print) | ISBN 9781492550990 (e-book)
Subjects: | MESH: Sports--psychology | Athletes--psychology | Psychology,
  Applied
Classification: LCC RC451.4.A83 (print) | LCC RC451.4.A83 (ebook) | NLM QT
  260 | DDC 616.890088/796--dc23
LC record available at https://lccn.loc.gov/2016044769

ISBN: 978-1-4925-2634-6 (print)

The web addresses cited in this text were current as of April 2017, unless otherwise noted.

Acquisitions Editors: Myles Schrag and Bridget Melton; **Developmental and Managing Editor:** Carly S. O'Connor; **Copyeditor:** Alisha Jeddeloh; **Indexer:** Katy Balcer; **Permissions Manager:** Dalene Reeder; **Graphic Designer:** Whitney Milburn; **Cover Designer:** Keri Evans; **Photographer (cover):** Jason Allen; **Photograph (cover):** © Human Kinetics; **Senior Art Manager:** Kelly Hendren; **Illustrations:** © Human Kinetics, unless otherwise noted; **Printer:** Sheridan Books

Printed in the United States of America   10 9 8 7 6 5 4 3 2 1

The paper in this book is certified under a sustainable forestry program.

Human Kinetics
Website: www.HumanKinetics.com

United States: Human Kinetics
P.O. Box 5076
Champaign, IL 61825-5076
800-747-4457
e-mail: info@hkusa.com

Canada: Human Kinetics
475 Devonshire Road Unit 100
Windsor, ON N8Y 2L5
800-465-7301 (in Canada only)
e-mail: info@hkcanada.com

Europe: Human Kinetics
107 Bradford Road
Stanningley
Leeds LS28 6AT, United Kingdom
+44 (0) 113 255 5665
e-mail: hk@hkeurope.com

For information about Human Kinetics' coverage in other areas of the world,
please visit our website: www.HumanKinetics.com   E6745

Assessment in Applied Sport Psychology is dedicated to two communities of people. First, it is dedicated to the sport psychology professionals worldwide who have inspired me and so many others to give our all in pursuit of our collective goal of helping athletes, coaches, and teams achieve their goals and dreams.

Second, this book is dedicated to the community of athletes, coaches, and parents who will be the ultimate recipients of what this book has to offer. Their passion, commitment, effort, sacrifice, and desire to be the best they can be provide the fuel that propels my colleagues and me to be the best we can be.

CONTENTS

PREFACE

Historically, the primary focus of graduate training in sport psychology has been to prepare graduates for academic careers in teaching and research. Over the last several decades, however, there has been a shift in training toward more applied work with athletes and teams, as evidenced by the establishment of the Association for Applied Sport Psychology (AASP), the establishment of Division 47 of the American Psychological Association (APA), and the creation by AASP of a certification program for professionals interested in applied sport psychology.

These graduate and certification programs have increasingly focused on preparing graduates for careers in sport psychology consulting. (In accordance with state laws restricting the use of *psychology* and *psychologist* to those professionals who are licensed psychologists, and for the sake of consistency of language, the terms *consulting* and *consultant* will be used throughout this book when referring to conducting assessments and providing services to athletes, coaches, and sport organizations.) This emphasis has resulted in extensive curricula with the objective of teaching students the knowledge and skills to help athletes and teams maximize performance and achieve greater success. These programs teach courses on subjects as wide ranging as motivation, confidence, counseling, leadership, and team cohesion, among many others.

Leaders in the field of applied sport psychology are attempting to create a model of graduate training that offers both curricular consistency and rigor in order to prepare graduates who enter the field to offer consumers uniformly quality services. This change is exemplified by the efforts since 2014 of the AASP, spearheaded by its founder, Dr. John Silva, to revamp curriculum development to better meet the needs of aspiring consultants. Part of this movement is a greater emphasis on practical skills, including assessment.

In an informal survey of members of the AASP and APA Division 47 listserv, both professors and students indicated that all graduate programs in applied sport psychology offer courses in assessment or include assessment in broader courses in applied sport psychology. However, the assessment coursework tends to focus on the scientific basis for assessment, including test measurement and validity and their use in research. Little emphasis has been placed on assessment as a means of evaluating and understanding individuals and teams in the real-world setting of consulting—despite the fact that the use of assessment in consulting is the intended purpose in these graduate programs.

It could be argued that assessment is essential to effective preparation because it is the foundation of effective work with athletes and teams. Why? Because without a clear understanding of a client, whether an individual athlete or a team, the most effective interventions can't be chosen and used.

One thing that has prevented a full appreciation of the value of assessment in the sport setting is a rather narrow view of what assessment comprises. Based on Taylor's review of the extant writings, his own experience as a consultant, and his teaching of an assessment course in a master's degree program in sport psychology in 2012 (from which this book idea emerged), the conventional wisdom is that assessment involves pencil-and-paper inventories (or their digital versions) or interviewing. Such a limited view of assessment prevents practitioners from taking advantage of a much wider range of information that can significantly deepen and broaden their understanding of their clients and their effectiveness in enhancing athletic performance.

Thus, the goal of *Assessment in Applied Sport Psychology* is to fill a void in our field's understanding of assessment, providing a book that plumbs the depth and breadth of this essential aspect of working with athletes, coaches, teams, and other stakeholders. A related goal is to provide academics, students, and professionals with a new and richer perspective on assessment and its vital role in the work of consultants.

What makes this book unique is its more expansive perspective of assessment, which goes well beyond the typical pencil-and-paper questionnaires and interviewing. This new vantage point provides a truly comprehensive understanding of the athlete. The book explores the traditional use of objective inventories and subjective assessment, but it also extends the notion of assessment to include

- personality and clinical assessment;
- psychophysiological measurement;
- observation of athletes in training and competition;
- corroboration from parents and coaches;
- coach and team effectiveness;
- parental involvement;
- use of assessment in sport organizations;
- talent identification;
- injury, rehabilitation, and pain;
- career transition; and
- consultant effectiveness.

Assessment in Applied Sport Psychology goes beyond the nuts and bolts of administering and evaluating assessment. It also explores other crucial issues in assessment, including ethical concerns and the impact of diversity on assessment and mental health screening.

This book provides students and professionals in our field with an increased appreciation for and an in-depth knowledge of essential issues related to understanding athletes and teams and a wide variety of assessment strategies. *Assessment in Applied Sport Psychology* has two fundamental objectives. The first is to help consultants gain a complete understanding of their clients through the use of a broad range of assessment tools. The second is to show them how to effectively and responsibly use assessments to better guide client conceptualization and intervention.

Book Structure

Assessment in Applied Sport Psychology is organized into three parts. Part I lays the groundwork for using assessment by exploring key contributors to its value, including the science and ethics, as well as the role of diversity, in responsible assessment. Part II examines the range of assessments you can use with athletes, including mental health screenings, personality tests, inventories, interviews, observations, and psychophysiological measures. Part III is devoted to special topics related to assessment, such as assessment of coaches, teams, and parents; talent identification; injury and concussions; career transitions; consulting with sport organizations; and consultant effectiveness.

Parts II and III offer a consistent structure that will help you gain the most value from the information provided. Each chapter in these sections includes sidebars that bring the assessments to life by providing examples of the use of the assessments within the athletic world and the benefits they offer to both the consultant and the clients. Chapters 4 through 15 feature chapter-ending tables called Assessment Tools and Their Availability, which provide specific information about the assessments, including the authors, purpose, references, and availability. Some assessments have "Contact the author" in the Availability column. These assessments are not readily available to the public and may require readers to submit requests directly to the authors of the assessments in order to obtain them. These requests will be granted at the discretion of the author of the assessment. Finally, each chapter concludes with a bulleted list of takeaways from the chapter.

Developing an Assessment Routine

An assessment protocol is much like the precompetitive routines that you help athletes develop. If you look at any group of athletes, all of their routines share two things. First, the shared goal is to maximally prepare the athletes for competitive success. Second, they share important components that are common to athletic readiness, including equipment, physical, and mental preparation. At the same time, for every group of athletes, you will find as many different precompetitive routines.

Similarly, there is no single ideal assessment or group of assessments for all consultants. You must choose yours based on your particular clientele and their needs and goals, as well as your theoretical and practical consulting orientation and your personality and interpersonal styles. The collective goal is to develop a comprehensive understanding of clients, with the aim of helping them achieve their athletic goals. The shared elements include the many psychological, emotional, behavioral, and social contributors to personal well-being and athletic performance that the assessments in this book intend to measure. But for any group of consultants, there are as many assessment protocols.

You want to create your own routine of assessments that is consistent with your education, training, and experience; your consulting style; and your clientele and their unique needs and goals. *Assessment in Applied Sport Psychology* was written to educate you about the wide range of assessment tools at your disposal and how you can use them ethically and effectively to foster a real understanding of your clients. The ultimate objective is to help you develop a comprehensive and deep portrait of your clients, with the goal of helping them become mentally prepared to perform their best and achieve their competitive goals.

eBook
available at
HumanKinetics.com

ACKNOWLEDGMENTS

I would first like to acknowledge the SportPsy listserv and the several essential things it provided in the creation of this book. I initially used the listserv to crowdsource the table of contents. What had begun as a 10-chapter book quickly grew to 17 chapters as colleagues from around the world suggested chapter topics that hadn't even occurred to me and that have added tremendously to the value this book will bring to our field. The listserv was also the resource from which I found colleagues with a generosity of spirit (and, realistically, the desire to add to their CVs for professional advancement and tenure, as well as personal satisfaction) who were willing to give their expertise and time in contributing to this book. As so many members of the listserv have experienced, whenever I have a question, there is always a colleague somewhere in the world willing to share their time and expertise to give me an answer.

I would also like to thank all 41 (yes, you read right, 41!) chapter authors for their remarkable commitment, egoless participation, collaborative spirit, quality writing, and (very importantly) adherence to deadlines. I always call this book *our* book, not *my* book, because it was a truly collective effort. I couldn't have done it without you!

I would like to express my deep appreciation for Carly O'Connor, our developmental editor at Human Kinetics, who steadily and joyfully shepherded all of us through the revision process that resulted in what I believe will be an important contribution to the field of applied sport psychology. In the previous books I have written and edited, there is always an unsettling sense of trepidation when the edited manuscript appears in my inbox and then when I first open the manuscript to confront the changes that are asked of us (my chapter contributors expressed the same feelings of uncertainty). Yet, Carly guided all of us through the revision process with a cool and compassionate hand, even when stress levels were high and emotions ran hot. As an author, when I finish a first draft of a book, I truly believe that it is exceptionally well written and that every word is essential and in its absolutely appropriate place. Yet, I can say without exception that every one of my books is always several magnitudes better when completed under the wise gaze of a skilled and experienced editor. Carly has unquestionably kept my streak of outstanding editors (and good fortune) intact.

A very special thanks and nod of gratitude to Myles Schrag, my acquisitions editor at Human Kinetics, without whom this book would never have come to fruition. His vision, determination, openness, tough love, voice of calm and reason, good cheer, and willingness to watch my back when I was challenged not only made this book possible but also a pleasure to be the editor of.

Finally, I would like to thank my wife, Sarah, and my daughters, Catie and Gracie, for their never-ending love and for their support of what has been (and will continue to be) the rewarding, yet sometimes quixotic, journey that is my career.

PART ONE

FOUNDATION OF ASSESSMENT IN SPORT PSYCHOLOGY CONSULTING

Part I lays the foundation of *Assessment in Applied Sport Psychology*. Chapter 1 offers a rationale for the role of assessment as a vital tool in sport psychology consulting for increasing understanding and explaining the practical value of your work. Chapter 2 details the science of assessment, providing you with a deeper appreciation of the quantitative and qualitative parameters of effective assessment. The goal of this chapter is to help you make informed decisions about the best assessment tools to meet the needs and goals of your clients.

Chapter 3 examines ethical issues that can arise when using assessment with an athletic population. It considers the primary ethical challenges that can occur and how you can best navigate the sometimes rocky ethical terrain you will face. Chapter 4 rounds out part I with an in-depth discussion of diversity in assessment. It challenges you to consider the impact of gender, race, religion, national identity, age, sexual orientation, language, and physical ability in your use of assessment with athletes.

CHAPTER 1

Importance of Assessment in Sport Psychology Consulting

Jim Taylor, PhD, CC-AASP

Thanks to Marshall Mintz and Michael Zito for their contributions to the Assessment Terminology section.

Is there anything more important to quality sport psychology consulting than assessment? To be sure, consultants need a deep knowledge of mental skills and how to use them with an athlete or team. Additionally, consultants must have a working knowledge of the sport in which their clients compete to ensure they offer information and mental tools to best enhance performance and enjoyment. However, as valuable as these aspects of consulting are, they would largely be for naught without effective assessment of the athletes or teams. Assessment is vital because it lays the foundation for all effective consulting: an understanding of the client.

Assessment Terminology

In your work with athletes, it is important that you and your clients share a common vocabulary. This appreciation of the language of assessment is important because it ensures understanding and acts as the foundation of knowledge that your clients will develop in your work together. This same approach applies to the relationship you will develop with *Assessment in Applied Sport Psychology* and its chapter authors. As this book explores the many facets of assess-

ment in consulting with athletes, coaches, teams, and others in the sport setting, it is essential to establish a common vocabulary so that you can gain the most from the information it offers.

To that end, we will delineate some key terminology that will form the basis of your knowledge as you explore and use assessment in your consulting. It is common in psychology to use the terms *assessment*, *measurement*, and *evaluation* interchangeably. However, these terms may have different meanings and constitute different professional activities. For instance, Cone (1995) characterizes *assessment* as "obtaining a snapshot-like view of a person at a moment in time in order to determine the person's status with respect to a cumulative knowledge or skill" (p. 201). Thus, you would perform an assessment to see where clients currently are on relevant sport psychological attributes.

Measurement, on the other hand, "can be seen as the dynamic act of charting changes in dimensional qualities of all or a portion of that repertoire over time" (Cone, 1995, p. 201). This distinction is subtle yet meaningful, characterized as the difference between the current state of a client (assessment) versus how that client has changed over the course of treatment (measurement). For example, you might measure confidence monthly during an intervention aimed at increasing an athlete's belief in his abilities, or you might measure an athlete's heart rate while under stress to track improvement due to a stress reduction program. These types of data collection can be useful for establishing baselines of psychological characteristics and tracking their trajectory over time.

Evaluation is the analysis, integration, and interpretation of the data collected from assessment or measurement. It involves using the gathered data to make a judgment about their meaning and value to clients. It creates a cohesive understanding of clients in relation to their performance challenges, needs, and goals. In a sense, evaluation is the end product of the data-collection process for the purpose of, for example, developing intervention plans.

Purpose of Assessment

To understand your athletes, you need a comprehensive knowledge of all aspects of the athletes that will affect their performance. This broad understanding involves who they are as athletes and, just as importantly, who they are as people. Assessment also tells clients a great deal about who you are and how you work and about your field more broadly.

Understanding the Person as an Athlete

The most obvious part of understanding involves the person as an athlete—that is, what makes her tick in training and competition. This understanding involves a wide range of psychology, including how athletes think, the emotions they experience, and the way they behave, particularly in the heat of competition. Specific components of athletes' psychology consist of their attitudes toward and relationships with success, failure, expectations, and competition. Mental factors that must be understood include motivation, confidence, intensity (e.g., energy, arousal, anxiety), focus, and emotions. Athletes' psychology can also include the mental tools athletes use in their preparation and performance, such as goal setting, mental imagery, routines, self-talk, and breathing. Furthermore, it can include their relationships with teammates, coaches, competitors, officials, and, importantly for young athletes, parents.

Even though consultants may be focusing on athletes' psychology, a true understanding of athletes must also include every area that affects performance, such as physical conditioning, technique, tactics, equipment, and team dynamics. Consultants need to know athletes' strengths and weaknesses in these areas, as well as how they approach their training and competitive performances.

Understanding the Athlete as a Person

In sport psychology there may be a tendency to view clients as athletes alone, forgetting that they are first and foremost people. For example, when athletes enter the field of competition, they don't leave their personness, so to speak, on the sidelines. Whoever they are as people will be expressed on the field as they pursue their athletic goals. Whatever weaknesses they hold as people, such as doubts, worries, or fears, will come out in their athletic performance. In a more positive light, whatever strengths they possess as people—whether determination, confidence, or resilience—will also emerge in practice and competition.

Just thinking about exploring the depth and breadth of a client's internal athletic life, much less her personal psyche, can be a daunting task. The athlete as person encompasses every aspect of who athletes are:

- Their innate dispositions, temperament, and tendencies (e.g., introverted or extroverted, stoic or emotional)
- Their values and priorities that act as signposts for their aspirations and goals
- Their beliefs about themselves (e.g., self-assessment, self-identity, self-esteem), which guide their internal dialogues, emotional reactions to situations, and the way they act on their world, interact with others, and perform in their sport
- The way they think and how this influences them both off and on the field (e.g.,

optimistic or pessimistic, critical or accepting, analytical or intuitive)

- Their emotional life, including their sensitivity, expressiveness, lability, and emotional reactions to setbacks and failure
- Their behavior in sport and nonsport settings
- The quality of their relationships and the way they interact with others (e.g., with empathy, support, divisiveness, or aggressiveness)

How Clients Understand Themselves

Self-knowledge on the part of athletes is an essential piece of the sport performance puzzle. Yet, the mental can lag behind the physical and technical facets of sport performance in terms of the athlete's appreciation, understanding, and development. Perhaps the most fundamental reason for this is that the physical and technical aspects of sport are readily observable and measurable. For example, if athletes want to determine their cardiovascular fitness, they can take a $\dot{V}O_2$max test. If they want to be evaluated technically, they can watch themselves on video or participate in biomechanical testing.

In contrast, the mental side of sport is quite ethereal; it can't be seen, touched, or measured directly. Also, whereas the physical and technical elements of sport are highly objective, the mental components are very subjective. From the outside, we can only indirectly measure an athlete's psychology. From the inside, athletes don't always have great insight into the psychological and emotional machinations that occur between their ears. In a sense, assessment can enable athletes to build a better relationship with themselves by helping them understand what makes them tick.

Assessment can be a powerful tool for helping athletes plumb the depths of their psyches both on and off the field. All assessment tools, whether interviews, mental status exams, personality tests, sport-specific inventories, or psychophysiological measures, can help athletes understand their mental strengths and areas in need of improvement. This understanding can

be valuable in several ways. Most obviously, assessment can clarify what areas athletes need to work on in their mental training. At a more basic level, effective assessment and the understanding it provides can explain to athletes why they do what they do mentally, such as why they get nervous before competitions or why they become frustrated when they can't readily learn a new technique. These realizations are often accompanied by the statement, "Now I know why I react that way!" From this epiphany and the greater understanding that psychological assessment provides, athletes gain the impetus and means to improve their strengths and alleviate their mental shortcomings.

How Clients Understand You

Assessment isn't just a unidirectional collecting of information in which you gather data about your client. Rather, it is a valuable tool for developing and strengthening the burgeoning relationship between you and your client. Assessment is a powerful way to begin building the connection, rapport, and trust that are so important for establishing an effective and comfortable professional relationship.

The assessments you use and the ways in which you collect information about your clients tells them a great deal about who you are as a person and as a professional. It is an opportunity for you to demonstrate appreciation for why your clients come to you. You can use assessments as a means of expressing concern and empathy for the difficulties that brought your clients to you. Assessment can also send the powerful message to clients that you understand them, and that understanding can act as the foundation for their belief that you can help them.

The assessment tools you use also educate clients about your areas of expertise, such as whether you focus on mental skills or administer psychophysiological protocols. Additionally, your choice of assessments reveals the mental areas that you believe are most important to athletic performance, such as motivation, confidence, focus, or mental imagery, and it communicates those areas that you intuit are at the heart of your clients' performance challenges, such as perfectionism or fear of failure. The assessments you select for clients give them their first hint at the intervention tools you may use (e.g., mental imagery, goal setting, cognitive restructuring) and how you may help the clients overcome their mental obstacles to achieve their athletic goals.

How Clients Understand Sport Psychology

As students or professionals in sport psychology, we have a clear and sophisticated understanding of what it is and how it can benefit athletes. However, clients who come to us for assistance related to the mental aspects of sport don't have this perspective. For many athletes, sport psychology is an amorphous concept; they only hold a vague sense that their mind is getting in the way of achieving their competitive goals. Yes, they know that the mental side of sport is important to athletic performance and success. At the same time, many would be hard pressed to provide an extensive accounting of what sport psychology entails, specific examples of mental factors that affect their performance, or mental skills they might use to improve their performance.

During the assessment, you evaluate your clients on many areas that are common to mental training programs offered by sport psychologists and mental coaches, including motivation, confidence, anxiety, focus, and mental imagery, as well as other performance-relevant areas such as perfectionism, fear of failure, and stress. As a consequence, assessment can provide clients with the opportunity to gain a better understanding of sport psychology, its components, its impact on their performance, and how it may benefit them. You are not only gaining a better understanding of your clients, but they are also learning more about all aspects of sport psychology. Thus, the assessment not only informs you about your clients and how best to assist them, but it is also provides them with an introduction to the field.

Practical Value and Use of Assessment

As you've just learned, assessment offers many benefits for both you and your clients in the early stages of a working relationship. At the same time, the value of assessment is its ability to offer useful information that will lead you and your clients to resolve the issues that led them to you for help. Assessment provides a process for garnering that information, from initial consultation and intervention to resolution and termination. With an appreciation for the value assessment provides your consulting work with athletes, you are better able to use the wide range of assessments discussed in this book.

Paint the Picture

The starting point for assessment is to paint a picture of who your clients are using a variety of parameters that are relevant to helping them. The assessments that act as the paint for this picture will depend on who you are as a person and a professional, your education and training, and the performance model that informs your work. The benefit of the broad-based approach to assessment advocated in this book is that the more paints you have on your palette, the more detailed and nuanced picture you can paint of your clients.

Perform Detective Work

Once you have created a portrait of your clients in broad strokes, the next step is to fill in the details by identifying the issues that have brought them to you. Here is where the detective work begins. Like Sherlock Holmes, you must uncover the clues that act as the starting point for learning your clients' primary issues. For example, if they describe precompetitive anxiety, what might its cause be? Pressure from parents, fear of failure, and lack of confidence are a few clues you might look for. Then you must use your deductive reasoning, much like the scientific method, to take the disparate information that comes from a comprehensive assessment and reduce it to some firm conclusions about the key factors that are affecting the client's performance. Additionally, this detective work should not be done solely by you; rather, it should be a collaborative effort in which your clients play Dr. Watson to your Mr. Holmes. Though you are the expert and bring an assessment repertoire to the consulting process, your clients bring the source of the information—themselves—and a valuable lens through which to look at their performance challenges and the conclusions you draw about them.

This detective work aims to uncover clues that lead you to the best conclusions about who your clients are and how their minds influence their athletic efforts. These clues can be obvious, such as learning through interviewing that a tennis player's parents yell at him if he loses a match. They may be subtle, such as a baseball pitcher having brief but consequential lapses of focus during a game. The clues may also be unclear and mystifying, such as a golfer getting upset and giving up after hitting a bad shot.

Identify Patterns

An essential part of this detective work is identifying patterns of thought, emotion, or behavior that point to the problem that has brought the client to you. As you assess your clients, you'll get a lot of white noise—that is, many possible clues that could lead you to believe some bit of information is relevant, such as the weather was bad on the day of a competition at which the client performed poorly, or a client was stressed out because of her school workload and didn't perform well. But these events in isolation should only be added to the "it's possible" list, without any definitive conclusions drawn.

A rule of thumb to use as you collect clues with clients is a variation of the Moscow rules, an axiom from the world of espionage: The first time is an accident, the second time is a coincidence, and the third time is a pattern. In other words, when a problematic thought, emotion, or behavior occurs three or more times, it is a powerful clue to add to your "it's likely" list and should be explored more deeply.

Rule Out Possible Causes

In addition to looking for clues you can use to rule in clients' key performance issues, another part of your detective work is to conduct assessments for the purpose of ruling out possible causes of the issues. This process of elimination is helpful in reducing the possible factors contributing to the performance problems. The ruling-out approach also ensures that you don't miss something important during the early stages of your consulting work with athletes.

For example, when you begin working with athletes, you might want to identify the most significant influences in their lives, whether parents, coaches, teammates, or others, to see if they are contributing to the performance challenges.

One area that is important to explore (and that chapter 5 addresses) is the presence of mental health issues such as anxiety, depression, eating disorders, substance abuse, or any other clinically diagnosable condition that could influence your clients' health, performance, and well-being. If you miss these concerns early in your work, you may be missing out on a likely contributor to your clients' performance; wasting your clients' time, energy, and money focusing on issues that aren't central to their challenges; working outside your professional expertise; and most importantly, putting your client at risk. As a consequence, gaining a thorough understanding of your clients' mental status should be one of the first steps in the assessment protocol.

You will also want to rule out any neurological concerns that might contribute to athletes' performance challenges and affect your understanding of and intervention with clients. Common concerns include learning differences, attention-deficit/hyperactivity disorder (ADHD), sensory disorders, and behavior on the autistic spectrum. As with mental health issues, missing this information can seriously compromise your understanding of and ability to help clients who come to you for guidance.

Despite the fact that athletes come to you for assistance with the mental side of sport performance, your rule-out list should include other significant contributors to their performance, including their physical health and fitness, technical and tactical capabilities, and sport equipment. Performance difficulties that athletes believe are psychological in nature are often actually related to one of the nonmental factors just mentioned. In these cases, communication and collaboration with the athlete's physician, conditioning coach, sport coach, and equipment adviser can help you rule in or rule out the influence of these areas on the athlete's current performance problems and guide your work moving forward. It may well be that some athletes who come to you don't need your help at all but rather need to improve their physical health or fitness, make technical or tactical gains, or adjust their equipment.

Uncover the Underlying Problem

In addition to collecting clues about the psychological or emotional issues that may be causing performance difficulties, you should also aim to identify your clients' "thing," meaning the underlying problem that is resulting in their inability to achieve their athletic goals. For example, let's say a figure skater experiences anxiety before her long program. Some consultants might use psychophysiological feedback technology to assess brain-wave activity, muscle tension, and breathing patterns. Others might assess the skater's thoughts and emotions before competition. Though these areas of assessment are worthy of exploration and may provide useful information, consider taking a preventive, reductionistic approach to athletic performance—that is, uncovering the causes of her unproductive thinking, interfering emotion, and physiological reactions as a first step to removing those causes, thus preventing them before they occur. An in-depth family history might reveal that the skater has type A parents and a highly competitive family culture that has led to the internalization of perfectionism and fear of failure. A thorough assessment that explores her "thing" would reveal the core cause of her performance anxiety—namely, unproductive attitudes and beliefs derived from her family's achievement dynamic—which would then inform a particular course of intervention.

Form a Preliminary Conceptualization

The goal of any assessment is to provide sufficient information to allow you to develop a preliminary conceptualization of the client. This conceptualization is your best interpretation of the assessment data as they relate to the client's performance difficulties—in other words, "From what I now know, I believe my client's performance challenges are caused by X."

This conceptualization is based on the totality of the information available early in your consultation in combination with your experience and professional judgment. The preliminary conceptualization usually occurs within the first few sessions and is based on the limited information that is collected to that point. The assessment process is ongoing, and additional information gained as you get to know your clients better—and they get to know themselves better—may cause you to modify your initial conceptualization of them as time goes by.

Develop an Initial Intervention Plan

The ultimate value of your assessment protocol, and the information gathered from it, is that it provides the early road signs toward the direction your work with your clients will take. In other words, based on your understanding of your clients, you develop an initial intervention plan to best solve their performance problems. This intervention is grounded in a melding of the assessment information with your intervention philosophy, education, training, and experience. The intervention plan is vital because it guides you and your clients on where and how to focus your energy and spend your time during the early stages of your work. Similar to the preliminary conceptualization, the initial intervention plan may change as you gather new information during subsequent work with your clients.

Give Clients Hope and Determination

Athletes often come to us because they are struggling with their performance and are looking for answers that can get them back on track. They are usually frustrated, worried, uncertain, and even afraid. In many cases, they feel helpless and hopeless because they don't understand why their performance has declined or how to turn things around. Your assessment can offer them the glimmer of hope that they are so in need of. What had been murky is now more understood. What had been ethereal is now more tangible. What had been overwhelming and scary is now more manageable and controllable. That moment when clients shift from hopeless to hopeful is the beginning of getting back on the road to their athletic goals.

With the information gained from the assessment, the preliminary conceptualization, and the initial intervention plan, you give clients the opportunity to regain the determination that was lost in their feelings of helplessness. This hope and determination then act as the fuel that propels them to do the work necessary to remove the psychological and emotional obstacles that have held them back. When you combine this renewed drive and commitment with the processes, strategies, and tools of our trade, you give them the means to overcome their challenges and return to and surpass their previous athletic form.

Foster Accountability

With the hope and determination that come from the assessment also comes a renewed sense of control—a sense that the clients can take action against the previously spectral forces that seemed determined to thwart their goals. The importance of accountability comes into play at this point as you transition from assessment to intervention. First, as you move from understanding your clients' performance challenges to helping to resolve them, you must demonstrate your accountability in this process. You can show clients the means by which they will surmount the obstacles through your initial intervention plan. You can also affirm your commitment to supporting your clients in this process. Finally, you can hold yourself accountable by creating a set of metrics (both objective and subjective) from the assessments that you and your clients can use to measure progress in your work together.

Of course, the ultimate accountability must come from the client. For positive change to occur, your clients must own the work that

you both do. All of the information gained from assessment and the intervention plan that emerges from it can empower your clients to embrace that accountability. This ownership means being fully committed to and engaged in the process of change. It means they are proactive in sharing ideas, feelings, and experiences. Ownership also entails your clients doing everything that you ask of them to help them achieve their athletic goals.

Assessment Skill Sets

Assessing clients isn't simply a matter of asking the right questions, using the right technology, or completing the right inventories. Rather, assessment is a complex process that requires many skill sets (see figure 1.1).

Data Collection

In its simplest form, assessment is about collecting relevant data. The data that you gather depend on which assessment tools you include in your protocol. The assessments you choose are determined by your approach to consulting, as well as your education, training, and experience. The various forms of data you collect may include neuro- and biofeedback, answers to questions about psychiatric information, responses to sport-specific and personality instruments, and observation of athletes in the field. Your ability to collect such diverse data and organize them into a cohesive body of information for the betterment of your clients will determine the value of your assessment protocol in your work.

Analysis

Information gathered from assessments of clients is, in its most basic form, disparate pieces of data that have little meaning in their own right. What

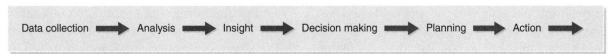

Data collection ➡ Analysis ➡ Insight ➡ Decision making ➡ Planning ➡ Action ➡

Figure 1.1 Assessment skill sets.

makes assessment data useful is your ability to analyze them in a way that results in identifiable patterns, clear conclusions, and actionable recommendations. This complex process can only occur with education, training, and experience; a deep understanding of various assessment modalities; and extensive knowledge of what the relevant information means in the context of your clients' challenges, needs, and goals.

Insight

Information and knowledge aren't enough to turn the assessment data into a coherent set of conclusions and intervention recommendations. You also need the ability to look at the diverse and often disconnected pieces of information in new ways within the context of your understanding of your clients. This insight, which requires creative thinking, is especially important when you have a client whose performance challenges are significant, complex, and without readily evident causes. This ability requires experience, resistance to quickly placing people into neat categories, and openness to looking at athletes as individuals who need a novel understanding of and approach to their unique challenges, needs, and goals.

Decision Making

Once you have a sound grasp of the assessment data you have collected, you must then determine how to best leverage the information. This decision-making process is sometimes simple and other times highly complex. The nature of the decision making depends on several factors related to both you and your clients. First, how you use the assessment data will depend on the clients' issues, such as whether the issues are related to performance, injury, or something else. Second, you must take into account the resources that clients bring to their work with you (e.g., maturity, motivation). Third, you must consider your experience and capabilities as a consultant and how you can weave the assessment information into your skill sets. Finally, you must decide how to translate the assessment data into a program of change that will help your clients achieve their goals.

Planning

Having made decisions about the meaning and value of the information gathered from the assessment, you can now take that information and formulate it into a compelling and actionable intervention plan. The plan must be compelling because it must inspire and motivate your clients to adhere to it. It must be actionable because your clients must have a clear understanding of how it will lead them to overcome their challenges and achieve their goals. In your planning, you must weigh what both you and your clients bring to the table, as well as practical considerations such as time, place, and support.

Action

All of the steps that have occurred thus far culminate in action, putting the data collection, analysis, insight and creativity, decision making, and planning into a form that empowers your clients to take identifiable steps toward surmounting their performance difficulties and achieving their athletic goals. How you operationalize the notion of action in your work depends on your consulting style and approach. For example, do you focus on mental skills such as goal setting, self-talk, relaxation, and mental imagery? Do you use biofeedback training? Do you rely more on traditional counseling strategies? What matters most in this step of the consulting process is that both you and your clients are confident that the action plan will produce the results they want.

Assessment Is Judgment

In its purest sense, assessment means making informed judgments about clients, what their most pressing concerns are, and how you can best address those concerns. In the context of consulting in sport, a judgment is the ability to form opinions, make considered decisions, and come to sensible conclusions based on available information about clients in combination with your education, training, and experience (American Psychological Association [APA], n.d.). This should result in the best choices for helping your clients meet their needs and goals.

The problem is that we humans are not the rational thinkers and dispassionate decision makers we would like to think we are, as first described by Kahneman and Tversky (1974) and popularized by Kahneman's 2013 bestselling book, *Thinking, Fast and Slow*. The premise of Kahneman's book is that we use fast and intuitive thinking (System 1) in most situations because it is efficient and sufficiently effective to meet our needs. Only when we are confronted with a difficult problem do we engage in more deliberate, effortful thinking (System 2). The conclusions drawn from this line of investigation are that we are riddled with cognitive biases and distortions that often result in flawed interpretations, analyses, and decisions. And these biases are as relevant in consulting as they are in any other aspect of life. This often-inaccurate thinking arises from several sources:

- Through evolution, we are driven by primitive needs and drives (e.g., the survival instinct) that can lead us to make decisions based on self-interest.

- We have evolved to reason adaptively (i.e., to reduce risks and costs) rather than rationally.

- Efficiency of decision making is as important as effectiveness (the faster we could make decisions when we were cave people, the better chance we had of survival).

- We often don't have sufficient information, resources, or time to arrive at the most rational decision; rather, we make the best decisions possible based on what we know in the amount of time we have available.

- We often engage in bad research, meaning we base our conclusions on, for example, insufficient or unrepresentative data points.

Research has identified hundreds of cognitive biases; however, there are 10 that appear to be particularly relevant for consulting in sport.

1. Confirmation bias—searching for or interpreting information in a way that confirms one's preconceptions (e.g., if the facts don't fit the theory, throw out the facts)
2. Anchoring—relying too heavily on one trait or piece of information when making decisions
3. Congruence bias—testing selected H_1 rather than alternative H_1 (rule out before ruling in)
4. Empathy gap—underestimating the influence or strength of feelings in oneself or others
5. Expectation bias—believing data that agree with one's expectations
6. Selective perception—allowing expectations to affect perception
7. Overconfidence effect—having excessive confidence in one's knowledge
8. Assumption of causality—seeing a causal relationship where one doesn't exist
9. Disregard of regression toward the mean—expecting extreme performance to continue
10. Mind reading—believing we can intuit other's thoughts, emotions, and intentions

A close look in the mirror will likely reveal your vulnerability to many of these biases in your work. Though research has demonstrated that it is difficult to overcome cognitive biases, some recommendations have emerged for making important decisions (Kahneman, Lovallo, & Sibony, 2011):

- Ask yourself what cognitive biases might influence your decision making.
- Play the devil's advocate with yourself.
- Assume you're not as confident or capable as you think you are (be humble).
- Actively seek out disconfirming information and listen to dissenting views.
- Reality-test your perceptions with others whom you trust and who have diverse experiences.
- Be methodical in your decision-making process.
- Don't make rushed decisions.

In addition to these suggestions for mitigating cognitive biases, Kahneman (2013) offers a handy rule of thumb that all consultants can benefit from. One might argue that inexperience can lead to poor decisions because those without much experience don't know what they don't know, so they rely on insufficient knowledge to make decisions. By extension, one could also argue that experience provides the knowledge necessary to make more sound decisions. However, Kahneman has suggested that experience creates more entrenched cognitive biases because it leads to excessive belief in what people think they know. This overconfidence can result in the belief that we can rely on System 1 thinking (fast and intuitive) to make important decisions when System 2 thinking (deliberate and effortful) would likely produce better results. Now for Kahneman's rule of thumb: If you are inexperienced, think. If you are experienced, think. Both inexperience and experience can make you susceptible to cognitive biases and distorted decision making. The best way to reduce the impact of cognitive biases on our thinking is to assume no decisions are easy and to immediately engage System 2 thinking (deliberate and effortful) in the decision-making process.

Assessment Toolbox

The intrusion of cognitive biases in the assessment process is why a broad-based assessment protocol is so important. There is a saying that if all you have is a hammer, everything looks like a nail. Hammers are useful tools but have limited utility; they are great for sinking nails in wood but can't do much else. Similarly, if you only use one assessment tool (i.e., a hammer), you will likely see all of your clients' problems through that lens (i.e., as nails) and will produce data that affirm your consulting view. In doing so, you may miss critical information that could help your clients. By creating an assessment toolbox with many evaluation tools, you mitigate the cognitive biases that are inevitable when you use only one tool, and you can collect data that will lead to a richer, more comprehensive conceptualization of who your clients are, what performance challenges they face, and how best to help them.

Assessment in Applied Sport Psychology offers many tools you can add to your assess-

ment toolbox. The coming chapters include assessments in the following areas:

- Diversity
- Mental health
- Personality
- Sport-specific inventories
- Interviewing
- Observation
- Neuro- and biofeedback
- Coach, team, and parent
- Talent identification
- Musculoskeletal injury
- Concussion
- Career transition
- Consulting in sport organizations
- Consultant effectiveness

From this well-stocked toolbox, you can select the assessment tools that will give you a thorough view of your clients, enabling you to make the most accurate decisions about the causes of their performance difficulties and the most effective course of action.

Choosing Assessment Tools

A major challenge in deciding which assessment tools to use is that there are so many to choose from that evaluate many types of information. Another challenge is figuring out their empirical and practical value in your work. One goal of *Assessment in Applied Sport Psychology* is to help you overcome these two challenges by informing you what the best assessment tools are—in terms of both scientific rigor and practical utility—and how to use them most effectively.

As part of this selection process, you should ask several questions to ensure you find the ideal match between your clients' needs and the best assessments in your toolbox.

Is It Valid?

When considering an assessment tool, you should ask an essential question that will act as the first gatekeeper of inclusion or exclusion:

Is the assessment valid? In other words, has it been tested scientifically and demonstrated its empirical validity and reliability (more on this in chapter 2)? Additionally, though an assessment may have been tested for validity on a general population, has it been evaluated with the population with which you are working?

Many assessment instruments are available that purport to measure a construct of interest in our field, whether motivation, depression, or team cohesion, to name a few. However, without a sound empirical foundation, assessments have little real value.

Is It Appropriate?

Not every assessment is suitable for every client. It is important to be sensitive regarding clients' age, gender, race, ethnicity, culture, religion, and sexual orientation (see chapter 4). For example, you may work with clients of varying ages, from preteens to mature adults. Assessments that are useful for one age group may not be suitable for another, and thus you should consider the chronological age, maturity, and education of your clients in determining the suitability of an assessment.

Assessments that are useful with one gender may not be so with the other. Be sure that your assessments take into consideration any gender differences that exist. It is also important to evaluate whether assessments have a gender bias that would skew their results favorably or unfavorably toward one or the other gender. Additionally, with the growing sensitivity of society toward issues of sexual orientation in our culture, you should consider the messages that assessments send to your clients. For example, assessments that use "he," "him," or "his" or items that refer to heterosexual relationships may offend those athletes who have a different sexual orientation.

Finally, given the increasingly diverse makeup of Western culture in the 21st century, cultural differences, including race, ethnicity, culture, and religion, must be considered. Assessments should be vetted for their sensitivity to cultural concerns and their ability, however inadvertent, to provoke discomfort among your clients.

Does It Match Client Goals?

A fundamental question you must ask is whether there is a match between a particular assessment and your clients' needs and goals. In other words, does the assessment serve a useful purpose in your work with your clients? Every tool in your assessment toolbox should serve a specific objective in helping you understand your clients (and helping them understand themselves). In addition, the information gathered from the assessment should play a central role in the preliminary conceptualization and the decision making and planning of the intervention program.

What Harm Could Come From Its Use?

No matter how innocuous an assessment tool might appear, it always has the potential to cause some sort of harm; for example, it could trigger an association with a painful past experience, a negative conception of the self, a recollection of a difficult relationship, or simply a release of the emotions that brought the client to you. Using an assessment without knowing your clients well and without considering the impact of the assessment on them may produce a reaction that is both unexpected and harmful.

Every time you consider adding an assessment to your toolbox, perform your due diligence and examine its strengths and potential for harm. This exploration can occur in several ways. First, examine the research on the assessment and see if any red flags or limitations come up. Second, based on your experience and knowledge of your clients, see if the assessment passes the duck test: If it looks like a duck and sounds like a duck, it's probably a duck. In other words, does it seem like a good tool for your purposes? Does it have basic face validity for your needs, or do you sense that it might cause harm, whether in its topical focus, its wording, or the responses it might elicit? Finally, obtain feedback from colleagues who have used the assessment and can describe how their clients have reacted to it.

Chapter Takeaways

- Assessment can be characterized as "obtaining a snapshot-like view of a person at a moment in time in order to determine the person's status with respect to a cumulative knowledge or skill."

- The goal of assessment is to develop a comprehensive understanding of the client as an athlete and as a person. In its purest sense, assessment is about making informed judgments about clients, what their most pressing concerns are, and how you can best address those concerns.

- Assessment enables clients to understand themselves, you, and the sport psychology work you are about to undertake with them.

- Assessment involves identifying patterns, ruling out causes, and identifying the underlying issue that brings the client to you.

- Assessment is the first step in the consulting process. It leads to an initial conceptualization and the development of a preliminary intervention plan.

- Skill sets necessary for effective use of assessments include data collection, insight, decision making, planning, and action.

- Our judgments of clients can be clouded by the cognitive biases that all human beings are vulnerable to. You should be aware of the impact of cognitive biases on your client assessments and take steps to mitigate those influences.

- An essential goal is to develop an assessment toolbox from which you draw appropriate assessments that best meet the needs and goals of your clients.

- Choosing an assessment tool should be based on whether it is valid and appropriate, there is a match between the assessment and the client's needs, and you have determined any potential risks for harm.

CHAPTER 2
Science of Sport Psychology Assessment

Anita N. Lee, DPE

Jim Taylor, PhD, CC-AASP

Choosing tools for your assessment toolbox isn't simply a matter of finding instruments that *seem* to fit your needs or *might* assess areas that are important for your work with athletes. To the contrary, assessment selection should be a rigorous process in which you scrutinize prospective tools to ensure they are valid and appropriate for their intended purpose.

This chapter focuses on the science of sport psychology assessment. It examines the selection of instruments to help you and your clients identify their performance challenges and provide direction on how to achieve their athletic goals.

When choosing an assessment in your consulting work with athletes or teams, you must consider four areas:

1. The purpose of the assessment (i.e., what you hope to learn from it)
2. The athlete or athletes you will be assessing (e.g., sport, skill level, age, maturity)
3. The environment in which the assessment will be administered (e.g., sport setting, team culture)
4. The risks of using the assessment

Assessment for Individuals Versus Groups

Sport psychology consultants have to deal with unique psychological issues of both individual athletes and groups. This section discusses the differences in selecting assessments for individual athletes versus groups of athletes. Athletes from individual sports are usually concerned about their own performance rather than group dynamics, cohesion, and other sport psychology determinants. Consultants need to know what determinants they want to assess and whether the assessment focuses on helping athletes to improve individual performance or to interact better with their groups to enhance group performance.

Additionally, consultants use assessments for a very different purpose—namely, to increase their understanding of their clients. For example, assessments can be used in the areas of mental health, personality, performance-related psychological states, intervention planning, and outcome evaluation (American

Educational Research Association [AERA], APA, National Council on Measurement in Education [NCME], & Joint Committee on Standards for Educational and Psychological Testing [JCSEPT], 2014), as well as for selection and screening in team settings.

A key issue in considering particular assessments is whether they were developed for identifying group or individual differences. Differences between groups of athletes found on an assessment may not predict differences among individual athletes and thus may not provide useful information when applied to individuals (Gardner & Moore, 2006, 2007). In many cases, findings from group assessments are presented collectively; as a result, their meaning to individual athletes is unclear.

Another important distinction involves the settings in which assessments are used for individuals or teams. Assessments for individual athletes are mainly for developing mental training programs, and assessments for groups are mainly for coaches and other team personnel to address team-level needs and goals. In contrast, assessments for consulting purposes are used in naturally occurring settings that lack any controls. Additionally, the information gathered may be influenced by any number of confounding factors about the athletes. These differences highlight the need to have a practical understanding of the science of assessment as it relates to its use in the consulting process with athletes.

Validity and Reliability of Assessments

As either a graduate student or professional in the field, we are going to assume that you took statistics in your training program. We are also going to assume that you studied validity and reliability as the foundations of effective assessment tools. We will further venture to guess that you found this topic rather dry and not of particular interest to your consulting work (apologies if we are being presumptuous).

However, we would also argue that the concepts of validity and reliability are central to your consulting work, especially in the assessment process. If you use information that is inaccurate or that presents a distorted view of your clients, you can't understand your clients effectively; if you don't understand them, you can't help them overcome their performance challenges and achieve their goals. Without the understanding that comes from information gathered from valid and reliable assessment tools, you are doing your clients a disservice and potentially acting unethically. Thus, we want to reintroduce validity and reliability to you in a concise and meaningful way that will enable you to fully appreciate them and apply them to your use of assessments in your work with athletes.

Validity

Validity is the most important information in determining whether you should use an assessment tool to evaluate a particular area of your clients. *Validity* refers to "the extent to which a test measures what it was intended to measure" (Gerrig & Zimbardo, 2002a, Validity section, para. 6). In other words, are you assessing what you really want to assess? For example, if you want to measure an athlete's confidence, is the instrument you're using actually measuring their confidence, or is it measuring some other variable? If you are not using a valid assessment, you don't know whether you are assessing what you want, and thus your assessment results and the conclusions you draw from them may not be valid. As a result, you are gaining no useful information about your client.

A common mistake made by untrained or inexperienced consultants involves selecting assessment instruments based on their topic, scope, and ease of administration, without considering their validity. We all might make the mistake of looking at an instrument and believing that if it appears to measure what we want it to measure (i.e., face validity), then it must do so. Returning to the duck example from chapter 1, just because it looks like a duck and sounds like a duck doesn't necessarily mean it's a duck. The bottom line is that you should be circumspect in using any assessment instruments that aren't demonstrably valid.

Given the importance of assessments, whether in developing hypotheses about the causes of performance problems, predicting competitive results, or evaluating future potential, you must ensure that every tool in your assessment toolbox meets the scientific rigors of validity testing. The validation process includes four types of validity: construct, content, criterion, and internal validity.

Construct Validity

Construct validity involves the extent to which an assessment measures the underlying construct, or idea, that it is intended to measure. For example, does an inventory designed to assess fear of failure adequately measure the theoretical concept of fear of failure developed by the researchers? The key value of construct validity is that the construct in question best explains the findings of research related to the construct and predicts future outcomes.

Content Validity

Content validity is how well the content of an assessment instrument reflects what you want to test. For example, if you want to test the anxiety level of an athlete a week before a critical competition, an assessment with a high degree of content validity will reflect the athlete's true anxiety level. Content validity involves three components of an assessment—domain clarity, content relevance, and content representativeness—that ensure the thematic content and specific item wording are related to the topic to be assessed.

Domain clarity is the extent to which the content of an assessment instrument is related to the construct being assessed. For example, is the assessment clearly written to assess state confidence level? Is the construct of an assessment clearly defined operationally and assessing what it claims to assess? In this stage, assessment developers reach out to experts to review the operational definitions and wording of an assessment instrument. Developers also propose what and how many constructs should be in an assessment.

After domain clarity is confirmed, content relevance needs to be ensured. Content relevance means the content agrees with and is meaningful to the construct represented in the assessment. Is the content logically relevant to what an assessment claims to assess? Assessment developers usually perform a pilot study to ensure the respondents understand the assessment content (Baumgartner, Mahar, Jackson, & Rowe, 2016). Content representativeness resides at the level of the assessment items. Each construct in an assessment instrument is reflected in multiple items. The item wording and content have to be appropriate, include the most important concepts, eliminate irrelevant content, and avoid duplicating other items.

Criterion Validity

Criterion validity is particularly important for consulting in sport because it involves how well an assessment correlates with some tangible measure of the construct being assessed; for example, is confidence related to better competitive results? Criterion validity has two components: concurrent validity and predictive validity. Concurrent validity is shown when an assessment is highly correlated with another measure that has already been judged as valid. For instance, in developing a measure of focus specifically for swimmers, the new instrument should correlate with a well-validated measure of focus in the general population of athletes. Predictive validity reflects how well an assessment can predict future events such as results from an upcoming competition.

Internal Validity

Internal validity means controlling potential confounding variables to increase the consistency and validity when administering the assessment instrument. For example, if you are going to use the assessment for comparison, such as in a team selection process, you must be sure of a high level of internal validity. Internal validity ensures that the setting, instructions, and administration procedures are consistent for all athletes tested and that potentially confounding influences are minimized as much as possible. For example, if you are assessing a group of athletes, internal validity requires administering the assessment at the same time of day during the same general time period (e.g., preseason).

Reliability

Reliability is "the degree to which a test produces similar scores each time it is used; stability or consistency of the scores produced by an instrument" (Gerrig & Zimbardo, 2002b, Reliability section, para. 20). In other words, does the assessment measure the same thing every time you use it? If it does not, it is not reliable. For quantitative psychometrics, reliability can be tests and represented by statistics. Cronbach's alpha (α) coefficient is a common statistic that is reported for items, subscales, or the entire assessment instrument on a range from 0 to 1, with the higher value representing greater reliability (Cronbach, 1951). Though there are many interpretations of the Cronbach alpha value for internal consistency (Cronbach, 1951; Nunnally, 1967, 1978), the first commonly used interpretation was presented by George and Mallery (2003), which stated that an alpha value less than 0.5 is unacceptable, between 0.50 and 0.59 is poor, between 0.60 and 0.69 is questionable, between 0.70 and 0.79 is acceptable, between 0.80 and 0.89 is good, and 0.90 or higher is excellent.

Determining the Value of Sport Psychology Assessments

As previously discussed, validity and reliability are important factors to consider when selecting assessments. As a consultant, you have neither the inclination nor the time to evaluate the validity of every assessment tool you might be interested in; you are not going to conduct validation research to determine which assessments are worthy. Rather, you should seek out other credible sources to make that determination.

For previous generations of consultants, this process was arduous, requiring extensive time in university libraries tracking down relevant scholarly articles and books demonstrating the validity of an assessment. Thankfully, due to the Internet, you now have at your fingertips all of the information necessary to draw reasonable conclusions about whether an assessment is valid and of value in your work with clients. A simple Internet search can be an easy first step in evaluating the validity of assessments you may want to add to your assessment toolbox. For example, a search for "validity Test of Attentional and

Interpersonal Style" (Nideffer, 1976, 1990, 1992, 1995) revealed a variety of sources discussing the theoretical and empirical foundations of this test. A word of caution here: Because search engines, such as Google, Bing, and Yahoo, base their search results on popularity, not scientific rigor, you must be a critical consumer to judge whether online sources are credible. You should not only use regular Internet search engines. Though you may find an assessment from such a search, its validity and reliability may not be clearly reported. You should review the original source because it provides complete information about how the assessment instrument was developed and validated.

To help mitigate these concerns about source credibility, you can use Google Scholar, another useful tool for evaluating the validity of assessments. This search engine focuses on scholarly publications, including journals and books, so your searches are more relevant and less likely to be contaminated by search engine optimization and popularity of sources. Once you find some relevant research articles online, you can use the reference lists of the articles to identify other pertinent articles that will lead to a reasonable conclusion about the validity and usefulness of a particular assessment tool.

Additionally, if you have access to a university library, you may use several helpful databases. Examples include Academic Search Premier, JSTOR, PsycINFO, and SPORTDiscus.

Critical Evaluation of Assessment Research

If you want to use assessments that are well validated and of the most value to your clients, you should read studies that have evaluated their validity. To discover as much as you can about the validity of an assessment, you can identify the key elements of a research article to get the information you need. Here are some tips to help you get the most out of articles in the shortest amount of time. Typically, these articles are divided into several standardized sections that you can dissect and digest efficiently: the introduction, methods, results, and discussion or conclusion.

- **Introduction.** As you scan the introduction, focus on the statement of the purpose of the assessment, its theoretical basis, and the hypotheses tested in the study. Consider if what you find is consistent with your intentions for using the assessment.

- **Methods.** In this section, you can obtain information about how the assessment was developed and the sample that was assessed to determine whether it is consistent with the clients you will be using the assessment with. You can also learn about the setting in which the assessment was administered to ensure that it is also consistent with your use with clients.

- **Results.** For psychometric development, this section frequently includes a dense array of statistical findings. Some readers may find this presentation daunting and even incomprehensible. If you have a basic understanding of the standard measures of validity, such as Cronbach's alpha coefficient, you can quickly judge the validity of an assessment. If you are not familiar or comfortable with the statistics that are presented, we recommend moving directly to the discussion or conclusion, where the results are encapsulated in a more understandable narrative.

- **Discussion or conclusion.** This section interprets the results in plain language. You should be able to ascertain the validity of the assessment here. Once you gather information on the use and validity of the assessment, you may want to return to the methods section and examine in more detail how the assessment was administered, any specific instructions that are given, and how to score and interpret its results.

Specificity of Assessment Instruments

Applied sport psychology is a dynamic discipline in which one size does not fit all. This notion is particularly relevant to the use of assessment in our field. The development of assessments in sport psychology can be based on sport generality or specificity and the demographics of an athletic population. An assessment that works for a general sport population may not work for your clientele and the specific requirements of their sport.

Most sport psychology assessment instruments are designed for a general population of athletes. Examples of these instruments include the following:

- Perceived Motivational Climate in Sport Questionnaire-2 (PMCSQ-2; Newton, Duda, & Yin, 2000)
- Task and Ego Orientation in Sport Questionnaire (TEOSQ; Duda, 1989; Duda & Nicholls, 1992)
- Test of Attentional and Interpersonal Style (TAIS; Nideffer, 1976)
- Group Environment Questionnaire (GEQ; Carron, Widmeyer, & Brawley, 1985)
- State Sport-Confidence Inventory (SSCI; Vealey, 1986a)
- Trait Sport-Confidence Inventory (TSCI; Vealey, 1986a)
- Competitive State Anxiety Inventory-2 (CSAI-2; Martens, Burton, Vealey, Bump, & Smith, 1990)

Many others are designed for use with a specific sport population, such as the following:

- Associative/Dissociative Scales for Triathlon Athletes (Bakker, van Diesen, Spekreijse, & Pijpers, 1993)
- Baseball Test of Attentional and Interpersonal Style (B-TAIS; Albrecht & Feltz, 1987)
- Diving Questionnaire (Highlen & Bennett, 1983)
- Golf Performance Survey (GPS; Thomas & Over, 1994)
- Basketball Concentration Survey (BCS; Bergandi, Shryock, & Titus, 1990)
- Tennis Test of Attentional and Interpersonal Style (T-TAIS; Van Schoyck & Grasha, 1981)

Sport-specific assessments will have greater validity and relevance in your work with athletes in a particular sport because the constructs and items of the assessment will be grounded in the unique characteristics of the sport.

When researchers develop an assessment instrument, they identify a target population for its use based on sport, age, school level, language, and so on. Or, they base their sample on the most available participants for the validation studies, such as college or high school athletes. Frequently, this demographic information is gathered as part of the assessment. When selecting assessment instruments, pay attention to the congruence between the population on which an assessment was validated and the particular clients you will use the assessment with. In some cases, an assessment may be effective for a certain population but not for your clients. With a basic knowledge of your clients' demographics, you can determine the fit of an assessment with their particular situation.

Quantitative and Qualitative Assessments

Quantitative assessments are usually questionnaires, surveys, or inventories that require users to answer questions with some form of numeric response that can then be coded and analyzed statistically. The advantages of quantitative assessments are that they can be more readily validated, can be administered and scored for groups of athletes, and can produce comparative norms (both between and within athletes). Disadvantages include the inability to customize the assessments for individual clients, use the information as it is gathered, and use the assessment process (i.e., the interaction between consultant and athlete) as another source of information.

Qualitative assessments consist of interviewing (see chapter 8) and observation (see chapter 9). This type of assessment produces open-ended responses to specific questions (interviewing) and behavioral information (observation). Qualitative assessments allow the collection of a richer array of information about athletes.

The open-ended nature of qualitative assessment allows for more detailed and nuanced exploration of athletes' psyches, including their thoughts and emotional experiences. It enables you to follow and expand on clues and insights that arise during the assessment and to more readily identify patterns and themes that would not be seen with quantitative assessment. Qualitative assessment can also be used to build rapport and trust between consultant and client. Qualitative assessment does, however, have drawbacks. For example, it is highly subjective in both collection and interpretation of the gathered information. As a result, it is vulnerable to cognitive biases such as those discussed in chapter 1. Additionally, qualitative assessment is time and energy intensive both in administration and analysis.

Response Options for Quantitative Assessments

Quantitative assessments can use several types of responses to item questions. The different response options offer different forms of answers to the questions.

Likert Scale

The Likert scale (Likert, 1932) is the most widely used survey scale. The number of choices in a Likert scale is usually odd, such as a 5-point, 7-point, or 9-point Likert scale. The most common Likert scale is the 5-point design, with *strongly disagree* and *strongly agree* at each end (see figure 2.1). Matell and Jacoby (1971) pointed out that the even-number Likert scale is dichotomous, while the odd-number scale is trichotomous. Due to the midpoint of the odd-number scale, Malhortra (2006) suggested that this design allows neutral, impartial, or no opinion from the responses. The selection of odd- or even-number Likert scales should be based on the needs and item contents (Losby & Wetmore, 2012). The items are usually statements rather than questions because the assessments are asking for agreement or disagreement. Additionally, some items are reverse scaled, meaning that a higher score may represent the worst or negative instead of the best or positive.

Strongly disagree	Disagree	Neutral	Agree	Strongly agree
1	2	3	4	5

Figure 2.1   Five-point Likert scale.

Symmetric Differential Scale

Symmetric differential scales are continua in which the two ends represent opposite meanings (Osgood, 1952, 1960, 1964; Osgood, Saporta, & Nunnally, 1956). For younger respondents, the answering scale may be pictures or photos (see figure 2.2).

Dichotomous Scale

Dichotomous scales have only two response choices (e.g., yes or no, agree or disagree). Dichotomous items are usually used for collecting demographic information, such as "What is your gender?" (female or male) and "Are you an athlete?" (yes or no).

Response Options for Qualitative Assessments

Qualitative assessment may use the verbal responses given by clients during interviews. Or, it may involve your impressions based on observation of athletes in training or competition.

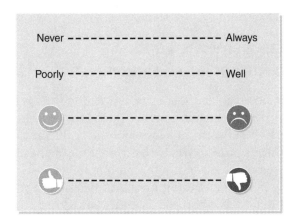

Figure 2.2   Sample differential scale items.

Interviewing

Interviewing (see chapter 8) can be conducted in several ways. Structured interviews follow a circumscribed process in which questions are asked in a specific order with the goal of obtaining particular information; they do not allow for deviation from the established protocol. These types of interviews are usually derived from lines of questioning that have been studied and validated empirically to produce an informational outcome.

Free-form interviewing is entirely unformatted. It begins with one or two evocative questions and relies on the initial responses and the consultant's experience and intuition to dictate the direction the interview takes and additional questions. This type of interviewing requires consultants to be highly attuned to their clients' answers and flexible with where the interview leads.

The open-ended nature of interviewing allows athletes to express their thoughts, feelings, and opinions in response to the questions, without the restrictions imposed by the limited response options of quantitative assessment. Though lacking the structure and cleanness of responses to quantitative assessments, the open-ended nature of interviewing allows you to gain deeper and more wide-ranging information about the athlete.

Behavioral Observation

An underappreciated form of assessment is behavioral observation, which involves gathering information about athletes by watching them in their natural settings of training and competition (see chapter 9). This allows you to see their emotions, behavior, performance, and interaction in the settings in which their performance challenges are most apparent. This information may also be collected via video recording.

Behavioral observation can be accomplished with formal or informal protocols. Formal protocols use structured checklists of relevant behaviors that can be manually recorded, codified, and analyzed. Informal protocols involve open-ended observation of behaviors and off-the-cuff data collection and analysis.

Assessment Myths

Consultants should be aware of the following three myths in order to avoid biases and unrealistic expectations when using assessments. Understanding these myths will help you make more informed assessment selections.

Assessments Occur in Perfect Conditions

Unlike other contributors to sport performance, such as strength and speed, assessment cannot usually evaluate and predict athletes' thoughts, emotions, or behavior with 100 percent accuracy due to the intangible nature of the mind. In other words, for most types of psychological assessment, direct measurement isn't possible. As a result, all information that is gathered through assessments must be interpreted in the context of the athlete as a whole person and the sport environment. Additionally, because most sport psychology assessments are indirect, information gained from athletes will be most valuable not in isolation but within a broader assessment net in which a large amount of diverse assessment information is collected, allowing for a thorough interpretation of the athletes in question. There are, however, exceptions to this myth, most notably psychophysiological testing and behavioral analysis, both of which provide direct, objective information about athletes' physiology and behavior.

Assessments Can Predict Athletic Performance

Considerable sport psychology research has demonstrated the ability of certain factors, such as confidence, anxiety, and focus (Boutcher, 1990; Craft, Magyar, Becker, & Feltz, 2003; Gould, Greenleaf, Chung, & Guinan, 2002; Hanin, 1980, 1986, 1997; Hardy, 1990, 1996; Jones & Hardy, 1990; Martin & Gill, 1991; McGrath, 1970; Moran, 1996; Spence & Spence, 1966; Vealey, 1986b, 2001; Wulf, 2007), to predict competitive performance differences among athletes. However, this predictive ability between groups of athletes does not mean competitive performance can be predicted at an individual level.

There are several reasons for this discrepancy. First, research assessing sport psychology assessments typically occurs in a controlled environment. In contrast, assessment used in consulting with athletes occurs in real-world settings in which many factors, both within and outside the control of athletes, may influence performance. Second, typical research on sport psychology assessment evaluates differences between groups rather than within individuals. As a consequence, most assessments aren't sensitive enough to separate the impact of various psychological influences on performance versus other contributing factors. Third, though mental aspects of sport have a demonstrable impact on performance, there are other factors, such as physical and technical, that play an equal or greater role in athletic performance. Unless these factors can be controlled, it is unlikely that psychological assessments of any sort can tease out the influences sufficiently to establish a practical relationship between psychological factors and performance, even if a statistical relationship can be seen.

Assessments Lead to Immediate Solutions

As noted in chapter 1, assessment is the initial step in the consulting process, and the end result is, hopefully, the resolution of the problems that athletes came to you for assistance in solving. So, assessment is not a panacea but rather a starting point for making informed decisions about understanding athletes and identifying their performance challenges. Assessments should not be used just once at the beginning of the process. Rather, they should be used on an ongoing basis to track athletes' relevant parameters and changes over time. Assessment then acts as the foundation for developing intervention plans that will lead clients to the successful resolution of their presenting issues and a return to athletic form and pursuit of their competitive goals.

Creating Your Own Assessments

If you are unable to find an assessment that meets your needs, you may feel compelled to create your own. Constructing your own assessment can be appealing in many ways; you can develop one to meet your specific needs, and it seems easy to do. However, the process of creating an assessment that is truly valid is time and energy intensive. Yes, you can make an assessment based entirely on face validity (i.e., the extent to which an assessment appears to measure what you want it to measure), but this is not a strong measure of validity, and what you think the assessment measures may not be what it actually measures (and it may not measure anything at all). As a result, if you use an assessment that hasn't been properly validated, you are gathering and valuing information that may not reflect anything of relevance to the client. Based on this line of reasoning, we strongly discourage this path of assessment selection.

Chapter Takeaways

- Consultants use assessments to increase their understanding of individual clients in the areas of mental health, personality, performance-related psychological states, intervention planning, outcome evaluation, and so on.

- Key issues to consider in selecting an assessment instrument include whether it was developed for identifying group or individual differences and whether it was tested in a controlled or naturally occurring environment.

- Assessment selection should be a rigorous process by which you scrutinize prospective tools to ensure that they are valid and appropriate for the intended purpose.

- Assessments can be either quantitative (e.g., questionnaires, surveys, inventories) or qualitative (e.g., interviewing, observation).

- Quantitative assessments can have various response options, including the Likert, symmetric differential, and dichotomous scales. Qualitative assessments can be either structured or free form.

- You can quickly determine the validity and value of an assessment instrument for your purposes by examining the introduction, methods, results, and discussion or conclusion of research papers.

- Validity and reliability are central to consulting work because they ensure accurate presentations of clients. We discourage you from developing your own assessment tools because of their lack of validity.

- Most sport psychology assessment instruments are designed for a general population of athletes, but some are sport specific. Information gathered through assessments must be interpreted in the context of the athlete as a whole person and the sport environment.

- You should not assume that assessments can predict performance.

- Assessments are just the first step in helping clients resolve their presenting issues and continue their pursuit of their competitive goals. They should be used on an ongoing basis to track progress.

CHAPTER 3

Ethical Issues in Sport Psychology Assessment

Marshall Mintz, PsyD

Michael Zito, PhD

Ethical behavior is the foundation of everything you do as a consultant, including assessment and intervention. Acting ethically in all aspects of your practice enables you to offer the highest quality services, products, and programs to help clients meet their needs while also ensuring that their welfare is your most important priority. Ethical practice is of particular importance to assessment because it is the starting point for all of your consulting work and its potential benefits for your clients. As Etzel, Yura, Perna, and Vosloo (2014) state, "It is necessary that professionals and professionals in the making be acutely aware of the many ethical and legal issues associated with the development and use of assessment devices (questionnaires, inventories, interviews)" (p. 190).

The purpose of this chapter is to identify and explore ethical concerns in your work with athletes, coaches, and sport organizations. Assessment is a complex, dynamic activity that requires knowledge of measurement and interviewing principles and skills, an awareness of human systems, and the competence to administer, score, interpret, and communicate the results. When consultants engage in assessment, they are bound by the ethical principles and current standards of their profession. Ethical assessment practices are important to examine because the use of assessments is common among consultants (66 percent) certified through the Association for Applied Sport Psychology (AASP) (O'Connor, 2004). Moreover, assessment acts as the foundation for all of your services, so ethical practices related to assessment set the tone for your work with clients.

Anyone may ask questions, conduct an interview, or administer an inventory or test. But when consultants ask questions, conduct interviews, and collect assessment data, the public must know and trust that the consultants have received education, training, and supervision that qualify them to carry out their work competently, ethically, and with the best interests of their clients in mind. Consultants know that assessment has a purpose, and they engage in the assessment activity only after they have taken personal responsibility for the ethical standards and practices of their profession.

Ethical Principles

The APA has established its Ethical Principles of Psychologists and Code of Conduct (2002), which act as the framework for this chapter. The AASP ethical guidelines (AASP, n.d.) are based primarily on those created by the APA.

The APA ethical principles consist of five tenets that are intended to "guide and inspire psychologists toward the very highest ethical ideals of the profession" (2002, p. 3). These principles are no less important in the use of assessment in consulting with athletes, coaches, and teams.

Principle A: Beneficence and Nonmaleficence

This principle asserts that consultants must "strive to benefit those with whom they work and take care to do no harm. . . . Because [consultants'] scientific and professional judgments and actions may affect the lives of others, they are alert to and guard against personal, financial, social, organizational or political factors that might lead to misuse of their influence" (APA, 2002, p. 3). You will likely face situations in your consulting work that bring two ethical challenges to light. The first challenge may occur when assessing athletes in a situation in which there are other stakeholders, such as coaches, parents, or teams, who have needs, intentions, and goals that conflict with those of the athletes. You may feel pressure to use the assessment findings in ways that aren't consistent with the best interests of the athletes.

A second ethical challenge may arise when your compensation is tied to your assessment procedures, which may create a tension between the goal of providing ethical, quality services and the need to build and sustain your consulting practice. This friction may compel you, whether consciously or unconsciously, to the unethical use of assessment procedures. An example of this would be using costly, revenue-producing assessment procedures, methods, or instruments when more appropriate cost-effective alternatives exist. In the authors' view, this should never be an issue under consideration. However, if you struggle with such a conflict, it is imperative you seek supervision and treatment to enhance your ethical behavior. In these situations, to act on any of these other motives would be unethical. You must be mindful of the ethical principle of beneficence, which requires you to place the needs of your clients first, resist those competing forces, and act solely in your clients' best interests.

Principle B: Fidelity and Responsibility

This principle states that consultants should "establish relationships of trust with those with whom they work . . . uphold professional standards of conduct, clarify their professional roles and obligations, accept appropriate responsibility for their behavior and seek to manage conflicts of interest that could lead to exploitation or harm" (APA, 2002, p. 3). Principle B is important for the assessment of clients because only their trust in you ensures their comfort in participating in the assessments and knowing that the results will be used responsibly. You can promote this trust by explaining your professional credentials and describing your expertise and experience with administering assessments.

Principle C: Integrity

This principle maintains that consultants should "seek to promote accuracy, honesty and truthfulness in the science, teaching and practice of psychology. In these activities [consultants] do not steal, cheat or engage in fraud, subterfuge or intentional misrepresentation of fact" (APA, 2002, p. 3). You should only use assessments in ways that are empirically or experientially supportable for your intended purposes. Additionally, you must speak honestly to your clients and other stakeholders about the reasons for assessment, the value it will bring, and any limitations that may exist. Moreover, you should take care not to use assessments in ways that are ethically questionable, such as in identifying talent (see chapter 12) or as leverage by a team against an athlete.

Principle D: Justice

This principle states that consultants should "exercise reasonable judgment and take precautions to ensure that their potential biases, the boundaries of their competence and the limitations of their expertise do not lead to or condone unjust practices" (APA, 2002, p. 3).

Because interpretation lies at the heart of assessments, you must stay vigilant against any biases you bring to your evaluations, including those grounded in your education and training, your theoretical orientation, and your perceptions of your clients both as individuals and as members of a group (e.g., sport, race, ethnicity, cultural background), as well the cognitive biases that we are vulnerable to as both people and professionals (Kahneman & Tversky, 1974). In addition, you should represent yourself accurately to the client in a way that is consistent with your education, training, knowledge, and experience with assessment.

Principle E: Respect for People's Rights and Dignity

This principle asserts that consultants must "respect the dignity and worth of all people, and the rights of individuals to privacy, confidentiality, and self-determination . . . are aware of and respect cultural, individual and role differences, including those based on age, gender, gender identity, race, ethnicity, culture, national origin, religion, sexual orientation, disability, language and socioeconomic status and consider these factors when working with members of such groups" (APA, 2002, p. 4). As noted previously, the ethics of privacy, confidentiality, and self-determination are most open to violation when assessments have been commissioned or will be used by stakeholders other than the clients. In addition, the role of diversity has taken center stage in recent years (see chapter 4). Given that the vast majority of the available assessments in sport have been evaluated with a largely homogeneous population, you should be sensitive to clients' receptiveness to and benefits from these assessments in your work with a diverse population.

Ethical Guidelines

In addition to these broad principles, the APA code of conduct identifies standards related to ethical use of assessment, which will serve as the basis for our discussion of ethics in assessment in this chapter. "The Ethical Standards set forth enforceable rules for conduct as psy-

chologists. The Ethical Standards are written broadly, in order to apply to psychologists in varied roles, although the application of an Ethical Standard may vary depending on the context" (APA, 2002, p. 2). These standards have greater depth and breadth than the APA ethical principles, which are "aspirational goals to guide psychologists toward the highest ideals of psychology" (p. 2).

The AASP ethics code offers similar ethical guidelines. Additionally, the *Standards for Educational and Psychological Testing* (AERA, APA, & NCME, 2014) also provide guidance on ethical use of assessment methods.

Titles, Qualifications, and Competence

One difference between a profession and a guild or collective is that a profession sets standards of practice and codes of ethics for its members. The standards and ethical codes are developed over a period of time, peer reviewed by the membership, and updated as times change. The APA Division 47 (Sport, Exercise, and Performance Psychology) and Division 42 (Psychologists in Independent Practice), the AASP, and other professional organizations worldwide continually make efforts to ensure strict and consistent ethical practice by members.

Your most basic ethical obligation is to represent yourself to the client in a manner consistent with your assessment experience, level of training, licensure, and allowable title designation for the jurisdiction in which you practice. In many jurisdictional laws, the terms *psychology*, *psychological*, and *psychologist* are protected. Using these terms implies that a consultant is a licensed or registered psychologist who has received the appropriate education, training, supervision, and experience to earn a license. If the consultant is not a licensed or registered psychologist, it would be unethical to use the restricted terms unless allowed by law. (For further guidance in this area, refer to Zito, Herzog, & Shipherd, 2013.)

According to Standard 2.01 of the APA guidelines, Boundaries of Competence, you should utilize specific aspects of your education combined with experiential learning, professional training, supervision experiences, and continuing education to guide your decisions concerning the populations and contexts in which you practice (APA, 2002). Given the diverse training of practitioners in our field, most notably the educational tracks of psychology and sport science, the issues of qualifications and competencies are paramount.

You should gauge how you select and conduct assessments based on your qualifications and competencies as determined by your education, training, supervised experiences, and professional licenses or certifications. If a professional assessment is not within your scope of training and professional development, you should not conduct formal assessments, or you should seek didactic supervision, training, and practice before conducting an assessment. Many assessments, such as those measuring personality and intelligence, require specific educational qualifications, including particular coursework, degrees, licenses, or certifications. Standard 9.07, Assessment by Unqualified Persons, specifies that only qualified people who have received appropriate training and supervision should conduct assessments.

Even for assessments that are not controlled or that do not require specialized training, a fundamental aspect of competence is education and training in the psychometric properties of assessment and interpretation (see chapter 2 for more details). Standard 9.05, Test Construction, refers to the importance of test construction knowledge and scientific understanding of statistical properties of a scale (APA, 2002). If the assessment instrument is normed, you should understand the relevant standard scores, the T-score distributions, and the meaning of clients' scores in relation to the normative data. If your goal is to predict future performance, you need to know if research on an assessment tool has shown predictive validity.

Effective assessment is as much an art as it is a science. The ability to interpret, analyze, organize, and develop intervention plans is essential for ethical use of assessments by qualified consultants. In addition to the coursework that lays the foundation for these competencies, supervised practica followed by didactic mentoring opportunities provide the experiences necessary to become competent in using appropriate assessment methods to accurately understand your clients.

Choosing Appropriate Assessment Methods

Ethical issues may vary depending on the client you will be assessing, the context in which the assessment will occur, and your professional qualifications and competencies. For example, ethical concerns related to competence may be relevant if you are asked to conduct a mental status exam for a potential referral but you don't have clinical or counseling psychology or other mental health licensure (see chapter 5 for more on mental health screening). Or, ethical issues of confidentiality may come into play when doing assessments on professional athletes that are paid for by their teams. In any case, to ensure the welfare of your clients, you must identify which ethical issues may present themselves and then apply the ethical standards and assessment guidelines to direct your professional decision making and actions in the selection and use of assessments (Hankes, 2012).

Two APA standards and the *Standards for Educational and Psychological Testing* (AERA, APA, & NCME, 2014) assessment guidelines are relevant to the ethical selection of assessments for athletes or other sport stakeholders. Standard 9.01, Bases for Assessments, requires you to ensure that all aspects of your practice that document findings, offer diagnostic impressions, and provide descriptive analysis of these impressions and findings are logical, professionally sound interpretations of reliable and valid assessment methods and strategies (APA, 2002). In other words, the judgments you make and the conclusions you draw about your clients should be grounded in a sound rationale for using the chosen assessments and the information you gather from those assessments.

To that end, as stated in the *Standards for Educational and Psychological Testing*, "Test users are well advised, and may be legally required, to consider other relevant sources of information on test takers, not just test scores. This addresses the importance of multi-method evaluation data gathering" (AERA, APA, & NCME, 2014, p. 112). A central strength of this book is that it provides the tools to develop and conduct ethically appropriate multimethod assessments that may include a detailed history, collateral information, interviewing, personality testing, sport-specific inventories, psychophysiological evaluation, and observation.

Standard 9.02, Use of Assessments, further mandates that the assessments you select should be extensions of empirically validated research findings related to the application and utility of the assessment methods (APA, 2002). Moreover, you should be cognizant of the match between the evaluation procedures and their fit with the members of the population they are being administered to (see chapter 2 for more on assessment psychometrics). Additionally, you should administer the assessments in a way that is intended by their design and that is sensitive to the unique characteristics and circumstances of your clients.

One ethical concern related to Standard 9.02 involves the use of assessments to predict future performance, something that professional sport teams attempt to do. The use of the Wonderlic Cognitive Ability Test is notable and ethically questionable. The Wonderlic is best known as an assessment used by the National Football League (NFL) as part of its Scouting Combine despite the fact that it has been proven to have no validity in predicting career success in professional football. For instance, a number of studies have found no significant relationship between Wonderlic scores and success (Adams & Kuzmits, 2008; Mirabile, 2005; Tymins & Fraga, 2014). This example highlights an important ethical issue. If you are asked to administer an evaluation instrument that will be used to predict future performance, but that instrument has not been validated as a predictor of future performance, it would appear that are you in violation of Standard 9.02.

Additionally, Dana (1994) has written about the importance of client diversity (e.g., racial, ethnic, cultural, religious, gender) in selecting assessment instruments (see chapter 4 for more information). Dana compellingly states that "ethical issues are emotionally charged and have sociopolitical implications in a climate of chaos and impending societal transformation. In addition, models for multicultural assessment practice are still in the process of being developed" (p. 349). Although Dana's points are now 20 years old, they remain as timely as ever. In deciding which assessments to use, Dana recommends that you consider the client not simply as an individual but as part of a cultural constellation with values, attitudes, and beliefs that may affect their experience with assessments. Assessment tools that are developed in a particular culture tend to reflect the language and values of that culture. For example, certain personality assessments that were developed in the United States are biased against minority cultures (Comer, 2014). Other possible considerations are the age appropriateness of a test, non-native-speaking language biases, the influence of socioeconomic status, and whether an assessment was normed on athletes with disabilities (physical or learning).

Client Welfare

Your fundamental ethical responsibility is the welfare of your clients. In traditional psychotherapy settings, it is easy to establish who the client is (excluding family therapy). In contrast, the sport setting adds complexity to who the client is because the athlete is often embedded in a system in which other stakeholders are invested (emotionally or financially) in your work with the athlete, such as parents, team owners, and coaches. As Knauss (2001) suggests, when administering assessments, you may face ethical dilemmas related to divergent needs of different stakeholders in your work. Although Knauss primarily addresses evaluations as a psychologist in school settings, her comments are equally relevant to consultants working in a sport setting. Specifically, sometimes the reasons for assessing athletes and what is in their best interests may be different from the goals of the coaches requesting the assessment or the organization paying for the assessment. Ethical consultation requires identifying who the client is and making it clear to all stakeholders (ideally in writing) the person you are ethically responsible to. This explicit declaration can help ensure that all stakeholders are aligned on the intention, purpose, and value of assessments; build trust and relationships; and prevent miscommunications and conflicts related to the use of the assessment information.

The APA ethical guidelines (2002) address several essential aspects of client welfare related to assessment. Standard 9.03, Informed Consent in Assessments, mandates informed consent in which clients are told they will be assessed and are offered a clear overview of the assessment process and its rationale. This should include language and concepts that the client can understand. Additionally, the fee structure, parameters for sharing information, and any questions should be discussed. The answers to questions should be framed in language and on a conceptual level that the client can comprehend. Moreover, consent requires "affirmative permission before action can be taken" (Bersoff & Hofer, 1990, p. 950). Written documentation of informed consent should contain the reasons for the assessment, a description of the specific assessments you will use, how and for what purpose the results will be used, and who will have access to the findings, without making promises or guarantees of any outcomes. Moore (2003) further asserts that informed consent should include "financial issues, description of services, detailed information regarding the likelihood of intervention success . . . and guidelines and limitations to confidentiality" (p. 603).

Standard 9.03 also requires sufficient opportunity for clients to ask questions and receive answers. Additionally, you should be sensitive to your own reactions to athletes' concerns about what is going to be done with the results of an assessment program. An open, empathic response to clients' concerns will send the message that you have their best interests at heart and will help engender trust in you.

Standard 9.04, Release of Test Data, addresses ethical concerns about how and to whom assessment data is released (APA, 2002). Regardless of your professional training, whether in psychology or sport science, the dissemination of assessment results must be conducted with transparency and with a primary focus on the welfare of the client. Standard 9.04 guards against the indiscriminate sharing of any type of raw data (e.g., interview information, answers to objective inventories, psychophysiological measures, behavioral observations) or analyses or evaluations derived from the data. The standard indicates that practitioners conducting assessments must carefully consider how and what information is released to whom, as well as the tone, breadth and depth, and context of this presentation. The reason for these considerations is to solely protect the client from harm, misuse, or misinterpretation of assessment findings, interpretations, and recommendations. Violations of how and what information is released have legal and financial consequences based on the laws of each state. In considering the best interests of the athlete, your decision to not share information (e.g., with team executives or coaches) may be in conflict with the interests of the organization. This ethical dilemma may produce strong reactions from the organization that hired you. Sometimes the conflict of interest between you and the organization that hired you may threaten your professional relationship, and in an extreme case it could result in your termination. To use a sport-related expression, sometimes not playing ball can get you fired!

Use and Interpretation of Assessment Results

Standard 9.06, Interpreting Assessment Results, relates to the interpretation of assessment results (APA, 2002). Everyone has used the phrase "It's all a matter of interpretation" in informal settings. Yet, this matter of interpretation is of the utmost relevance in professional assessment. The interpretation of assessments, whether in client notes, formal reports, or automated output of computerized inventories, must be held to the same ethical standards because these analyses often provide more information about clients than the raw data from which they are gleaned. As mentioned earlier, your own potential biases also need to be considered as a factor in interpretation, and interpretation should be a data-driven process whenever possible.

Standard 9.09, Test Scoring and Interpretation Services, addresses the sale and purchase of assessment and scoring services that may yield automated reports (APA, 2002). This standard indicates that those offering assessment and scoring services for use by other professionals must be clear about the empirical characteristics and limitations of the assessment method. Furthermore, the training and experience necessary to administer and interpret the method should be communicated to those purchasing assessment services. This standard helps ensure that users can make informed, ethical decisions about which assessments best meet the needs and goals of their clients.

It is rare for consultants to develop and use their own formal assessments. As a consequence, consultants generally choose assessment instruments from those available for purchase or for free. Therefore, it is the consultants' responsibility to understand their role in the application, interpretation, and use of the materials. This responsibility is inherent, whether the consultant personally scores and interprets results or uses automated or other services. In all cases, you have an ethical obligation to have a deep understanding of the assessments you use, including their procedures, psychometrics, qualifications required, analytics, and limitations. The aim of this ethical obligation is to ensure that users have a comprehensive understanding of all aspects of the assessments so they can use them ethically with their clients.

Moreover, it is unethical to merely parrot the automated results generated by some assessment instruments, which are often overly broad and lack clear relevance to individuals. The nuances and complexities of an individual's behavior cannot be readily captured by these boilerplate reports. When interpreting results of an assessment tool, you need to consider the unique attributes and circumstances of individual clients, including test-taking abilities, life situation, and cultural and language differences. Finally, you are ethically bound to respect the copyright of assessment developers and only use assessments that you have legally purchased or that are freely available.

Standard 9.10, Explaining Assessment Results, addresses the issue of explaining assessment results to clients (APA, 2002). It states that consultants should make all reasonable efforts to ensure the assessment results are disseminated appropriately to the client or the designated individual receiving feedback (e.g., parent, coach, physician). In some circumstances, which are not relevant for most sport contexts, neither the client nor the client's representative will be the recipient of assessment results. This can be the case in some organizational consulting, preemployment or security screenings, and forensic evaluations. These latter circumstances would likely be the purview of a licensed psychologist or other health professional and require a clear explanation in advance.

The explanation of the assessment results should be introduced before the assessments are administered so that clients can understand the benefits of the assessments and how, when, and where they will learn the results. This process should also include how the assessments will be used, such as to inform an intervention plan that you will develop for your clients based on the results.

Assessment Security

Standard 9.11, Maintaining Test Security, requires consultants to ensure that test materials and other assessment techniques are kept secure and their integrity maintained (APA, 2002). Some vendors have periodic updates and renorming of their scoring sections that require purchasing the latest version of the instrument. In compliance with the Health Insurance Portability and Accountability Act (HIPAA), the consultant must consider security (physical and online) and other legal requirements. After you have obtained test results and they have been put to use with clients, you must ensure that all test materials (e.g., the instruments themselves, testing protocols, scoring manuals, client responses, client notes, analyses that resulted from the assessments) are protected from breaches of any sort, including breaches of physical and online storage. This is particularly a concern due to the increased use of online assessment and storage, where security breaches are not uncommon, and you are ethically bound to ensure that all components of the assessments that you administer to your clients are safe in perpetuity.

When Ethical Dilemmas Arise

Ethical dilemmas may arise in consulting for several reasons. First, ethical principles, standards, codes, and guidelines as detailed by the APA, AASP, and other professional organizations impose structure and behavioral conditions on decision making when conducting assessments in the sport setting. For example, they would govern your decision making if you experienced the previously discussed tension between the best interests of your clients and financial pressures you might feel as the owner of a consulting practice. If such temptations to place your financial needs ahead of your clients' needs arise, we encourage you to review the appropriate ethical guidelines and seek supervision to guide you toward the most ethical decisions, always acting in the best interests of your clients.

Second, working with athletes can involve many stakeholders (e.g., athletes, coaches, administrators, parents, media), who often have differing, and sometimes conflicting, motives and goals. For example, as discussed earlier, there may be conflict concerning the identification of who the client is and who thus requires your ethical consideration and protection. This situation can arise when your client differs from the person (e.g., parent) or organization (e.g., team) paying for your services. As a result of holding the financial responsibility for your assessment work, a stakeholder other than the athlete may expect access to or control over the results, resulting in a breach of confidentiality and privacy.

Third, you may be asked to conduct an assessment using instruments that lack validity for the requested purpose (e.g., the Wonderlic). Fourth, your role as a consultant for a high-profile sport organization, such as a collegiate or professional team, in which you may garner media attention, may challenge your clients' rights to confidentiality and privacy.

Regardless of the ethical dilemmas that arise, the fact that you recognize them speaks volumes to your integrity and your concern for your clients' welfare. When faced with ethically challenging situations, there are several steps you can take to ensure you are adhering to accepted ethical principles and guidelines. First, you should review the relevant APA and AASP ethical codes, as well as other professional assessment guidelines, to better understand the circumstance that has raised an ethical red flag. Second, we advise you to consult with a mentor or peer who has significant supervised assessment experience and expert knowledge of ethical guidelines. A trusted, knowledgeable, and experienced colleague can offer a dispassionate, reasoned perspective on the ethical situation in question. This consultation enables you to step outside your emotional engagement with the situation (and we assure you that it can be emotional) and gain a more impartial perspective on the ethical issue at hand. An effective consultation can allow you to

- sort out your thoughts and feelings related to the situation,
- clarify your needs and goals,
- identify the specific ethical issues and their causes,
- reality-test your perceptions of the situation to ensure an accurate representation of the conflict,
- illuminate and mitigate personal biases and distortions,
- specify the ethical standards being challenged, and
- assist in making sound decisions that will resolve the ethical dilemma.

Ultimately, a consultation with a trusted colleague can help you engage in rational problem solving and decision making with the goal of resolving the ethical dilemma and acting in the best interests of your client.

Chapter Takeaways

- Ethical behavior in your role as a sport psychologist or professionally trained consultant is the foundation of everything you do as a provider of assessment and intervention services.

- The most basic ethical obligation is to represent yourself to the client in a manner consistent with your assessment experience, level of training, licensure, and allowable title designation for your jurisdiction. Your fundamental ethical responsibility is the welfare of your clients.

- Ethical practice is of particular importance to assessment because it is the starting point for all of your consulting work and the potential benefits that will accrue for your clients. Assessment is a complex, dynamic activity that requires knowledge of measurement and interview principles and skills, an awareness of human systems, and the competence to administer, score, interpret, and communicate the results.

- You will likely be presented with situations in your consulting work that raise two ethical challenges. One is assessing athletes when there are other stakeholders who have conflicting needs, intentions, and goals. The other is when a tension arises between the goal of providing quality services and the need to build and sustain your consulting practice. This friction may compel you, whether consciously or unconsciously, to the unethical use of assessment procedures.

- You must be mindful of the ethical principle of beneficence, which requires you to place the needs of your clients first, resist competing forces, and act solely in your clients' best interests.

- When consultants ask questions, conduct interviews, and collect assessment data, the public must know and trust that the consultants have received education, training, and supervision that qualify them to do so ethically and with the best interests of their clients in mind.

- The APA general principles consist of five tenets that are intended to "guide and inspire psychologists toward the very highest ethical ideals of the profession" (APA, 2002, p. 3).

- Ethical issues may vary depending on the client you are assessing, the context in which the assessment occurs, and your professional qualifications and competencies.

- Multimethod data gathering should be the cornerstone of your assessment process, which includes a detailed history, collateral information, interviewing, administration of assessment devices, and observation, so as to maximize the validity and reliability of your evaluation.

- The APA ethics code provides guidance for psychologists and standards of ethical professional conduct that can be applied by the APA and by other bodies that choose to adopt them.

- When ethical dilemmas arise, you should review the relevant APA ethical codes and seek consultation with a mentor or peer who has significant supervised assessment experience and expert knowledge of ethical guidelines.

CHAPTER 4
Diversity in Sport Psychology Assessment

Latisha Forster Scott, PhD

Taunya Marie Tinsley, PhD

Kwok Ng, PhD

Jenny Lind Withycombe, PhD, CC-AASP

Melanie Poudevigne, PhD, FACSM, CC-AASP

An appreciation of the athlete's worldview, as well as an awareness of the consultant's own assumptions, values, and biases, is necessary to establish a healthy relationship with clients and to develop culturally appropriate intervention strategies and techniques aimed at enhancing athletic performance. The purpose of this chapter is to examine the role of diversity and culture in sport psychology assessment. A systematic developmental framework for assessment of athletes from diverse cultural backgrounds will be provided. We will examine cultural diversity and sport psychology assessment and provide information on cultural sport psychology competencies. You will become aware of cultural, individual, and role differences within the athlete population, including those based on gender, language, disability, race, and spirituality and religion, and how to consider these factors when working with athletes.

Marginalization of Cultural Diversity in Sport Psychology and Assessment

Culture is used throughout this chapter to refer to identity characteristics encompassing such elements as a person's gender, race, sexual orientation, religion, age, national identity, language, spirituality, and ability. The role of culture is often marginalized or not addressed at all in sport psychology assessment. Issues of self-esteem, self-concept, self-image, and athletic identity are examined throughout the literature, but usually from a point of reference from the dominant culture (Ram, Starek, & Johnson, 2004). This lack of culturally relevant information disregards the present diversity of athletics. Standard concepts, instruments, and procedures in which the dominant group is considered the norm are not always appropriate for examining the collective behavior of those who have cultural perspectives that are historically and often radically different. To increase empirical knowledge and provide relevant data, social scientists must give more credence to the cultural factors endemic to the diverse communities from which athletes come.

Consultants need to carefully consider the significance of identity politics as they are expressed, reproduced, or resisted in sport. The systems of domination and subordination that people must function within play a role in their development. Therefore, to understand the behaviors of athletes, it is important to understand their collective experiences, attitudes, and behaviors as they seek to succeed in environments that often assign them a subordinate status. These experiences are sources of stratification that will alter the life choices and perceptions of each athlete. It would be naive for a consultant to ignore these influences on assessments and the range of interventions that are used.

Multicultural Sport Psychology Competencies

The fields of sport psychology and cultural psychology and counseling are influenced by the history of general psychology, and recognition of the hegemonic history of this field is critical. The development of multicultural counseling and cultural sport psychology (CSP) marks a paradigm shift in the way sport psychology consultants work within their various fields. The majority of these consultants are white, male, able-bodied, Christian, and upper middle class, yet the majority of athletes (and to some extent coaches) represent significant diversity in all these areas. Few consultants are trained in CSP and are often uncomfortable tackling issues that fall outside the dominant paradigms under which they were trained (Schinke & Hanrahan, 2009). It is important for consultants to not only be aware of their own cultural influences but also do their best to increase their knowledge of the athlete's cultural background. International status, race, ethnicity, gender, primary language, and religion, to name a few, can influence athletes' goals for participating and competing in sport (Cole & Tinsley, 2009; Steinfeldt, Reed, & Steinfeldt, 2010). Additionally, minority

groups, including athletes, can face oppression, prejudice, and discrimination (Simons, Bosworth, Fujita, & Jensen, 2007). By extending the principles of multicultural counseling and cross-cultural psychology to the athlete population, consultants are in a better position to respond to the unique needs and goals of athletes and to enhance the quality of their services (Ward, Sandstedt, Cox, & Beck, 2005).

The American Counseling Association (ACA) recognized a need for specialized training in sport counseling more than 25 years ago (Nejedlo, Arredondo, & Benjamin, 1985). In 2005, Tinsley developed the multicultural sports counseling competencies and their four dimensions. Additionally, Ward et al. (2005) identified several essential competencies for psychologists working with athletes.

Tinsley

- *Multicultural sports counseling competencies* are defined as the extent to which the counselor has developed and integrated the awareness, knowledge, and skills, while maintaining a positive counseling relationship, necessary to work with the athlete population.

- *Multicultural awareness* is defined as proactive multicultural sensitivity and responsiveness toward athletes, extensive interactions and life experiences with sport and athletes, broad-based cultural understanding, advocacy within institutions, enjoyment of the athlete population, and an increase of athletes as clients.

- *Multicultural counseling knowledge* is defined as the ability to conduct culturally relevant case conceptualization and treatment strategies, assess cultural information, and conduct multicultural counseling research with the athlete population.

- *Multicultural counseling skills* are defined as the successful retention of athlete cases, recognition of and recovery from cultural mistakes, use of nontraditional assessment methods, counselor self-monitoring, and tailoring of structured versus unstructured counseling sessions to the needs of athletes.

- *Multicultural counseling relationship* is defined as the counselor's interaction process with athletes, such as the counselor's trustworthiness, comfort level, stereotypes of athletes, and worldview.

Ward et al.

- Sport psychologists recognize that clients' athletic identity may be as important to the counseling process as their race, gender, age, and so on.
- Sport psychologists respect coaches' helping practices and organizational help-giving resources.
- Sport psychologists respect clients' beliefs and values regarding physical and mental training.
- Sport psychologists are aware of their values and biases as they relate to athletes and the sport environment.
- Sport psychologists do not automatically assume that clients' presenting issues are clinical in nature.
- Sport psychologists acknowledge the existence of a distinct sport and athlete culture.
- Sport psychologists understand the influence of the athletic environment on their clients.
- Sport psychologists understand and respect organizational and institutional regulations that may govern a client's behavior.
- Sport psychologists understand how race, culture, and ethnicity affect the appropriateness of counseling treatments for their clients.
- Sport psychologists have had supervised experience counseling athletes.
- Sport psychologists refer clients to more qualified professionals when appropriate.
- When a dual relationship is unavoidable, sport psychologists place importance on maintaining the effectiveness of their counseling relationship with their clients.
- Sport psychologists take into account cultural differences when selecting particular techniques and theoretical frameworks for work with clients.

- Sport psychologists know how and when to intervene with institutions and organizations on behalf of their clients while appreciating the complexity of confidential issues in a sport environment.
- Sport psychologists take responsibility for educating clients, whether they are athletes, coaches, or organizations, about the counseling process.
- Sport psychologists ethically seek consultation with coaches regarding clients' treatment when appropriate.
- Sport psychologists use those counseling theories and techniques that are most compatible with athlete culture.

The competencies identified by Tinsley (2005) and Ward et al. (2005) are categorized within the domains of attitudes and beliefs, knowledge, and skills, and they promote counseling awareness and sensitivity within the sport culture. More specifically, Ward et al.'s competencies were designed to help counseling professionals not trained in sport psychology to identify areas where further education, training, and experience are needed to ensure effective and ethical service delivery. Developing such competencies will help psychologists and students not trained in sport psychology identify areas in which they need further education, training, or experiences in order to competently work with clients; further define the specialty of athlete counseling; and help athlete clients, as well as nonathlete clients, distinguish among available psychological services (Ward et al., 2005).

Overview of Multicultural Assessment

This section provides an overview of issues pertaining to gender, language, disability, race, and religion. The goal is to enhance your levels of cultural competency, which will better prepare you to utilize tools for multicultural assessment.

Gender and Sex

As stated by Ryba, Schinke, and Tenenbaum (2009), "Much of the knowledge base in sport and exercise psychology was developed by inference from positivistic research and practice with white male athletes" (p. 3). Failing to address gender identity in sport and exercise psychology diminishes the diversity of gendered experiences within sport.

Sex constitutes a person's biology, whereas *gender*, or more appropriately, *gender identity*, refers to a person's sense of him or herself as male or female, masculine or feminine. Historically, men used males exclusively as their sample populations in devising the majority of early psychological theories; women were seen as merely variations from the norm (Hyde, 2005). Even when women were included in the research process, traditional gender roles and identity constructions were used (Hyde, 2005). For example, Gill and Kamphoff (2010) explain that studies in the sport and exercise literature from the 1970s often relied on stereotypical masculine and feminine characteristics such as personality traits. Because female athletes often had elevated scores in the categories of assertiveness and competitiveness, they were described as being more masculine, a finding that still has significant psychological and sociocultural ramifications. The authors further explain that recent studies have now examined male and female athlete competitiveness independent of these so-called masculine and feminine personality traits (Gill & Kamphoff, 2010). Using the Sport Orientation Questionnaire (SOQ; Gill & Deeter, 1988), which measures sport achievement orientation, similarities and differences between male and female athletes on dimensions of competitiveness can be explored independent of socially normed beliefs about men and women (Gill & Kamphoff, 2010).

Gender biases influence the topics that scholars consider important to study, the theoretical constructs guiding their research, the selection of sample populations, and the analysis and implications of data (Matsumoto & Juang, 2008). Differences in social roles, societal expectations, opportunities to learn, and biological characteristics might confound assessment responses and interpretations for males and females. Furthermore, gender bias can occur in the design, selection, administration, and interpretation of an assessment, meaning that different norms, additional or multiple

indicators, and multiple interpreters might be necessary to ensure valid assessments (Linn & Kessel, 2006).

When a psychological instrument is developed in one society (e.g., the United States) with one population (e.g., middle-class, Christian, able-bodied white men) and is applied to a different society (e.g., Nicaragua) and a different population (e.g., working-class Latina women), reliability and validity cannot be assumed. In its most general form, bias is "a lack of correspondence between the observed scores of subjects from different cultural populations and the domain of generalization" (van de Vijver & Poortinga, 1997, p. 29). The most common reason for bias is the unfounded assumption of the generalizability of psychological constructs and theoretical underpinnings (van de Vijver & Poortinga, 1997). Although today's studies include far more diversely gendered samples, gender stereotypes remain a core part of how we see the world. Studies by Williams, Satterwhite, and Best (1999) spanning more than two decades demonstrate the pervasive and stable nature of gender stereotypes around the world and across time. According to the results of the Williams et al. (1999) studies,

> men are generally viewed as active, strong, critical, and adult like, with psychological needs such as dominance, autonomy, aggression, exhibition, achievement, and endurance. Men are also associated more with the personality traits of conscientiousness, extroversion, and openness. Women are generally viewed as passive, weak, nurturing, and adaptive, with psychological needs such as abasement, deference, succorance, nurturance, affiliation, and heterosexuality. They are also associated with higher scores on personality traits of agreeableness and neuroticism. (Matsumoto & Juang, 2008, p. 170)

Stereotypes such as these often play a significant role in psychological assessment development, research, and interpretations, particularly in sport settings where hegemonic ideologies remain strong (Matsumoto & Juang, 2008).

Despite the growth of feminist research in areas such as multicultural and cross-cultural psychology, reviews of publications and conference programs confirm a continued lack of diversity in sport psychology research and practice (Ryba et al., 2009). Diversifying sport psychology does not merely mean including women in studies. It means "diversifying against the backdrop of the cultural turn and a serious engagement with a reexamination of ontological, epistemological, analytical, and political underpinnings of sport psychological research" (Ryba et al., 2009, p. 6). For example, early sport psychology research focused exclusively on gender differences between the sexes: personality and roles (e.g., Bem Sex-Role Inventory), competitive orientation (e.g., SOQ), self–perceptions in sport, and physical activity and body image (Gill, 2007). Today's research emphasizes the importance of social context and processes and demonstrates that males and females are "more alike than different on psychological variables, and overstated claims of gender differences cause harm and limit opportunities" (Hyde, 2005, p. 569).

"How males and females think they differ is more important than how they actually differ" (Ryba et al., 2009, p. 64). And by extension, the conscious and unconscious beliefs of those who select, administer, and interpret the results of psychological assessments in sport settings have an impact on the understanding of clients and the profession (Fuentes & Adames, 2014). It is critical to carefully consider sex and gender issues in clinical and applied practice. As Ryba and colleagues (2009) state, we must consider the "cultural context and social practices that permeate and constitute the individual psyche" (p. ix). The use of psychological assessments is an integral part of consulting; however, we must proceed with caution. Considerations regarding gender and assessment are briefly summarized in table 4.1.

Language

Adopting the practices of the world's leading sport psychology assessments is strategically desirable because these practices are based on reliable, validated existing samples. The question is whether these practices are effective in other areas of the world where different national cultures influence different value systems. It is worthwhile to investigate whether the same questionnaire measures the same constructs in different cultural systems.

Cluster analysis is popular in psychology. This analytical procedure examines varying motivational behavior and profiles of athletes in sport psychology. However, relatively little research has been conducted in the cross-cultural context. Research is needed for each construct equivalence across diverse cultural groups.

Motivation has the most cross-cultural validation. For example, Brière, Vallerand, Blais, and Pelletier (1995) created the Échelle de Motivation dans les Sports (EMS) to assess self-determination in sport. This instrument is based on the Academic Motivation Scale (AMS;

Table 4.1   Key Components of Gender Reflexivity in Assessment

Theoretical constructs	Instrument	Consultant
Are the theories that underpin the development of the assessment culturally reflexive?	Were different sexes and gendered samples assessed during the creation of the instrument?	What are my potential sex and gender biases?
Were different sexes and gender orientations included in the development of the theory?	Is this instrument valid and reliable across populations with differing sexes and genders?	What impact might my biases have on my research, practice, choice of assessments, interpretation of results, and so on?
How were sex and gender defined?	Does it make sense to have more than one consultant interpret the results before drawing conclusions?	How will I minimize the influence of my positionality on my understanding of the subject's assessment and subsequent care?

Vallerand, Pelletier, et al., 1992) in the English version of l´Échelle de Motivation en Éducation (EME; Vallerand, Blais, Brière, & Pelletier, 1989). The EMS measures intrinsic and extrinsic motivation and was translated into English by Pelletier and colleagues (1995) as the Sport Motivation Scale (SMS). With regard to the validity and reliability of the SMS, factor-analytic studies have supported the seven-factor structure, which was then used to develop the Behavioral Regulation in Sport Questionnaire (BRSQ). The BRSQ has better cross-cultural validity compared with the SMS when measuring motivation (Lonsdale, Hodge, & Rose 2008).

When looking for universality of a construct across countries, Scholz, Doña, Sud, and Schwarzer (2002) demonstrated that several prerequisites must be considered: "First, a culturally sensitive adaptation of the instrument, which is superior to a literal translation, is made for all languages and second, it has the same structure across cultures, which is especially important when dealing with multidimensional instruments" (p. 249). Today, the Bandura self-efficacy scales (2006) remain the only universal confidence scales to be translated and validated cross-culturally. The Profile of Mood States (POMS) from McNair, Lorr, and Droppleman (1971) also seems to be a universal measure of moods such as anxiety, depression, fatigue, vigor, and anger but requires further cross-cultural investigation.

Many of the current theories and constructs in exercise and sport psychology were developed in English-speaking countries and therefore tested psychometrically in westernized regions. The extent to which cultural bias may exist is largely unknown for most questionnaires. Assuming that a mere translation of a questionnaire will suffice is naive because it can lead to inaccurate cross-cultural inferences. There is a clear need to develop valid and reliable cross-cultural questionnaires to assist with assessments accounting for cultural differences. A questionnaire should only be generalized once cross-cultural validation is demonstrated. To date, sport psychology assessments are mostly based on single-nation samples. Methodology, validation, and equivalency should be meticulously studied across constructs to better appreciate the world's cultural wealth in sport psychology.

Disability

The United Nations (UN) Convention on the Rights of Persons with Disabilities states that "persons with disabilities include those who have long-term physical, mental, intellectual or sensory impairments which in interaction with various barriers may hinder their full and effective participation in society on an equal basis with others" (UN, 2008, Article 1). Descriptions of the term *disability* are often needed in the literature, and the *Publication Manual of the American Psychological Association, Sixth Edition* (APA, 2010) provides guidelines for using the person-first approach, focusing on the individual rather than the disability. Guidelines 13 through 17 are explicit to testing and assessment in the APA *Guidelines for Assessment of and Intervention with Persons with Disabilities* (APA, 2016). Using correct terms is important to the profession; however, the publication manual only provides guidance for writing about disability. The situation can be very different when working with athletes with disabilities. Studies from the perspective of athletes in disability sport indicate that some athletes do not approve of the person-first approach (Peers, Spencer-Cavaliere, & Eales, 2014). As such, it is important to know how your clients with disabilities use language to describe their needs.

Another consideration is finding out what it means for the athlete to have an athletic identity. For some people with disabilities, athletic identities will vary. Some may have a nonathlete identity, some may see the athlete as a future self, and some may view the present self as athlete (Perrier, Smith, Strachan, & Latimer-Cheung, 2014). For example, in media coverage and on billboards around London and the rest of the United Kingdom during the 2012 Paralympic Games, images of Paralympians with the tagline of *Meet the Superhumans* were visible almost everywhere (Walker, 2012). This was one type of athletic identity that bolstered the image of people with disabilities. Within the supercrip theory, people with physical disabilities are not expected to take part and excel in activities like sport, nor is it considered normal for them to do so. However, athletes who overcome this and go onto the larger stage in sport have been framed as supercrips in the same way that Superman had superpowers over the average human (Silva & Howe, 2012). Although athletic prowess is a major feature in athletic identity for people without disabilities, the external perception of overcoming disability to compete in sport is unique to athletes with disabilities, and consultants should consider how athletes identify within this framework.

Athletes' relationships with coaches and managers may also be problematic; recent surveys indicate that coaches lack sufficient knowledge about disabilities (Dieffenbach & Statler, 2012). Few coaches have disabilities themselves, and thus it may be more difficult for some coaches to recognize and understand the specific challenges a disabled athlete is facing. However, this may arguably be a good thing because the sporting identity of disability sport is not completely framed around the disability (Howe, 2008), and thus the athlete excels beyond limited expectations. In addition, there must be heightened trust between the athlete (e.g., biomedical history, sport identity and competencies) and the coach for high performance (Peters & Kohe, 2016). Meaningful assessments in this realm of coach–athlete relationships provide valuable insights in applied practice.

Currently, elite disability sport is organized for competition through a system of complex classifications. The purpose of classification is to provide an equal playing field based on the sport-specific capabilities of the athlete (Tweedy & Vanlandewijck, 2009). However, these classifications are constantly evolving. Following changes to a classification system, athletes who were once the best in their classification level may find they become some of the worst in the revised class (Jobling, 2012). Throughout these changes during an athlete's career, psychological assessments may need to be revisited.

Race

Sport mimics the greater society wherein the problems of prejudice, discrimination, and racism continue to exist. According to Coakley (2007), sport organizations possess patterns of discrimination and racism similar to those found in the larger social environment. Media exposure of some racially diverse athletes in certain sports lead many to believe that sport

is relatively free of the racism that is found in other aspects of life. However, upon closer look, it is clear that racial and ethnic minority athletes are largely absent from many sports, and those who participate often face some form of racial treatment and discrimination (Lapchick, 2015). Issues of race and ethnicity contribute to the inequities found in sport, and racism can exist at the individual, institutional, and cultural levels of sport (Brooks & Althouse, 2000; Captain, 1991).

Examples of racism in sport include the following:

- Overt or covert denial to participate in a sport, team, or league based on race
- Social isolation of racial minority athletes in and out of a sport setting
- Name-calling by teammates, coaches, opponents, fans, or referees
- Unequal pay or notoriety for the same services and accomplishments
- Stacking in particular player positions
- Limited opportunities at the athletic, managerial, and administrative levels
- Perpetual beliefs about natural and unnatural physical and intellectual abilities
- Systemic cultural, economic, and political forces that limit opportunities to participate in local, national, and international levels of sport

Historically, discussions of race assumed that groups of people have a biological basis of identification that sets them apart from other groups (Oomen, 1994). These biological traits are usually observable in skin color, nasal index, lip thickness, and hair texture. However, more recent scholarship argues that there is greater biological overlap and similarity than difference between the so-called races, which weakens any definition of race that relies solely on biology (Ponterotto, Utsey, & Pederson, 2006). Hence, the term *race* does not exclude aspects of social, political, and cultural commonality. Race is arguably a sociopolitical construction used to divide people along dominant and subordinate lines (Jones, 1997).

Ethnicity is the identification with a group of people who share a common background of certain beliefs, values, customs, language, religion, territory, and historical experiences (Tatum, 2003). The terms *race* and *ethnicity* are often used interchangeably; however, *race* usually implies some biological basis for identification, and *ethnicity* focuses more on shared cultural experiences, with less emphasis on physical difference. It is important to understand the greater context in which race and ethnicity are being discussed, because some societal practices differentiate and oppress along the lines of ethnicity versus race. It is also important to know that people may be of the same race but different ethnicities.

Jones (1997) asserts that racism occurs at the individual, institutional, and cultural levels. A racist individual believes that one is superior or inferior based on some physical trait that determines social, moral, and intellectual qualities and presumes that these qualities are a legitimate basis for one's inferior or superior status. Institutional racism involves those established laws, customs, and practices that systematically reflect and produce racial inequalities. These racialized practices can either be overt or covert, intentional or unintentional. The intent of a law or practice does not have to be intentionally racist, but if it has clear and recognizable racialized effects, it is therefore racist. Cultural racism is the cumulative effect of individual and institutional racist beliefs and practices that favor the dominant group. Racialized customs become so ingrained in the culture that certain practices go unquestioned or unchecked and are simply considered the norm, wherein racialized viewpoints are reproduced from one generation to the next.

It is important to consider the meaningfulness of race and racism in athletes' lives, particularly if athletes assert some level of significance to race and the conditions of their lives in and out of sport. *Racial identity development* refers to the process of defining for oneself the significance and social meaning of belonging to a racial group (Tatum, 2003). *Racial identity saliency* refers to the extent to which a person's race is relevant to self-concept. The degree to which race is salient to a person has implications for the way events are construed and the resulting behavior (Sellers, Rowley, Chavous, Shelton, & Smith, 1997). Racial identity saliency is not

stagnant for an individual or group. Therefore, the degree to which racial identity has occurred in a positive or negative manner needs to be taken into consideration when counseling or assessing those who identify with specific racial or ethnic groups.

Racial identity developmental processes have the potential to greatly influence an athlete's sport experiences both positively and negatively. *Acculturation* refers to the extent to which ethnic minorities participate in the dominant cultural traditions (acculturated), remain immersed in their own cultures (traditional), or become bicultural (participate in both) (Landrine & Klonoff, 1994). It is important to identify where a client falls within this framework so that certain behaviors can be better understood. Never assume that athletes take pride in identifying with their ethnicity or have positive feelings associated with their racial group. The degree of racial pride and racial saliency will vary from one athlete to another (Helms, 1995). Keep in mind that many racial and ethnic minorities are socialized into the larger society, which often devalues the beliefs and practices of their racial and ethnic groups. Thus, many develop unhealthy ways of being and are faced with conflict in trying to negotiate between the groups they identify with.

Coping skills play a significant role in the ability to survive in a system that has historically devalued a particular race or ethnic group. Individual, family, community, and organizational styles of coping have assisted racial and ethnic minorities in dealing with poverty, discrimination, racism, and various forms of political and economic forces that work against them (Daly, Jennings, Beckett, & Leashore, 1995). Understanding how racial minorities respond to living in a society that has worked systematically to oppress their existence is crucial in gaining insight into the process of a maturing self-identity. The psychology of oppression is important in understanding the behavior of racial and ethnic minorities because there is a constant struggle for them to exist in a dominant culture that seeks to deny their legitimacy (Baldwin, 1980). There is no complete separation of one's racial identity and athletic identity. Helping an athlete develop effective coping skills when it comes to race and racism can often be the difference between having a long-term successful athletic career versus one that is cut short.

Spirituality and Religion

Consultants work with athletes who hold widely differing values and beliefs about their sporting and everyday life, and it is inevitable that a significant number of athletes will also have spiritual or religious beliefs (Watson & Nesti, 2005). Research has shown that spirituality plays an important role in enhancing sport performance and contributing to personal growth and well-being (Dillon & Tait, 2000). Additionally, current research indicates that spirituality and religion have a positive impact on both mental and physical health and that spiritual well-being is strongly associated with psychological factors related to athletic performance (Hall & Edwards, 2002; Storch, Kolsky, Silvestri, & Storch, 2001). Thus, consultants need to understand that spiritual and religious matters are therapeutically relevant, ethically appropriate, and significant topics to assess, either quantitatively or qualitatively, when developing culturally appropriate interventions and responding to the unique needs of athletes.

Religion and spirituality are interrelated but are conceptualized differently. Although research has shown that spirituality is positively associated with good physical and psychological health, the definitions of spirituality and religion are varied. For the purpose of this chapter, *spirituality* will be used to describe one's "search for meaning and purpose in human existence. It includes the development of a deep appreciation for the depth and expanse of life and natural forces that exist in the universe" (Hettler, 1976, p. 55). Furthermore, it can be defined as a sense of relatedness and connectedness to others and the fostering of body and soul through a stress-buffering effect (Ridnour & Hammermeister, 2008). *Religion*, on the other hand, is denominational, external, cognitive, behavioral, ritualistic, and public. It provides a social context within which a set of beliefs, practices, and experiences occurs. Religion is institutional and creedal, and it is typically socially defined. It offers a structure for human spirituality, including narratives, symbols, beliefs, and practices that are embedded in ancestral traditions, cultural traditions, or both.

Once the definitions of spirituality and religion have been clarified, consultants can understand that their clients, as well as themselves, will present widely differing ideas about religion, spirituality, and the relationship between the two. To practice ethically and competently, it is necessary to discern a client's unique experience of this relationship (quantitatively, qualitatively, or both), understanding that an athlete can be both spiritual and religious, spiritual but not religious, religiously tolerant and indifferent, religiously antagonistic, or religious but not spiritual (Cashwell & Young, 2011). Additionally, consultants may want to consider integrating the Competencies for Addressing Spiritual and Religious Issues in Counseling into their practice. The Association for Spiritual, Ethical, and Religious Values in Counseling (ASERVIC) has outlined these competencies (i.e., culture and worldview, self-awareness, human and spiritual development, communication, assessment, diagnosis, and treatment) to honor "diversity and embrace a cross-cultural approach in support of the worth, dignity, potential, and uniqueness of people within their social and cultural contexts" (ACA, 2014, p. 3; ASERVIC, 2015). More specifically, the ASERVIC competencies state, "During the intake and assessment processes, the professional counselor [or sport psychology consultant in this case] strives to understand a client's spiritual and/or religious perspective by gathering information from the client and/or other sources" (ASERVIC, 2015).

The ASERVIC competencies are intended to be used in conjunction with evidence-based counseling and psychological approaches that align with best practices in psychology and counseling, including sport psychology and sport counseling (ASERVIC, 2015). More specifically, the APA (2002) included religion, a subset of spiritual well-being, in its ethical principle on respect for people's rights and dignity. Furthermore, the recent call for positive psychology provides further support for the argument that the spiritual side of human existence plays an important role in fostering not only mental health and physical well-being but excellence in human activities as well (Ridnour & Hammermeister, 2008).

Developing Action Plans to Deal With Racial or Religious Conflicts

Remember that the saliency of race and religion will be different for each athlete, and the level of acculturation will vary. Help athletes identify whether or not what they are experiencing stems from individual, institutional, or cultural practices. Which of these do the athletes have any control over or are able to deal with directly? Help the athletes identify support systems. Are there nearby clubs, organizations, or functions relative to the athletes' race or religion that they can join? Help the athletes identify places of worship and places to purchase personal items such as hair products, foods, or religious items that may not be available in typical stores. Help the athletes identify psychological safe places and allies within the team or organization and cooperatively develop a plan of action to deal with conflict that may continue to arise.

Assessment Tools

Unless otherwise noted, all of the assessment tools discussed in the following sections have sound psychometric properties. These include acceptable validity, reliability, and internal consistency.

Gender and Sex

Currently, there are no sport assessments used specifically to explore the saliency of gender in sport contexts. Following the feminist movement of the 1960s, a recognition of the use of primarily male samples to test and validate psychological assessments encouraged psychologists and counselors to validate such assessments using sex- and gender-diverse samples. Many sport assessments have been adjusted according to sex similarities and differences and are now considered valid and reliable. At present more work needs to be done to explore the impact of varied gender conceptions and identities in psychological assessments in general and in sport.

Language

Guillemin, Bombardier, and Beaton (1993) recommend sensitivity to the translation of questionnaires. They suggest following the scenarios presented in table 4.2.

The chapter-ending tables Assessment Tools and Their Availability and Assessment Tools for Non-English Speakers and Their Availability detail various sport psychology constructs and assessment tools, their respective reference and acceptable validity in the appropriate language for non-English speakers, and their availability. The assessments in the tables were chosen based on their free access online, the 10 most spoken languages in the world, and the top 10 languages used the most for translations with questionnaires. Consultants should also visit the free online article from Acquadro, Conway, Hareendran, and Aaronson (2008), which details methods to translate questionnaires for use in multinational research.

Disability

Sport psychology assessment tools specifically for athletes with disabilities are not well produced, often because of low sample sizes or a lack of generalizability due to the types of disabilities involved in studies (Semerjian, 2009). In the majority of cases, common assessment instruments that have sound reliability and validity can also be applied to athletes with disabilities (Dieffenbach & Statler, 2012). One area for caution is the functional limitations of the athlete (Hanrahan, 2005).

Across various health professions, including psychology, the International Classification of Functioning, Disability and Health (ICF) of the World Health Organization (WHO; 2001) is used to gain a better understanding of functional limitations. In this model, disability is no longer only a medical condition, nor is it just due to societal barriers. The ICF model is a biopsychosocial-spiritual approach in the context of ethics, human rights, and legal frameworks. It is a classification system whereby all people fit into a spectrum of functioning, disability, and health. There are six interacting components: health condition, body structure and functions, activities, participation, environmental factors, and

Table 4.2   Scenarios Where Cross-Cultural Adaptation May Be Required

Use of a questionnaire in a new population	Resulting changes			Adaptation required	
	Culture	Language	Country of use	Translation	Cultural adaptation
Use in same population; no change in culture, language, or country from source	—	—	—	—	—
Use in established immigrants in source country	✓	—	—	—	✓
Use in other country with same language	✓	—	✓	—	✓
Use in new immigrants, not English-speaking but in same source country	✓	✓	—	✓	✓
Use in another country and another language	✓	✓	✓	✓	✓

Adapted from Guillemin, Bombardier, and Beaton 1993.

personal factors. The ICF also offers a common language for professionals, support members, and athletes, enabling people to work together to provide full participation (Bickenbach, 2012). The International Paralympic Committee (IPC) believes it is important to use the language of the ICF, not least in the international acceptability of the ICF as well as the translations offered by WHO partners (Tweedy & Vanlandewijck, 2009).

One useful area of the ICF lies in the global mental domain, which would be helpful in highlighting the ability of athletes to use their mental capacities when taking an assessment. Athletes with moderate, severe, or complete limitations in their mental capacities may struggle to comprehend assessment tools. Additionally, there is a sensory and pain domain, which can provide insight when addressing tools related to psychological disorders. Consultants may, at times, trust too many of their own specialized tools rather than provide consistency and rely upon the global assessments that are used and shared by other health professionals. Other bodily functions and structures may also limit the use of certain assessment tools; therefore, consultants will find the ICF useful when assessing athletes with disabilities.

During the assessment phase of a consultation, use the ICF to consider whether a pen-and-paper format can be used. Following are some other questions to consider: Can the assessment tool

Assessment in Action

Identifying the Functional Limitations of Clients

This exercise can help identify the functional limitations of clients and provide a common language so teams can work together to provide full support. According to the ICF (WHO, 2001) all people fit on a spectrum of functioning, disability, and health. The six interacting components of the ICF include health condition, body structure and functions, activities, participation, environmental factors, and personal factors (Bickenbach, 2012). Discuss each of these components with your clients and have them describe any functional limitations. Then have the clients explain what it means for them to be athletic in light of these limitations. This exercise can help clients develop a sense of purpose, as well as aid in the identification of necessary support systems for success.

be used in the way it was meant to be? In what ways can the assessment tool be modified? Can the athlete hold a pen steadily enough to complete the assessment tool? Will bias result if the assessment tool is read aloud? Does the client have sufficient patience or dignity to complete the assessment tool in the original or modified way?

Race

Most of the current instruments that exist examine race, racism, and racial identity development outside the sport context (Forster-Scott, 2005). The Saliency of Race in Sport Questionnaire (SORIS-Q) explores the role that race and racial identity play in sport. The SORIS-Q examines these issues within the sport context, determining the extent to which issues of race are perceived to play a role in a sport participant's experiences.

The SORIS-Q is based on the theory of nigrescence and the Cross Racial Identity Scale (CRIS; Vandiver, Cross, Worrell, & Fhagen-Smith, 2002). Nigrescence models of racial identity development have six stages, as described in table 4.3.

The SORIS-Q is worded so that it can be used with anyone. Athletes are able to self-identify their race or ethnicity, and there are no specific references to any racial or ethnic group in any of the statements. Hence, the SORIS-Q can provide way to assess the impact of race-related issues when working with athletes. Future research with this instrument will include more diverse racial and ethnic sampling.

Spirituality and Religion

The most researched instrument on spirituality and religion to date, the Spiritual Well-Being Scale (SWBS; Ridnour & Hammermeister, 2008) consists of two subscales. The first subscale measures religious well-being as it relates to the subjects' relationship with a higher power (God) in regard to commitment, behavior, communication, cooperation, level of friendship, or degree of intimacy. The second subscale measures existential well-being, or the subjects' environmental relationship, meaning the conditions that affect the way people live and how satisfied they are in life. The SWBS consists of 20 items using a 6-point Likert-type scale (1 = strongly disagree; 6 = strongly agree).

The Duke Religion Index (DRI; Koenig, Parkerson, & Meador, 1997), a five-item scale, was used to investigate three major domains of religion (organizational, nonorganizational, and intrinsic religiosity) in a sample of elite

Table 4.3   SORIS-Q Subcategories and Sample Statements

SORIS-Q subcategory	SORIS-Q statement
Saliency (SRQS)	My racial identity is important to me.
	I always identify myself in terms of my race.
Pre-Encounter (SRQPE)	Race is not an issue in sport.
	Sport participation is the ideal way to move ahead and be successful in life.
Encounter (SRQE)	I have personally experienced racism in sport.
	I have been told to distance myself from my race or culture in order to be successful in sport.
Immersion/Emersion (SRQIE)	I have chosen not to participate in sport because of racism.
	I choose not to socialize with other athletes (sport persons) outside of competition and practice because of racial or cultural differences.
Internalization (SRQI)	I believe that it is important to celebrate my racial or ethnic identity and still participate in sport with different people.
	I have learned things about my race or culture that have helped me to deal with problems related to race in sport.
Fillers of Interest	I feel like I have to "play down" aspects of my race or culture when I am socializing with other athletes.
	I sometimes feel isolated from teammates or other athletes (sport persons) because of racial or cultural differences.

college athletes and nonathletes (Storch et al., 2001). "Organizational religiousness has traditionally been defined as the frequency with which one attends formal religious services. Non-organizational religiousness, in contrast, has been defined in terms of the amount of time spent in private religious activities such as prayer or meditation. Intrinsic religiousness has been conceptualized as the degree to which one integrates their religiousness into their life endeavors" (Koenig, Parkerson, & Meador, 1997; Storch et al., 2001, p. 347).

The DRI included the following questions and statements: "How often do you attend religious services or meetings?" (6-point Likert scale); "How often do you spend time in private religious activities such as prayer, meditation or Bible Study?" (6-point Likert scale); "In my life, I experience the presence of the Divine" (5-point Likert scale); "My religious beliefs are what really lie behind my whole approach to life" (5-point Likert scale); and "I try hard to carry my religion into all other dealings in life" (5-point Likert scale) (Koenig et al., 1997). The study found that male and female athletes reported higher degrees of organizational, nonorganizational, and intrinsic religiousness compared with male nonathletes. These results may help consultants understand that religion may provide athletes with a sense of security and order in life and that athletes may turn toward religious and spiritual beliefs for guidance when coping with uncertainty (Storch et al., 2001).

The Spirituality in Sports Test (SIST) was developed by Dillon and Tait (2000) in conjunction with the Zone Test (ZT) for the purpose of determining whether there is a relationship between spirituality and the experience of being in the zone in a team sport (Watson & Nesti, 2005). Dillon and Tait (2000) consider *being in the zone* to be synonymous with the concept of flow, whereas *spirituality* (or religiosity) is "defined as experiencing the presence of a power, a force, an energy, or a God close to you" (p. 93). Given these definitions, Dillon and Tait asked athletes to indicate how often, if ever, they use or look to this kind of experience in various situations they would be likely to encounter as a participant in a team sport. Results from their study showed a statistically significant relationship between scores on the SIST and the ZT (Dillon & Tait, 2000; Watson & Nesti, 2005).

Watson and Nesti (2005) commended Dillon and Tait (2000) for addressing a much-needed area of research on spirituality and being in the zone in team sport. However, one limitation of their study was the use of questionnaires to measure the experiential states of spirituality and being in the zone. Additionally, researchers on flow in sport and spirituality in psychology "have voiced concerns about utilizing quantitative instruments to measure experiential states" (Watson & Nesti, 2005, p. 233). Thus, future research on spirituality in sport psychology (and consultants working with athletes) may benefit from collecting supporting qualitative data, adding depth and meaning to quantitative results.

Implications for Consultants

Athletes are born with specific attributes such as social class, sex, birth date, race, disability, spirituality, and religion. These attributes are sources of stratification that will alter life choices and perceptions for each athlete, and it would be naive to ignore their influences on assessments.

Cultural influences undeniably change the meaning of heterogeneity in diversity. In light of this socialization, consultants need to take a more functionalist approach to assess who plays sport and what happens when they do, which processes are influencing sustainable participation, and what happens to individuals when they are playing. Sport matters differently in different locations for different people. The way an athlete relates to a sport must be understood within historical and political contexts and their significance in time and social place. Consultants should be sensitive to the social and cultural diversity of athletes to better understand the individuals, community, or society they come from.

Consultants should embrace the mix of physical, cultural, social, religious, and political differences influencing assessments. Combating discrimination starts with the perception of the construct categories of an individual's gender, disability, race, and culture.

Consultants should be sensitive about who makes the rules, how power operates, and the existence of inequalities, especially when it comes to labor relations in sport. The issue of commodifying the self and sport should be clarified with a client to better understand the nature of the sport participation and how it could potentially influence the meaning of assessments.

Future Directions for Professional Development

There is a need for graduate training and professional development opportunities to better prepare consultants to assess diverse athletes and teams. Course content that explores current sport psychology issues in diversity needs to be developed and introduced early on.

It is important for consultants to not only be aware of their own cultural influences but also do their best to increase their awareness and knowledge of a client's cultural background. Gender, language, race, ethnicity, disability, international status, spirituality, and religion can all affect athletes' goals (Cole & Tinsley, 2009). By extending the principles of multicultural consulting and introducing a more cross-cultural approach to sport psychology, consultants will be better positioned to respond to the developmental needs of athletes, to facilitate effective assessment, and to improve the quality of their services (Ward et al., 2005).

Our final recommendation for consultants who work with athletes is to increase their research activities in diversity and make a point to be more inclusive. More importantly, we encourage past, current, and future graduate students to publish their theses and dissertations looking at important sport psychology assessments including race, gender, sex, language, disability, spirituality, and religion.

Assessment Tools and Their Availability

Assessment tool	Construct	Author and reference	Availability
Spiritual Well-Being Scale (SWBS)	Existential well-being and religious well-being	Ellison, C.W. (1983). Spiritual well-being: Conceptualization and measurement. *Journal of Psychology and Theology, 11*(4), 330-340. Ridnour, H., & Hammermeister, J. (2008). Spiritual well-being and its influence on athletic coping profiles. *Journal of Sport Behavior, 31*(1), 81-92.	For purchase at www .lifeadvance.com/ spiritual-well-being-scale/3-the-spiritual-well-being-scale.html
	The SWBS consists of two subscales: (1) Religious Well-Being as it relates to the subjects' relationship with a higher power (God) in regard to commitment, behavioral, communication, cooperation, level of friendship, or degree of intimacy, and (2) Existential Well-Being, which measures the subjects' environmental relationship, meaning the conditions surrounding people that affect the way they live and their satisfaction in life.		
Duke Religion Index (DRI)	Organizational, non-organizational, and intrinsic religiosity	Koenig, H.G., Parkerson, G.R., & Meador, K.G. (1997). Religion index for psychiatric research. *American Journal of Psychiatry, 153*, 885-886. Storch, E.A., Kolsky, A.R., Silvestri, S.M., & Storch, J.B. (2001). Religiosity of elite college athletes. *The Sport Psychologist, 15*, 346-351.	Full measure in Koenig et al. article; http://dx.doi.org/10.1176/ajp.154.6.885b
	The DRI is used to investigate three major domains of religion: (1) organizational, (2) nonorganizational, and (3) intrinsic religiosity.		
Spirituality in Sports Test (SIST)	Spirituality or religiosity; experiencing the presence of a power, a force, an energy, or a God close to you	Dillon, K.M., & Tait, J.L. (2000). Spirituality and being in the zone in team sports: A relationship? *Journal of Sport Behavior, 23*(2), 91-100.	Full measure in article
	The SIST is used to determine if there is a relationship between spirituality and the experience of being in the zone in team sport.		

Assessment Tools for Non-English Speakers and Their Availability

Language	Availability
Sport Motivation Scale (SMS) (motivation)	
Arabic	Bayyat, M.M., Almoghrabi, A.H., & Ay, K.M. (2016). Preliminary validation of an Arabic version of the Sport Motivation Scale (SMS-28). *Asian Social Science, 12:7*, 186-196
	Free at www.ccsenet.org/journal/index.php/ass/article/download/58526/32583
Bengali	Khalil, N.L.B.M. (2015). *The influence of reward and leadership style on the extrinsic motivation among royal Malaysian police officers* (Unpublished doctoral dissertation). Universiti Utara Malaysia.
	Contact the author
Chinese	Li, C., Kawabata, M., & Zhang, L. (2016). Validity and reliability of the Sport Motivation Scale-II for Chinese athletes. *International Journal of Sport and Exercise Psychology*, March, 1-14.
	Full measure in article; http://dx.doi.org/10.1080/1612197X.2016.1153130
French	Brière, N.M., Vallerand, R.J., Blais, M.R., & Pelletier, L.G. (1995). Développement et validation d'une mesure de motivation intrinsèque, extrinsèque et d'amotivation en contexte sportif: L'Échelle de Motivation dans les Sports (EMS). *International Journal of Sport Psychology, 26*, 465-489.
	Contact the authors
German	Burtscher, J., Furtner, M., Sachse, P., & Burtscher, M. (2011). Validation of a German version of the Sport Motivation Scale (SMS28) and motivation analysis in competitive mountain runners. *Perceptual and Motor Skills, 112*(3), 807-820.
	Full measure in article; http://dx.doi.org/10.2466/05.06.25.PMS.112.3.807-820
Italian	Candela, F., Zucchetti, G., & Villosio, C. (2014). Preliminary validation of the Italian version of the original Sport Motivation Scale. *Journal of Human Sport and Exercise, 9*(1), 136-147.
	Full measure in article; http://dx.doi.org/10.4100/jhse.2014.91.14
Malay	Teo, E.W., Khoo, S., Wong, R., Wee, E.H., Lim, B.H., & Rengasamy, S.S. (2015). Intrinsic and extrinsic motivation among adolescent ten-pin bowlers in Kuala Lumpur, Malaysia. *Journal of Human Kinetics, 45*(1), 241-251.
	Contact the authors
Portuguese	Bara Filho, M., Andrade, D., Miranda, R., Núñez, J.L., Martín-Albó, J., & Ribas, P.R. (2011). Preliminary validation of a Brazilian version of the Sport Motivation Scale. *Universitas Psychologica, 10*(2), 557-566.
	Full measure in article; SICI: 1657-9267(201108)10:2<557:PVOSMS>2.0.TX;2-Z
Spanish	Granero-Gallegos, A., Baena-Extremera, A., Gómez-López, M., Sánchez-Fuentes, J.A., & Abraldes, J.A. (2014). Psychometric properties of the "Sport Motivation Scale (SMS)" adapted to physical education. *Journal of Sports Science & Medicine, 13*(4), 801.
	Full measure in article; PMCID: PMC4234949
Behavioral Regulation in Sport Questionnaire (BRSQ) (motivation)	
Arabic	Khalaf, S.B.H. (2014). Arabic women's participation in sport: Barriers and motivation among Egyptian and Kuwaiti athletes. Unpublished doctoral dissertation. University of Wales, Bangor, UK.
	Free at http://e.bangor.ac.uk/5026/1/Thesis%20final%20version%20with%20vaiva%20corrections.pdf
Chinese	Chung, P.K., & Dong Liu, J. (2012). Examination of the psychometric properties of the Chinese translated Behavioral Regulation in Exercise Questionnaire-2. *Measurement in Physical Education and Exercise Science, 16*(4), 300-315.
	Free at http://derwinchan.iwopop.com/Motivation-BRSQ; must request password

Language	Availability
Behavioral Regulation in Sport Questionnaire (BRSQ) (motivation) *(continued)*	
French, Greek, Spanish	Viladrich, C., Appleton, P.R., Quested, E., Duda, J.L., Alcaraz, S., Heuzé, J.P., et al. (2013). Measurement invariance of the Behavioural Regulation in Sport Questionnaire when completed by young athletes across five European countries. *International Journal of Sport and Exercise Psychology, 11*(4), 384-394.
	Full measure in article; http://dx.doi.org/10.1080/1612197X.2013.830434
Portuguese	Monteiro, D., Moutão, J., & Cid, L. Validation of the Behavioral Regulation Sport Questionnaire (BRSQ) in a sample of Portuguese athletes. *Revista de Paicologia del deporte*. Submitted for publication.
	Contact the authors
Task and Ego Orientation in Sport Questionnaire (TEOSQ) (motivation)	
German, Bengali	Asghar, E. (2011). *A comparative study of multidimensional talent in field hockey at development stage between the players of Germany and Pakistan* (Unpublished dissertation). University of Leipzig, Germany.
	Contact the author
Italian	Bortoli, L., & Robazza, C. (2003). Orientamento motivazionale nello sport. *Giornale Italiano di Psicologia dello Sport, 3*, 63-67.
	Contact the authors
Korean	Kim, B.J., & Gill, D.L. (1997). A cross-cultural extension of goal perspective theory to Korean youth sport. *Journal of Sport and Exercise Psychology, 19*, 142-155.
	On p. 56 of the book available at http://book.naver.com/bookdb/book_detail .nhn?bid=1273512
Portuguese	Fonseca, A.M., & de Paula Brito, A. (2005). The issue of the cross-cultural adjustment of instruments for psychological evaluation in national sport contexts—The case of the Task and Ego Orientation in Sport Questionnaire (TEOSQ). *Psychologica, 39*, 95-118.
	Contact the authors
Spanish	Balaguer, I., Castillo, I., & Tomas, I. (1996). Analysis of the psychometric properties of the Task and Ego Orientation in Sport Questionnaire (TEOSQ) in its Spanish version. *Psicologica, 17*, 71-81.
	Contact the authors
Self-efficacy scales (confidence)	
25 languages, including French, Spanish, German, Greek, Hungarian, Hindi, Malay, Italian, Japanese, Korean, Portuguese, and Russian	Scholz, U., Doña, B.G., Sud, S., & Schwarzer, R. (2002). Is general self-efficacy a universal construct? Psychometric findings from 25 countries. *European Journal of Psychological Assessment, 18*(3), 242-251.
	Free at http://userpage.fu-berlin.de/~health/selfscal.htm
Competitive State Anxiety Inventory-2 (CSAI-2) (anxiety)	
Chinese	Peili, Z. (1994). The revised Chinese norm of the Competitive State Anxiety Inventory (CSAI-2). *Psychological Science, 6*.
	For purchase at http://en.cnki.com.cn/Article_en/CJFDTOTAL-XLKX406.006.htm; contact the author for free version

(continued)

ASSESSMENT TOOLS

Assessment Tools for Non-English Speakers and Their Availability *(continued)*

Language	Availability
Competitive State Anxiety Inventory-2 (CSAI-2) (anxiety) *(continued)*	
German	Stöber, J., Otto, K., Pescheck, E., Becker, C., & Stoll, O. (2007). Perfectionism and competitive anxiety in athletes: Differentiating striving for perfection and negative reactions to imperfection. *Personality and Individual Differences, 42*(6), 959-969.
	Free at www.erzwiss.uni-halle.de/gliederung/paed/ppsych/bericht07.pdf
Portuguese	Coelho, E.M., Vasconcelos-Raposo, J., & Mahl, Á.C. (2010). Confirmatory factorial analysis of the Brazilian version of the Competitive State Anxiety Inventory-2 (CSAI-2). *Spanish Journal of Psychology, 13*(01), 453-460.
	Contact the authors
Competitive State Anxiety Inventory-2 Revised (CSAI-2R) (anxiety)	
French	Martinent, G., Ferrand, C., Guillet, E., & Gautheur, S. (2010). Validation of the French version of the Competitive State Anxiety Inventory-2 Revised (CSAI-2R) including frequency and direction scales. *Psychology of Sport and Exercise, 11*(1), 51-57.
	Full measure in article; http://dx.doi.org/10.1016/j.psychsport.2009.05.001
Malay	Bagherpour, T., Hashim, H.A., Saha, S., & Ghosh, A.K. (2012). Effects of progressive muscle relaxation and internal imagery on Competitive State Anxiety Inventory-2R among taekwondo athletes. *International Proceedings of Economics Development & Research, 30*, 218.
	Contact the authors
Spanish	Andrade, F.E., Lois, R.G., & Arce, F.C. (2007). [Psychometric properties of the Spanish version of the Revised Competitive State Anxiety Inventory-2 with athletes]. *Psicothema, 19*(1), 150-155.
	Contact the authors
Profile of Mood States (POMS) (emotion/mood)	
Arabic	Aroian, K.J., Kulwicki, A., Kaskiri, E.A., Templin, T.N., & Wells, C.L. (2007). Psychometric evaluation of the Arabic language version of the Profile of Mood States. *Research in Nursing & Health, 30*(5), 531-541.
	Contact the authors
Chinese	Chen, K.M., Snyder, M., & Krichbaum, K. (2002). Translation and equivalence: The Profile of Mood States short form in English and Chinese. *International Journal of Nursing Studies, 39*(6), 619-624.
	Contact the authors
French	Fillion, L., & Gagnon, P. (1999). French adaptation of the shortened version of the Profile of Mood States. *Psychological Reports, 84*, 188-190.
	Full measure in article; http://dx.doi.org/10.2466/pr0.1999.84.1.188
German	Albani, C., Blaser, G., Geyer, M., Schmutzer, G., Brähler, E., Bailer, H., & Grulke, N. (2005). [The German short version of "Profile of Mood States" (POMS): Psychometric evaluation in a representative sample]. *Psychotherapie, Psychosomatik, Medizinische Psychologie, 55*(7), 324-330.
	Contact the authors
Italian	Nasta, M.T., Grussu, P., Quatraro, R.M., Cerutti, R., & Grella, P.V. (2002). Cholesterol and mood states at 3 days after delivery. *Journal of Psychosomatic Research, 52*(2), 61-63.
	Contact the authors

Language	Availability
Profile of Mood States (POMS) (emotion/mood) *(continued)*	
Japanese	Yokoyama, K., Araki, S., Kawakami, N., & Tkakeshita, T. (1990). [Production of the Japanese edition of profile of mood states (POMS): Assessment of reliability and validity]. *Nihon Koshu Eisei Zasshi, 37*(11), 913-918.
	Contact the authors
Korean	Yeun, E.J., & Shin-Park, K.K. (2006). Verification of the Profile of Mood States-Brief: Cross-cultural analysis. *Journal of Clinical Psychology, 62*(9), 1173-1180.
	Contact the authors
Portuguese	Azevedo, M.H., Silva, C.F., & Dias, M.R. (1991). O Perfil de Estados de Humor. Adaptação à população Portuguesa. *Psiquiatria Clínica, 12*, 187-193.
	Contact the authors
Spanish	Andrade, E., Arce, C., Torrado, J., Garrido, J., De Francisco, C., & Arce, I. (2010). Factor structure and invariance of the POMS mood state questionnaire in Spanish. *Spanish Journal of Psychology, 13*(01), 444-452.
	Contact the authors
Test of Attentional and Interpersonal Style (TAIS)	
French, Chinese, Italian, Japanese, Spanish, German	Nideffer, R.M. (2007). Reliability and validity of The Attentional and Interpersonal Style (TAIS) inventory concentration scales. In D. Smith & M. Bar-Eli (Eds.), *Essential readings in sport and exercise psychology* (pp. 265-277). Champaign, IL: Human Kinetics.
	Contact the author
Athlete burnout inventory (burnout)	
Arabic	Altahayneh, Z.L. (2003). *The effects of coaches' behaviors and burnout on the satisfaction and burnout of athletes* (Doctoral dissertation). Retrieved from the Florida State University Database. (FSU_migr_etd-0005 [IID]).
	Free at http://diginole.lib.fsu.edu/islandora/object/fsu%3A168048
Chinese	Chen, L.H., Kee, Y.H., & Tsai, Y.M. (2008). Relation of dispositional optimism with burnout among athletes. *Perceptual and Motor Skills, 106*(3), 693-698.
	Contact the authors
French	Isoard-Gautheur, S., Oger, M., Guillet, E., & Martin-Krumm, C. (2010). Validation of a French version of the Athlete Burnout Questionnaire (ABQ): In competitive sport and physical education context. *European Journal of Psychological Assessment, 26*(3), 203.
	For purchase at http://psycnet.apa.org/index.cfm?fa=buy.optionToBuy&id=2010-14573-007
German	Ziemainz, H., Abu-Omar, K., Raedeke, T.D., & Krause, K. (2004). *Zur Prävalenz von Burnout aus bedingungsbezogener Perspektive* [Burnout in sports—The prevalence of burnout from an environmental perspective]. *Leistungssport, 34*, 12-17.
	Contact the authors
Italian	Vitali, F., Bortoli, L., Bertinato, L., Robazza, C., & Schena, F. (2014). Motivational climate, resilience, and burnout in youth sport. *Sport Sciences for Health, 11*(1), 103-108.
	Contact the authors

(continued)

Assessment Tools for Non-English Speakers and Their Availability *(continued)*

Language	Availability
Athlete burnout inventory (burnout) *(continued)*	
Japanese	Yamada, Y., & Hirosawa, M. (2009). Does Typus Melancholicus determine characteristics of athlete burnout symptom and its process among Japanese university athletes? *Journal of Human Ergology, 38*(2), 67-79.
	Contact the authors
Korean	Cho, S. (2014). *A self-determination theory perspective on burnout among Korean athletes: Perceived coaching behaviors and satisfaction/thwarting of psychological needs* (Unpublished dissertation). Florida State University, Tallahassee, FL.
	Contact the author
Portuguese	Bertoldi, R. (2014). *Fatores preditores do burnout em atletas: Um estudo com atletas brasileiros profissionais de futsal* (Unpublished dissertation). Universidade Federal do Rio Grande do Sul, Brazil.
	Free at www.lume.ufrgs.br/handle/10183/106581
Spanish	Arce, C., De Francisco, C., Andrade, E., Seoane, G., & Raedeke, T. (2012). Adaptation of the Athlete Burnout Questionnaire in a Spanish sample of athletes. *Spanish Journal of Psychology, 15*(3), 1529-1536.
	Free at www.redalyc.org/pdf/172/17224489059.pdf

Chapter Takeaways

- The impact of culture is marginalized or not addressed at all in sport psychology research and assessment.

- Consultants need to carefully analyze the significance of identity politics as they are expressed, reproduced, and resisted in sport. The development of multicultural counseling and CSP marks a paradigm shift in the way sport psychology consultants work within their various fields.

- By extending the principles of multicultural counseling and the CSP approach to the athlete population, consultants may be better positioned to respond to the unique needs of athletes and to enhance the quality of their services.

- Sport is a heavily gendered space. Ensure all assessments are valid and reliable using both male and female populations for testing.

- Translating written questionnaires into another language does not necessarily mean the translated assessment will keep intact its contents and psychometrics. Consultants working with foreign clients should check for the validity of the translated assessment.

- Disability sport has its own form of classification. Working with other health care professionals is advised with the ICF.

- Racial and cultural identity are part of a multilayered identity. Racial identity saliency will vary across a life span, within groups, and between groups. The SORIS-Q is a tool that can be used to examine race-related issues in sport.

- Consultants need to consider the meaningfulness of race to athletes, the athletes' level of acculturation, and the types of coping skills athletes use when facing particular circumstances relative to their racial and cultural backgrounds.

- Spirituality and religion are therapeutically relevant, ethically appropriate, and significant topics in applied sport psychology with culturally diverse populations.

- Spirituality and religion have a positive impact on mental and physical health, and they are strongly associated with psychological factors related to athletic performance.

PART TWO
ASSESSMENT TOOLS

Part II introduces the six ways you can assess an athlete: mental health screening, personality tests, sport-specific objective measures, interviewing, observation, and applied psychophysiology. Each chapter in this section provides a rationale for the strengths and weaknesses of each approach. Each also offers recommendations of well-established assessments that have proven useful in sport psychology consulting.

CHAPTER 5
Mental Health Screening: Identifying Clinical Issues

Erin N.J. Haugen, PhD, LP, CC-AASP

Jenni Thome, PhD

Megan E. Pietrucha, PsyD

M. Penny Levin, PhD

"The most profound aspect of mental illness is that it occurs in people who are otherwise functioning well, even in those possessing outstanding abilities in specialized and creative endeavors" (Burton, 2000, p. 61). Anyone can be vulnerable to mental illness, including athletes. Unfortunately, sport culture perpetuates a stigma that athletes with mental health difficulties are not mentally tough, are weak, and cannot participate in sport (Markser, 2011). Not only are these assumptions incorrect, they contribute to athletes avoiding or delaying mental health treatment until the problem becomes severe. To complicate matters, mental health symptoms can also be misdiagnosed as physical in nature (e.g., diagnosing depression as overtraining syndrome), resulting in inappropriate or misdirected treatment, which can exacerbate the psychological difficulties. The sooner difficulties are identified, the sooner athletes can receive appropriate treatment and improve their prognosis.

A mental health screening helps identify potential issues early, allowing you to treat those issues if you are appropriately trained or to refer the athlete to a professional with specialized mental health training if you are not. It is also important to remember you can't treat a bullet wound with a bandage; mental health problems can be complex even when not readily apparent. There is no need to abandon your performance work with the athlete until the mental health problem is fixed. This can be an important time to work closely with the mental health professional and other providers as necessary to help the athlete in a holistic manner. Therefore, screening for mental health difficulties is both ethically responsible and in the best interests of your athletes, and it should be conducted as part of the initial intake and during the first few sessions of consulting work.

Inherent in the screening process is developing a network of competent, reliable, trustworthy mental health providers (ideally ones who also have experience working with athletes). Most referrals for athlete mental health originate from coaches, athletic trainers, team physicians, family members, or teammates rather than the athletes directly. Getting to know your referral sources can be invaluable when referring athletes, largely because athletes may be more likely to see a mental health professional if you have a personal connection with the referral source. Other sources of collaboration include student health centers, counseling centers, and state psychological associations.

This chapter reviews mental health difficulties commonly experienced by athletes and recommends screening measures. Inventories were chosen based on their usefulness, ease of use, popularity, and use with athletes. Unless otherwise noted, all of the assessment tools in this chapter have sound psychometric properties, including acceptable validity, reliability, and internal consistency.

Finally, this chapter is not devoted to conducting mental status exams or diagnosing mental illness, both of which require clinical or counseling psychology training and licensure as a psychologist or other mental health professional (e.g., licensed counselor). Rather, the recommended measures are intended to be used by nonlicensed individuals as tools for screening mental health difficulties to identify people at risk for them. Specific diagnoses are best left to trained professionals who engage in comprehensive evaluations of mental health.

Stress

The central concern in addressing stress among athletes is differentiating reasonable responses to the rigors of training and competition from those that suggest a need for psychological evaluation and treatment. According to one model, stress results from an imbalance between perceived demands and the individual's perception of the resources available for coping with the demands (Matheny, Aycock, Curlette, & Junker, 2003). Athletes choose to place themselves in stressful situations and are generally able to manage these experiences effectively, but failure to recover from training-related stress may result in burnout and a decrease in sport performance (Kellman & Kallus, 2001). At times, outside concerns such as family conflict or financial problems can cause stress, placing additional demands on athletes while also taxing the resources they have available. Internal issues such as medical problems, insomnia, perfectionism, disorganization, or negative self-talk can also become sources of stress. Additionally, an underlying disorder such

as anxiety or depression may exacerbate stress reactions when other stressors increase.

Understanding stress in athletes is important for several reasons. Acute stress reactions are associated with an increase in heart rate, blood pressure, and cortisol production (McEwen, 2008). Elevated levels of cortisol are related to a wide range of health-related problems, such as insomnia, obesity, and depression (Gold & Chrousos, 2002). In athletes, prolonged psychological distress is linked to injury and illness and may predict injury (Andersen & Williams, 1988). It is also associated with difficulties with affect, attention, memory, behavior, and burnout (Gil-Monte & Peiró, 1998; Perna & McDowell, 1995).

Generally speaking, athletes become stressed when they feel incapable of meeting competitive demands and anticipate a negative outcome (Scanlan, 1982). Andersen and Williams (1988) suggest this reaction results from the relationship among a range of factors, including the athlete's personality, coping resources, competitive situation, and personal history. Success or failure to cope with stress, both personally and in terms of sport performance, can result from either internal factors (e.g., cognitive assessment of the situation, perceived intensity of stressors; Anshel & Sutarso, 2007) or situational factors (e.g., competitive situation, athlete's overall life).

One measure that can be used to evaluate stress in athletes is the Perceived Stress Scale (PSS-10; Cohen & Williamson, 1988). The PSS-10 is a 10-item self-report inventory that measures perception of and ability to cope with stress over the past month. Although this inventory does not have cutoff points for referral, normative data are found in the scoring materials. The PSS-10 is easily administered and readily available. Because the time frame is one month, results cannot be generalized over time; however, the PSS-10 can be administered periodically as athletes' circumstances change. This inventory can help identify athletes who are having difficulty coping with stress, which can be a precursor to other mental health issues.

Another inventory that can be used to screen for stress is the Recovery-Stress Questionnaire for Athletes (RESTQ-Sport; Kellman & Kallus,

2001, 2016). Part of a broader family of inventories designed to evaluate stress and recovery, the RESTQ-Sport was designed to measure stress and recovery specifically in athletes. It identifies the extent to which athletes are physically or mentally stressed, along with their current capabilities for recovery. Social and emotional stress is also evaluated. The RESTQ-Sport is available in 36-, 52-, and 76-item versions. It has been used widely across sports and in many countries (Martinent, Decree, Isoard-Gautheur, Wired, & Ferrand, 2014).

Depression and Suicide

Major depression (also referred to as *depression*) is a period of at least two weeks with depressed mood or loss of interest or pleasure in nearly all activities and five of the following symptoms in the same two-week period (APA, 2013):

- Change in weight or appetite
- Change in amount of sleep
- Psychomotor agitation or retardation
- Fatigue or loss of energy
- Feelings of worthlessness or inappropriate guilt
- Difficulty concentrating or indecisiveness
- Recurrent thoughts of death, suicidal ideation, or a suicide attempt or plan to die by suicide

Although it is common for people to have transient depressed moods, particularly in relation to stressors, it is not considered a depressive episode until symptoms are associated with significant life interference or distress for a majority of the two-week period.

Many studies evaluate depressive symptoms in athletes using screening questionnaires, which are not diagnostic by nature. Using screening questionnaires, researchers found rates of depression in athletes ranging from 15 percent to 27 percent in a variety of samples across cultures (Gulliver, Griffiths, Mackinnon, Batterham, & Stanimirovic, 2015; Proctor & Boan-Lenzo, 2010). Although prevalence rates vary, the evidence clearly suggests a substantial number of athletes report clinical symptoms of depression.

Several factors are important to consider when monitoring symptoms of depression in athletes. Female athletes tend to report higher levels of depressive symptomatology than male athletes, and freshman athletes report higher levels of depressive symptoms than upperclassmen (Yang et al., 2007). Athletes in individual sports endorse more depressive symptoms than those in team sports (Nixdorf, Frank, Hautzinger, & Beckmann, 2013). There is also evidence that current college athletes are more likely to report symptoms of depression than retired college athletes (Weigand, Cohen, & Merenstein, 2013), although depression certainly exists among retired athletes. Finally, research suggests high comorbidity between depression and other difficulties, such as sport-specific stress, anxiety, and substance use (Nixdorf et al., 2013; Schaal et al., 2011).

Several sport-related variables are associated with depressive symptoms. Research strongly suggests that injured athletes (concussed and nonconcussed) report higher levels of depression than noninjured athletes (Gulliver et al., 2015; Vargas, Rabinowitz, Meyer, & Arnett, 2015), and this trend has also been reported in samples of retired athletes (Kerr, Marshall, Harding, & Guskiewicz, 2012). Other psychosocial factors may trigger a depressive episode for athletes, particularly in times of transition (Reardon & Factor, 2010), high stress (Galambos, Terry, Moyle, & Locke, 2005), competitive failures, (Hammond, Gialloreto, Kubas, & Davis, 2013), and retirement from sport (Kerr et al., 2012).

One example of a screening measure used to evaluate depression is the Center for Epidemiological Studies Depression Scale Revised (CESD-R; Eaton, Muntaner, Smith, Tien, & Ybarra, 2004). The CESD-R is a 20-item self-report inventory used to evaluate symptoms of depression in adolescents and adults and is one of the most widely used measures of depression. Total scores range from 20 to 60, and a total score of 16 or above is associated with a depression diagnosis.

Given that the presence of suicidal ideation or behavior is a criterion of depression, it is natural to assess suicide in the context of depression. At the same time, suicidal ideation or behavior may occur in the presence of other disorders, and you are encouraged to screen athletes for suicide whenever necessary. Athletes generally have a lower risk of death by suicide than nonathletes (Rao, Asif, Drezner, Toresdahl, & Harmon, 2015; Sabo, Miller, Melnick, Farrell, & Barnes, 2005). Death by suicide accounted for 7 percent of National Collegiate Athletic Association (NCAA) deaths from 2002 to 2012, and males were more than three times more likely than females to die by suicide (Rao et al., 2015). Female athletes may attempt suicide more frequently than nonathletes (Kokotalio, Henry, Koscik, Flemming, & Landry, 1996), and male athletes may have a higher rate of severe injury when attempting suicide in comparison to nonathletes (Sabo et al., 2015). Factors such as being a multisport athlete (Sabo et al., 2015), playing football (Rao et al., 2015), and experiencing sport-related loss (Smith & Millner, 1994) are associated with higher rates of suicidal behavior and death by suicide in athletes.

Suicide can be difficult to evaluate, even for trained professionals. It is important to take any endorsement regarding suicide (ideation, plan, or behavior) seriously and refer any athlete you are concerned about to a qualified mental health professional as soon as possible. Contrary to popular belief, talking about suicide does not promote thoughts or increase the risk of suicide. Suicide items are often embedded within depression screening inventories. Although this can be a useful way to identify at-risk athletes, it may be insufficient. Therefore, it may be useful to include an additional screening inventory when concerned about suicidality. If you have little or no education or training in broader mental health issues, you should seek consultation with a qualified mental health professional for any questions or concerns about addressing suicide.

An example of a screening measure for suicide is the Suicidal Behaviors Questionnaire-Revised (SBQ-R; Osman et al., 2001). The SBQ-R is a four-item inventory that addresses four dimensions of suicidality in adolescents and adults: lifetime suicidal ideation or attempt, frequency of suicidal ideation in the past 12 months, threat of suicide attempt, and self-reported likelihood of future suicidal behavior. The developers found a score of ≥7 led to 93 percent sensitivity and 95 percent specificity. At the same time, it is important to address endorsement of items at any level.

Anxiety

Competitive anxiety has been the subject of numerous theoretical discussions and empirical studies over the years (see chapter 7), but significantly less attention has been paid to anxiety disorders in athletes (Reardon & Factor, 2010). Anecdotally, athletes are often more comfortable seeing a consultant for issues related to competitive anxiety than more general mental health concerns; this may be because competitive anxiety is a common experience in sport. Competitive anxiety is situation specific and relatively short in duration; that is, it only arises in the context of sport competition and doesn't last beyond the competition. In contrast, anxiety disorders are ever present, persistent, and have a more debilitating impact on athletes' lives both in and away from the competitive arena. Competitive anxiety and anxiety disorders may be closely linked in that competitive anxiety may emerge from an anxiety disorder and increase to a clinical level.

The *Diagnostic and Statistical Manual of Mental Disorders, Fifth Edition*, or *DSM-5* (APA, 2013), includes diagnostic criteria for three anxiety disorders reviewed in this chapter:

1. **Generalized anxiety disorder (GAD):** This disorder is characterized by persistent and uncontrollable worry most of the time accompanied by associated symptoms (e.g., easily fatigued, mind going blank, irritability).
2. **Panic disorder:** This disorder is characterized by the presence and fear of panic attacks (i.e., somatic symptoms, such as difficulty breathing, feeling disoriented) that peak within 10 minutes.
3. **Social anxiety disorder:** Also called *social phobia*, this disorder is characterized by fear and anxiety in social and evaluative situations that is out of proportion to the situation. People with social anxiety disorder tend to avoid these situations or endure them with intense anxiety.

There is little research examining prevalence rates of anxiety disorders in athletes, and existing research used screening measures to estimate prevalence rates. Female athletes generally report higher levels of anxious symptomatology than male athletes, although the trend varies depending on the disorder. The following rates have been identified for clinical levels of anxiety symptoms in athletes: GAD is found in up to 7 percent of men and 10 percent of women, social anxiety disorder is found in approximately 14 percent of men and 15 percent of women, and panic disorder is found in up to 3 percent of men and 6 percent of women (Gulliver et al., 2015; Schaal et al., 2011).

Several sport-related factors are associated with anxiety disorders. First, symptoms of anxiety are common during the injury rehabilitation process, and symptoms of competitive anxiety may play an important role in susceptibility to injury (Andersen & Williams, 1988). Injured athletes also report higher symptoms of GAD than noninjured athletes (Gulliver et al., 2015). Second, anxiety may be associated with burnout; athletes who perceive their anxiety as debilitating are more likely to report burnout than athletes who do not experience their anxiety in that manner (Wiggins, Lai, & Deiters, 2005). Finally, athletes in aesthetic sports may experience higher levels of generalized anxiety symptoms (Schaal et al., 2011).

A number of screening measures have been developed to evaluate the anxiety disorders mentioned earlier. Examples of these tools include the following:

- **Generalized Anxiety Disorder 7 (GAD-7; Spitzer, Kroenke, Williams, & Lowe, 2006).** The GAD-7 is a seven-item self-report inventory developed to screen adults in primary care settings for symptoms of generalized anxiety. Spitzer and colleagues found that a score of ≥10 indicates probable diagnosis of GAD. Gulliver et al. (2015) used this measure to evaluate generalized anxiety symptoms in a sample of athletes and used a total score ≥7 to identify clinical levels of GAD. This inventory has also been translated into several languages.

- **Panic Disorder Severity Scale—Self-Report (PDSS-SR; Houck, Spiegel, Shear, & Rucci, 2002).** The PDSS-SR is a five-item self-report inventory used to screen for panic disorder symptoms in adults. Items are scored using a Likert-type scale, and the developers recommend using a score of ≥8 for referral. This scale was used in one study of elite athletes (Gulliver et al., 2015) examining clinical anxiety levels. The study found that more than 4 percent of athletes in the sample reported clinical levels of panic disorder, and 10 percent experienced strong somatic symptoms of anxiety (including panic attacks) in the previous week.

- **Social Phobia Scale (SPS-6; Peters, Sunderland, Andrews, Rapee, & Mattick, 2012).** The SPS-6 is a six-item self-report inventory evaluating fears of general social interaction. The developers found a score of ≥2 was associated with a social phobia diagnosis. Given the evaluative nature of social phobia, it may also be beneficial to use measures evaluating competitive anxiety (see chapter 7) when screening for social phobia.

Disordered Eating and Eating Disorders

Disordered eating and eating disorders include a range of abnormal eating and weight-control behaviors, including restriction of food intake, bingeing and purging behaviors, and other compensatory behaviors such as excessive exercise, laxative use, and diuretic use. These symptoms are typically accompanied by body dissatisfaction. The *DSM-5* (APA, 2013) includes diagnostic criteria for four eating disorders and related concerns reviewed in this chapter:

1. **Anorexia nervosa (AN):** This disorder is characterized by distorted body image and excessive dieting behavior leading to significantly low body weight, with an accompanying fear of becoming fat or gaining weight.
2. **Bulimia nervosa (BN):** This disorder involves a repetitive cycle of dysregulated eating, including recurrent episodes of

binge eating followed by compensatory behaviors such as vomiting, laxative abuse, or excessive exercise.

3. **Binge eating disorder (BED):** This disorder involves recurrent episodes of binge-eating behaviors without compensatory purging or nonpurging behaviors following the binge and is more common than AN and BN combined.

4. **Avoidant/restrictive food intake disorder (ARFID):** This eating or feeding disturbance may include a lack of interest in food, avoidance of food based on sensory characteristics, and concern about aversive consequences of eating. This leads to significant weight loss, nutritional deficiency, dependence on nutritional supplements, and marked interference with psychosocial functioning.

Concerns about body image and eating pathology are often comorbid with other mental health issues, including depression, anxiety, and low self-esteem (Johnson & Wardle, 2005; Thome & Espelage, 2004).

Research regarding the prevalence of eating disorders among athletes is conflicting due to a range of methodological limitations (Nattiv et al., 2007). Some well-designed studies suggest that eating disorders such as AN and BN may be more prevalent among athletes than nonathletes, with higher rates among female athletes than male athletes and elite versus recreational athletes (Knapp, Aerni, & Anderson, 2014; Sundgot-Borgen & Torstveit, 2004). Some studies suggest eating disorder prevalence rates of 25 to 31 percent among elite athletes, compared with 5 to 9 percent in control groups. Eating disorders are more prevalent among athletes in lean and aesthetic sports such as cross country running, gymnastics, and figure skating (46.7 percent) compared with athletes in nonlean sports (19.8 percent) and controls (21.4 percent) (Torstveit, Rosenvinge, & Sundgot-Borgen, 2008).

Because athletes often engage in high levels of exercise, have lower body-fat percentages, and tend to eat healthily to gain muscle mass for their sport, it can be difficult to identify athletes struggling with eating concerns. Further, several traits of a so-called good athlete (e.g.,

excessive exercise, perfectionism, overcompliance) are similar to traits found among people with AN and may be valued and reinforced by coaches, trainers, and teammates (Thompson & Sherman, 1999). Red flags in nonathlete populations (e.g., amenorrhea, low blood pressure, low resting heart rate) may be attributed to the athlete's activity status rather than identified as indicators of eating concerns (Maron & Pelliccia, 2006).

Given the short- and long-term physical and psychological risks of eating disorders, it is essential to recognize individuals with such symptoms and encourage them to seek treatment. The American College of Sports Medicine (ACSM; Nattiv et al., 2007), National Athletic Trainers' Association (NATA; Bonci et al., 2008), and the International Olympic Committee (IOC, 2009) advocate for screening of eating disorders during the preparticipation evaluation and periodically thereafter. However, there is no consensus about how this should be done or which screening tools should be used. Ideally, screening and assessment should include multiple sources of information and be sensitive to the athlete's age and competitive level (Mitchell & Robert-McComb, 2014).

A number of assessment and screening tools have been developed and validated for the general assessment of eating disorders, and many have been used in studies with athletes (see Pope, Gao, Bolter, & Pritchard, 2014). Examples of these tools include the following:

• **Eating Attitudes Test (EAT-26; Garner, Olmstead, Bohr, & Garfinkle, 1982).** The EAT-26 is a 26-item self-report screening tool of eating disorder symptoms. A total score of ≥20 is recommended for referral for additional assessment by a trained clinician. It also evaluates extreme weight-control behaviors, which may be red flags indicating the need to meet with a qualified professional. It can be administered in individual or group settings by mental health professionals, school counselors, coaches, or others with an interest in screening and referral for additional evaluation for eating disorders. This measure has been used in a variety of cultures with male and female athletes.

- **Eating Disorders Examination Questionnaire (EDE-Q; Fairburn & Beglin, 1994).** The EDE-Q is a 41-item self-report questionnaire designed to evaluate the frequency of disordered eating behaviors over the past 38 days. It is different from the EAT-26 in that it evaluates eating behaviors and body dissatisfaction. It has been used in research with male and female athletes.

- **Female Athlete Screening Tool (FAST; McNulty, Adams, Anderson, & Affenito, 2001; Robert-McComb & Mitchell, 2014).** The FAST is a 33-item questionnaire developed to identify eating pathology and atypical exercise and eating behaviors in female athletes. In a small group of female athletes, subclinical scores were 77 to 94 and clinical scores were >94 (Robert-McComb & Mitchell, 2014).

One criticism of using general eating disorder assessments is that athletes may appear more pathological than they are; for example, high levels of exercise in an athlete may have little to do with manipulating weight (Thompson & Sherman, 2014). There has also been little cross-validation in athlete populations. Therefore, several athlete-specific screening tools have been developed. Unfortunately, athlete-specific

---

| **Assessment in Action** |

Screening With One Inventory

You are working with a 19-year-old gymnast who has recently suffered a stress fracture, has been performing poorly lately, and has lost a significant amount of weight this season. You feel the athlete trusts you, and you share concerns about a potential eating disorder. The athlete reports she has been trying to eat less to lose fat and look better for competition. The athlete agrees to take the EAT-26 and scores a 40, which suggests she should meet with a mental health professional for further assessment. You refer the athlete to the university counseling center for further assessment.

---

screening tools for eating disorders typically have less established psychometric properties and may be based on outdated diagnostic criteria. Therefore, the measures recommended in this chapter were chosen for their utility in screening for eating disorders and their sound psychometric properties. It would be prudent to incorporate more than one screening tool when assessing athletes for eating disturbances given the aforementioned concerns.

Attention-Deficit/ Hyperactivity Disorder

Attention-deficit/hyperactivity disorder (ADHD) is a neurodevelopmental disorder commonly diagnosed in children, but it can also be present in adulthood. It is characterized by persistent symptoms of inattention (e.g., careless mistakes, not listening, easily distracted), hyperactivity, and impulsivity (e.g., fidgeting, difficulty remaining seated, talking excessively) that contribute to life impairment or distress. Symptoms of ADHD are persistent and present in multiple settings (APA, 2013).

Similar to depression and anxiety, there is no epidemiological research examining the prevalence of ADHD in athletes. Researchers suggest the prevalence of ADHD may be higher in athlete populations compared with nonathletes (Burton, 2000). Some authors also suggest athletes with ADHD may have advantages such as heightened reaction time, quick decision making, and creative problem solving, particularly in sports such as hockey and soccer (Parr, 2011). However, there are no concrete data suggesting athletes with ADHD have distinct performance advantages.

Although ADHD is typically diagnosed in childhood, some athletes may not be diagnosed until young adulthood for a variety of reasons. Athletes may have subthreshold symptoms that do not fully manifest until the demands of their environment are greater than their coping capacities (Parr, 2011). Such examples exist during the transition to college, when the student-athlete is balancing the demands of multiple rigorous roles. Academic difficulties may then increase the stress level of the student-athlete because eligibility is threatened (White, Harris, & Gibson, 2014). Athletes with ADHD may also be misdiagnosed with behavioral difficulties; they are often seen as problem children due to poor attention and impulse control.

One example of a screening measure for ADHD is the Adult ADHD Self-Report Scale (ASRS-v1.1; Kessler et al., 2005). The ASRS-v1.1 is a self-report inventory designed to evaluate symptoms of ADHD in adult community samples. The screening version is six items, and cutoff scores are identified on the inventory as part of the scoring rubric. This inventory is available in several languages and can be used to screen for ADHD symptoms in adults, college students, and adolescents.

A second screening measure that can be used for ADHD is the Conners' Adult ADHD Rating Scales (CAARS; Conners, Erhardt, & Sparrow, 1999). There are two types of forms: self-report and other report. Both types come in short, long, and screening versions. The self-report screening version (CAARS-S:SV) is most appropriate for screening of ADHD symptoms in athletes. The CAARS-S:SV contains the 30 items that best differentiate people diagnosed with ADHD. There is also an inconsistency index that is used to evaluate validity of responses. T-scores ≥65 can be used to identify athletes for referral. The CAARS-S:SV can be administered in paper, online, or with software formats and is available in various languages.

One challenge of using screening inventories for ADHD is the high degree of symptom overlap between ADHD and other disorders, such as anxiety and depression. In addition, ADHD screening inventories are typically face valid, so symptoms can be endorsed easily (Sullivan, May, & Galbally, 2007). Therefore, referral for a comprehensive evaluation is recommended to differentially diagnose various mental health conditions and to screen out individuals seeking stimulant-based ADHD medications for nontreatment purposes (e.g., performance enhancement, weight loss).

Substance Use and Abuse

According to the *DSM-5*, substance use disorders involve cognitive, behavioral, and psychological symptoms suggesting a person continues to use the substance despite these use-related difficulties. There are 10 classes of substance use disorders (e.g., alcohol, opioids, stimulants), and each is measured on a continuum from mild (two to three symptoms) to severe (six or more symptoms). A substance use problem often consists of a problematic pattern of use (e.g., social impairment, risky use, failure to fulfill obligations), tolerance, and withdrawal (APA, 2013).

Much of the available information about substance use and athletics is a product of research within the collegiate student and student-athlete populations. Males and lacrosse players report the highest rates of substance use (NCAA, 2014). Athletes report using alcohol, marijuana, and smokeless tobacco most frequently (Green, Uryaz, Petr, & Bray, 2001; Hainline, Bell, & Wilfert, 2014; NCAA, 2014). Some studies found up to 80 percent of athletes use alcohol (Green et al., 2001; NCAA, 2014), and athletes may engage in binge drinking at higher rates than nonathletes (Hainline et al., 2014). Use of other substances is generally lower in athletes compared with nonathletes, although this depends somewhat upon competitive level (Green et al., 2001; NCAA, 2014).

Although a large percentage of research examining the use of substances in athletes is related to performance enhancement (i.e., doping), substance use among athletes can occur for many reasons that are not related to sport participation or performance enhancement. An athlete's psychological response to injury may result in problematic substance use. Treatment for injury and pain management often includes prescription pain medication, and student-athletes are prescribed narcotics at higher rates than nonathletes (Putukian, 2014). Nonprescribed use of narcotics, as well as ADHD medications, is a concern because these medications have a high risk of addiction. Athletes may also use substances to build muscle and control weight (Berger, Pargman, & Weinberg, 2007).

Social reasons for substance use can include peer pressure, modeling of drug use behaviors, and fun or experimentation (Berger et al., 2007). College student-athletes are susceptible to heavy (i.e., binge) drinking and the faulty belief that this behavior is common and acceptable among students. The negative impact of alcohol abuse is well documented among collegiate athletes and continues to be a concern for coaches, administrators, athletic trainers, and parents (Green et al., 2001).

Athletes may also use substances for psychological reasons, such as coping with painful emotions, low confidence, and fear of failure, stress, and underlying mental health issues (e.g., anxiety, depression; Berger et al., 2007). The term *dual diagnosis* is used to describe coexisting diagnoses of substance abuse and mental illness. The relationship between substance use and other mental health conditions is complex, but substance abuse can occur as a form of self-medication for existing psychological conditions. Substance use can worsen and may also trigger the onset of psychological symptoms. This is especially true for athletes in their late teens or early twenties, a common time for the onset of mental health problems.

Because young adults do not tend to identify themselves as having alcohol or substance use problems, detecting problems can be difficult and often occurs after negative consequences from alcohol and substance use. Therefore, it may be beneficial to screen for substance use difficulties where alcohol-related injuries or illnesses may be present, such as in the training room, the sports medicine clinic, and the strength and conditioning gym. Should screening confirm suspected problems with substance use, an appropriate referral to a substance abuse professional should be made for additional assessment and treatment options. Examples of screening measures for substance use and abuse include the following:

- **Alcohol Use Disorders Identification Test (AUDIT; Babor, Higgins-Biddle, Saunders, & Monteiro, 2001).** The AUDIT is a 10-item self-report inventory identified as the gold standard for detecting alcohol misuse. It is effective at identifying less severe forms of drinking across a range of countries and populations (Dhalla & Kopec, 2007). The AUDIT can be adapted for use by nonhealth professionals, can be used in a variety of settings, and can be self-administered. A score of ≥8 in adults is recommended for referral (Babor et al., 2001), and a score of ≥2 is recommended for people aged 14 to 18 (Knight, Sherritt, Harris, Gates, & Chang, 2003).

- **Drug Abuse Screening Test (DAST; Skinner, 1982).** The DAST was developed as a brief screening for drug abuse or dependence disorders, not including alcohol and tobacco. It is most useful in settings where seeking treatment for drug problems is not the individual's goal (Skinner, 1982), such as sport settings, and it can be used with older adolescents and adults. The DAST can be administered in self-report or interview format and includes a 10-, 20-, and 28-item screening, so it can be tailored to the needs of the environment, consultant, and athlete.

Assessment in Action

Screening With Multiple Inventories

You conduct an intake with a 21-year-old soccer player who is experiencing a decrease in performance and difficulty concentrating in practice and class. He also reports low mood and use of alcohol. As part of the intake process, you administer the CESD-R, GAD-7, ASRS-v1.1, and AUDIT. He scores in the clinical range for depression, ADHD, and alcohol use. You refer him to a local psychologist for a psychological evaluation to aid in diagnostic clarification and treatment planning, and you continue working on performance-related issues with the athlete while the evaluation is completed.

Assessment Tools and Their Availability

Assessment tool	Construct	Author and reference	Availability
Perceived Stress Scale (PSS-10)	Stress	Cohen, S., & Williamson, G. (1988). Perceived stress in a probability study of the United States. In S. Spacapan & S. Oscamp (Eds.), *The social psychology of health* (pp. 31-67). Newbury Park, CA: Sage.	Free at www.mindgarden.com
	The PSS-10 is a 10-item self-report inventory designed to evaluate perception of and ability to cope with stress in the past month.		
Recovery-Stress Questionnaire for Athletes (RESTQ-Sport)	Stress	Kellmann, M., & Kallus, K.W. (2016). The Recovery-Stress Questionnaire for Athletes. In K.W. Kallus & M. Kellmann (Eds.), *The Recovery-Stress Questionnaires: User manual* (pp. 86-131). Frankfurt am Main: Pearson Assessment & Information GmbH.	For purchase at www.pearson assessment.de
	The RESTQ-Sport is a self-report inventory designed to evaluate stress and recovery in athletes. It is available in three item lengths and is used across a range of sports and countries.		
Center for Epidemiological Studies Depression Scale Revised (CESD-R)	Depression	Eaton, W.W., Muntaner, C., Smith, C., Tien, A., & Ybarra, M. (2004). Center for Epidemiologic Studies Depression Scale: Review and revision (CESD and CESD-R). In M.E. Maruish (Ed.), *The use of psychological testing for treatment planning and outcomes assessment* (3rd ed., pp. 363-377). Mahwah, NJ: Erlbaum.	Free at www.cesd-r.com
	The CESD-R is a 20-item self-report inventory used to screen for depression. It is one of the most widely used measures for depression.		
Suicidal Behaviors Questionnaire-Revised (SBQ-R)	Suicide	Osman, A., Bagge, C.L., Gutierrez, P.M., Konick, L.C., Kopper, B.A., & Barrios, F.X. (2001). The Suicidal Behaviors Questionnaire-Revised (SBQ-R): Validation with clinical and nonclinical samples. *Assessment, 5,* 443-454.	Contact the author
	The SBQ-R is a four-item inventory addressing four dimensions of suicidality.		
Generalized Anxiety Disorder 7 (GAD-7)	General anxiety and worry	Spitzer, R.L, Kroenke, K., Williams, J.B.W., & Lowe, B. (2006). A brief measure for assessing generalized anxiety disorder. *Archives of Internal Medicine, 166,* 1092-1097.	Free at www.phqscreeners.com
	The GAD-7 is a seven-item self-report inventory designed to screen for symptoms of generalized anxiety. Several languages are available.		
Panic Disorder Severity Scale—Self-Report (PDSS-SR)	Somatic anxiety and panic	Houck, P.R., Spiegel, D.A., Shear, M.K., & Rucci, D. (2002). Reliability of the self-report version of the Panic Disorder Severity Scale. *Depression and Anxiety, 15,* 183-185.	Contact the author
	The PDSS-SR is a five-item self-report inventory used to screen for panic disorder symptoms (i.e., somatic symptoms of anxiety).		

Assessment tool	Construct	Author and reference	Availability
Social Phobia Scale (SPS-6)	Social phobia	Peters, L., Sunderland, M., Andrews, G., Rapee, R.M., & Mattick, R.P. (2012). Development of a short form Social Interaction Anxiety Scale (SIAS) and Social Phobia Scale (SPS) using nonparametric item response theory: The SIAS-6 and SPS-6. *Psychological Assessment, 24,* 66-76.	Full measure in article; http://dx.doi.org/ 10.1037/ a0024544
		The SPS-6 is a six-item self-report inventory designed to evaluate fears of general social interaction.	
Eating Attitudes Test (EAT-26)	Eating disorders	Garner, D.M., Olmsted, M.P., Bohr, Y., & Garfinkel, P.E. (1982). The Eating Attitudes Test: Psychometric features and clinical correlates. *Psychological Medicine, 12,* 871-878.	Free at www.eat-26.com (for inventory) and http://river-centre.org/Docs/ EAT-26Scoring-10-16-08-dg.pdf (for scoring)
		The EAT-26 is a 26-item self-report screening tool of eating disorder symptoms and extreme weight-control behaviors.	
Eating Disorder Examination Questionnaire (EDE-Q)	Eating disorders	Fairburn, C.G., & Beglin, S.J. (1994). Assessment of eating disorder psychopathology: Interview or self-report questionnaire? *International Journal of Eating Disorders, 16,* 363-370.	Free at www.credo-oxford.com/7.2.html
		The EDE-Q is a 41-item self-report inventory designed to evaluate maladaptive eating behaviors and body dissatisfaction.	
Female Athlete Screening Tool (FAST)	Eating disorders	McNulty, K.Y., Adams, C.H., Anderson, J.M., & Affenito, S.G. (2001). Development and validation of a screening tool to identify eating disorders in female athletes. *Journal of the American Dietetic Association, 101,* 886-892. Robert-McComb, J.J., & Mitchell, J.J. (2014). Menstrual dysfunction screening and management for active females. In J.J. Robert-McComb, R.L. Norman, & M. Zumwalt (Eds.), *The active female: Health issues across the lifespan* (pp. 93-109). New York: Springer.	Free; see McNulty et al. (2001) for inventory and Robert-McComb & Mitchell (2014) for scoring
		The FAST is a 33-item questionnaire designed to evaluate eating pathology, atypical exercise, and maladaptive eating behaviors in female athletes.	
Adult ADHD Self-Report Scale (ASRS-v1.1)	ADHD	Kessler, R.C., Adler, L., Ames, M., Demler, O., Faraone, S., Hiripi, E., . . . Walters, E.E. (2005). The World Health Organization Adult ADHD Self-Report Scale (ASRS). *Psychological Medicine, 35,* 245-256.	Free at www.hcp.med.harvard.edu/ncs/asrs.php
		The ASRS-v1.1 is a six-item self-report inventory designed to screen for symptoms of ADHD. It is available in multiple languages.	

(continued)

Assessment Tools and Their Availability *(continued)*

Assessment tool	Construct	Author and reference	Availability
Conners' Adult ADHD Rating Scales—Self-Report: Screening Version (CAARS-S:SV)	ADHD	Conners, C.K., Erhardt, D., & Sparrow, E. (1999). *CAARS Adult ADHD Rating Scales: Technical manual*. New York: Multi-Health Systems.	For purchase at www.mhs.com
	The CAARS-S:SV is a 30-item screening inventory for ADHD, and there are longer and other-report versions. It can be administered in multiple formats and languages. Special qualifications (training in tests and measurement) may apply to purchase this inventory.		
Alcohol Use Disorders Identification Test (AUDIT)	Substance use (alcohol)	Babor, T.F., Higgins-Biddle, J.C., Saunders, J.B., & Monteiro, M.G. (2001). *The Alcohol Use Disorders Identification Test: Guidelines for use in primary care* (2nd ed.). World Health Organization (WHO). Retrieved from www.talkingalcohol.com/files/pdfs/WHO_audit.pdf.	Free at http://apps .who.int/iris/ bitstream/10665/ 67205/1/WHO_ MSD_MSB_01.6a .pdf
	The AUDIT is a 10-item self-report inventory for screening alcohol consumption, drinking behavior, and alcohol-related problems.		
Drug Abuse Screening Test (DAST)	Substance use (drugs)	Skinner, H.A. (1982). The Drug Abuse Screening Test. *Addict Behavior, 7*, 363-367.	Free at www .integration .samhsa.gov/ clinical-practice/ screening-tools
	The DAST is a 28-item self-report screening for drug abuse or dependence disorders, not including alcohol and tobacco. It is also available in a 10-item version (DAST-10).		

Chapter Takeaways

- Mental health difficulties are not readily identified in athletes due to a variety of factors, including shame and fear of stigma. Therefore, screening as part of the intake process can help identify symptoms and facilitate referrals to qualified mental health professionals.

- Screening for stress in athletes is important because stress may be a precursor to other mental health conditions or may be exacerbated when mental health conditions already exist.

- Even though death by suicide may be less common in the athlete population, suicide attempts may be more frequent and more severe than for nonathletes. If there is any question about suicide, refer to a mental health professional immediately.

- Given the strong relationship between injury and mental health symptoms, screening measures should be given to athletes once an injury is sustained.

- Female athletes are more likely to report symptoms of depression, anxiety, and disordered eating than male athletes.

- The risk of eating disorders among athletes is elevated in certain aesthetic and lean sports and with increasing levels of competition, and there are high levels of comorbidity with other mental and physical health concerns.

- Measures used for the screening of eating disorders may be general or athlete specific, and it is prudent to incorporate several screening measures with any given athlete.

- Athletes may report attentional difficulties for a variety of reasons, including ADHD. A comprehensive evaluation by a mental health professional can aid in diagnosis.

- Athletes use substances for a variety of reasons. They report using alcohol, marijuana, and smokeless tobacco most frequently and may engage in higher rates of binge drinking than the average college student.

CHAPTER 6

Personality Tests: Understanding the Athlete as Person

James Tabano, EdD

Steve Portenga

Athletes seek the services of sport psychology consultants because they are struggling in some aspect of their performance, are performing below expectations, or are no longer making progress toward their goals, and they believe these difficulties are due to psychological obstacles. Assessment is invaluable in identifying the causes of the performance difficulties, particularly because there can be so many possible causes both within and outside of athletes. Additionally, assessment data will help the consultant identify what the athlete needs to learn or change to perform better.

The ability to evaluate athletes in a meaningful way is based on the theories consultants use to understand the psychology of high performance. However, most psychological theories (from Freud and Jung to Rogers and Maslow) were developed to explain general personality development for the purpose of achieving such ethereal outcomes as happiness, well-being, or self-actualization (Ewan, 1998). Correspondingly, most personality assessments are designed to help understand roadblocks related to these goals, not for the purpose of understanding athletic performance. Given that personality is such a powerful influence on athletes' thoughts, emotions, and behavior, assessments aimed at

understanding athletes must include personality data that are conceptualized with the psychology of high performance in mind above and beyond general theories of personality.

Personality has been defined as "important, relatively stable characteristics within the individual that account for consistent patterns of behavior" (Ewan, 1998, p. 2). This chapter draws on this definition and focuses on personality characteristics of athletes. Personality is a widely researched topic in sport psychology due to its relationship to many aspects of behavior and its ability to explain why people act the way they do (Ahmetoglu & Chamorro-Premuzic, 2013). For the same reasons, personality is also an important topic for sport psychology consulting.

The assessment of personality in sport has a long history, reaching back to the 1930s and Coleman Griffith, who is considered the founding father of sport psychology (Razon & Tenenbaum, 2014). Informed by the general personality theories of the time, researchers attempted to identify the sporting personality. Given that these theories address general psychological functioning, not performance, the data did not find evidence of a unique sport or athlete personality, nor did they find evidence to accurately predict performance (Razon & Tenenbaum, 2014).

Although assessing the range of traits associated with personality can be daunting, there are many benefits to doing so. Personality assessment can add another rich data point to consultants' ability to understand, predict, train, and maximize performance-relevant behavior (Nideffer & Sagal, 2001). Personality assessment can provide athletes, coaches, and consultants with a better understanding of how the athletes think, feel, behave, and perform in the competitive world. When athletes walk onto the field of play, they don't leave their personness, so to speak, on the sideline. Rather, they bring everything that they are, including their personality, to all that they do athletically, whether in training or competition.

Personality influences attitude, motivation, confidence, focus, emotions, resilience, teamwork, and performance under pressure, as well as many other psychological components of athletic participation. These attributes may not always be directly relevant in the moment of performance, but they nonetheless have a significant influence on the path taken by athletes as they approach, for example, the first pitch, serve, snap, or tee. Personality assessment can help athletes increase their self-awareness by revealing parts of themselves they may not be fully aware of. It can also help you by identifying personality strengths and roadblocks to achieving their athletic goals. Finally, personality assessment can help in building a relationship between consultant, athlete, and coach. When you sit down with an athlete (and coach) to review the assessment, a deeper understanding and a deeper relationship can develop, facilitating resolution of the performance challenges and putting the athlete back on the road to achieving competitive goals.

When examining personality traits within a specific subpopulation such as athletes, the focus on performance outcomes makes the competitive context a critical variable of personality assessment. A basic inquiry may seek to identify what traits compose the athlete's personality and how these affect athletic preparation and performance. The measurement tools often employed for discerning personality traits of athletes were

Assessment in Action

Utility of Personality Assessment of Athletes

Vealey (1989) pointed out that personality and sport research must continue to shift from a trait paradigm to interactionism. Consequently, much of sport personality profiling has provided descriptive and predictive data but less intervention information. Effective personality assessment creates an organized, descriptive structure of an athlete's traits and behaviors. But if the practitioner cannot use this personality map to bring the client into a joint intervention strategy, the bridge from theory to practice will be thwarted. Thus, sport psychology consultants can create more effective mediation protocols for their clientele if they take the time to fully assess the athlete's personality through any number of scales and inventories discussed in this chapter. By taking a more holistic understanding of the athlete as a person, the consultant's intervention can be more comprehensive and effective. The enduring personality constructs must be considered because they affect the athlete's behavior and cognitions beyond the training facility and playing field.

originally applied to the general population. It remains a deductive challenge to interpret these global personality measures in the rarified context of sport. Yet, there is little doubt that personality plays an influential role in athletic performance. As a result, some researchers have contributed to a more sport-specific examination of personality that has direct relevance to consultants working with athletes to maximize competitive performance.

This chapter first describes the history of personality assessment in sport. Then it explores several personality traits that are central to understanding athletes and their performances. It also provides a detailed accounting of the personality assessments that best measure these attributes for the purpose of helping athletes remove roadblocks and pursue their athletic goals. Unless otherwise noted, all of the assessment tools in this chapter have sound psychometric properties, including acceptable validity, reliability, and internal consistency. All information (e.g., location, availability) for the assessment tools in this chapter can be found in the chapter-ending table Assessment Tools and Their Availability.

History of Personality Assessment in Sport

Given all the theories that set out to explain human personality, the concept of personality defies a single unified structure. Hogan (1976) called the concept of personality "poorly defined" and "lacking borders with ambiguity at its edges" (p. 152). Within personality, the various constructs act as its distinct and measureable features. They can also interact and combine into more complex operations of thinking, emotions, behavior, and performance. Additionally, these constructs should not be assessed in isolation from the effects of social context or the complex environments in which athletic performance occurs. Consequently, engaging in personality assessment can be daunting, yet it can still be a source of valuable data about athletes. Like genome mapping, which has a finite number of active elements with innumerable possible interactions, personality assessment identifies those individual traits that collectively compose personality.

Personality assessment has a long history in sport psychology, including using traditional instruments to map athletes' personalities. Many of these measures can be traced back to Cattell's 16 Personality Factors (16PF; Cattell & Eber, 1966). One study of athlete personality using Cattell's 16PF (Valliant, Simpson-Housley, & McKelvie, 1981) reported that athletes were more dominant and self-assured, though less imaginative, than the general population. Valliant and Simpson also found personality differences based on individual versus team sports. Specifically, individual Olympic athletes demonstrated higher intelligence, higher ego strength, and higher dominance than team-sport athletes.

Other assessments have been developed that have proven to be more expedient without sacrificing statistical rigor. The five-factor model (FFM; McCrae & Costa, 1999), the Big Five personality traits (Morizot, 2014), and the Big Five Inventory (BFI; John, Donohue, & Kentle, 1991) are some of the assessment measures that tap into the predominant personality constructs of extraversion, agreeableness, conscientiousness, neuroticism, and emotional stability. Though well vetted among the general population, personality profiling and the use of these assessments have not been fully explored by the sport psychology field.

Eysenck, Nias, and Cox (1982) reported that athletes tend to be extroverted yet lower in neuroticism and anxiety than nonathletes. They also identified other important personality factors in athletes, including assertiveness, sensation seeking, and competitiveness, though these constructs showed no specific relationships to sport performance, such as reduced anxiety and depression. Rapalyea (2010) used profiling in a study of NCAA Division I athletes and reported low neuroticism, high extraversion, and more agreeableness than nonathletic undergraduates. For the sport psychology consultant, personality profiling may be useful in the design and implementation of intervention programs to improve performance.

Self-Esteem

Self-esteem has been defined as "a person's appraisal of his or her value" (Leary & Baumeister, 2000, p. 2). It reflects what people think and feel about themselves and their sense of worth in the world. People's actions and decisions can be directed by a desire to see themselves as worthy or valuable (Crocker & Park, 2004; Leary & Baumeister, 2000). Some psychologists have viewed the pursuit of self-esteem to be such a strong driver of one's thoughts, emotions, and behaviors that they have conceptualized it as a basic human need (Maslow, 1968).

Successes in aspects of life that influence the athlete's self-esteem feel good and are rewarding (Crocker & Knight, 2005). Although high self-esteem is not directly related to academic achievement, good job performance, or leadership (Baumeister, Campbell, Krueger, & Vohs, 2003), these positive feelings can be motivationally reinforcing (Crocker & Knight, 2005). Perhaps more importantly, low self-esteem can be a risk factor for depression (Sowislo & Orth, 2013) and aggression (Lee, 2014). Athletes with lower, unstable views of themselves are at risk of these views interfering with their sport development and their performance. If these athletes do not have sufficient experiences that they can view as positive and reinforcing, they may decide to discontinue their sport participation (Sowislo, Orth, & Meier, 2014). Athletes with lower, unstable self-esteem may also be less able to stay focused on their performance and may instead be caught up thinking about their sense of self.

It can be beneficial to assess an athlete's self-esteem to be aware of the potential for that athlete to lose motivation or be vulnerable to distractions while performing. Athletes with lower, unstable self-esteem should be engaged in conversation to understand where they draw their sense of self from and to understand why it might be unstable. Helping athletes develop a more positive and stable sense of themselves based on areas of their lives beyond sport can help them develop a solid foundation of self-esteem that is strong and resilient in the face of the many challenges presented by sport (Sowislo et al., 2014).

One example of an assessment used to measure self-esteem is the Rosenberg General Self-Esteem Scale (RSES; Rosenberg, 1965), which is perhaps the most widely used general measure of self-esteem (Alessandri, Vecchione, Eisenberg, & Łaguna, 2015). According to Rosenberg (1965), the scale assesses the "feeling that one is good enough" (p. 31). It is a 10-item instrument that consists of a 4-point Likert scale ranging from strongly disagree to strongly agree. The scores for all 10 items are totaled, and higher scores relate to higher self-esteem. Although Rosenberg originally constructed this scale for use on adolescents, it has been more widely applied since its inception.

Studies using the RSES with athletes have found it to be a valid measure of general self-esteem. Although it may not capture aspects of self-esteem specific to sport achievement, it does measure overall self-esteem. It appears the RSES can provide important information when working with athletes. For instance, a study of NCAA Division I athletes found that clinically significant depression symptoms were predicted by low scores on the RSES (Armstrong & Oomen-Early, 2009). Intercollegiate athletes with low RSES scores have been found to also have high scores on maladaptive perfectionism, as will be discussed in more detail later in this chapter (Gotwals, Dunn, & Wayment, 2003).

The RSES seems to be valid for a number of populations. For example, reports on the construct validity of the RSES using a sample of NCAA wheelchair athletes found the scale was useful in investigating global self-esteem in this population (Vermillion & Dodder, 2007). The RSES is a quick, validated way to get a general sense of athletes' self-esteem. Consultants can use the RSES to get a general snapshot of how athletes view themselves and their self-worth.

Another assessment used to measure self-esteem is the Coopersmith Self-Esteem Inventory (CSEI; Coopersmith, 1967). Before developing his self-esteem inventory, Coopersmith (1959) argued that self-esteem poses a conceptual problem and that studies of self-esteem are difficult to evaluate due to ambiguity and multiple interpretations. When the CSEI was published, he defined *self-esteem* as a measure of evaluative attitudes toward the self. Coopersmith (1967) developed the scale to measure the extent to which people believe themselves to be capable, significant, successful, and worthy.

The later version of the CSEI (Coopersmith, 1981) expanded the scope of the inventory to academic and adult life. Two forms of the CSEI were created. The School Form is used with children aged 8 to 15 and contains 58 items: 50 self-esteem items and 8 lie-scale items measuring student defensiveness and test wiseness. There is a short version of the School Form that has only 25 items and lacks the lie scale and subscores. The Adult Form of the CSEI is used with people aged 16 and older and contains 25 items adapted from the shorter School Form. All the forms are designed to measure the evaluative attitudes of self in society, school, family, and personal experience.

There has also been research supporting the value of the CSEI with athletes. Kerr and Goss (1997) investigated possible relationships between locus of control, self-esteem, and trait anxiety of young, elite, female gymnasts (30 11- to 17-year-olds) using the CSEI as one of the measures. There was a significant positive relationship between locus of control and self-esteem; as athletes sense a loss of control, their self-esteem declines as well. Thus, perceptions of loss of control may be a risk factor for low self-esteem. Additionally, there was a significant inverse relationship between self-esteem and trait anxiety, meaning as self-esteem rose, trait anxiety declined. In other words, athletes' confidence in their abilities mitigated anxiety. Extending this connection, if athletes lose their sense of control, their anxiety increases. Additionally, using the CSEI on a group of 50 field hockey players pre- and postseason, Kolt and Roberts (1998) found evidence of a relationship between low self-esteem and more severe sport injuries. They concluded that sports medicine professionals should consider this link and assess self-esteem when developing rehabilitation protocols. For further discussion of assessing psychosocial factors related to sport injury and rehabilitation, refer to chapter 13.

Perfectionism

Perfectionism is a personality trait in which people set impossibly high performance goals and devalue themselves if they fail to achieve them (Frost, Marten, Lahart, & Rosenblate, 1990). Perfectionists use these demanding standards as a basis for their self-evaluation. Perfectionism is generally agreed upon by researchers to be a multidimensional trait (Stoeber, 2014). One dimension has been termed *perfectionistic strivings* or *personal standards perfectionism* (Gaudreau & Thompson, 2010). This dimension represents the positive aspects of perfectionism, such as setting high standards and striving to attain them. The other common dimension is termed *perfectionistic concerns* or *evaluative concerns perfectionism*. This dimension represents the negative aspects of perfectionism and "entails a socially prescribed tendency to perceive that others are exerting pressure to be

perfect, combined with a propensity to evaluate oneself harshly and to doubt one's capacity to progress towards elevated standards" (Gaudreau & Thompson, 2010, p. 532).

Although there is some evidence that personal standards perfectionism has positive effects on sport participation, such as higher levels of general positive affect, academic satisfaction, self-determination, and goal progress (cf. Gaudreau & Thompson, 2010), there is a strong correlation between perfectionistic strivings and perfectionistic concerns (Gotwals, Stoeber, Dunn, & Stoll, 2012), suggesting that perfectionistic strivings are not as positive as originally believed. Although seemingly positive, personal standards perfectionism can become emotionally exhausting due to the effort and energy expended to pursue unrealistically high standards (Flett & Hewitt, 2014). Thus, the challenge for perfectionistic athletes (and the sport psychology consultant working with them) is to maximize the positive aspects of personal standards perfectionism while minimizing the negative impacts of evaluative concerns perfectionism (Gotwals et al., 2012).

Perfectionism is clearly a concern in sport; a recent study found that almost two out of every five athletes had unhealthy perfectionism (Dunn, Causgrove Dunn, Gamache, & Holt, 2014). Another study by Rasquinha, Dunn, and Causgrove Dunn (2014) reported that higher levels of competitive sport are associated with higher perfectionistic strivings. Athletes with an unhealthy perfectionistic approach react to self-described failures with self-criticism and frustration, dwell on the negatives, and may become depressed (Hill, Witcher, Gotwals, & Leyland, 2015). These athletes respond to challenges in their performances with responses that are not helpful to improvement, such as avoidant and disengagement-oriented coping (Dunn et al., 2014). High perfectionistic concerns are also associated with fear of failure and low self-esteem (Sagar & Stoeber, 2009).

One example of an assessment tool used to measure perfectionism is the Multidimensional Perfectionism Scale (MPS; Hewitt & Flett, 1991). The MPS measures three trait dimensions of perfectionism: self-oriented, other oriented, and socially prescribed. As an assessment tool for athletes, the MPS can explore motivational and cognitive aspects of behavior in training and competitive situations and associate these characteristics with the performance difficulties for which athletes are seeking help. There are common characteristics for high scorers in any of the three subscales compared with group norms. High scores in the self-oriented scale reflect athletes who have unrealistically high expectations of themselves and are compulsively driven to succeed with little sense of satisfaction. An elevated other-oriented score indicates athletes who externalize the characteristics of the self-oriented scale, meaning their expectations of others, such as teammates and coaches, are unrealistic, and others are also expected to strive compulsively toward their goal. For high socially prescribed scores, athletes perceive others as wanting them to be perfect, often fearing rejection if they make mistakes or fail.

Further discerning these dimensions of perfectionism for athletes, Flett and Hewitt (2005) "summarized contemporary research on perfectionism in athletes and exercisers, and concluded that perfectionism is primarily maladaptive" (p. 17). Consequently, elevations in the subscores in the MPS can indicate possible performance, personal, or interpersonal difficulties for athletes, thereby identifying potential problem areas in terms of thinking, emotions, and behavior that could produce performance roadblocks.

The latest version of the MPS is available in hand-scored, online, and software formats. The scale is appropriate for adults aged 18 and older and averages 15 minutes to administer. More information on the MPS, including where to purchase it, can be found in the chapter-ending table Assessment Tools and Their Availability. There is also a useful interpretive report online that offers a complete MPS subject scoring and interpretation example.

The Frost Multidimensional Perfectionism Scale (FMPS) is another multidimensional self-report scale of perfectionism. The FMPS contains 35 items categorized into six subscales: Concern over Mistakes (CM; 9 items), Personal Standards (PS; 7 items), Parental Expectations (PE; 5 items), Parental Criticism (PC; 4 items), Doubts about Actions (D; 4 items), and Organization (O; 6 items). Frost et al. (1990) recommend that the O scale be excluded from the total score because it is only remotely connected with the other five subscales. The first five subscales embody the essential dimensions of the FMPS. When the scores for the O scale are eliminated, there are 29 scored items for the FMPS, and scores range from 29 to 145. Each answer option is a 5-point Likert scale ranging from strongly disagree to strongly agree.

Research examining the FMPS in sport settings (Frost & Henderson, 1991) looked at the relationship between perfectionism and reactions to competitive athletics. Results indicated that, for the 40 female athletes sampled, those who were rated high on Concern over Mistakes reported more anxiety with less athletic confidence. These subjects also reacted negatively to their mistakes and engaged in negative thinking 24 hours before competition. A high score on Personal Standards was associated with an orientation toward athletic success, as well as more ideation of perfection before competition.

Fear of Failure

Although most athletes focus on opportunities for success in their sport, many are also keenly aware of the possibilities for failure. Moreover, a substantial number of athletes are becoming increasingly attentive to and fearful of the consequences of failure. Conroy, Willow, and Metzler (2002) state that a fear of failure involves "threats to an individual's ability to accomplish one or more personally meaningful goals when one fails in a performance" (p. 76). An early conceptualization of fear of failure by Atkinson (1957) viewed it as a unidimensional psychological construct driven by a person's desire to avoid shame and humiliation. Conroy, Poczwardowski, and Henschen (2001) explored fear of failure in more detail and concluded that it comprises more than just shame avoidance. They found that, in addition to shame, consequences of failure include tangible losses, feelings of losing control, damage to interpersonal relationships, emotional costs, and negative self-evaluations.

Unlike many other personality constructs, considerable research has explored the impact of fear of failure among athletes. Much of this research has supported the complexity of the construct and its multidimensional nature. Fear of failure in athletes has been associated with decreased sport performance in both adolescent (Sagar, Busch, & Jowett, 2010) and adult (Stoeber & Crombie, 2010) athletes, increases in test anxiety (Elliot & McGregor, 1999), poor academic achievement and surface learning (Diseth & Kobbeltvedt, 2010), negative physical and mental health outcomes (Elliot & Church, 2003), burnout (Rainey, 1995), adoption of avoidance achievement goals (Conroy & Elliot, 2004), pessimism and self-handicapping (Martin & Marsh, 2003), and generalized interpersonal distress (Conroy, Elliot, & Pincus, 2009). Considering the importance of fear of failure in the context of sport, Conroy (2001) holds that the construct offers sport psychology consultants the opportunity to foster athletes' development because of the athletes' investment in their sport participation.

Fear of failure seems to pose significant psychological and emotional challenges for athletes and as a result poses challenges for consultants who attempt to mitigate its effects on their clients' athletic experiences (Fox, 2003). Brewer (2008) cautions that fear of failure can be easily overgeneralized and ambiguous. More importantly, Brewer raises the critical question as to what constitutes failure. Failure may be in the eye of the beholder; coaches, competitors, parents, and spectators all have their own definitions of failure that may differ from each other. Simple win-or-lose outcomes do not render clear judgments for failure. With outcome judgments of failure less clear, context and perception are important factors when evaluating failure. For example, a runner may finish third in a meet yet post her best career time. Was the result a success or a failure? It depends on who is judging and the standard of success that is held.

Fear of failure can have significant negative consequences for athletes. As mentioned previously, prolonged fear of failure can lead to dropping out of sport due to burnout. Paradoxically, fear of failure increases the chances that athletes will experience failure due to its debilitating impact on their thinking, emotions, behavior, and performance. They are more likely to set maladaptive goals that increase stress and distract from performance success (Wikman, Stelter, Melzer, Hauge, & Elbe, 2014). Although some fear of failure can be motivating, it often ends up a destructive construct in postperformance evaluation (Rebar & Conroy, 2013).

An example of an assessment used to measure the fear of failure is the Performance Failure Appraisal Inventory (PFAI). Conroy et al. (2002) formulated the PFAI as a multidimensional measure of fear of failure. The PFAI was developed based upon Lazarus' (1991) cognitive-motivational-relational theory of emotion. The authors created 25 items for the PFAI that identify five negative consequences of failure: experience of shame or embarrassment, devalued self-esteem, uncertainty about the future, loss of interest by other important people, and upsetting other important people.

The PFAI comes in both long and short forms. Both forms use a response scale ranging from –2 (do not believe at all) to +2 (believe 100% of the time). The middle response is 0 (believe half the time). The scoring template offers equations for the factors measured by the scale. The short form produces only one scoring equation that reflects the grade for the general fear of failure factor rather than scores for the five subscales. The PFAI was normed on 440 male and female college students. Research by Gucciardi, Mahoney, Jalleh, Donovan, and Parkes (2012) examined the PFAI constructs among 423 elite athletes across various team and individual sports. These authors reported three perfectionism profiles: nonperfectionists, maladaptive perfectionists, and adaptive perfectionists. These perfectionism profiles were examined against various motivational orientations: achievement goals, fear of failure, and motivation regulation.

Need for Control

Conceptually, control is needed to act on choices (Leotti, Iyengar, & Ochsner, 2010). It is through making choices that we act on and with our world. Leotti and colleagues further contend that beyond a psychological desire, the need to control is biologically motivated; we are wired by evolution to exert control over our environment. It has been repeatedly argued that "the perception of control is not only desirable, but it is likely a psychological and biological necessity" (Leotti et al., 2010, p. 457).

The desire of people to exercise control over themselves and the world around them is also a personality trait (Kelly, 1955) that has been well researched (Deci, 1972). The adverse effects of a perceived lack of control over oneself and one's environment were demonstrated by the research of Seligman (1975), where extended exposure to uncontrollable negative stimuli had debilitating effects on performance, emotional well-being, and cognitive functioning. Conversely, if people believe they have control over the negative stimuli, even if they don't in reality, the dysfunctional effects are less evident.

A sense of control on the part of athletes has important implications for many aspects of their sport lives. The perception of control has an impact on a variety of psychological parameters, including motivation, confidence, arousal, focus, emotions, and resilience. It is also expressed in athletes' motivation to practice and prepare, trust in their ability to overcome challenges, respond positively to the pressures of competition, and react constructively to failures and setbacks.

Formulated by Burger and Cooper (1979), the Desirability of Control Scale (DCS) measures a person's desire to exercise control. The underlying premise of the scale is that perceived control has a direct relationship with reactions and outcomes. Greater perceived control leads to more positive reactions and outcomes and vice versa for lower perceived control. A particular distinction the authors make is that the perception of control is as important as actual control. In other words, the benefits associated with control occur when people believe they have control over a situation, even when they objectively do not.

The DCS consists of 20 items using a 7-point scale ranging from "This statement doesn't apply to me at all" (1) to "This statement always applies to me" (7). The scoring requires adding all items for a single control score. The reported norms for college students on the DCS as reported by Burger and Cooper (1979) is around 100 points, with a standard deviation of 10. The higher the score, the more people need to feel control over life events.

Low scores on the DCS have been found to be related to physical and mental well-being, low burnout rates, and job satisfaction (Dvash & Mannheim, 2001). In a study of the psychometric properties for the DCS, Thomas, Buboltz, Teague, and Seeman (2011) used an exploratory factor analysis to identify three factors in the scale: leadership, decision avoidance, and destiny control. The overall scale score is commonly used to measure the subject's desire for control, but these researchers urged caution in focusing on this score because it tends to diminish the multidimensionality of the DCS.

Assessment Tools and Their Availability

Assessment tool	Construct	Author and reference	Availability
Rosenberg Self-Esteem Scale (RSES)	Self-esteem	Rosenberg, M. (1965). *Society and the adolescent self-image*. Princeton, NJ: Princeton University Press.	Free at PsycNET.org
	The RSES was developed for adolescents but effectively extended to athletes as well as other subpopulations (e.g., students); there is some application in the literature to athletes.		
Coopersmith Self-Esteem Inventory (CSEI)	Self-esteem	Coopersmith, S. (1981). *Self-esteem inventories*. Menlo Park, CA: Mind Garden.	For purchase at www.mindgarden.com
	The CSEI was initially intended for the general population but further developed for adults and children with additional use with athletes. Two short forms are available, one for school-aged children (8-15) and one for adults (>16).		
Multidimensional Perfectionism Scale (MPS)	Perfectionism	Hewitt, P.L., & Flett, G.L. (2004). *Multidimensional Perfectionism Scale*. North Tonawanda, NY: Multi-Health Systems.	For purchase at www.mhs.com
	The MPS focuses on motivation and cognitive aspects of behavior in training and competition. There is significant reported use for the athletic population.		
Frost Multidimensional Perfectionism Scale (FMPS)	Perfectionism	Frost, R.O., Martens, P., Lahart, C., and Rosenblate, R. (1990). The dimensions of perfectionism. *Cognitive Research and Therapy*, 14(5), 449-468.	For purchase at link.springer.com
	Perfectionism is a major diagnostic criterion. It major dimension which is particularly relevant to athletics and performance, is the fear of making mistakes. The MPS with its 5 sub scales delineates this multidimensional construct.		
Performance Failure Appraisal Inventory (PFAI)	Fear of failure	Conroy, D.E., Willow, J.P., & Metzler, J.N. (2002). Multidimensional fear of failure measurement: The Performance Failure Appraisal Inventory. *Journal of Applied Sport Psychology*, 14(2), 76-90.	For purchase at www.tandfonline.com
	The PFAI is a self-report scale with six subscales, with the sixth scale cited as problematic to the overall score. It is frequently applied to athletes of all levels and ages.		
Desirability of Control Scale (DCS)	Need for control	Burger, J.M., & Cooper, H.M. (1979). The desirability of control. *Motivation and Emotion*, 3(4), 381-393.	Free at PsycNET.org
	The DOCS is widely used on athletes at all levels. It is offered in both long and short forms, both reported in application to athletes. It assumes perception of control is as important as actual control.		

Chapter Takeaways

- Because personality is such a powerful influence on athletes' thoughts, emotions, behavior, and performance, personality assessments are useful for gaining a comprehensive understanding of athletes.

- Personality influences attitude, motivation, confidence, focus, emotions, resilience, teamwork, and performance under pressure, as well as many other psychological components of athletic participation.

  - The ability to evaluate athletes in a meaningful way is based on the assumption that consultants rely on both general theories of personality and their understanding of the psychology of high performance.

  - Past research has not found evidence of a unique sport personality because it has been predominantly based on theories that address general psychological functioning, not performance.

  - Personality assessment can provide a better understanding of how athletes think, feel, and behave in the competitive world; help athletes increase their self-awareness; and help build a relationship between consultant, athlete, and coach.

  - Personality attributes may not always have a direct impact on athletic performance, but they have a significant influence on the path taken by athletes as they approach competition.

  - Personality traits that appear to be most relevant to athletic performance include self-esteem, perfectionism, fear of failure, and need for control.

- Self-esteem reflects what people think and feel about themselves and their sense of worth in the world.

- Perfectionism is a personality trait in which people set impossibly high performance goals and devalue themselves if they fail to achieve them.

- Fear of failure is grounded in athletes' beliefs in the consequences of failure, including shame, tangible losses, feelings of losing control, damage to interpersonal relationships, emotional costs, and negative self-evaluations.

- Need for control is founded in the belief in one's ability to exert control over the environment and to produce desired results that are essential for well-being, healthy functioning, and optimal performance.

CHAPTER 7
Inventories: Using Objective Measures

Graig M. Chow, PhD
Todd A. Gilson, PhD

In sport settings, quantification is routine and is used in nearly every aspect of preparation and performance. Athlete and team outcomes are compiled into win–loss standings; performances during practices and competitions are assessed in relation to goals; detailed training programs are created to help athletes develop the physical skills necessary for sport success; the dietary intake of athletes is scrutinized to achieve the optimal balance of protein, carbohydrate, and fat; and data-driven analytics from games has become a staple at the professional level and is steadily gaining traction at every level of sport. Through detailed assessment, athletes, coaches, and teams can better understand their strengths and deficiencies in order to improve performance and achieve greater success.

In addition to physical measures and assessment for other contributors to athletic performance, there is also a need for objective psychological measures. When consulting with athletes, you can use psychological assessment tools for a variety of purposes. For instance, a downhill skier experiencing worry or tension during competition can be assessed using a questionnaire about competitive anxiety to provide understanding of how her anxiety levels affect her performance. A marathon runner can learn how fatigue and lethargy may indicate burnout. A swimmer can develop mental skills to bolster concentration during long races, and the effectiveness of each strategy can be assessed and examined after performances. As a whole, objective measures help you better assess the needs of your clients and develop more effective intervention plans. As aptly stated by Silva, Metzler, and Lerner (2011), it should not be a question of whether or not you should use objective psychological measures in your applied work; rather, the central consideration is choosing which measures meet the needs and goals of the athletes with whom you work.

In this chapter, we discuss sport-specific inventories you can use to assess your clients. The list of objective measures presented is by no means exhaustive; we focused on those that are most commonly used by consultants and that offer the greatest utility in applied work with athletes. We begin with a brief discussion of practicality when determining which inventory to select. Benefits of using objective measures in consulting with athletes are then highlighted. We close by discussing several psychological assessment tools that can be used for a variety of purposes. It is our hope that readers will benefit from an enhanced understanding of how to select and use appropriate, objective sport-specific inventories and why they are an essential component of effective consulting with athletes.

Importance of Practicality When Choosing Assessments

Chapter 2 examines the psychometric properties of objective assessments, so we will not duplicate its discussion. Though not a psychometric property per se, practicality is an important factor to consider when choosing an assessment tool to use with clients. Practicality includes convenience, interpretability, and cost. In particular, an assessment has low practicality if it is too long, time consuming, complex, or uninteresting to readily administer to athletes. It is also impractical if it causes athletes to become bored and unmotivated, leading them to provide inaccurate responses and thus invalidate the purpose of the assessment. A measure ought to be readily interpretable, such that administration instructions are clearly outlined, scoring keys are available, and sufficient guidance for how to use the inventory and understand the results is provided (Kothari, 2004). An assessment is also considered to have low practicality if it must be purchased for administration when an equally good inventory exists in the public domain. Finally, practicality means that the results of the assessment provides real value to you and your clients in terms of understanding the athletes, planning interventions for them, and helping them achieve their goals.

Benefits of Objective Measures in Consulting With Athletes

Assessment in Applied Sport Psychology discusses a variety of assessments to consider and use in your applied practice, including mental status exams, interviews, psychophysiological tests, observation, and objective psychological measures, with each having unique advantages and disadvantages. The type of assessment or combination of assessments you use will depend on your knowledge and competency, the purpose of the assessment, clients' individual needs and goals, practicality, and perceived utility. Objective measures have certain characteristics that, among the constellation of assessments available, make them particularly valuable in working with athletes.

Perhaps the strongest rationale for using objective measures is that many derive from a current theoretical perspective where the construct has been operationally defined and antecedents and outcomes of the constructs have been empirically validated; in other words, most objective inventories are valid and reliable. For instance, if an athlete scores relatively low on a measure that was based on sound theory, areas to discuss and target for intervention are guided by the theoretical framework. This reflects the scientist-practitioner approach. In addition, many objective measures have been shown to predict important sport-related outcomes such as performance (Weinberg & Williams, 2010). Thus, an improvement in scores from objective measures is likely to correspond to meaningful changes in desired outcomes.

Objective measures can also help you better understand athletes' self-perceptions of presenting concerns and validate information obtained through observations, interviews, or discussions with coaches, parents, or teammates. Often, athletes present to a consultant with a concern that can be conceptualized in terms of different yet related constructs. For example, there are several reasonable explanations for why an athlete is experiencing debilitating precompetitive anxiety, such as a fear of failure, parental pressure, lack of preparation, or low confidence. You can measure each of these constructs to identify the ones to target for intervention, as well as rule out other potential explanations. Further, convergence between scores derived from inventories and other forms of assessment (e.g., interview, observation) provides clear direction for you and the athlete, while discrepancies provide an opportunity for you to discuss and clarify inconsistencies with the athlete to ensure client needs are appropriately met.

Athletes constantly receive detailed, objective feedback about their physical skills and performance in order to facilitate improvement and performance. Likewise, you can use results obtained from objective psychological measures to promote athletes' awareness of their mental strengths and areas for improvement. If weaknesses in particular attributes are discovered, we recommend that you normalize the experience provided that normative data exist or you have prior experiences using the inventory with athletes. Providing the results to athletes can assist with the development of intervention goals and plans and selection of appropriate techniques to employ. Administering objective psychological measures at predetermined phases of consultation (e.g., preintervention, six weeks into treatment, postintervention) allows you and the athlete to monitor progress and make any necessary modifications, and ultimately it helps you evaluate the effectiveness of your consulting and interventions.

Finally, a distinct advantage of using objective measures is the ability to conduct assessments often, in short time periods, and with large numbers of athletes. Most of the objective measures discussed in this chapter can be completed in less than 15 minutes. When you are working with a large group of athletes, it is usually impractical to meet with each athlete individually due to time constraints. Employing an objective measure in these situations is a useful method to gain an understanding of athletes' strengths and weaknesses, as well as the issues most prevalent at the group level. The information gleaned from this assessment allows you to design and implement group interventions to meet the needs of the majority of athletes.

Assessment Tools for Individual Athletes

Numerous inventories can be used in consultation with athletes. In this section, we discuss sport-specific measures that offer the greatest utility across a variety of situations and clients. Most of the objective psychological measures presented here have undergone adequate to extensive psychometric analysis to establish their validity and reliability. Given the importance of practicality, brief measures are described for certain constructs that you may wish to consider

depending on the purpose of assessment or time constraints. This section focuses on measures that are useful in initial sessions with athletes, as well as those that assess important psychological constructs, skills, and techniques.

Assessing Readiness for Sport Psychology

One area you should consider assessing before or during the first session is athletes' level of motivation to engage in sport psychology services. Such motivation is shaped in part by their attitudes toward sport psychology and their readiness for change. Some athletes hold positive views about sport psychology and are intrinsically motivated to work with you, whereas others experience stigma and are reluctant to meet with you, especially if they have been forced to see you by their parents or coach. Assessing athletes' attitudes toward consultation and their readiness to engage in mental skills training is essential for identifying and addressing barriers, as well as tailoring appropriate interventions.

Consultation

As mentioned, when beginning the consulting process, an important step to consider is assessing the athlete's openness and attitudes toward sport psychology services. Accordingly, the Sport Psychology Attitudes-Revised form (SPA-R; Martin, Kellman, Lavallee, & Page, 2002) is a 25-item measure that assesses stigma tolerance, confidence in the consultant, personal openness, and cultural preference. It was developed using high school and college athletes from a variety of sports, and it has been confirmed with a large sample of high school, club, and college athletes from the United States, United Kingdom, and Germany. The psychometric properties of the SPA-R are adequate, although the coefficient alpha for the personal openness subscale was marginal (Martin et al., 2002). You can use the SPA-R to understand how athletes and their significant others feel about seeking consultation or whether the athletes prefer that significant others do not know about their work with you. This information is valuable for addressing perceived barriers to initiating consultation, such as stigma and confidentially.

The SPA-R is also beneficial for understanding athletes' expectations of and receptivity toward sport psychology, their opinions about other cultures and races, and how comfortable they are working with a consultant of a different ethnicity. If you are concerned about practicality, there is support for using each subscale independently if you prefer.

Mental Training

The transtheoretical model (Prochaska & DiClemente, 1983) posits that behavior change involves a progressive transition through a series of successive stages: precontemplation, contemplation, preparation, action, and maintenance. Research supports the value of assessing clients' stage of change and tailoring interventions based on clients' readiness (Norcross, Krebs, & Prochaska, 2011). Failure to match an intervention to the athlete's current stage of change may result in negative outcomes, including premature termination (Swift & Greenberg, 2014).

The Stages of Change for Psychological Skills Training (SOC-PST; Leffingwell, Rider, & Williams, 2001) evaluates the motivational readiness of athletes to engage in consultation. It uses 3 items to address each stage of change (e.g., precontemplation, contemplation, action, maintenance), resulting in a simple 12-item measure. Items specific to the preparation stage are not included. The SOC-PST was developed and cross-validated on two samples of NCAA Division I student-athletes. To determine an athlete's current stage of change, you can use the highest subscale standardized score (i.e., T-score). Notably, the SOC-PST measure has been found to predict subsequent initiation of sport psychology services, with athletes in the contemplation, action, and maintenance stages being two to three times more likely than precontemplators to initiate individual consultation in the year following assessment (Leffingwell et al., 2001). In addition to using the SOC-PST to tailor your interventions to match stage of change, you can also use it to evaluate the effectiveness of your interventions in terms of moving athletes to later stages of change.

The Stages of Change Questionnaire is a brief, ordered scale that you can use to assess athletes' regular use of mental skills training according to all five stages of behavior change (Grove, Norton, Van Raalte, & Brewer, 1999). Clients are asked to circle the number on a 5-point ladder (0-4) that best describes their current use of mental skills training (e.g., 1 = "I do not use regular mental skills training, but I have been thinking about starting within the next six months", 4 = "I regularly use mental skills training and have done so for longer than six months"). This allows you to classify the athlete into one of the five stages of change.

Assessment in Action

Identifying Athletes' Readiness for Consulting

During an intake session, sport psychology consultants can sometimes become so focused on the presenting concern and appropriate intervention that they fail to assess where the client is at in terms of motivation for change. Through interviewing and using measures such as the SPA-R (Martin et al., 2002) or the SOC-PST (Leffingwell et al., 2001), you can gain a deeper understanding of an athlete's readiness to engage in sport psychology consulting. Match the intervention to your client's current readiness level and attitudes toward sport psychology. For example, motivational interviewing is beneficial for athletes in the precontemplation or contemplation stage. By tailoring interventions this way, you reduce the likelihood of premature termination and move the athlete to higher stages of change.

Assessing Psychological Constructs

As a consultant, you are interested in understanding and enhancing athletes' psychological contributors to sport performance. State measures assess how athletes feel at a specific moment in time, whereas trait measures assess how athletes generally feel or their predispositions to experience certain psychological states.

This distinction is important to consider when choosing appropriate measures to use with athletes. The objective measures reviewed in this section represent some of the most commonly targeted psychological constructs for intervention, including motivation, confidence, anxiety, concentration, commitment, and burnout.

Motivation

Motivation is one of the most salient psychological constructs that you can quantify in athletes. Understanding athletes' motivation provides insight into why and how they initiate action, the direction and magnitude of the effort displayed, and how they respond to challenges and setbacks (Roberts, Treasure, & Conroy, 2007). To this end, there are several inventories based on various theoretical frameworks for better understanding the process of motivation.

To best understand the trait motivational tendencies of an athlete from a self-determination theory (SDT) perspective (Deci & Ryan, 2000), questionnaires that assess intrinsic and extrinsic motivation are most relevant. The Sport Motivation Scale-28 (SMS-28; Pelletier et al., 1995) is a commonly used measure that has demonstrated sound validity for athletes of both sexes and is appropriate to use when translated into other languages. However, one criticism of the SMS-28 is that it does not adequately measure the most autonomous form of extrinsic motivation— integrated motivation. This form of motivation is important when both athletes and coaches share the same end goals (e.g., improvement, winning), and it explains why athletes may continue to persist even if they have little control in outlining the process used for goal accomplishment.

To address this issue, the Sport Motivation Scale-6 (SMS-6) was developed by Mallett, Kawabata, Newcombe, Otero-Forero, and Jackson (2007). This 24-item measure includes questions more appropriate for experienced athletes and also has the ability to assess varying striations of intrinsic motivation (i.e., knowledge, stimulation, accomplishment). Yet, the SMS-6 also has its share of limitations. In particular, the content validity of some questions may be inadequate. In the SMS-6, questions developed to measure amotivation actually appear to assess a decrease in intrinsic motivation. Furthermore, the constructs of identified regulation and intrinsic motivation lack discriminant validity with the well-known concept of flow states, meaning the SMS-6 may actually assess elements of flow and not facets of motivation outlined within the framework of SDT.

Finally, the Behavioral Regulation in Sport Questionnaire (BRSQ-6 and BRSQ-8) is a measure developed for elite athletes (Lonsdale, Hodge, & Rose, 2008). The distinguishing feature between the two versions is the ability to collect data on the three forms of intrinsic motivation (i.e., knowledge, stimulation, and accomplishment), with the BRSQ-8 being multidimensional and the BRSQ-6 focused on intrinsic motivation as a solitary construct. Regardless of the version used, the BRSQ includes questions related to all forms of extrinsic motivation and is fairly short, with four items per subscale. On the other hand, psychometric testing has produced mixed results related to construct validity; thus, more work is warranted with this measure.

Motivation inventories can also be designed within the framework of achievement goals (i.e., the desired outcome for each participant during a competition or performance). The Task and Ego Orientation in Sport Questionnaire (TEOSQ; Duda, 1989) is the seminal measure in sport psychology in this area. Simple and effective, the 13-item TEOSQ provides information related to how athletes define success in their sport and produces subscale scores for task and ego orientation. The Perception of Success Questionnaire (POSQ) is similar to the TEOSQ in theoretical design, length, and implementation with athletes, with the contrasting feature being that the construction of the POSQ was made with solely athletes in mind (Roberts, Treasure, & Balague, 1998). Though a TEOSQ question for ego orientation phrased as "I am the only one who can do the play or skill" is appropriate in sport, research has also used the TEOSQ in physical education settings to examine the achievement goals of youth participants. A similar question in the POSQ reads, "I outperform my opponents," which is better suited to the world of athletics. Both the TEOSQ and POSQ reflect trait or dispositional measures of motivation. Goal states are often measured by rewording the stem of an existing goal orientation measure to obtain a state assessment (Roberts et al., 2007).

In recent years, an expanded view of achievement goals has gained popularity, adding approach or avoidance in relation to task- and ego-orientation goals (Elliot & McGregor, 2001). To address this expanded understanding, the Achievement Goals Questionnaire for Sport (AGQ-S) was designed using a 2 × 2 framework where individuals can be strong or weak in each achievement goal orientation, as well as strive toward accomplishment or seek to avoid failure when engaging in a task (Conroy, Elliot, & Hofer, 2003). As the name implies, the AGQ-S phrases items to be relevant for athletic competitions, and predictive validity is quite extensive when the 2 × 2 framework is used (for a review, see Roberts et al., 2007). Criticisms of the AGQ-S center on the somewhat inconsistent findings with approach-related goals and individuals' perceptions of competence.

Confidence

Confidence is another critical construct separating athletes who succeed from those who fail. Psychological assessment of confidence can be identified as state and fluctuate based on current perceptions (e.g., self-efficacy), or it can be identified as trait and be more dispositional in nature (e.g., sport confidence). It can also be measured at the individual or team levels. This chapter only discusses individual-level confidence inventories (for a review of group or team confidence, see chapter 11).

The Trait Sport-Confidence Inventory (TSCI; Vealey, 1986) was conceptualized to ascertain individuals' beliefs about being successful in sport. Because athletes in multiple sports can use this measure, question stems remain fairly general and ask respondents to indicate their perceptions in comparison to the most confident athlete they know. The TSCI has demonstrated adequate psychometric properties in testing and has been shown to predict athletes' state-level sport confidence both before and after competition. Building on the TSCI, Vealey, Hayashi, Garner-Holman, and Giacobbi (1998) developed the 45-item Sources of Sport-Confidence Questionnaire (SSCQ) and empirically tested it with

high school and collegiate athletes. From four iterations of data collection, it was noted that athletes derived confidence in their sport from nine distinct sources: physical and mental preparation, social support, mastery, demonstration of ability, physical self-presentation, environmental comfort, vicarious experiences, coach leadership, and situational favorability. Thus, by using this measure, consultants can gain insight into the factors that influence athletes' confidence and specific areas to target for intervention.

For assessing confidence from a state perspective, Vealey (1986) developed the State Sport-Confidence Inventory (SSCI) with the purpose of measuring athletes' confidence immediately before a competition; however, the SSCI has not demonstrated strong relationships with performance. This may be because it was developed using similar guidelines to those of the TSCI, where athletes rate their confidence in comparison to the most confident athlete they know. The decision to use a norm-referenced scale (i.e., comparison to others) may cloud the relationship between athletes' behavior, performance, and eventual outcome with their confidence in the here and now. Consequently, consultants seeking a measure of state confidence with stronger predictive validity may wish to consider self-efficacy scales and the guidelines put forth by Bandura (2006).

Anxiety

Competitive anxiety is a well-known psychological construct in athletics. Researchers have discovered that anxiety can be experienced at a cognitive or somatic level (Martens, Vealey, & Burton, 1990). This negative emotion is essential to consultants' work with athletes because the emotional response and then cognitive appraisal of a situation often dictate competitive results (Landers & Arent, 2010). Thus, through the use of inventories, you can gauge athletes' anxiety levels and determine their optimal level for competitive performances.

As with the concept of confidence, athletes can experience state or trait anxiety. Measures of state anxiety assess how anxious an athlete feels at a particular moment in time, often before a competition. Thus, administration, responses, and calculated scores are specific to a certain situation and time. The Competitive State Anxiety Inventory (CSAI-2; Martens, Burton, Vealey, Bump, & Smith, 1990) is one of the more popular measures of state anxiety. This 27-item questionnaire includes subscales in cognitive anxiety, somatic anxiety, and a related component of self-confidence that can be independently calculated, providing a detailed snapshot of an athlete when the situation calls for a paper-and-pencil test.

In recent years, the factorial structure and inclusion of specific questions based on researcher assumptions in the CSAI-2 have come under increased scrutiny, leading to the Competitive State Anxiety Inventory-2 Revised (CSAI-2R; Cox, Martens, & Russell, 2003). An enhanced methodology was the driving force behind the development of this updated version, including a more rigorous analytic technique and the use of calibration and validation samples that were independent. Based on the results of Cox et al. (2003), these considerations produced a more psychometrically sound—and shorter—instrument while still adhering to the overall structure of cognitive anxiety, somatic anxiety, and self-confidence subscales found in the original CSAI-2.

Because state anxiety levels can fluctuate moment by moment, you may find it useful to use brief measures that athletes can complete immediately before competition. The aforementioned point is a methodological limitation of the CSAI-2 and the CSAI-2R; however, the Mental Readiness Form-3 (MRF-3; Krane, 1994) and the Anxiety Rating Scale (ARS; Cox, Russell, & Robb, 1998) allow for quick and easy assessments of anxiety while still drawing upon the CSAI-2 as a framework. The MRF-3 and MRF-Likert version contain only three items (one each for cognitive anxiety, somatic anxiety, and self-confidence) with bipolar anchors. In the MRF-3, the bipolar continuous scales (i.e., worried–not worried, tense–not tense, confident–not confident) are separated by a 10-centimeter line on which athletes simply mark a spot corresponding to how they feel, with scores ranging from 1 to 100. Alternatively, the MRF-Likert uses the same anchor words, but athletes respond on an 11-point Likert-type scale. Both the MRF-3 and MRF-Likert have adequate concurrent validity and are not influenced by social desirability bias. Similarly, the ARS is a three-item measure that was developed by examining the best three items from each CSAI-2 subscale and then collapsing these items into one question. Athletes indicate their perceived level of anxiety and confidence using a rating of perceived exertion (RPE) response system that ranges from 1 (not at all) to 7 (intensely so). Although these brief measures of anxiety have adequate validity, note that they only focus on intensity for the given construct and cannot provide the richness of data supplied by the CSAI-2 or the CSAI-2R.

Trait anxiety, which is more inherent in a person's disposition, as opposed to being triggered by a situation or environment, is also an important construct to consider. Measures of trait anxiety assess how anxious athletes usually feel before or while competing in their sport. The Sport Competition Anxiety Test (SCAT) is a 15-item, unidimensional measure of trait anxiety composed of a simple 3-point response scale; participants respond to each statement regarding if they rarely, sometimes, or often feel this way when competing in their sport (Martens, 1977). SCAT scores of less than 17 reflect a low level of trait anxiety, scores of 17 to 24 reflect an average level, and scores of more than 24 reflect a high level. A benefit of the SCAT is that norm-referenced inferences can be made to many populations; however, this measure only assesses anxiety as a single dimension and therefore disregards other forms of anxiety and their consequences.

More recently, the Sport Anxiety Scale-2 (SAS-2; Smith, Smoll, Cumming, & Grossbard, 2006) has been developed to quantify anxiety levels of athletic participants. The SAS-2 includes 15 items and assesses cognitive anxiety, somatic anxiety, and concentration disruption that can occur from experiencing anxiety. Two major advantages of this inventory are the applicability of this questionnaire with children as young as nine years old and the ability to use results to predict future state anxiety scores. Scores from the SAS-2 can be used to assess the effectiveness of anxiety reduction methods on athletes' anxiety levels before an impending performance or competition. Further, if you are concerned with social desirability, the directions provided in the SAS-2 help normalize anxiety in an attempt to generate accurate responses, stating that "Many athletes get tense or nervous before or during games, meets, or matches. This happens even to pro athletes."

Concentration

Through education and implementation of techniques, consultants aim to help athletes identify what to focus on and where to direct that focus while simultaneously ignoring irrelevant cues. Focusing on correct opponents, plays, and objects during sport performance is a significant component of success. To address these issues, you should gain a better understanding of the attentional selectivity of your athletes and any deficiencies that may exist.

Nideffer (1976) developed the Test of Attentional and Interpersonal Style (TAIS) for assessing individuals on six attentional styles (broad-external, external-overload, broad-internal, internal-overload, narrow-focus, and reduced-focus), and this measure continues to be the go-to inventory for those who seek to better understand how people concentrate. At 144 questions and 17 subscales, TAIS is a lengthy measure that should primarily be used for diagnosing attentional problems and not for drawing relationships to a performance. It can be a useful tool to educate athletes about effective and ineffective attentional styles and the dimensions of attention, such as width (broad-narrow) and direction (internal-external), and then assist them in identifying the type of focus needed for various sport skills or situations. This information can help you determine the skills and situations where athletes are focusing appropriately and those where athletes are lacking optimal focus and then identify possible reasons for this (e.g., anxiety).

Although TAIS results can highlight how using the correct attentional style affects the quality of athletes' performances, sport-specific TAIS measures, in tennis, baseball, soccer, and rifle shooting, have not undergone rigorous psychometric validation (Albrecht & Feltz, 1987; Etzel, 1979; Fisher & Taylor, 1980; Van Schoyck & Grasha, 1981). Additionally, TAIS requires a fee, and the administrator must have earned at least a master's degree in psychology or educa-

tion with training in assessment practices or be a current member of an organization adhering to the AERA, APA, and NCME Standards for Educational and Psychological Testing.

Commitment and Burnout

Most athletes will reach a point in their careers where they question their continued participation or experience symptoms of burnout. As a consultant, you are well suited to address these issues. In the area of commitment, Scanlan, Chow, Sousa, Scanlan, and Knifsend (2016) developed the Sport Commitment Questionnaire-2 (SCQ-2) to help understand the psychological state of athletes who continue their involvement in sport. The authors extended the original SCQ to create a 58-item measure assessing 10 sources and two types of commitment based on multiple rounds of psychometric testing with adolescent athletes in various sports and from diverse ethnic backgrounds. Scanlan and colleagues highlight how to use the SCQ-2 with athletes during intake sessions to understand the extent to which they are committed to continued sport involvement. Because the SCQ-2 assesses both the types as well as the sources of commitment, administering it to athletes who are reporting low commitment may provide insight into the factors you can target for enhancement.

Athletic burnout can have serious consequences, ranging from a temporary break from competition to quitting altogether due to prolonged and unmanageable stress, constrained sport commitment, lack of motivation, overtraining, and underrecovery. Raedeke and Smith (2001, 2009) developed the Athlete Burnout Questionnaire (ABQ) to assess burnout in athletes. The ABQ is consistent with the athlete-specific conceptualization of burnout syndrome and includes three subscales: emotional and physical exhaustion, reduced sense of accomplishment, and sport devaluation. It is a simple 15-item measure in which athletes respond to the question stem of "How often do you feel this way?" using a 5-point Likert-type scale ranging from almost never to most of the time or almost always. The ABQ has been shown to be valid and reliable even when data are collected remotely (e.g., over the Internet). Additionally, items can be customized to specific sports.

Because of this feature, the ABQ has been used with a wide variety of athletes across many ability levels in many sports. Although normative cutoff values for ABQ scores are presently not available, high burnout is typically characterized as scores at the response midpoint (i.e., 3 = sometimes) or higher on all three subscales. Perhaps the biggest downside of the ABQ is that the measure and instructions are only provided as a manual for purchase (see the chapter-ending table Assessment Tools and Their Availability for information).

Mental Skills and Techniques

A cornerstone of consultation is the development and enhancement of mental skills (e.g., productive thinking, energy management) by teaching, modeling, and employing a variety of techniques designed to influence these skills (e.g., goal setting, imagery, self-talk, relaxation). An aim of mental skills training is for athletes to achieve self-regulation, mastery, and, ultimately, automaticity in using the mental skills and techniques during competitive situations. For this to occur, techniques must be regularly and systematically practiced. Thus, in addition to assessing athletes' strengths and weaknesses, many of the measures presented in this section can be used to evaluate the level and frequency of mental skills and techniques used by your clients.

Several comprehensive inventories are available for assessing a broad range of mental skills and techniques at once, and there are also instruments that assess one particular mental skill or technique. Comprehensive inventories are particularly advantageous for identifying athletes' strengths and weaknesses across several mental skills deemed important for sport performance. However, a limitation of comprehensive tools is that they do not provide in-depth assessment on particular mental skills and techniques the way focused assessments do.

Comprehensive Measures

Assessing athletes' use of psychological methods is important before, throughout, and following implementation of a psychological skills training program. The Test of Performance Strategies (TOPS 2; Hardy, Roberts, Thomas, & Murphy, 2010) is a popular inventory for assessing the frequency with which athletes use a range of mental skills and techniques in both practice and competition. The TOPS 2 includes 64 items with eight practice and eight competition subscales. The subscales include

1. self-talk,
2. emotional control,
3. automaticity,
4. goal setting,
5. imagery,
6. activation,
7. relaxation, and
8. attention control (practice) and negative thinking (competition).

The TOPS 2 is essentially two separate scales: one for practice and the other for competition (the authors caution against summing the practice subscales and the competition subscales to obtain an overall score of athletes' use of mental skills and techniques). Thus, depending on the time of season or target of intervention, it may be appropriate to use one of the scales alone or both scales at once. Employing both scales is powerful for identifying patterns of consistencies (or inconsistencies) in athletes' mental skill and technique utilization in practice and competition. Importantly, TOPS subscales have been found to predict performance and differentiate athletes across skill levels, with athletes who are most skilled reporting the greatest use of mental skills and techniques (Hayslip, Petrie, MacIntire, & Jones, 2010).

Version 3 of the TOPS (TOPS 3; Thomas, Hardy, & Murphy, 2007) has 68 items, still with the same eight subscales as previous versions of the instrument. Users receive information regarding how to interpret scores, subscale definitions, and a profile of mental skills and techniques used for practice and competition. There is also an option to compare individual scores with various group norms, including sport and competition level. We were unable to locate any published studies examining the psychometric properties of the TOPS 3.

Information on obtaining the TOPS 3 is available in the chapter-ending table Assessment Tools and Their Availability.

The Ottawa Mental Skills Assessment Tool-3 (OMSAT-3*; Durand-Bush, Salmela, & Green-Demers, 2001) includes 48 items and 12 mental skill subscales grouped under three broader factors:

1. Foundation skills (goal setting, self-confidence, commitment)
2. Psychosomatic skills (stress reactions, fear control, relaxation, activation)
3. Cognitive skills (imagery, mental practice, focusing, refocusing, competition planning)

Scores on the OMSAT-3* subscales significantly discriminated between elite and competitive athletes (Durand-Bush et al., 2001). More recently, the OMSAT-3* was used in a multifaceted mental skills training program with the Canadian national short-track speedskating team as part of a monitoring strategy in which individual profiles for each athlete were developed for a yearly evaluation process (Beauchamp, Harvey, & Beauchamp, 2012). Users who complete the OMSAT-3* receive a summary profile that includes scores on the 12 mental skill subscales, a visual graph, and an interpretation of scores based on each mental skill.

In comparison to the TOPS and OMSAT-3*, the Athletic Coping Skills Inventory-28 (ACSI-28; Smith, Schutz, Smoll, & Ptacek, 1995) is a comprehensive measure of mental skills that is shorter in length and available at no cost. The ACSI-28 reflects a trait measure of mental skills and includes seven subscales:

1. Coping with adversity
2. Peaking under pressure
3. Goal setting and mental preparation
4. Concentration
5. Freedom from worry
6. Confidence and achievement motivation
7. Coachability

A general measure of psychological coping skills, personal coping resources, can be derived by summing the subscales, although we recommend calculating and interpreting the subscales independently. The subscale for coping with adversity is particularly useful for understanding how an athlete's emotions, thoughts, arousal, and mood are affected by challenging situations, while the subscale for peaking under pressure is beneficial for identifying how athletes appraise, react to, and perform in stressful situations. The coachability subscale is particularly novel and is helpful for understanding how an athlete responds emotionally and behaviorally to the coach's advice, instruction, and criticism. The ACSI-28 has been shown to predict athletic performance and sport career longevity (Smith & Christensen, 1995).

To evaluate the effectiveness of sport psychology interventions or workshops or programs that incorporate them, or to better understand your athletes' strengths and weaknesses, you can assess mental toughness and its components with objective measures. Despite the widespread use of the phrase *mental toughness* in the sport world, there is no single accepted definition. It has been conceptualized as a state of mind, as a personality trait, and as a set of psychological characteristics. Jones, Hanton, and Connaughton (2007) offer what appears to be the most rigorous definition: "having the natural or developed psychological edge that enables you to, generally, cope better than your opponents with the many demands (competition, training, lifestyle) that sport places on a performer and, specifically, be more consistent and better than your opponents in remaining determined, focused, confident, and in control under pressure" (p. 247). The Mental Toughness Questionnaire (MTQ48; Clough, Earle, & Sewell, 2002) is based on the 4Cs model of mental toughness (control, challenge, commitment, confidence) and assesses total mental toughness and the following six subcomponents:

1. Emotional control
2. Life control
3. Challenge
4. Commitment
5. Confidence in abilities
6. Interpersonal confidence

Strengths of the MTQ48 include its psychometric properties; feedback of results for athletes and their coaches, including suggestions for development; and efficiency (it takes approximately eight minutes to complete). Results are provided in comparison to established norms. In addition to the 48-item version, there is also an 18-item version, but it has no subscales. To purchase and administer the MTQ48, you must be a licensed user, which involves attending a training program on its use.

Though not necessarily an inventory, performance profiling is a popular and useful objective assessment tool that you can use to identify and understand areas requiring improvement and maintenance in athletes. The technique generates valuable information that can guide the development of your interventions and consultations. Performance profiling is commonly employed by first eliciting athletes' perceptions of the qualities they believe are fundamental to the success of elite athletes in their sport. Then the athletes provide self-ratings on these qualities, which are displayed on a visual profile to represent their strengths and weaknesses in a graphic format. Modest support for the validity and reliability of performance profiling has been demonstrated (Doyle & Parfitt, 1996, 1997; Gleeson, Parfitt, Doyle, & Rees, 2005).

Gucciardi and Gordon (2009) revised the performance profiling technique to facilitate a deeper understanding of the content and structure of the athlete's perspective by creating a three-stage model for a more thorough evaluation. In stage 1, you introduce the performance profiling technique to athletes, including explaining its purpose in assessing their strengths and areas in need of improvement. In stage 2, you assist athletes in generating a list of key qualities of an elite performer in their sport (similar to the original technique). For each key quality (e.g., self-belief), athletes provide a description of its personal meaning and then generate the opposite quality (e.g., self-doubt) and a description of it. In the last step of stage 2, athletes rank the generated constructs (each key quality and opposite quality) in order of importance and provide general ratings of importance. In stage 3, athletes rate themselves on each of their generated constructs. An extension of this approach consists of comparing athletes' self-assessments with those of their coach.

Performance profiling helps athletes (with assistance from the consultant) identify those mental skills and techniques that are important in their sport, and self-assessments obtained throughout consultation can be used to evaluate the effectiveness of your interventions and athletes' progress. Further, due to its efficiency of administration and scoring, performance profiling can be useful for work with both individual athletes and teams.

Assessment in Action

Using the Revised Performance Profiling Technique

This technique can help identify an athlete's strengths and weaknesses in psychological, physical, technical, and tactical areas (Gucciardi & Gordon, 2009). The profile generated not only facilitates the athlete's self-awareness and intrinsic motivation, it also gives the practitioner a deeper understanding of the athlete's psychological framework and sport participation. Discuss with your client why each quality was selected and its personal meaning, and explore discrepancies between the anchors of each bipolar construct as well as between the athlete's current self-ratings and desired self-ratings. Processing the profile with your clients enhances the working alliance, provides a foundation for goal setting, and assists in the selection of interventions.

Individual Mental Skills

When working with athletes on specific mental skills or techniques, it can be beneficial to obtain a more in-depth assessment than comprehensive measures provide. In this section, we discuss measures of individual mental skills, including self-talk, mental imagery, and mindfulness.

Self-Talk

Self-talk is an important psychological technique in both the performance realm and in the acquisition of new skills (Tod, Hardy, & Oliver, 2011). To this end, various self-talk questionnaires have been developed to help you and your athletes better understand their self-talk tendencies. Two of the most prominent are the Self-Talk Use Questionnaire (STUQ; Hardy, Hall, & Hardy, 2005) and the Automatic Self-Talk Questionnaire for Sports (ASTQS; Zourbanos, Hatzigeorgiadis, Chroni, Theodorakis, & Papaioannou, 2009). The STUQ is a 59-item measure with several sections focusing on how often athletes use self-talk, why athletes use self-talk in both practice and competition, how athletes engage in self-talk, and the content of athletes' covert and overt self-talk. Responses are made on a 9-point Likert scale (or in the case of self-talk content, percentages related to positive, neutral, and negative self-talk). In initial testing, the STUQ has demonstrated adequate content validity and test–retest reliability.

The ASTQS is a measure of self-talk that is trait in nature and was designed to assess the underlying structure of self-talk statements. In developing the ASTQS, athletes from both individual and team sports who competed regionally, nationally, and internationally recorded their self-talk statements at the end of a competition. Athletes' reflections were then used by researchers to generate the 40 items of the ASTQS, in which participants respond about the frequency of each form of self-talk on a 5-point Likert scale. Through a series of studies, an eight-factor model of thoughts was established, with four positive categories (psych up, confidence, anxiety control, and instruction), three negative categories (worry, disengagement, and somatic fatigue), and one neutral category (irrelevant thoughts). The ASTQS can help consultants develop more precise self-talk interventions for improved athletic performance.

Mental Imagery

Mental imagery is a central component of mental skills training. Consultants should devise and implement individualized imagery scripts with a variety of imagery content and clearly defined outcomes for their clients. However, before developing an individualized imagery script, you should assess the imagery capabilities of your athletes, regardless of their competitive level (MacIntyre et al., 2013). This allows you to design the script according to the client's ability to image. For instance, if an athlete has good imagery ability, you might include a greater number of sensory modalities and longer imagery duration (Williams, Cooley, Newell, Weibull, & Cumming, 2013). Several objective measures are available for assessing athletes' imagery ability.

The Vividness of Movement Imagery Questionnaire (VMIQ) was revised (VMIQ-2; Roberts, Callow, Hardy, Markland, & Bringer, 2008) based on current imagery perspective and modality conceptualizations. The VMIQ-2 assesses athletes' imagery ability in 12 movements (e.g., running, jumping sideways, kicking a ball in the air) along three subscales: internal visual imagery, external visual imagery, and kinesthetic imagery. When completing the VIMQ-2, the athlete is asked to image each of the 12 movements in these three ways (i.e., internal, external, kinesthetic) and rate the vividness of each image on a 5-point Likert scale.

Whereas the VMIQ-2 is a measure of movement imagery ability that requires no actual physical movement, the Movement Imagery Questionnaire—Revised (MIQ-R, Hall & Martin, 1997) involves physical movement. The MIQ-R comprises eight items: four that assess visual imagery ability and four that measure kinesthetic imagery ability. Athletes are asked to perform a simple motor movement. They are then instructed to either see themselves performing the movement as clearly and vividly as possible or to feel themselves performing the movement. Unlike the VMIQ-2, the MIQ-R requires athletes to rate the difficulty of seeing or feeling the movement rather than the vividness. In addition, the MIQ-R does not distinguish between visual imagery perspectives.

Besides imagery ability, you may be interested in assessing your clients' imagery use. The Sport Imagery Questionnaire (SIQ; Hall, Mack, Paivio, & Hausenblas, 1998; Hall, Stevens, & Paivio, 2005) measures the frequency with which athletes use the cognitive and motivational functions of imagery. The SIQ consists of 30 items and the following five subscales:

1. Cognitive-specific: measures imaging particular skills
2. Cognitive-general: focuses on imaging strategies
3. Motivational-specific: assesses imaging particular goals
4. Motivational-general-mastery: addresses imaging mastering in competitive situations
5. Motivation general-arousal: assesses imaging the excitement and emotions of competing

Importantly, the SIQ has demonstrated predictive relationships with sport performance (Martin, Moritz, & Hall, 1999). The SIQ test manual (Hall et al., 2005) includes the questionnaire with instructions and a rating chart, a scoring section to calculate imagery performance, an overview of the purpose and function of the SIQ, and comprehensive chapters on understanding imagery, the methods involved in both developing and using the SIQ, and the psychometric properties and normative data of the SIQ. If you are working with young athletes (aged 7-14), you can use the Sport Imagery Questionnaire–Children's Version (SIQ-C; Hall, Munroe-Chandler, Fishburne, & Hall, 2009) to assess imagery use along the same five dimensions as the SIQ.

Mindfulness

Mindfulness-based interventions designed to enhance sport performance and well-being have become increasingly prevalent in consulting (e.g., Gardner & Moore, 2007). The Mindfulness Inventory for Sport (MIS; Thienot et al., 2014) comprises 15 items with three subscales: awareness (e.g., "I am aware of the thoughts that are passing through my mind"), nonjudgmental attitude (e.g., "When I become aware that I am angry at myself for making a mistake, I criticize myself for having this reaction"), and refocusing ("When I become aware that I am not focusing on my own performance, I am able to quickly refocus my attention on things that help me to perform well"). Athletes rate each statement in terms of how well it reflects their recent experience, ranging from 1 (not at all) to 6 (very much). You can use the MIS to evaluate the effectiveness of your mindfulness-based interventions. Preliminary support for the factorial validity of the MIS and the internal consistency and reliability of the subscales has been demonstrated, and subscales of the MIS displayed significant correlations with flow, worry, concentration disruption, and perfectionism (Thienot et al., 2014).

Assessment Tools and Their Availability

Assessment tool	Construct	Author and reference	Availability
Sport Psychology Attitudes-Revised (SPA-R)	Attitudes toward consultation	Martin, S.B, Kellman, M., Lavallee, D., & Page, S.J. (2002). Development and psychometric evaluation of the Sport Psychology Attitudes-Revised Form: A multiple group investigation. *The Sport Psychologist, 16*, 272-290.	Full measure in article; http://dx.doi.org/10.1123/tsp.16.3.272
	The SPA-R assesses athletes' stigma tolerance, confidence in the consultant, personal openness, and cultural preference. It is beneficial to administer it during the first session to understand the client's receptivity and perceived barriers toward sport psychology consultation.		
Stages of Change for Psychological Skills Training (SOC-PST)	Readiness to engage in psychological skills training	Leffingwell, T.R., Rider, S.P., & Williams, J.M. (2001). Application of the transtheoretical model to psychological skills training. *The Sport Psychologist, 15*, 168-187.	Full measure in article; http://dx.doi.org/10.1123/tsp.15.2.168
	The SOC-PST evaluates the motivational readiness of athletes to engage in sport psychology consultation. Identifying the stage of change (precontemplation, contemplation, action, maintenance) the client is at allows practitioners to tailor interventions appropriately.		
Sport Motivation Scale-6 (SMS-6)	Motivation	Mallett, C., Kawabata, M., Newcombe, P., Otero-Forero, A., & Jackson, S. (2007). Sport Motivation Scale-6 (SMS-6): A revised six-factor sport motivation scale. *Psychology of Sport and Exercise, 8*, 600-614.	Full measure in article; http://dx.doi.org/10.1016/j.psychsport.2006.12.005
	The SMS-6 allows practitioners to assess athletes' motivation on a continuum ranging from amotivation to intrinsic motivation; however, care should be taken because the validity of some subscales has been questioned.		
Achievement Goals Questionnaire for Sport (AGQ-S)	Motivation	Conroy, D.E., Elliot, A.J., & Hofer, S.M. (2003). A 2 × 2 Achievement Goals Questionnaire for Sport: Evidence for factorial invariance, temporal stability, and external validity. *Journal of Sport & Exercise Psychology, 25*, 456-476.	Full measure in article; http://dx.doi.org/10.1123/jsep.25.4.456
	The AGQ-S provides an in-depth analysis of both approach and avoidance tendencies related to goal orientations for athletes. Criticisms of the measure rest with the ability to fully delineate between approach-style goals using the AGQ-S.		
Trait Sport-Confidence Inventory (TSCI)	Confidence	Vealey, R.S. (1986). Conceptualization of sport-confidence and competitive orientation: Preliminary investigation and instrument development. *Journal of Sport Psychology, 8*, 221-246.	Full measure in article; http://dx.doi.org/10.1123/jsp.8.3.221
	The strength (and weakness) of the TSCI is that because of the general phrasing of its questions, it can used for a wide variety of sports, which also means it lacks specifics for any one sport or performance realm.		
Competitive State Anxiety Inventory-2 Revised (CSAI-2R)	Anxiety	Cox, R.H., Martens, M.P., & Russell, W.D. (2003). Measuring anxiety in athletics: The revised Competitive State Anxiety Inventory-2. *Journal of Sport and Exercise Psychology, 25*(4), 519-533.	Full measure in article; http://dx.doi.org/10.1123/jsep.25.4.519
	The CSAI-2R is a psychometrically sound instrument for assessing anxiety; however, because anxiety fluctuates moment to moment, the measure may be somewhat cumbersome to use immediately before an athlete's performance.		

Assessment tool	Construct	Author and reference	Availability
Test of Attentional and Interpersonal Style (TAIS)	Concentration	Nideffer, R. (1976). Test of Attentional and Interpersonal Style. *Journal of Personality and Social Psychology, 34*, 394-404.	For purchase at https://goo.gl/5a7MHa
	A thorough measure that assesses a person's attentional style, TAIS is only available for purchase. Furthermore, because of its length, it should be used for diagnostic purposes only.		
Sport Commitment Questionnaire-2 (SCQ-2)	Commitment	Scanlan, T.K., Chow, G.M., Sousa, C., Scanlan, L.A., & Knifsend, C.A. (2016). The development of the Sport Commitment Questionnaire-2 (English Version). *Psychology of Sport and Exercise, 22*, 233-246.	Full measure in article; http://dx.doi.org/10.1016/j.psychsport.2015.08.002
	A detailed measure that can provide information on both the types and the sources of sport commitment, the SCQ-2 is useful for identifying why athletes persist in sport. It is particularly advantageous for clients who are considering discontinuing sport participation.		
Athlete Burnout Questionnaire (ABQ)	Burnout	Raedeke, T.D., & Smith, A.L. (2009). *The Athlete Burnout Questionnaire manual*. Morgantown, WV: Fitness Information Technology.	For purchase at https://goo.gl/57vqxS
	A simple and customizable questionnaire, the ABQ allows the practitioner to customize questions based on the situation; however, the measure must be purchased for use.		
Test of Performance Strategies (TOPS)	Psychological skills	Hardy, L., Roberts, R., Thomas, P.R., & Murphy, S.M. (2010). Test of Performance Strategies (TOPS): Instrument refinement using confirmatory factor analysis. *Psychology of Sport and Exercise, 11*, 27-35.	For purchase at www.topsfirst.com
	The TOPS measures athletes' use of mental skills and techniques in both practice and competition. Psychometric properties of the TOPS 3 are unknown.		
Ottawa Mental Skills Assessment Tool-3 (OMSAT-3*)	Psychological skills	Durand-Bush, N., Salmela, J.H., & Green-Demers, I. (2001). The Ottawa Mental Skills Assessment Tool (OMSAT-3*). *The Sport Psychologist, 15*, 1-19.	For purchase at https://mindeval.com
	The OMSAT-3* is a comprehensive measure that assesses 12 mental skills. These mental skills are grouped under three broader factors: foundation skills, psychosomatic skills, and cognitive skills.		
Self-Talk Use Questionnaire (STUQ)	Self-talk	Hardy, J., Hall, C.R., & Hardy, L. (2005). Quantifying athlete self-talk. *Journal of Sports Sciences, 23*, 905-917.	Full measure in article; http://dx.doi.org/10.1080/02640410500130706
	The STUQ measures how frequently athletes use self-talk, why athletes use self-talk in both practice and competition, how athletes engage in self-talk, and the content of athletes' covert and overt self-talk.		

(continued)

Assessment Tools and Their Availability *(continued)*

Assessment tool	Construct	Author and reference	Availability
Vividness of Movement Imagery Questionnaire-2 (VMIQ-2)	Imagery ability	Roberts, R., Callow, N., Hardy, L., Markland, D., & Bringer, J. (2008). Movement imagery ability: Development and assessment of a revised version of the Vividness of Movement Imagery Questionnaire. *Journal of Sport & Exercise Psychology, 30,* 200-221.	Contact the first author of article; http://dx.doi.org/10.1123/jsep.30.2.200
	The VMIQ-2 assesses athletes' ability in internal visual imagery, external visual imagery, and kinesthetic imagery. Assessing the imagery capabilities of athletes allows practitioners to create individualized imagery scripts.		
Mindfulness Inventory for Sport (MIS)	Mindfulness	Thienot, E., Dimmock, J., Jackson, B., Grove, R., Bernier, M., & Fournier, J. (2014). Development and validation of the Mindfulness Inventory for Sport. *Psychology of Sport and Exercise, 15,* 72-80.	Full measure in article; http://dx.doi.org/10.1016/j.psychsport.2013.10.003
	The MIS assesses three dimensions of mindfulness: awareness, nonjudgmental attitude, and refocusing. It is more trait-like in nature because athletes rate each statement in terms of how well it reflects their recent experience; it is not intended to assess mindfulness after a specific competition or event.		

Chapter Takeaways

- When deciding which inventories to use with athletes, consider carefully your knowledge and competency in the particular measure, the purposes of psychological assessment and how the measure can be used to achieve these purposes, and how the results will be used.

- The practicality of assessment measures depends on convenience, interpretability, and cost; the practitioner will have to balance the costs and benefits of these factors when making a selection.

- Objective measures can assist with identification of athletes' psychological strengths and weaknesses, case conceptualization, selection of interventions, creation of intervention goals and plans, and evaluation of intervention effectiveness.

- Key psychological constructs (e.g., motivation, confidence, anxiety) related to sport performance can be accurately assessed using objective measures. From these assessments, a comprehensive strategy can be developed to address the unique needs of each athlete.

- Objective measures should never be used in isolation. Instead, measures highlighted in this chapter should be used in conjunction with other assessment methods, such as interviews and observations, to gain the most accurate and in-depth understanding of athletes.

CHAPTER 8

Interviewing:
Asking the Right Questions

Jim Taylor, PhD, CC-AASP

Duncan Simpson, PhD

Angel L. Brutus, PsyD, LPC, CRC, DCC

As you are seeing as you read this book, many assessment tools are available that can assist you in understanding your clients and identifying the psychological, emotional, behavioral, psychophysiological, and performance challenges they face (Cormier & Cormier, 1991). The specific uses, advantages, and limitations of many of these tools and methods are discussed in other chapters.

Although these traditional tools and methodologies are effective in providing information about specific psychological constructs (e.g., motivation, confidence) and clinical issues (e.g., depression, eating disorders), they often limit the client's responses to the parameters of the questions being asked, the behaviors being observed, and the psychophysiological reactions being measured. Furthermore, "although psychological tests can assist clinicians with case formulation and treatment recommendations, they are only tools. Tests do not think for themselves, nor do they directly communicate with [clients]" (Meyer et al., 2001, p. 153). As a consequence, it is not surprising that many consultants believe interviewing should be a primary form of information gathering and should be used in conjunction with other assessment tools to maximize

the value they bring to their clients (Rosqvist, Björgvinsson, & Davidson, 2007).

In its exploration of interviewing as an assessment tool in applied sport psychology, this chapter is composed of two primary content areas. The first part of the chapter provides a broad examination of the interviewing process, including information about best practices, listening skills, and concerns related to diversity, among other important topics. The second part of the chapter offers the Sport Interviewing Protocol (SIP), a newly developed, comprehensive interviewing protocol you can use while working with clients.

Importance of Client Information

The significance of interviewing lies in understanding that clients' descriptions are essential to understanding their experiences (Pollio, Henley, & Thompson, 1997) and the meaning of their experiences to their current performance challenges. Interviewing is the best way to plumb the depth and breadth of your clients' experiences and their meaning in order to understand the challenges that brought them to you for help

(Rosqvist et al., 2007). In fact, Kvale (1996) describes interviews as "a construction site of knowledge" (p. 2) because what should be of interest to you is "finding out who a person is, what they do, how they do it, why they do it, and perhaps if the opportunity arose, what they would do differently" (Crandall, 1998, p. 155). Having this knowledge and level of understanding will provide the basis for developing a comprehensive view of your clients, which will then inform your efforts to meet their needs and help them achieve their goals.

Best Practices of Interviewing

We advocate the use of interviewing as an assessment tool in consulting; however, unlike other forms of assessment such as objective inventories, interviewing is as much an art as a science (Potter & Hepburn, 2005). The setting in which the interview is conducted, how the interview questions are asked, and your vocal tone, emotional inflection, body language, and reactions to the questions all play a significant role in clients' willingness to share their experiences with you and the information you garner from the interviewing process. Certainly, education and training play a role in your interviewing skills. At the same time, your skill as an interviewer is also influenced by who you are as a person, such as your confidence, emotional openness, and empathy.

Because of these concerns, we advise you to weigh carefully the benefits and potential drawbacks to using interviews as an assessment tool with your clients (Potter & Hepburn, 2005) and honestly consider your competencies as an interviewer. In this chapter, we outline some of the significant issues regarding interviewing as an assessment tool in consulting. We also offer what we consider to be best practices for its use.

Your Background

Your educational background, qualifications, training, and experience will influence the approach you take to using interviewing with your clients (Cleary, Mechanic, & Weiss, 1981). For example, if you are primarily trained in the sport sciences with expertise in mental skills training, you may interpret your client's use of the word *anxiety* differently than someone who is trained in clinical psychology. As a consequence, you must be aware of how your professional experiences will inform the intention and direction, as well as the structure, content, and process, of your interviewing.

The particular questions you pose to your clients are important in the consultation process. At the same time, the way you present the interview questions and how you react to the clients' responses are of equal or perhaps greater importance. The latter part of the interviewing experience is as much influenced by who you are as a person as by who you are as a consultant.

Self-reflection plays a key role in making this connection between the influence of your personness and your consultantness, so to speak. Consider the overt attributes you communicate to clients when you meet with them:

- Are you serious and intense or lighthearted and relaxed?
- Are you stoic or emotionally expressive?
- Are you process oriented or goal directed?
- Are you cerebral or soulful?
- Are you challenging or accepting?
- Are you tough or gentle?

Be aware that these are not either–or attributes; rather, they lie along a continuum, and you may be a combination of both to varying degrees. These qualities of who you are will emerge in the interviewing process, permeate your relationship with your clients, and express themselves throughout your consulting work.

Setup Phase

The initial assessment session with new clients sets the tone for whether and how your consultation moves forward. As a consequence, there are several important questions to consider in the setup phase of the consultation:

- Who is initiating the consultation, and how will this affect the client's motivation and receptiveness toward working with you?

- Based on the information you gather from your first contact with the client (e.g., age, maturity, athletic experience), how will you structure the interview to build an initial alliance of trust and collaboration and gain the most information?
- How much does the client understand about the interviewing process, and what can you say to put the client at ease about this early stage of the consultation?
- How can you best communicate to your client about confidentiality and how the information from the interview will be used?

The atmosphere you create for clients plays a major role in how they respond to your interviewing and the initial impressions they develop about you as a professional and as a person, as well as about how you might help them. It also influences the clients' comfort in answering what may be personal and perhaps uncomfortable questions. One way to mitigate clients' resistance to answering your questions is to prepare them for the interviewing process that lies ahead. You can shape their expectations by acknowledging that some of your questions may seem intrusive or cause discomfort. The more they understand about what lies ahead in their work with you, the more receptive they will be to your efforts to help them.

Your Questions

There are two components to the questions you ask during an interview. The first is *what* questions you ask—that is, the content of the questions in your interviewing protocol. As Taylor and Schneider (1992) describe in the Sport-Clinical Intake Protocol (SCIP), you should create an interviewing protocol that represents your approach to consulting and that will elicit the responses you need to make a comprehensive and accurate evaluation of clients' performance challenges. Your interviewing protocol should provide a framework for your information gathering, but it should also be adaptable to the needs and goals of individual clients.

Second, you must consider *how* you ask the questions, which potentially influences the responses you receive (Thomas & Pollio, 2002). One way to understand this process is to consider the answers that your questions allow. For example, asking "Did you win?" only allows for a yes-or-no response. Moreover, it communicates a very different set of priorities than "Can you describe your last competition?" or "How did you perform in your last competition?" You want to ensure that your questions do two things. First, they should convey to your clients what you believe is important (e.g., winning versus performance). Second, they should elicit as much relevant information as possible related to the question (e.g., thoughts, emotions, and behaviors surrounding the performance).

The effectiveness of an interview depends on your ability to ask the right questions in the right way to draw out the most detailed and accurate information about your clients' experiences and challenges. Only with this information will you be able to gain a detailed understanding of who your clients are and what challenges they are facing, with the goal of helping them overcome the challenges and achieve their athletic goals.

Accuracy of Client Information

The primary purpose of using an assessment tool is "to generate data which give an authentic insight into people's experiences" (Silverman, 2001, p. 143). Interviewing allows you to explore your client's lived experiences in detail and at every level, such as their thoughts, emotions, and actions. Importantly, interviewing gives you the opportunity to explore deeply personal and sensitive issues that could not be obtained through the other forms of assessment discussed in this book. Both types of assessment in combination enable you to fully see clients' internal and external worlds from their perspective (Rubin & Rubin, 2012).

Though interviewing lacks the objectivity and scientific rigor of pencil-and-paper inventories and psychophysiological measures, it must still be used in a scrupulous manner that pays close attention to the accuracy of the information provided by your clients. Validity was discussed in detail in chapter 2, so here we will simplify the concept of validity for the purpose of interviewing and ask, "Are the data we are receiving accurate?" (Shea, 1998).

The interviewing process is a constructive activity between you and your clients (Holstein & Gubrium, 2011), and there are many reasons why clients may distort the information they provide (Shea, 1998). For example, they may wish to make a positive impression on you, they may feel embarrassment or shame over sharing uncomfortable aspects of their lives, or they may be unwitting victims of the unconscious cognitive biases that distort their memories and interpretations of their life experiences. Thus, it is up to you to judge the accuracy of the information being divulged by clients. You must take into account the client's intellectual functioning, attention to detail, motives to lie, and overall level of honesty (Akiskal & Akiskal, 1994). Furthermore, the athlete may downplay issues in order to appear normal and to avoid the stigma that often accompanies seeking psychological services.

Other assessment tools use embedded social desirability measures and statistical techniques to establish accuracy (i.e., validity and reliability). However, for interviewing, *you* serve as the instrument, which makes accuracy more difficult. As Holstein and Gubrium (2011) suggest, "The challenge lies with extracting information as directly as possible, without contaminating it" (p. 153) with your own professional or personal biases.

You are not immune to subjectivity and bias, and you will inevitably filter the information you receive from clients through the lens of your professional education, training, and personal life experiences. Moreover, as noted in chapter 1, cognitive biases are part of every aspect of our thought processes (Kahneman & Tversky, 1974). Your challenge is to minimize the impact of the professional and personal lens through which you see your clients' information, open yourself to the information you receive from your clients unfiltered, and evaluate this information as objectively as possible.

Creswell and Miller (2000) discussed various strategies to enhance accuracy that are frequently used by qualitative researchers, and these strategies are equally relevant for consulting. The first strategy is *prolonged engagement and persistent observation* of your clients, which will allow you to build trust, learn about the culture in which your clients live and perform, and allow you more opportunities to judge whether they are being authentic.

The second strategy is *triangulation*, the notion in which *Assessment in Applied Sport Psychology* is grounded. Triangulation involves collecting information from multiple sources (e.g., objective inventories, biofeedback, input from other individuals, direct observations of clients in practice and competition) to corroborate your interview findings (Creswell & Miller, 2000).

Third, you can engage in *peer review* while maintaining confidentiality. This strategy involves discussing your clients with trusted colleagues to reality-test your interpretations and to obtain different perspectives on your clients' issues (Creswell & Miller, 2000). Fourth, as recommended by Kahneman, Lovallo, and Sibony (2011), you must continually recognize your own *biases* that have shaped your delivery and interpretation of the interviews.

Finally, you must develop *rich and thick descriptions* of your clients and their issues (Creswell & Miller, 2000). Detailed note-taking will help you record your client's perceptions and will aid your memory in constructing an accurate narrative when you return to your notes for further evaluation and interpretation. The content of your notes could include behavioral observations, specific thoughts and emotional reactions from clients, and your initial impressions and insights.

Basic Listening Skills

Regardless of your theoretical orientation, your primary skills should involve keen listening. Gathering information during an interview is not just about the direct information the clients provide but also the subtle information that is the subtext of the interview. These valuable indirect clues include clients' choice of words, emotional content of their responses, body language, voice inflection, hesitations, pressured or rushed speech, difficulties accessing information, tangential references, and digressions. It is often the indirect and unspoken information that provides texture and color to

Developing Your Active Listening Skills

This exercise can enhance your active listening skills as well as strengthen your ability to demonstrate interest in clients' experiences, concerns, and presenting issues. And, it will assist you in better understanding your clients' needs and goals, which will lead to a more effective conceptualization and intervention plan (McNaughton et al., 2008). Create a list of 10 active listening statements and then try to integrate them into your next session with a client. Be sure to use a range of open-ended questions, paraphrases, and summaries.

the broad strokes of clients' spoken responses and deepens your understanding of their experiences and perspectives.

Furthermore, you should engage in active listening, which involves probing, summarizing, and paraphrasing the client's responses for clarification (McNaughton, Hamlin, McCarthy, Head-Reeves, & Schreiner, 2008). Examples of active listening statements include "What I hear you saying is . . . ," "Let me see if I've got this right . . . ," and "What you're telling me is. . . ." Active listening sends a powerful message to clients that you are hearing what they have to say, you are entirely engaged with them, you are fully present, and you understand them. This message increases their comfort with you, builds trust and rapport, and increases their willingness to open up and be authentic as you continue building the consultant–client alliance.

Multicultural Awareness

Consulting is a dynamic interaction in which clients bring backgrounds and experiences that may be different from your own in terms of age, gender, race, class, socioeconomic status, sexual orientation, religion, marital status, and so on. As described in chapter 4, there has been a concerted effort in recent years to understand issues of diversity in consulting with athletes (Hylton, 2013; Schinke & Hanrahan, 2009). These differences are no less important in the interviewing process. It is essential to acknowledge, discuss with your clients, and incorporate these differences into your interviewing protocol to gain a richer understanding of your clients and they of you.

Designing an Effective Sport Interviewing Protocol

Effective interviewing cannot be accomplished with an off-the-cuff approach to asking questions. Rather, interviewing should begin with the creation of a comprehensive, structured, and in-depth interviewing protocol that will ensure maximal information gathering, resulting in a deep and broad understanding of clients' experiences. Effective interviewing protocols are as varied as there are consultants working with athletes. At the same time, as alluded to in the preface, interviewing protocols are like athletes' precompetitive routines—they are unique to each consultant yet share many common elements. Your theoretical orientation, approach to consulting, and professional experiences will determine your competencies (Prout & Wadkins, 2014), inform the development of your interviewing protocol, and shape your interviewing style.

We encourage you to draw on your professional, athletic, and life experiences as you design an interviewing protocol that fits your consulting approach and personality. At the same time, like the precompetitive routine just mentioned, we encourage you to build your protocol around some important categories of information that are essential for a comprehensive understanding of the athletes with whom you work.

Sport-Clinical Intake Protocol

Interviewing techniques designed specifically for the athletic population formally began more than two decades ago by one of this chapter's coauthors with the publication of the Sport-Clinical Intake Protocol (SCIP). The authors of the SCIP argue that the benefits of interviewing as an assessment tool are enhanced by customizing the interview protocol to meet the unique needs and goals of the athletic population. In response to the need to cast a wide net to gather information from athletes that includes data from both their athletic and personal lives,

> the SCIP has several objectives: (a) acquire both sport-specific and clinical information, (b) incorporate the sport-specific and clinical avenues of inquiry into an organized framework that is non-threatening to the client, (c) provide information that will enable the professional to determine the true nature of the problem, thereby allowing for the decision to treat or refer the client, and (d) to give the professional sufficient understanding of the client in order to develop an initial treatment direction. (Taylor & Schneider, 1992, p. 318)

The SCIP identified seven areas of information gathering that encompass the range of athletes' life experiences:

1. Presenting problem: a cursory description of the problem that brought the client to you
2. Athletic history: relevant background on the client's athletic development and experiences
3. Family and social support: the role that family and others play, both supportive and discouraging, in the pursuit of client's athletic goals
4. Health: the presence of physical problems, such as fatigue, burnout, injury, or illness, that might cause the presenting problem
5. Important life events: past events that may have shaped the client's current athletic experiences
6. Changes prior to onset of presenting problems: changes in the client's athletic, personal, or social life that may have precipitated the presenting problems
7. Details of presenting problem: an in-depth exploration of the presenting problem and its impact on thinking, emotions, behavior, and performance

Sport Interviewing Protocol

Though the SCIP continues to offer the most thorough accounting of the interview process to date, after more than 20 years, the original codeveloper and his two coauthors of this chapter believe it could use an upgrade that would provide additional important information to make it an even more compelling and useful tool in consultants' toolboxes. Taking the many strengths of the SCIP, we developed an updated protocol that we call the *Sport Interviewing Protocol*, or *SIP*. The SIP consists of 11 areas that are relevant for gaining a comprehensive understanding of your clients, and each area is discussed in the sections that follow. Sample questions are included in the following sections, but the complete SIP can be found at the end of the chapter. We suggest you pick and choose specific elements of the SIP to develop a personalized interviewing protocol that best fits your approach and meets the needs and goals of your clients.

Demographics

Demographic information may appear to be the most mundane of all the information you gather during the interviewing process. However, it is often a gateway to more probing questions and more relevant information. Though some demographic information can be easily captured on an intake form, we suggest you make it part of your interviewing protocol because you can use these comparatively benign questions to make clients feel at ease before you present more pointed questions later in the interview.

To illustrate the deeper value of demographic information, let's consider how some of this data can be used to elicit additional useful information. The gender (Hays, Maynard, Thomas, & Bawden, 2007), race and ethnicity (Omi & Winant, 2015), age (Voight, 2014), and education of your clients may have implications for the types of interventions you use. For example, age will play in an important role regarding a client's level of self-awareness and emotional maturity, which would influence the vocabulary you use and the depth of the questions you ask.

Paying attention to and elaborating on seemingly minor details also signifies to clients that you are listening and are interested in learning their story, thus helping to establish rapport and trust. For example, if the client provides a cell phone number with an area code different from his current place of residence, that is a great opportunity to learn more about his geographical history and factors that contributed to his relocation.

Overview of Presenting Issues

With each step further into the interview, you gain richer and more textured information. However, information without context has limited value. As a consequence, early in the interviewing process it is useful to gain a preliminary understanding of why the client has sought your help. Simple questions such as "Why are we here?" and "Can you tell me a little about what's going on with you in your sport?" can begin the conversation about the performance challenges your clients are facing and their own theories about their causes. Once you know the outline of the presenting issues, you can place the information garnered from the remainder of the interview in the context of the presenting issues. Key questions may include "What is the presenting problem and when did it begin?", "How often does it occur?", and "What do you believe is the cause?"

Previous Experience With Sport Psychology

Knowing what experiences clients have had with psychology in general and sport psychology in particular is helpful in understanding what preconceived notions, expectations, or fears they may bring to your relationship. Those experiences will shape their perceptions of you and can either act as a catalyst or an impediment to your work with them.

Without any exposure to our field, clients likely enter the relationship and your work together without any real understanding of what lies ahead, though they may have a vague sense of what sport psychology is and what you might do. A series of targeted queries such as "What do you hope to get out of our work?" and "Do you have any concerns about our work?" can

ensure they begin with a positive attitude and an open mind.

Athletic History

To help clients get where they want to go, it is essential that you learn where they have come from. To that end, a thorough understanding of their athletic history can put all of the information you gain from the interview into context and perspective. Performance challenges do not occur in a vacuum but rather are part of athletes' arc of participation in their sport. Asking questions such as "How did you get involved in your sport and at what age?" and "What were some of the high and low points of your career?" can give you an understanding of the trajectory of their athletic lives. Furthermore, this information will provide useful clues about the causes of their challenges and how best to address them.

It is also worthwhile to explore clients' nonsport history to identify any important life events that may contribute to performance challenges. Examples include relocations, divorce, and health changes.

Athletic and Life Goals

Having learned where your clients have been in their athletic lives, you can then learn about what their athletic goals are (e.g., "What are some of your big goals for this season?") and where they hope to go in their sport (e.g., "What is your dream goal for your sport participation?"). This information also puts their current performance challenges in perspective because it allows you to see where they were, where they are now, and how far they have to go. You can get a sense of how realistic their goals are given their current developmental arc and their performance challenges. This information enables you to evaluate how big these challenges are relative to their goals and assists you in determining how heavy a lift your work will be, so to speak, to help them progress toward those goals.

In addition to athletic aspirations, most athletes have other life goals they are pursuing, whether educational or professional. By learning about their long-term life goals, you can gauge the role that sport plays in their lives and connect the dots among their interests, passions, and pursuits.

Physical Health

Though consultants focus on the mental aspects of sport performance, the reality is that sports are fundamentally physical activities. Thus, the physical aspects of sport play an essential role in athletes' performance efforts. Moreover, before you look for psychological causes of performance challenges, you should first rule out any physical causes. For example, an inability to focus may be due to a lack of sleep. Or, a decline in confidence and performance could be the result of a lingering injury. To that end, a thorough assessment of your clients' physical status (i.e., health, training intensity and recovery, injuries, sleep, eating, drug and alcohol use) will provide valuable information about potential physical contributors to their performance challenges. It will also help paint a more complete picture of who they are as people and as athletes.

Mental Health

Though athletes come to consultants for help in overcoming performance challenges, they often don't have a clear understanding of what is actually causing the problem. As a result, you should not assume that performance difficulties are simply deficits of mental skills or are even sport related. For example, if a client has sought your help for significant precompetitive anxiety, you would want to explore whether she has a history of anxiety outside sport or whether there is a family history of anxiety (Pinel, 2011). The same is true for familial substance use, mood disorder manifestations, and other potential symptoms (Butcher, Mineka, & Hooley, 2010). Whether or not you are a trained mental health professional, your foremost responsibility is your clients' mental health and well-being. Additionally, early recognition of broader mental health issues will have an immediate impact on your course of action (see chapter 5 for more on mental health assessment).

If you are able to rule out any mental health concerns, you can move directly to addressing performance challenges. However, if there is some evidence of mental health issues, you have

several options based on your education and training. If you are a licensed mental health professional, you can either treat those mental health issues first or incorporate them into your overall intervention plan. If you are not a licensed mental health professional, you can find an appropriate referral and then decide whether continuing to work on the performance challenges is reasonable. If you do not have clinical or counseling experience with the ability to readily recognize and diagnose mental health problems, asking the right questions, such as "Have you ever seen a mental health professional for issues unrelated to sport? If so, for what, when, for how long, and what was the outcome?", is essential to getting a sense of whether mental health issues are present, which will guide you in how you proceed.

Family Background and Social Support

Athletes don't train, perform, or live in a vacuum. Rather, their athletic lives are part of a social system of family, friends, coaches, teammates, and others who influence how they perform in their sport, how they function in their lives, and how they feel about themselves as people. A thorough understanding of your clients' family life and social support system is essential for painting a robust picture of the many systems they navigate (Steele, 2011).

As you gather this information, a social network will take shape in which you and your clients can identify those people who have the greatest influence, as well as the nature and quality of that influence. This portrait provides insights into the messages clients have received from their social world that have shaped who they are as athletes and people. Importantly, asking the right questions, such as "What is your relationship with your parents and siblings?", can illuminate how certain obstacles (e.g., perfectionism, fear of failure, negativity) may have developed and how they can be eliminated.

From this information, you can also identify the people in your clients' social world who have the greatest influence on various aspects of their athletic lives and can be targeted for support. For example, you may ask "How satisfied are you with the support you receive from your family, friends, coaches, teammates, and others?" You can then formulate an intervention plan that not only focuses on what your clients can do but also reshapes their social world to remove possible causes of their performance challenges, thus marshaling the clients' internal and external resources to clear the path to their athletic goals.

Performance Assessment

Just as a conditioning coach would conduct a thorough testing regimen to identify athletes' physical strengths and weaknesses, consultants should administer an analogous assessment program as a part of their initial interviewing protocol to help identify clients' sport-related mental strengths and weaknesses. Though other forms of assessment that are discussed throughout this book may evaluate the same areas, we have found that including performance assessment, a kind of physical testing for the mind, in your interviewing protocol allows you to identify key areas and then immediately explore them in greater depth to produce valuable information about athletes' perspectives, perceptions, and performances.

We model this performance assessment on performance profiling (see chapter 7) and have clients rate themselves on a scale of 1 to 10 in a variety of relevant psychological and performance areas. Though we encourage you to develop your own list of items to assess based on your education, training, and approach to sport performance, here is a list of areas that we find most beneficial: motivation, confidence, intensity (i.e., arousal, energy, anxiety), focus, emotions, mental imagery, routines, perfectionism, fear of failure, and need for control.

Changes Prior to Onset of Performance Challenges

As alluded to in chapter 1, being a consultant means playing detective as you collect clues to solve the case; think of it as the case of the missing performance. In addition to the general information that you collect as part of the SIP, you must also gather more granular information (i.e., specific to when the problems began) that will hopefully uncover the most direct cause of the performance problems. Assuming that the performance challenges haven't always

been there (which is most often the case), the most fundamental question that you can ask is "What changed just before the onset of your performance challenges?" If you can help clients answer this question, you will be well on your way to solving the case and helping them return to athletic form.

The difficulty is that there may be no obvious clues as to even the general area of the cause. Moreover, the complexity of sport means that there can be many possible causes (e.g., equipment and coaching changes), including those that may not be even remotely related to the psychology of sport (e.g., relationships with significant others). Given the complicated nature of sport, you have to examine every possible area that might have changed, possibly causing the decline in performance. For example, you might ask, "Have there been any changes in your sleeping or eating patterns?" and "Have you noticed any changes in your emotions?"

Detailed Exploration of Presenting Issues

Equipped with a wide range of information about your clients collected from the early phases of the SIP, you now have a detailed portrait of just about every important aspect of your clients' athletic and personal lives. You now have a broader understanding that is necessary to delve deeply into the issues for which they sought your help.

This phase of the interview involves three important areas of inquiry. First, you want to gather more facts about the performance challenges—what actually happens when these difficulties arise? Second, you want to listen carefully to the clients' perspectives and interpretations of their issues. Often, athletes' perceptions of the challenges provide clues as to their causes. Third, you want to be attuned to their emotional reactions as they describe and reexperience their challenges. All of these sources of information will likely coalesce around an initial hypothesis of the cause. From this preliminary theorizing, in subsequent sessions you can guide your clients toward further exploration, information gathering, and detective work that will ultimately lead to an intervention plan to resolve the performance challenges.

Assessment Tools and Their Availability

Assessment tool	Construct	Author and reference	Availability
Sport-Clinical Intake Protocol (SCIP)	Interview protocol	Taylor, J., & Schneider, B.A. (1992). The Sport-Clinical Intake Protocol: A comprehensive interviewing instrument for sport. *Professional Psychology: Research and Practice, 23,* 318-325.	Full protocol in article
	The SCIP was designed specifically for the athletic population. The protocol is based on 7 key informational areas: presenting problem, athletic history, family and social support, health, important life events, changes prior to onset of presenting problem, and details of presenting problem.		

Chapter Takeaways

- Interviewing should be the primary form of information gathering and should be used in concert with other assessment tools to maximize the value of information solicited from clients.
- Your educational background, qualifications, training, and experience will influence the approach you take to interviewing.
- Consider what questions you will ask and how you will ask the questions.
- It is up to you to judge the accuracy of the information divulged by clients.
- Your ability to listen openly and intently to clients provides you with more useful information beyond just the words that are spoken.
- Individual differences such as age, gender, race, ethnicity, class, socioeconomic status, sexual orientation, religious beliefs, marital status, and many other social categories may intersect in how clients experience their performances and how they interact with you.
- The Sport Interviewing Protocol (SIP) is an updated version of the SCIP. It is designed to collect a wide range of information that will guide you in understanding your clients and developing effective intervention plans.
- The SIP can be used as a template for interviewing, but it should be customized to fit your education, background, experience, approach, and style, as well as (and most importantly) the needs and goals of your clients.

Sport Interviewing Protocol (SIP)

1. Demographics
- Name
- Gender
- Age
- Race/ethnicity
- Address/phone number/e-mail address
- Sport/level
- School/level/major/favorite courses
- Marital status
- Work status/position
- Emergency contact: name, relationship, phone numbers

2. Overview of Presenting Issues
- Describe presenting problem.
- How often does it occur?
- When did it begin?
- How intense is the problem on a scale of 0-10?
- How long has it lasted?
- Where does it occur?
- What do you believe is the cause?

3. Previous Experience With Sport Psychology
- What is sport psychology, and what does it involve?
- What, if any, has been your experience with sport psychology? For example, have you ever attended a workshop, taken a course, or worked with a sport psychology consultant before?
- How would you characterize that experience, either good or bad?
- What do you hope to get out of our work?
- Do you have any concerns about our work?

4. Athletic History
- How did you get involved in your sport and at what age?
- At what age did you make a serious commitment to your sport?
- How did you progress up the ranks of your sport?
- What were some of the high points of your career?
- What were some of the low points of your career?
- What is your current status in your sport?
- What are your strengths (i.e., enable you to experience success)?

- What are your weaknesses (i.e., prevent you from experiencing success)?
- Why do you participate, and have your reasons changed at any point?
- Is there any non-sport-related life history that might be helpful for me to know about (e.g., relocations, divorce, health changes)?

5. Athletic and Life Goals
- What is your dream goal for your sport participation?
- How confident are you that you can achieve your dream goal?
- What are some of your outcome goals for this season?
- What are some of your process goals (that is, what you need to do to accomplish your outcome goals)?
- What strengths do you bring that will help you achieve your goals?
- What obstacles might prevent you from reaching your goals?
- What other life goals do you have, such as for education, future career, and hobbies or other passions?

6. Physical Health
- Overall health status

  How is your health presently?

  When was your last physical examination? Did anything arise?

  Have you had any major health issues in the past that may affect you now?
- Training: Are you able to recover effectively after practice and competitions?
- Injuries

  What injuries have you had in the past and when?

  Do you have any injuries at present? If so, how do these injuries affect your training and competitive performances?
- Sleep

  How are you sleeping lately?

  Are you tired often?

  Do you have difficulties getting to sleep?

  Do you sleep too much?

(continued)

6. Physical Health *(continued)*

- Sleep

    Are you waking up during the night?

    Has your sleeping changed recently?

    Before falling asleep, what thoughts are going through your mind?

    Do you wake up and have trouble falling back to sleep? If so, why (thoughts, emotions)?

    Have you been having any dreams lately? If so, what was in your dreams?

    If sleep difficulties are present, how do they affect your training and competitive performances?

- Eating

    Describe your eating habits (i.e., what, when, and how much you eat).

    How has your appetite been?

    Have you had any recent changes in your body weight?

    Have your eating habits changed?

    Do you take any vitamins or supplements? If so, which ones and why?

    Has your eating influenced your training and competitive performances?

- Alcohol and drug use

    Do you drink alcohol? If so, how much and how often?

    Do you take prescription, recreational, or performance-enhancing drugs? If so, what kind and how often?

    If alcohol or drug use is present, how do they affect your training and competitive performances?

7. Mental Health

- Have you ever seen a mental health professional for issues unrelated to sport? If so, for what, when, for how long, and what was the outcome?

- Have you ever struggled with mental health issues but decided not to seek professional help? If so, why not?

- Is there any history of mental health issues in your family (e.g., depression, anxiety, substance abuse)?

- Do you have any diagnosed mental illness presently (e.g., depression)?

- Do you have any diagnosed learning challenges (e.g., ADHD, dyslexia)?

- How would you rate your general happiness (1-10 scale)?

- How would you rate your general level of life stress (1-10 scale)?

- How would you rate your ability to cope with life stress (1-10 scale)?

- Do you experience extended periods in which you are very sad, uncomfortably anxious, or can't let go of certain thoughts?

- Have you ever had thoughts of suicide? If so, when, what caused it, did you ever develop a concrete plan, and did you seek help?

- Are there any areas of your life in which you feel like you are struggling and can't find solutions?

8. Family Background and Social Support

- Family

    Tell me about your parents (i.e., married or divorced, ages, quality of their relationship, educational background, current occupations, your relationship with them).

    Tell me about your siblings (i.e., same questions as for parents).

    What is your relationship with your parents?

    What is your relationship with your siblings?

    What is your family's history of sport participation?

    What is your parents' previous athletic experience?

    What is your parents' current participation in sport?

    What is your parents' involvement in your sport participation (e.g., coach, management, administration)?

    What is your siblings' participation in sport?

    What role does your sport participation play in your family members' lives?

- Social support

    How many and what quality of friendships do you have within sport?

    How many and what quality of friendships do you have outside sport?

8. Family Background and Social Support *(continued)*

- Social support

  What are other sources of support you have?

  How satisfied are you with the support you receive from your family, friends, coaches, teammates, and others?

- Coaches

  How would you describe your relationship with your coach(es)?

  How long have you been working with your current coach(es)?

  What are the strengths of your coach(es)?

  What are the weaknesses of your coach(es)?

  Is there anything you would change about your relationship with your coach(es)?

- Teammates

  How would you describe your relationship with your teammates?

  How long have you been with your current team?

  Is there anything you would change about your relationship with your teammates?

9. Performance Assessment

- Motivation
- Confidence (self-talk)
- Intensity (i.e., arousal, energy, anxiety)
- Focus
- Emotions
- Mental imagery
- Routines
- Perfectionism
- Fear of failure
- Need for control

10. Changes Prior to Onset of Performance Challenges

- Physical

  Sleep and fatigue

  Eating

  Illness

  Injury

  Prescription side effects

- Athletic

  Physical conditioning

  Technique

  Tactics

  Quality and quantity of training

- Mental

  Motivation

  Confidence

  Intensity

  Focus

  Emotions

  Precompetitive routines

- Equipment

  New equipment

  Change in old equipment

- Competitive

  Competitive level (e.g., regional, national)

  Stage of competitive season

  Current performance level (e.g., winning record, performance statistics)

- Social and environmental

  Changes in relationships: family, friends, school, work

  Team: teammates or coaches

  New relationships

  Training and competitive sites

- Changes in cognition, affect, and behavior

  Changes in cognition (e.g., negative, obsessive)

  Changes in affect (e.g., sadness, anger, joy)

  Changes in behavior (e.g., routines, habits)

11. Detailed Exploration of Presenting Issues

- Indicate a typical situation in which the problems arise. What was going on at the time?

  Competitive setting

  Competitive scenario

  Key factors that were present

- Personal influences

  Thoughts

  Emotions

  Behavior

  Physical experience

- Social influences

  What other people were around you?

  What were they doing?

  How did they affect you?

(continued)

113

Sport Interviewing Protocol (SIP) *(continued)*

11. Detailed Exploration of Presenting Issues *(continued)*

- Consequences

   What happened after the problem occurred?

   What kinds of thoughts and feelings did you have?

   How did others react?

- Greater exploration

   Has this happened in the past? When and why?

   When does it occur (e.g., practice, particular competitions)?

Is there a consistent pattern of occurrence?

What sorts of things are going on when the problem is at its worst?

What sorts of things are going on when the problem gets better?

What do you believe are the causes of your performance challenges?

What do you believe you can do to get over the problem?

What do you want to accomplish by being here?

CHAPTER 9

Observation:
Seeing Athletes on the Field

Tim Holder, PhD

Stacy Winter, DProf

Brandon Orr, PhD

Maximizing athletic performance is the often stated goal of consulting. As a consultant, you may achieve this objective through the identification and enhancement of athletes' thoughts, emotions, and behaviors (Anderson, Miles, Mahoney, & Robinson, 2002). Psychological assessment is, therefore, an important component of consulting. It allows you to collect various forms of information about athletes to identify and understand the causes of their performance difficulties (Beckmann & Kellmann, 2003; Tkachuk, Leslie-Toogood, & Martin, 2003), as well as the means to help them remove those obstacles and clear the path toward their athletic goals. From this information, you can conceptualize clients' issues and choose interventions that directly target the factors impeding their progress.

A challenge for you, and everyone in our field, is that those performance difficulties are often grounded in causes—namely, thoughts and emotions—that aren't readily measured. Thus, the conclusions you draw are based on indirect and potentially biased or inaccurate information gathered through, for example, interviewing and objective inventories. In contrast, observation is an often neglected assessment tool that can provide clear information about athletes based on their overt behavior.

Observation has long been used as an assessment method to aid in understanding people through the collection of behavioral evidence. This objective is primarily achieved by watching and listening to athletes in practice and competitive settings, though it can also include observing them in any context that might provide useful information about who they are and how they respond to the world around them.

Across a range of allied professions, the impact of observation on human effectiveness is clear. For example, observation of school classrooms (Gresham, 2011), psychiatric patients (Lewis-Smithson, Mogge, & LePage, 2010), family interactions (Markman, Leber, Cordova, & St. Peters, 1995), and medical students training to become physicians (Hauer, Holmboe, & Kogan, 2011) provides insight into the many areas where observation is seen as a valuable method of collecting data to enhance performance.

Observation is also an extensively used assessment tool for recording and evaluating behavior in sport. Spectators are observing their team playing in a competition and applauding or vilifying their team based on what they have witnessed (Bowker et al., 2009). Coaches are viewing the execution of technique and observing the pattern of play during a competition in order to enhance the tactical and technical precision of their players (Wang & Straub, 2012). In addition, performers are observing the movements of their opponents to anticipate and respond to their next action (Savelsbergh, Williams, van der Kamp, & Ward, 2002). It is clear that many stakeholders in sport are making observations frequently for a variety of purposes.

Observation is also regularly stated as one of the predominant assessment modalities used by consultants (Watson & Shannon, 2010). Arguably, the importance of observation has arisen as a result of the unique demands that accompany working with athletes to maximize performance. For example, unlike traditional psychology practice, which occurs almost exclusively in an office setting, sport psychology consultants often work with athletes in their practice and competition settings, thus providing opportunities to not just hear retrospectively about their athletic experiences but to actually observe them as they happen (Gardner, 2009).

Underlying Professional Philosophy

Direct assessment of client behavior through observation becomes increasingly important when considering your philosophical approach as a consultant. An effective professional philosophy can aid you in every aspect of your work, from understanding what the athlete is experiencing to applying interventions in practice (Poczwardowski, Sherman, & Ravizza, 2004). Observation can assist you in this process because your ability to take general information and commonly used techniques and apply them to the specific needs of the athletes and demands of the sport contribute to your effectiveness as a consultant (Taylor, 1995). Moreover, the athletes' needs and sport demands are best identified through observation.

Cognitive behavioral therapy (CBT) is the most prevalent philosophical approach in consulting (Hemmings & Holder, 2009). A CBT perspective emphasizes the interactions between current situations, cognitions, emotions, and behavior. It further proposes that athletes' behaviors are subjectively and cognitively mediated through their perceptions (Beauchamp, Halliwell, Fournier, & Koestner, 1996; Cohn, Rotella, & Lloyd, 1990). If all people have a unique perception of their surroundings, the CBT framework provides a clear rationale to observe specific behavioral issues within the client's sporting context. A primary advantage of observation over other assessment tools (e.g., self-report instruments, interviewing) is that it is direct and allows for the simultaneous generation of information on athletes' personal, physical, and social environments (McKenzie & van der Mars, 2015). Observation can be a valuable strategy for collecting data to advance your understanding of your clients, as well as how their environment influences their cognitions, emotions, and sport-related behavior.

Use and Benefits of Direct Observation

Observation provides the only assessment opportunity for you to immerse yourself and witness client behaviors firsthand in the rich and dynamic setting of the sporting environment (Gee, 2011; Hauer et al., 2011). Direct observation can assist you in gathering a range of performance-related information. Useful data may be obtained through observation of the athlete during practice and competition. You can informally spend time on the field with your clients during training to make observations about their behaviors and interactions, or you can engage in more systematic observation by documenting specific competition information. If you operate under the assumption that athletes on the field are inseparable from who they are off the field, you can also gather helpful information by observing them in non-sport-related settings such as at meals, with family, and at school. Regardless, this real-time, in vivo assessment provides unambiguous behavioral information within and outside the athletic arena (Taylor, 1995). Four categories of observational data can be collected during this assessment:

1. Behavioral manifestations (e.g., body language, verbalizations, emotional expressions) of psychological contributors to performance, including motivation, confidence, anxiety, focus, and emotions
2. Athletes' ability to maintain consistency and respond to setbacks in training and competition, as well as the factors that may influence both
3. Behavioral habits of athletes before and during competitions, including precompetitive routines and other competitive habits
4. Interactions with teammates, coaches, parents, and stakeholders

Effective consulting requires you to gain entry into the consulting process, establish trusting relationships with athletes and other stakeholders (e.g., parents, coaches, administrators, teammates), and gather relevant information about your clients' capabilities, needs, and goals. Furthermore, Ravizza (1988) has acknowledged a need for compatibility between athletes' needs, the provider's delivery style, and environmental requirements. All these factors can be aided by observation. You can create observation opportunities from practice, competitions, and traveling with a team with the express goal of immersing yourself in an athlete's life. The end result is an observational data set that is both wide and deep (Hauer et al., 2011).

Consultants interested in behavioral analysis have used direct observation as a primary assessment tool to enable "precise, quantitative recording of the behaviors of interest" (Hawkins, 1986, p. 333). Such an approach to the assessment of human behavior clearly has strengths, but it also has limitations. One restraint is that through this assessment method, "One can record yelling, pushing, or hitting but not anger; similarly, smiling but not happiness" (Tryon, 1998, p. 82). As a result, observation is often criticized because of its inability to causally account for invisible factors such as cognition and intention, and it is therefore viewed as speculative (Gillham, 2008). However, it should also be recognized that standardized questionnaires may pres-

ent hypothetical, fabricated scenarios to the client, and interviews are generally conducted in an environment far removed from the client's sporting world. Thus, it has been argued that observation exceeds all other assessment measures for identifying the actual contexts in which these interactions occur (McKenzie & van der Mars, 2015).

Congruence in Assessment Information

Quantitative assessment using self-report questionnaires has generated hugely contrasting attitudes within consulting (Beckmann & Kellmann, 2003). A vast array of measures have been developed to assess athletes' thoughts, emotions, and attitudes before, during, and immediately after a competition and to determine the most significant contributors to successful or unsuccessful athletic performance. One limitation of these instruments is that they are based on self-report and as a result may be biased or inaccurate. For example, athletes may respond in ways that are inconsistent with the reality of the situation as a means of managing the impressions that you or others have of them, responding in socially desirable ways, or malingering (Leffingwell, Durand-Bush, Wurzberger, & Cada, 2005). Or, they may respond in ways that they believe are expected of them or to obtain your approval or that of others such as coaches. In contrast, behavior is more difficult to manipulate or distort. As a result, assessing athlete behavior through observation may be more accurate than self-report methodologies. As a direct method, observation can provide objective information with strong internal validity—that is, what you see is what you get (McKenzie & van der Mars, 2015). Conversely, clients' verbal reports and understanding of their behavior and interactions is not always congruent with their observed behavior (Gillham, 2008). It is therefore imperative that you are not fully satisfied with clients' accounts of their behavior and that you are aware of the opportunities provided by effective observation (Watson & Shannon, 2010).

Triangulation of Assessment Information

The value of any psychological assessment lies in how well it measures what it is supposed to measure. Interviews and standardized pen-and-paper protocols (or their digital counterparts) have been researched extensively and are considered to provide increased knowledge and understanding of the client (Lines, Schwartzman, Tkachuk, Leslie-Toogood, & Martin, 1999). However, both these types of assessment depend on how self-aware athletes are and to what degree they have insight into what affects their performances. Their value also depends on clients' willingness to be honest in response to the questions. As a consequence, although these assessments can provide valuable information, these resources should be qualified and informed by other sources of information in practice to ensure their accuracy. Observation of behavior, which athletes are less able to consciously control or manipulate, allows for comparison with the information gathered from interviews and questionnaires (e.g., self-perceptions, attitudes, beliefs), thus allowing for the triangulation of assessment data, which in turn enables a more comprehensive and accurate account of athletes' presenting issues (Hemmings & Holder, 2009).

On a similar note, during observational assessment it is necessary to obtain sufficient data to ensure its validity and reliability. For example, to determine whether observed behaviors are consistent across time or simply an artifact of the particular training situation, you should observe across a number of comparable sporting conditions. Additionally, observation should occur in a variety of settings (e.g., training, competitions) to assess the cross-situational consistency of observed behaviors. This approach enables you to ensure the accuracy of your observations and, as a result, strengthens the conclusions you draw from them, thus resulting in greater understanding of and more effective interventions for your clients (Taylor, 1995).

Monitoring and Evaluating Intervention Effectiveness

Despite the widespread use of psychological assessment in consulting, concerns exist whether current assessment tools are sensitive enough to measure changes in athletes engaged in mental training programs (Leffingwell et al., 2005). Consultants spend valuable time working to understand clients and provide suitable interventions to improve mental skills and performance, but they would remain uninformed if they did not evaluate the intervention effectiveness. Observation can also help increase the value of the assessment evidence for intervention planning and evaluation. For example, if you have implemented an intervention to mitigate a client's negative emotional reactions to a mistake during competitions, behavioral observations following the client's mistakes can help you determine whether the intervention has produced the desired improvement in his emotional reactions to mistakes (see chapter 17 for more on assessment of consultant effectiveness).

Observing across multiple practices or competitions allows you to monitor targeted behaviors and the subsequent success of implemented interventions. This strategy can also be supplemented by verbal feedback from the athletes and coaches to provide subjective support to the intervention effectiveness. Furthermore, visual demonstrations of improvement via video evidence can provide powerful reinforcement and incentive for clients to continue to implement interventions and maintain the progress they have made.

Categories of Observational Assessment

An additional benefit of observation as an assessment mode is that it can apply to a wide range of settings and circumstances. This enables you to glean a greater scope of observational information within the assessment process.

The following sections describe two categories you can use when exploring and developing observation with your clients. A fundamental distinction can be made between a more global, environment-focused observation and a more granular, personal or interpersonal interaction. The former category is best described as a macro-level observation, where the intention is to understand and explore the fullest range of information possible within the context of your applied work. For example, you may be present prior to training, observe a training session, and observe what happens after the session has been completed. In contrast, micro-level observations focus on more subtle verbal and nonverbal behaviors and communications. For example, you may observe the emotional reactions and body language of a client when she describes being criticized by a coach.

Macro-Level Observations

As mentioned, macro-level observations focus on understanding the overall context within which the individual client or team functions. When using this observational strategy, an important concept to consider is that of contextual intelligence (Brown, Gould, & Foster, 2005), which directs your efforts toward a range of relevant factors, including communication links, decision-making hierarchies, interpersonal relationships, and other factors within the sport environment.

Contextual Intelligence

The value of a contextual intelligence framework cannot be underestimated for the collection of relevant observation information. The advantages of this framework are apparent when the components of contextual intelligence are considered. The acronym *SPAM* has been put forward to encapsulate the four components needed to establish optimal contextual intelligence (Brown & McDaniel, 1995): **s**tructure, **p**atterns, **a**ttitudes, and **m**eans of influence (SPAM). Each characteristic adds to your macro-level understanding of the performance environment in which you are working and observing.

Structure This feature of the contextual intelligence framework identifies the importance of the overall organization of the environment in which you are observing. This information includes a full range of potential characteristics, such as who the leaders are and who carries out what tasks, as well as features such as how flexible the structures are and what initiates change in that context. For example, in observing the structure of a team during practice, you may be more aware of who initiates and coordinates the training sessions.

Patterns This framework feature takes into consideration the patterns of action within the context; as such, it considers what changes over time and how those changes take place. Specifically, observation could focus on the ways in which review and evaluation of a competition performance is conducted and how this may change based on the competitive result. This facet exemplifies the need for ongoing, consistent observations to maximize contextual understanding.

Attitudes This component identifies the importance of understanding the values and beliefs held by those within the context. Understanding how attitudes influence the structures and patterns is key to effective consultation within any context. If effective information about attitudes can be obtained during the assessment process, it can provide an effective platform for ongoing observation and intervention. Central (but not exclusive) to the understanding of attitudes is information collected through observation. For example, you may identify aggressive attitudes in a varsity men's team that differ significantly from a junior varsity team, and this observation may become apparent in competition more than in training.

Means of Influence The final aspect of the conceptual intelligence framework considers the understanding of how change occurs and who and what can influence that context. Understanding through whom and how influence can be achieved is another central facet to maximizing contextual intelligence and optimizing observation and intervention within that context. Observing a sporting context with an eye toward establishing the means of influence can enhance your assessment. For example, through observation you can see and hear the athletes and coaches who assert the most influence, both overtly and subtly, on the dynamics of a team.

As you can see from the framework just described, you can customize your approach to observation in any sporting context. This framework can focus the observation strategies put into place and help make sense of complex, dynamic situations and their environment. There is a paucity of academic literature attesting to the impact of contextual intelligence within sport, but consideration of cultural influences and organizational effects has begun to emerge within the literature in the last decade (e.g., Fletcher & Wagstaff, 2009).

Assessment in Action

Establishing an Enhanced Contextual Intelligence

A contextual intelligence approach can help to establish important features of the performance environment. Practitioners can focus their observations to gather information relative to structure, patterns, attitudes, and means of influence. You should observe the performance environment in as many of its subcontexts as possible, including practice, competition preparation, competition itself, and social environments. Accessing this breadth of relevant contextual information can provide a clarity of understanding that enhances decision making in applied practice and improves the effectiveness of ongoing work.

Macro-Level Observation Contexts

Taking a more pragmatic approach based on the foundation of contextual intelligence, macro-level observations can take place in various environments that enhance the understanding you gain from your observational assessment. Macro-level contexts include practice, competitive, and social environments.

Practice Setting When working with individual athletes or teams, attending and immersing yourself in the practice context can make significant contributions to your understanding (Bull, 1995). Depending on the sport, practices may provide significantly more opportunities than competitions because some sports involve far more time practicing than competing. In contrast, some sports may compete two or three times a week and spend less time in practice. Whatever the athlete or team may offer to you, practices can provide valuable assessment information.

At practices, there may be numerous areas where you might direct your observations:

- Motivation of your clients during practice
- Relationships between clients and teammates and coaches
- Specific communications between clients and coaches
- The extent to which clients demonstrate effort and persistence
- Responses of clients to challenges at practice
- Clients' commitment to quality practice

Practice observations can be guided by prior information or can provide the starting point for initial assessment. For example, you may be aware that a client has been considering quitting due to a lack of motivation. For this athlete, you may be primarily interested in how she responds to challenging circumstances within practice environments in addition to her punctuality and attitude toward others on the team.

Competitive Setting The competitive setting is a key example of an athletic environment where macro-level observation can be critical to understanding an individual or team client. You can gather a wealth of useful information from observation of a competition:

- Preparation strategies
- Emotional expressions before competition
- Emotions and behavior during competition
- Interactions between athletes and teammates and coaches
- Coping with travel to and from competitive venues
- Using practice opportunities within a competitive schedule

Assessment in Action

Tracking an Important Behavior in Training Scenarios

This approach to observation assists in the assessment or monitoring of a particular sporting behavior. This can be particularly important in a practice context where a macro-level observation can be focused on a particular performer's behavior. For example, a performer may have difficulty receiving corrective feedback from coaches. The practitioner can use a simple, bespoke observation instrument to chart the behavior over time both within and across practice sessions. Such an approach can assist performers in monitoring improvements in behavior and potentially relate these improvements to other important characteristics, such as relationships with coaches and overall contributions to performance.

Of the preceding list, it is clear that some contextual components may be more or less relevant to your observations. This relevance may be led by previous interactions that identify the most useful competitive features for a specific client at that particular time. For example, if you are working with a team rife with intrateam competition and conflict, then a key focus for competition observations may be interactions between teammates and between coaches and teammates. This dynamic may lead you to direct your observational efforts in a particular way to identify any observable causes of conflict toward which you may direct your intervention efforts.

Social Context   In addition to observation within traditional sporting environments such as practice and competition, there are also benefits to observation within off-field social contexts. Such opportunities may be rare, depending on the nature of your consulting work, or they may be readily available if you have consistent contact with a particular athlete or team. Scenarios that may be of additional benefit in a social context could be how athletes are involved in

- travel,
- meals,
- lodging, and
- downtime.

The challenge for you is to remain open to a range of information in these social contexts. There may be surprising differences in the behaviors of athletes outside the traditional role-driven sporting environments of practice and competition. As a consequence, you can benefit from being receptive to a broad range of valuable information that could be garnered while observing athletes or teams rather than narrowly focusing on specific elements.

There are ethical considerations, such as boundary issues, to consider when you are involved in social contexts with clients outside the sport setting. However, there are clear advantages to being present (when appropriate) at such social contexts as a means of collecting a more diverse range of observations.

Micro-Level Observations

In addition to macro-level observations, there are significant benefits to be gained from micro-level observations, meaning the opportunities to gain understanding of the client through observations within one-to-one consultations. Such situations are clearly fertile ground for gathering information through interviewing skills such as effective questioning, clarification, and summarizing (Katz & Hemmings, 2009).

Nonverbal Information

Interviews are essential to one-to-one assessment and enable the practitioner to hear clients' responses to the questions, leading to significant gains in understanding of their thinking, emotions, and behavior (see chapter 8 for more on interviewing). At the same time, a significant component of the information communicated between two people goes beyond the words they use and incorporates a range of nonverbal information (Lloyd & Trudel, 1999; Petitpas, Giges, & Danish, 1999). Therefore, micro-level observations within a consulting situation can be influential in giving you additional information and expanding your understanding of the client (Rosenfeld & Wilder, 1990). Specifically, observation of the client at a micro level can benefit greatly from listening to the emotional content of clients' words and gathering information from body language, voice tone and inflection, gestures, and subtle changes in facial expression (Ekman, 2003; Sauter, Eisner, Ekman, & Scott, 2010).

Active Listening

Active listening is often considered foundational to the effectiveness of consulting (Murphy & Murphy, 2010). The skill of active listening is usually applied through the verbal skills of summarizing, paraphrasing, and clarifying. It is beyond the scope of this chapter to provide a detailed examination of these verbal skills (see Hargie, 2006; Katz & Hemmings, 2009); however, a significant component of active listening relies on effective micro-level observations that can provide insight into communications from clients. The component of active listening of interest here is that of reflection resulting from emotional listening.

Emotional listening can provide an opportunity to move beyond the content of the information offered by clients (factual listening) and consider what other messages they might be communicating. This sensitivity can offer even more information to help you understand your clients, their challenges, and their experience. To maximize this benefit, you should consider the relevance of a range of observational cues available in your consulting sessions. In addition to those mentioned previously (e.g., body language, voice, gestures), you may also observe shifts in the emotional status of your clients through changes in posture, skin color, and breathing (see Ekman, 2003; Hargie, 2006).

Finally, macro- and micro-levels of observation are not distinct categories but rather ways of organizing how you use observation in your work. In reality, you will apply the macro- and micro-level forms of observation in all consulting settings; that is, you can observe micro-level information in macro-level settings and vice versa. For example, you can view body language and posture during competitions, and you can use contextual intelligence (SPAM) in your consulting sessions with clients.

Observation Assessment Tools

Thus far, the chapter has highlighted that a primary function for the sport psychology consultant is to identify and understand clients' individual needs as a baseline to move toward achieving their athletic goals (Austin & Carr, 2000). Furthermore, priority has been placed on observing clients in their natural practice and competitive settings, unrestrained by formal procedures or protocols. Direct observation allows you to focus on the visible manifestations of their thoughts, emotions, and behavior within and outside the context of their specific sport (Gee, 2011; Watson & Shannon, 2010).

A systematic approach to observation helps you objectively record and evaluate behaviors in a more formal and structured way (DeMarco, Mancini, Wuest, & Schempp, 1996). Systematic observation is rooted in observation measures that have been empirically assessed, and thus are statistically valid and reliable, so they can be generalized to a broader population or used to make predictions regarding certain behaviors in a given context (e.g., Tenenbaum, Ecklund, & Kamata, 2012). The following sections highlight measures that lend themselves to a systematic approach to observation. These observation assessment tools are provided so you can incorporate observational approaches into your assessment practices in a more structured way. In addition, strengths and weaknesses of the measures are identified.

Self-Talk and Gestures Rating Scale

The Self-Talk and Gestures Rating Scale (STAGRS; Van Raalte, Brewer, Riviera, & Petitpas, 1994) was developed to record tennis players' self-talk and gestures; all aces, games, sets, and service breaks; and a running tally of the match score. The measure allows you to examine the relationship between clients' self-talk and their performance. Specifically, the scale provides a system that organizes tennis players' self-talk and gestures into three categories:

positive, negative, or instructional. The initial correlation and regression models demonstrated support for the hypothesis that self-talk direction aids in understanding (and hopefully even predicting) athletic performance (Van Raalte et al., 1994). Furthermore, lower occurrence of negative self-talk was found in players who performed well in competition; however, no difference was demonstrated in the use of positive self-talk between winning and losing players.

Multidimensional Motivational Climate Observation System

The Multidimensional Motivational Climate Observation System (MMCOS; Smith et al., 2015) assesses the motivational sport environment influenced by the coach. Given that sport performance contains an interpersonal component involving athletes' relationships with teammates, coaches, and opponents, attention should be paid to the coaches' behavior, including language and action. The MMCOS involves two high-order factors (empowering and disempowering), seven environmental dimensions (e.g., task and ego involvement, relatedness), and 32 low-order coaching strategies (e.g., use of extrinsic rewards, language, instruction). These facets of coaching are then coded into dimensions of empowering or disempowering as related to achievement goal orientation and self-determination principles. The MMCOS does not measure athlete sport behavior in relationship to sport coaching. However, if the focus of your work is working with coaches, then this observation tool can provide highly relevant behavioral information. Similar observation instruments have been influential in establishing effective coaching behaviors since the 1970s (e.g., the Coaching Behavior Assessment System [CBAS]; Smith, Smoll, & Hunt, 1977).

Precompetition and Competition Behavior Checklist

Compiled by Rushall (1979), this checklist involves presenting a series of statements to athletes, to which they respond "Always," "Occasionally," or "Never." The checklist enables athletes to establish how they prefer to prepare and behave in competitive situations. Examples of statements include "I get nervous before an important competition" and "When I am tired, I concentrate on technique." Though established and widely accepted as a valid assessment tool, this checklist is generic across all sports. It has clear face validity in the context of competitive sport; however, it does not lend itself so readily to contextualized investigation of the specific sport or the targeted behaviors sought in an individualized behavior intervention. As such, it is less serviceable to the customized measures central to sporting observation.

In general, such checklists are used on the grounds that they have acceptable reliability and validity, although their predominant focus tends to be the cognitive strategies of athletes. Furthermore, they are generic and involve self-reporting, and therefore they do not lend themselves to the bespoke nature of observation tools necessary for developing interventions for athlete behavior.

Limitations and Concerns

Despite our argument that observation is a powerful means of gathering information about athletes, we would be remiss if we didn't also discuss its key limitations as an assessment within consulting. This final section of the chapter addresses those limitations and identifies possible advances in the use of observation for future practice.

Accuracy

A potential limitation concerns the way in which observable behavior can be interpreted. As we have seen in this chapter, observation can focus on a variety of behavioral and environmental factors. However, it is clear that the contribution of observation to assessment information is grounded in the behavior of those being observed. It has long been recognized that the behaviors exhibited within any context are at best an approximation of the experience of the person being observed (Gillham, 2008). Additionally, when athletes know they are being observed, they may consciously or unconsciously alter their behavior to present a more positive impression, which may not accurately reflect their typical behavior. As a result, the consultant's observations may be erroneous, leading to an inaccurate representation and understanding of their clients.

Another limitation involves not the observed but the observer. As discussed in chapter 1, the notion of an objective, impartial observer is illusory. In reality, consultants bring professional and life experiences, as well as a range of cognitive biases that influence perception, interpretation, evaluation, and decision making, that shape what behaviors are observed and how those behaviors are interpreted. As a consequence, you must question and triangulate the reliability of your observations to ensure their accuracy.

Lack of Triangulation

The assessment of behavior through observation can open up a wealth of possibilities in understanding the athlete experience. However, observation is only one of many potential contributors to your identification and understanding of your clients' needs. For example, the observation of body language in a client does not provide direct or necessarily accurate information related to the client's cognitive, emotional, or psychosocial functioning at that time. What may be relevant from the observation of body language is the identification of potential avenues for further discussion with the client. For example, a practitioner may benefit from a reflective conversation with a client who consistently turns his back on a coach when receiving feedback in practice. This approach could lead to triangulation and enhanced understanding by using multiple assessments in the assessment process.

Observation as a Skill

Another limitation of observation as an assessment tool is that it is a skill that develops with experience. The skill sets required to conduct effective observation are varied. Moreover, they necessitate education, training, supervision, and experience to become a skilled observer. Such training enables you to be more confident that the observational information you gather has significant accuracy and thus can aid in the conceptualization of your clients.

Literature from allied professions can assist in the development of observational skills (Smith et al., 1977; Wood et al., 2004), but it is critical that consultants have training that develops specific skills relevant to appropriate contexts within sport. Such training can assist you in better understanding the range and complexity of athletes and sport environments you encounter in your consulting. Moreover, appropriate training will enable you to fully develop your professional skills, allowing clients to benefit from this expertise that provides insights and information above and beyond what is available through other modes of assessment.

Paucity of Evidence

The final limitation to discuss is the confidence with which you can use observation opportunities from an evidence-based position (Winter & Collins, 2015). At present, it is unclear how consultants are able to develop these observation skills due to the paucity of academic literature and educational guidelines addressing their development in consulting. As the profession expands, such skills will require a greater body of evidence to support them and professional guidelines for the training and development of observation. Currently there is a concerning gap that exists between what is possible from the perspective of consultants and what has been demonstrated with research evidence. A significant challenge for the profession is to develop an evidence base for the use of observation in a similar manner to that which has been developed for other forms of assessment such as questionnaires and interviews (Katz & Hemmings, 2009; Tenenbaum et al., 2012). The possibilities of using observation in an evidence-based way are clear and exemplify the advantages of observational assessment opportunities.

Assessment Tools and Their Availability

Assessment tool	Construct	Author and reference	Availability
Sport-specific check-lists	Athlete behavior assessment	Martin, G.L., Toogood, A., & Tkachuk, G.A. (1997). *Behavioral assessment forms for sport psychology consulting*. Winnipeg, MB: Sport Science Press.	Various checklists throughout book
		This book provides a number of checklists for use in observation across a range of sports.	
Self-Talk and Gesture Rating Scale (STAGRS)	Athlete behavior assessment	Van Raalte, J.L., Brewer, B.W., Rivera, P.M., & Petitpas, A.J. (1994). The relationship between observable self-talk and competitive junior tennis players' match performances. *Journal of Sport and Exercise Psychology, 16*, 400-415.	Full measure in article; https://doi.org/10.1123/jsep.16.4.400
		The STAGRS enables the tracking of sport-specific behaviors relevant to tennis regarding observable self-talk and gestures. Adaptation for other sports is required.	
Multidimensional Motivational Climate Observation System (MMCOS)	Athlete behavior assessment	Smith, N., Tessier, D., Tzioumakis, Y., Quested, E., Appleton, P., Sarrazin, P., Papaioannou, A., & Duda, J. (2015). Development and validation of the multidimensional motivational climate observation system. *Journal of Sport and Exercise Psychology, 37*, 4-22.	Full measure in article; https://doi.org/10.1123/jsep.2014-0059
		In line with achievement goal theory and SDT, the MMCOS enables the measurement (through observation) of the coach-created motivational climate in sport. Observers code the coach's behaviors in relation to a range of motivational climate factors.	
Precompetition and Competition Behavior Checklist	Athlete behavior assessment	Rushall, B. (1979). *Psyching in sport: The psychological preparation for serious competition in sport.* London: Pelham Books.	Full measure in book
		This checklist provides a semistructured questionnaire for performers to establish the types of behaviors and interactions they use in precompetition and competition. It is flexible enough to be used across a range of sports.	

Chapter Takeaways

- Observation has long been used as an assessment method to aid in understanding people through the collection of behavioral evidence.

- A primary advantage of observation over other assessment tools (e.g., self-report instruments, interviewing) is that it is direct and allows for the simultaneous generation of information on athletes' personal, physical, and social environments.

- The benefits of observation include understanding the clients' world, assessing the accuracy of other assessment information in the real world, and monitoring the effectiveness of interventions.

- Observation provides the only assessment opportunity for you to immerse yourself and witness client behaviors firsthand in the rich and dynamic setting of the sporting environment.

- Observation assessment provides valuable information but should be triangulated with other forms of assessment to ensure its accuracy.

- Macro-level observations enable broader understanding of the sporting environment and the development of conceptual intelligence.

- Micro-level observations allow you to gather verbal and nonverbal information from clients during consulting sessions, practices, and competitions.

- Customizing observation protocols to the specific needs of clients and demands of their sport is recommended.

- There are limitations to the effective use of observation, including the accuracy of interpretation, consultants' observation capabilities, and paucity of research evidence and training guidelines on which to develop observation practice.

CHAPTER 10

Applied Psychophysiology: Using Biofeedback, Neurofeedback, and Visual Feedback

Sheryl Smith, PhD, BCB, CC-AASP

Melissa Hunfalvay, PhD, CC-AASP

Tim Herzog, EdD, CC-AASP

Pierre Beauchamp, PhD, CC-CSPA

Psychophysiology is the study of the mind–body relationship. The central nervous system (CNS) and the peripheral nervous system (PNS) regulate brain and body processes, respectively. Much of what they do is below the level of our conscious awareness, but not, as we are discovering, beyond our conscious influence. Psychophysiological assessment provides objective data about an athlete's psychological and physical functioning, both at baseline and under stress. These measurements allow consultants to help athletes improve focus, control intensity, and maximize motor efficiency and performance. The goal is for athletes to move into a state of automaticity in which they attend to precisely the right environmental details that allow for the selection and execution of appropriate movements.

Psychophysiological assessment data are the foundation of arousal management, cognitive flexibility training, and vision training, a set of interventions that help athletes improve their training and competitive performances. More specifically, by using psychophysiological data as the basis for a feedback training regimen, athletes learn to reduce cognitive intrusion into the attentional resources necessary for quality sensorimotor performance. Training with perceptual-cognitive data also improves anticipation, pattern recognition, and decision making, which are all essential skills for successful athletic performance. This chapter introduces the types of psychophysiological data that sport consultants collect, the training interventions that they enable, and the benefits that athletes derive from them.

Stress Response and Self-Regulation

A major benefit of psychophysiological assessment is the identification of various elements of the stress response that are threats to athletic performance. While the specific nature of the stress response may vary from person to person, high sympathetic nervous system arousal generally consists of a combination of the following:

- Elevated heart rate and respiration
- Decreased heart rate variability (HRV)
- Increased muscular tension
- Increased sweat production
- Reduced blood flow to the periphery
- Decreased skin temperature

Cognitive changes may include the following:

- Attention can become blank or race internally with anxious rumination.
- Attention can become inflexible and narrowly focused on perceived threats, possibly to the exclusion of other relevant stimuli.

All of these elements can interfere with athletic performance. The solution for managing these disturbances is increasing one's self-regulation capacity. For example, both Porges (1995) and Thayer and Lane (2000, 2009) emphasize the role of the vagus (10th cranial) nerve in mediating autonomic arousal. The vagus nerve exerts a parasympathetic inhibitory effect by acting as a brake on sympathetic arousal. When there is vagal influence on sympathetic activity, it enables flexibility of attention, allowing attention to move effectively and efficiently from visceral awareness to appropriate situational cues. Psychophysiological assessment makes it possible to strengthen the ability to voluntarily elicit this vagal influence. Biofeedback, neurofeedback, and visual feedback are psychophysiological assessments that provide unique opportunities for athletes to enhance self-regulation.

Biofeedback

Biofeedback refers to the feedback of PNS activity for the sake of enhanced awareness and influence over these functions. Psychophysiologists use sensitive electronic equipment to measure biological markers such as heart rate, HRV, skin conductance (SC), and peripheral temperature. When athletes are given assessment data in real time, it provides them with a means of expediting psychophysiological self-regulation.

The technology of biofeedback holds great promise for sport psychology practitioners, specifically for psychological skills training, stress management, and self-regulation. Reviews in the sport science literature have highlighted the benefits of biofeedback (Blumenstein, 2002; Zaichkowsky, 1982). *Biofeedback* is a comprehensive term that often includes neurofeedback. In this chapter, *biofeedback* refers to the feedback of PNS activity and *neurofeedback* refers to CNS feedback.

Neurofeedback

Neurofeedback refers to information gathered from neural activity in the brain for the purpose of increasing awareness and influence over these processes. Neurofeedback uses highly sensitive instruments to measure brain activity associated with athletic performance. When possible, athletes are monitored during their athletic performance. When this is not possible, athletes experience their performance through simulations such as video replay or imagery.

Visual Feedback

Also referred to as *perceptual-cognitive assessment*, visual feedback involves using technology to measure sensory perception and cognitive processing of that sensory information. Athletes use this information to perform a variety of sport skills and goal-directed movements. The objective of visual feedback and training is to enhance the ability of athletes to perceive and process information in the most effective and efficient way that will ultimately lead to improved performance. The preponderance of work in this area involves visual focus, which is a critical component of attention and is the gateway for information processing. Visual assessment data are interpreted into meaningful, understandable feedback and delivered immediately to the athlete. Remote eye trackers can provide gaze replay within a minute, and mobile eye trackers can provide gaze replay within five minutes, though analysis of this data takes longer.

Benefits of Psychophysiological Assessment

Psychophysiological assessments provide data on athletes' current functioning in comparison to their baseline, their optimal performance state, and their stress response patterns. These data guide interventions in the psychophysiological areas that are impeding performance.

Readiness to Perform

Psychophysiological assessment data, particularly resting HRV, indicate fitness level and readiness to perform. Measurement of the heart's interbeat interval (IBI) and its variability has been shown to be an excellent indicator of the health, fitness, and stress state of athletes. HRV parameters can indicate reduced functional state due to fatigue, acute psychological and physical stressors, or both (Schmitt et al., 2013). Supine and 45-degree-tilt positions during five-minute HRV measurements can both assess overtraining. An athlete's deviation from baseline measures of HRV can guide coaching decisions about training loads and recovery (Tuominen, 2007).

Successful Performance States

Not all psychophysiological assessments seek to identify threats to performance. Psychophysiological monitoring before, during, and after performances reveals optimal states for anticipation, initiation, and recovery (Dupee & Werthner, 2011; Wilson & Shaw, 2012a). Research has found that in precision sports such as shooting, sensitive measurement of brain and body responses that are below the perceptual threshold can often detect small differences that may distinguish successful and unsuccessful performances (Wilson & Shaw, 2012a). Small differences in brain states, detected by frequency and location of neural activity, can then be associated with the athlete's best performances. Likewise, in sports such as tennis and golf, differential relaxation and differences in forearm or trapezius tension levels may reveal the optimal grip tension during swing and recovery.

Problematic Stress Responses

A psychophysiological stress profile provides objective data about how athletes' brains and bodies respond to acute stressors. A stress profile includes short-term activation levels and recovery times of the muscular, nervous, and cardiovascular systems and indicates athletes' current ability to upregulate the parasympathetic activity. This profile can be used to identify strategies for self-regulation training, which can remediate maladaptive patterns and build on individual strengths. For example, using strain gauges and surface electromyography (SEMG) assessment of the accessory muscles of breathing, athletes can learn to identify and modify dysfunctional breathing patterns in response to stress (Peper & Tibbetts, 1997). The following areas for targeted self-regulation training are revealed in a stress profile.

Muscle Tension

SEMG feedback provides data about muscle tension that is more objective than self-report and more sensitive than observation of successful gross movement (Sime, 1985). Assessing muscle activation levels though SEMG monitoring shows athletes that their actual muscle tension can differ from their perceived muscle tension, which in many cases may be maladaptive (Harvey & Peper, 2012). Energy expenditure errors similarly become recognizable through monitoring and feedback (Whatmore & Kohli, 1968). SEMG training can increase muscular efficiency by eliminating residual tension. Training that includes contraction and relaxation repetitions helps combat the typically low awareness of excess muscle tension (Wilson & Peper, 2014), and it has been found to improve the smoothness, tempo, and power of golf strokes (Arave, 2012).

Respiration and Heart Rate

Respiration feedback allows athletes to increase awareness of their breathing, including maladaptive breathing patterns and the stressors that trigger them. Heart rate feedback enhances awareness of the cardiac cycle. Knowledge of the timing of heartbeats, for example, benefits archers and shooters who seek to maximize their accuracy by timing their triggering to a specific point in the cardiac cycle (Landers, 1985; Mets, Konttinen, & Lyytinen, 2007).

Emotional Self-Regulation

HRV training increases athletes' ability to generate emotional responses that are appropriate for the task at hand. HRV is modifiable by training (Lehrer & Gevirtz, 2014), especially when this training is enhanced by real-time cardiac and respiratory data. Higher baseline HRV is correlated with resiliency and recovery from the stress response, emotional buffering of physical and interpersonal threat (Gyurak & Ayduk, 2008; Hansen, Johnsen, & Thayer, 2003), and increased ability to adaptively regulate emotions (Appelhans & Luecken, 2006; Thayer & Lane, 2009). Increases in activated HRV prior to the performance of a task improve the ability to buffer threat and manage pressure-related arousal and response (Thayer & Lane, 2009). Evidence is accumulating that also supports HRV as an index of emotional adaptability and self-regulatory capacity (Thayer, Ahs, Fredrickson, Sollers, & Wager, 2012). Psychophysiological assessments that indicate low HRV suggest the athlete would benefit from an HRV resonance frequency assessment (see the Respiratory Sinus Arrhythmia section) and an educational modality for circular and abdominal breathing (Lehrer et al., 2013).

Flexibility of Focus

Athletes seek the ability to regulate and adapt their attention as needed so that they are attending to the most important task-relevant cues in any given situation. Autonomic flexibility, as measured by the ability to increase or decrease HRV, has been shown to reflect the ability to make appropriate attentional shifts in response to environmental cues (Cribbet, Williams, Gunn, & Rau, 2011; Hansen et al., 2003; Marcovitch et al., 2010). Increased flexibility of focus, appropriate attention, and quiet mind are more specifically trained through neurofeedback. In this process, attentional states are modi-

fied through operant conditioning by rewarding the EEG (electroencephalography) frequencies with which they are associated (Monastra et al., 2005; Thompson & Thompson, 2003, 2007).

Behavioral Impulsivity

The ability to inhibit behavioral impulsivity (Sterman, 1966) and the ability to maintain a calm, alert focus (Thompson & Thompson, 2007; Wilson et al., 2011) are associated with increased ability to voluntarily produce changes in cortical activity in the 12 to 14 Hz (Hertz) range over the sensorimotor strip (sensorimotor rhythm, or SMR). In addition, theta (4-7 Hz) suppression and beta-1 (16-20 Hz) enhancement over the central and frontal regions of the brain are associated with increases in sustained attention and behavioral control of impulsivity (as reviewed by Lubar, 2003, and Monastra, 2003). Athletes with decreased impulsivity demonstrate better judgment and control in critical game situations (e.g., the ability to control aggression while checking vulnerable players in ice hockey).

Imagery Capacity

Mental imagery tends to be enhanced by occipital increases in the high theta and low alpha ranges (Wilson & Shaw, 2012b). Neurofeedback training in these ranges is done to enhance imagery ability.

Anticipatory Anxiety

Palmar sweat, or SC, levels during imagery of athletic performance may reveal specific components that invoke a disabling anticipatory stress response (Peper & Schmid-Shapiro, 1997). Once identified, athletes engage in calming or focus training while watching video or mentally rehearsing these performance components and getting feedback from the corresponding tracings of their skin conductance on the training monitor.

Biofeedback and Neurofeedback Assessment

Psychophysiological assessment and training tools, including biofeedback and neurofeedback, are increasingly integrated into sport psychology services for both professional and Olympic athletes (Beauchamp, Harvey, & Beauchamp,

2012; Blumenstein, Bar-Eli, & Tenenbaum, 1997; Collins, 1995; Dupee & Werthner, 2011; Lagos et al., 2011; Pusenjak, Tusak, Leskovsek, & Schwarzlin, 2015; Strack, 2003; Wilson & Peper, 2011; Zaichkowsky, 1982). In the biofeedback and neurofeedback domain, there are many clinical software packages designed for therapy and diagnosis (e.g., ADHD; Schwarz & Andrasik, 2003). However, in the optimal performance domain, fewer have been developed with the goal of performance enhancement in sport.

Psychophysiological Assessment Packages

Many consultants who are trained in psychophysiological assessment create their own protocols tailored to their areas of interest. This can be done with the general software that comes bundled with biofeedback hardware (signal acquisition encoder and processor). Alternatively, you can use one of the commercially developed assessment and training suites intended for athletes (examples can be found in the chapter-ending table Assessment Tools and Their Availability). These assessments are composed of assessment scripts and training screens, and they often use sport-specific contexts for both assessment and training. However, diligence is advised regarding software and hardware compatibility before making such a purchase.

Assessment Scripts

Scripted sessions are standardized assessments and follow-up sessions. Time- and event-based scripts let you run automatic sessions that guide clients through predefined sequences of activities. Standardized scripts ensure athletes are following the same instructions and process before each assessment so you can meaningfully compare data across sessions. A stress profile is an example of a script.

Training Screens

Individual training screens allow for flexible training routines. Biological data from the athlete are compiled and shown on a monitor. Athletes are instructed to keep their levels above (or below) a baseline that has been set by the consultant. Depending on the type of software, a reward will occur as a result of successful psychophysiological self-management. The practitioner can focus on specific skills and choose different reward systems. Upon completion, the data from these saved screens can be used to demonstrate an athlete's progress. Using these training screens, protocols for self-regulation can be designed for individual use or, for example, for an Olympic Training Center that has several thousand athletes and many coaches using the equipment. Performance coaches can follow a predetermined protocol designed to deliver a 10-week self-regulation program for an entire team.

Training screens are generally bundled according to level of difficulty and complexity. For example, in HRV training, the first competency athletes learn is to use abdominal breathing with a pacer. Once athletes have mastered this skill, they typically move on to a resonance frequency assessment, and then to using resonance frequency breathing to shift into higher HRV in stressful contexts. Using a competency approach, athletes enhance their perceptions of efficacy while building self-regulation skills.

Biofeedback and Neurofeedback Assessment Modalities

Psychophysiological assessment and training are done with a polygraph. A polygraph is a machine that measures various physiological functions, or modalities. Sensors placed over the area of interest transmit signals to an encoder. The encoder samples the incoming data, digitizes it, and sends it to software, which displays it on a monitor. Athletes and sport consultants observe real-time measurement of psychophysiological processes at a sensitivity not otherwise possible.

Muscle Activation

SEMG measures muscle activation in microvolts (μV) using sensors placed on the skin over the muscle of interest. Monitoring muscle activation during movement and psychological tasks reveals maladaptive muscle habits, such as guarding, that reduce flexibility and energy efficiency. Ideally, resting muscle is inactive. Residual muscle tension indicates that athletes may benefit from training on muscle tension awareness. For example, athletes train to recognize and produce the right electromyography (EMG) level for the quickest reaction-time start in the 100-meter dash.

Skin Conductance

An electrodermograph measures the degree of electrical conductivity across the hand. Eccrine glands produce tiny amounts of sweat in response to sympathetic nervous system activation, which increase the electrical conductivity of the skin. Sometimes referred to as an *electrodermal response*, or *EDR*, skin conductance (SC) is measured in microsiemens (µS). SC is a measure of arousal, whether positively or negatively experienced. It is useful in assessing reactivity and quieting. SC is often used to reveal stress points in an athletic performance, either in anticipation or in review of the performance. For example, it can be used during start simulation training to increase an athlete's ability to maintain focus within a specified arousal threshold.

Temperature

Skin temperature is measured with a thermistor, usually placed on a finger. As blood vessels dilate or constrict, temperature increases and decreases accordingly. Hand cooling indicates sympathetically activated vasoconstriction. It is normal for hand temperature to cool in response to the presentation of acute stressors, and it is desirable for that cooling to slowly reverse into a warming trend during recovery periods. Athletes who practice learned hand warming modulate their stress response before performance and hasten their recovery afterward.

Respiration

Respirometers (strain gauges) indirectly measure mechanical changes in breathing. Of particular interest are the relative contributions of diaphragmatic breathing and thoracic breathing. Using the accessory muscles of breathing when not under conditions of exertion is often a sign of stress response. Monitoring the respiration rate of athletes before they start their routines can identify hyperventilation and excessive anxiety and can guide interventions.

Blood Volume Pulse

A photoplethysmographic sensor, placed on one finger or the earlobe, uses infrared light to detect blood volume changes in response to each heartbeat. Blood volume pulse (BVP) is a noninvasive measure of heart rate and HRV. BVP demonstrates rapid changes in heart rate in response to precompetitive anxiety and decreases in heart rate during rest and recovery. Though it is less accurate than electrocardiography, it is often more practical for applied use with athletes.

Electrocardiography

The electrical activity of the heart is recorded by several electrodes placed on the skin over the cardiac muscle. Electrocardiography (ECG) measurement of heart rate and interbeat variability is preferable to BVP for research-grade HRV assessment because it provides a clear signal for measurement. A measure of electrical activity, an ECG gives a precise measurement of the depolarization of cardiac muscle. In contrast, BVP is a measure of blood volume changes in the arteries and capillaries.

Heart Rate Variability

Heart rate variability (HRV) represents the ability of the heart to flexibly respond to situational demands. A dynamic equilibrium between sympathetic (excitatory) nervous system influences and parasympathetic (inhibitory) influences is associated with autonomic balance and emotional flexibility. Heart rate varies with breathing. Healthy, nonstressed hearts accelerate during inhalation (to capitalize on the influx of oxygen) and decelerate during exhalation. Slow breathing lengthens this cycle and increases the variability of the beat-to-beat interval. Measurement of IBI (interbeat interval) can be accomplished using ECG and measuring from peak to peak (the R spikes, as depicted in figure 10.1) or by using photoplethysmography (PPG) with the peaks of the BVP signal.

Athletes with high HRV are said to be recovered. Those with low HRV most likely need more recovery time between intense workouts for best training results.

Respiratory Sinus Arrhythmia

Respiration-driven changes in heart rate acceleration and deceleration are called *respiratory sinus arrhythmia*, or *RSA*. The breathing frequency at which RSA is greatest is called the *resonant frequency* and is associated with a state of calm readiness in athletes. This ranges from 4.5 to 7.5 breaths per minute for adults (Lehrer et al., 2013; Lehrer & Gevirtz, 2014). RSA assessment reveals the resonant breathing frequency for individual athletes by leading them with a breathing pacer through rates from approximately 8 breaths per minute to 4 breaths per minute. An example of an athlete's individualized resonance frequency report is illustrated in figure 10.2. The key to recognizing the resonance frequency in this figure is to look for the bar with the tallest *black* segment (Low Frequency component). In this case, it also happens to be the tallest bar in the figure.

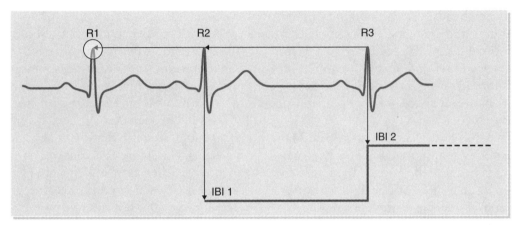

Figure 10.1   Sample R-R interval measurement in milliseconds, demonstrating variation in heartbeat intervals.

Reprinted, by permission, from Didier Combatalade, 2010, *Basics of HRV manual* (Montreal, Quebec: Thought Technology).

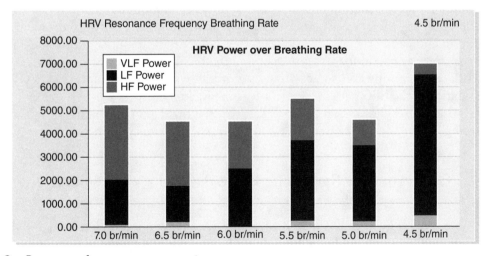

Figure 10.2   Resonance frequency assessment.

Reprinted, by permission, from P. Beauchamp, 2017, Peak Performance Suite.

Electroencephalography

In neurofeedback, electrodes are placed on the scalp to record the amplitude (in microvolts) of brain activity in that location in a process called *electroencephalography*, or *EEG*. The results are expressed in frequency bands (often represented by Greek letters) that reflect different types of thinking and attention (see table 10.1). For example, active problem solving correlates with the 15 to 18 Hz frequency band, whereas calm, focused attention correlates with activity in the 13 to 15 Hz band. By calculating the ratios between bands, you can obtain estimates of attentional and imagery abilities, efficient problem solving, and the tendency to try too hard or engage in self-judgment or rumination. (For a comprehensive treatment of EEG assessment and neurofeedback, see Thompson & Thompson, 2003.)

Standard, full-head electrode arrays use 24 or more sensors. A quantitative EEG (qEEG) presents this data in a visually understandable brain map, as opposed to lines of raw data. However, for cost and efficiency, many consultants use fewer sensor placements located over specific brain areas of interest. Common locations for sensor placement are on the top of the head, the sensorimotor cortex (Cz), the motor strip (Fz), and the left temporal lobe (T3).

One Hz bins EEG assessment is a brief, one-site assessment of brainwave frequencies in increments of 1 Hz, rather than larger bands. It is useful for checking the current state of an athlete's brain function and can indicate atypical responding that may be useful for single-Hertz up-training or down-training (Wilson & Shaw, 2011). Examination of the EEG data in combination with the athlete interview may reveal areas for skill training.

Currently, there are no published norms for athletes by sport. However, a few studies have reported EEG patterns that differentiate high performers from low ones (Babiloni et al., 2010; Wilson, Ainsworth, & Bird, 1985), and a general EEG pattern in elite athletes is beginning to emerge (Wilson & Shaw, 2011; Wilson & Somers, 2011).

Psychophysiological Stress Profile

Monitoring all of the previously mentioned modalities, a stress profile typically includes assessment for baseline values in eyes-open and eyes-closed conditions and then a series of stressful tasks followed by recovery periods. The goal is to determine which stress responses are most prominent and to assess how efficiently athletes can return to baseline after the stressor has been removed. Through this process, an individualized profile of stress response is generated. Resting arousal levels are different when the eyes are open than when they are closed. The purpose of the eyes-closed condition is to check for an increase in alpha-wave activity over the visual cortex. Alpha-wave activity is suppressed when the athlete has open eyes and is processing visual stimuli. Some assessments include an imagery task that indicates the athlete's current imagery ability and its representation in the EEG data.

The types of stressors in these stress assessments include cognitive tasks, such as the Stroop test, which requires the inhibition of a dominant learned response, and mathematical calculations under time pressure. Emotional tasks such as the recall of a positive or negative event or the anticipation of an unpleasant event may also be included.

Figure 10.3 is an example of the result generated by a scripted psychophysiological stress

Table 10.1   EEG Frequency Ranges for Sport Psychology Consulting

Theta 4-8 Hz	Low alpha 8-10 Hz	High alpha 11-12 Hz	SMR 13-15 Hz	Beta 15-18 Hz	High beta 19-22 Hz	Busy brain 23-25 Hz
Drifting, wandering mind, frustration disinhibition	Imagery, calm, relaxed	Calm, relaxed	Ready to pounce, sport ready	Processing information, scanning	Trying too hard, anxiety	Evaluation, rumination, negative thoughts

Adapted, by permission, from V. Wilson, *Optimizing performance and health suite.*

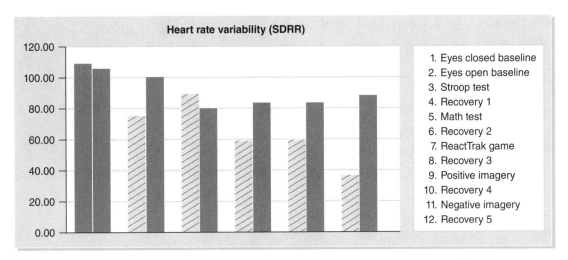

Figure 10.3   Changes in HRV over time in response to stressful events and recovery periods. The measurement of HRV used here is SDRR, which is the standard deviation (variability) of the R-R intervals and is measured in milliseconds. The first two bars (reading from left to right) represent eyes-closed and eyes-open baseline conditions. Each of the next bars represents a stressful activity (slanted lines) followed by a recovery period.

Reprinted, by permission, from P. Beauchamp, 2017, *Peak Performance Suite*.

profile (PSP). The figure represents the HRV response to a seven-activity PSP contained in the Peak Performance Suite. This protocol assesses the athlete's response to a variety of stressors, with a recovery phase (represented by bars with slanted lines) interposed between each stressor. In the figure, the athlete's HRV begins to decrease with successive stressors. However, this athlete is able to maintain good relative levels of HRV by using her breathing effectively between stressors. It is common to do a preintervention and postintervention PSP to demonstrate the athlete's progress. The physiological signals that can be charted for each activity include all of the modalities mentioned previously.

Unscripted in-context stress assessments employ the same multimodal recording while the athlete is in the practice venue or, less frequently, during competition (van der Lei & Tenenbaum, 2012). In these situations you can discover important physical and social stimuli that influence arousal or attention. For example, the calming or disrupting effect on an athlete's composure of a coach's comment or a parent's shout from the stands is revealed during concurrent psychophysiological recording.

Assessment in Action

Using Video Recordings to Detect Problematic Stress Responses

Athletes frequently have access to video recordings of their performances. Monitoring their psychophysiological responses while they are viewing themselves performing allows them to understand their reaction to stress-evoking components and the point at which they begin to anticipate those stressors. Conducted in conjunction with a second monitor that plays a video of athletes' competitive performances, athletes can review the salient points of their successful and unsuccessful performances and the associated differences in their physiology (for example, the Best v. Worst script in Peak Performance Suite software). Often athletes are not aware of their arousal and breathing changes during the stressful moments in competition. Desensitization with self-regulation training can then be an effective intervention.

Biofeedback and Neurofeedback Training With Athletes

The purpose of these assessments is to identify problematic mental states, such as rumination, self-judgment, or worry, that interfere with optimal performance and subsequently target them in training. Existing abilities such as self-calming, focus, and imagery can also be augmented with biofeedback training. The principle behind training guided by psychophysiological assessment is that an increase in an athlete's ability to self-regulate arousal and attention improves performance in competition (for a review of biofeedback- and neurofeedback-related performance improvements, see Blumenstein, 2002, and Vernon, 2005). Biofeedback training with athletes generally starts in an office or lab, where the process of biofeedback is explained and initially experienced. In this controlled environment, athletes learn to become aware of their psychophysiological states and how to regulate them. Athletes progress through incremental levels of difficulty and improve their awareness and control over their psychophysiology. Physiological feedback is then gradually delayed and eventually removed to prevent dependence on feedback guidance and to promote self-sufficiency.

To facilitate transfer of this awareness and mastery from the office to more realistic sport situations, the training context begins to increasingly resemble the competitive context in which these skills will be used. Practicing changes in mental state with imagery of competitive situations, video of past performances, and actual performance simulations sets the stage for the transfer of these skills to the practice and competitive arenas. After this transition, athletes apply their new skills to their practice and competitive efforts until the skills become automatic in their training and competitive routines. The following is an example of a biofeedback training protocol for heart rate (Beauchamp et al., 2012).

HRV Training Protocol

Assessment: PSP profile with scripted HRV assessment

Education: influence of respiration on SNS activation, diaphragmatic and resonant

Assessment in Action

Using Visual Imagery and HRV Biofeedback to Learn Feared Skills

Athletes in dangerous sports can have difficulty learning or relearning a skill that risks injury. When fear is inhibiting motor programming and execution, explicit motor imagery rehearsal under calm conditions can reduce the fear associated with the skill. Education, assessment, and resonant frequency breathing are used to develop and strengthen the ability to shift into high HRV. During psychophysiological monitoring, this calming skill is applied to guided imagery of the difficult movement. Interaction with the consultant between trials allows discussion of the key factors in maintaining both a good level of HRV and a high level of engagement with the imagery. Athletes proceed to self-guided imagery under calm conditions. After they are confident they can experience strong imagery while calm, they gradually increase their arousal levels with the goal of being able to dependably engage in high-quality imagery while experiencing the physiological signs of anxiety. The result is increased confidence in performing well under stress.

---

breathing technique, benefits of shifting into higher HRV

Training: breathing exercises at athlete's individualized resonance frequency with psychophysiological feedback guidance and homework (breathing pacer mobile app)

Simulation: progressive exposure to sport context stressors

Integration: transfer into training routine and daily life micro-situations

Evaluation: follow-up five-minute HRV assessment

In a similar way, neurofeedback can help athletes gain awareness of and train relevant brainwave frequencies at specific brain locations to enhance the types of attention and focus

Assessment in Action

Neurofeedback and Target Sports

An EEG stress assessment identifies problematic areas of cognitive flexibility for athletes in target sports. Next, EEG monitoring while aiming and shooting, plus athlete self-report, reveals the cognitive experiences that distinguish good shots from less accurate ones. The results of these assessments guide the subsequent neurofeedback training. Practicing raising alpha waves and SMR and lowering beta waves, for example, increases the ability to shift into that mental state when desired. This cognitive shift is added to the preshot routine to improve accuracy and confidence.

required by their sport. These training protocols are individually developed for athletes based on their psychophysiological stress assessment profiles. Generally, neurofeedback training may include variations of these protocols designed to do the following:

- Reduce internal distraction (suppression of 8-10 Hz low alpha) and increase calm focus (elevation of 12-15 Hz SMR) prior to execution of a motor task.

- Increase calm external awareness (elevation of 11-12 Hz high alpha) and (13-15 Hz SMR) and decrease worry (19-35 Hz).

- Move in and out of a state of problem solving (16-18 Hz) or mental work (39-41 Hz). Athletes practice clearing their minds and refocusing.

- Augment imagery skills (increase 6-10 Hz theta-alpha). Closed eyes strengthen this ability.

Visual Assessment

The fastest muscle movement in the human body is a saccade at 1,000 degrees per second (Holmqvist & Nystrom, 2011). The purpose of a saccade is to move the eye from one relevant location (or cue) to another. An athlete's ability to track objects and react appropriately develops with experience and at an individualized pace. Visual attention, perceptual information processing, and response selection can be disrupted by anxiety and distraction. Training to improve the allocation of attentional resources can enhance the development of these skills and protect them against the effects of pressure (Vine, Moore, & Wilson, 2014).

Benefits of Visual Search Assessment

Effective use of visual gaze behaviors (see table 10.2) and, in turn, the assessment of perceptual-cognitive skills, provides the following benefits:

- **Anticipation:** Looking at the right spot at the right time and making sense of what is seen enhances the ability to predict future events (Farrow & Abernathy, 2002; Savelsbergh, Williams, van der Kamp, & Ward, 2002).

- **Attention:** Efficient use of attentional resources involves focusing on the most important cues while ignoring distractions to take in the minimum amount of essential information. This results in the most efficient processing (Williams & Davids, 1998).

- **Memory:** Synthesis of past events into meaningful chunks of information enables athletes to employ effective strategies and tactics (Abernathy, Baker, & Cote, 2005).

- **Pattern recognition:** The ability to read plays based on experience (North & Williams, 2008) allows athletes to synthesize patterns and learn from them.

- **Problem solving:** The ability to conceptually organize thoughts based on visual information processing influences athletes' ability to determine what has worked and what hasn't (McPherson & Kernodle, 2003).

- **Decision making:** Athletes with effective perceptual-cognitive skills can read, anticipate, and make accurate decisions quickly (Vaeyens, Lenoir, Williams, Mazyn, & Philippaerts, 2007).

Table 10.2   Characteristics of Visual Perception (Gaze Behaviors) for Expert Athletes Compared With Less Experienced Athletes

Experts	Less experienced
Fewer visual cues	Many more visual cues
High consistency in visual search	High variability in visual search
View cues in the same order	View cues in varying order
Accurate interpretation of what is seen	Guesswork
Look only at relevant cues	Many irrelevant cues
Consistent eye routines	Unsystematic visual search; no routines

- **Situational awareness:** The ability to perceive and understand the environment (Caserta & Abrams, 2007) improves as athletes know what is visually important and what to ignore.

- **Motor efficiency:** The result of effective perception and cognition in sport is often motor efficiency (Williams & Ericsson, 2007).

- **Stress reduction:** A further benefit of effective perceptual-cognitive skills is reduced stress (Gerstenberg, 2012). Being more focused and reducing information processing can lead to a cascading reduction in stress (Vickers & Lewinski, 2012).

- **Alertness and resilience:** The ability to stay alert over time is an important benefit of perceptual-cognitive skills. In any situation with a potential for fatigue, the more efficient the perceptions, cognitions, and motor responses, the greater the alertness and resilience (Williams, Hodges, North, & Barton, 2006).

Eye Tracking

Unlike biomechanical changes, which are readily observable, visual and cognitive processes are not so easily scrutinized. An eye tracker is a special pair of glasses that records athletes' point of gaze upon the environment, taking pictures of the location of the gaze at various frame rates (e.g., 60 times per second), similar to a camera. Eye-tracking technology enables us to make three types of visual feedback assessments.

Gaze Location

An eye tracker examines the location of a person's focal vision (gaze point) within an environment to determine if the subject is attending to the appropriate cues (see figure 10.4). For example, research has demonstrated that looking at the contact point when returning a serve in tennis assists in ball tracking (Murray & Hunfalvay, 2016). In baseball, the pitcher's hand positioning on the ball helps hitters determine the type of pitch that will be thrown (Takeuchi & Inomata, 2009).

Assessment of visual feedback gaze location using eye trackers is based on research using temporal occlusion (Farrow, Abernathy, & Jackson, 2005), where the task being viewed is stopped at various points before completion and athletes are asked to extrapolate information about what will happen in the future, such as the direction a ball will travel. Visual feedback is also based on cue occlusion (also called *spatial occlusion*) research (Muller & Abernathy, 2006), where important cues are blocked from view to determine their impact on performance. These assessment paradigms measure performance outcomes using additional tools such as pressure-sensitive floor mats and infrared beams that detect response time (Williams & Ericsson, 2005).

Common assessments of gaze error include missed cues, scattered visual search, and late tracking. Missed cues (see figure 10.5) are often caused by a lack of perceptual-cognitive expertise or a failure to understand what the cue reveals, why it is important, and how it can be used to improve performance.

a

b

Figure 10.4 *(a)* Minor League Baseball aggregate visual search cues versus *(b)* Major League Baseball aggregate visual search cues. Major leaguers demonstrate attention to fewer and more localized visual cues.

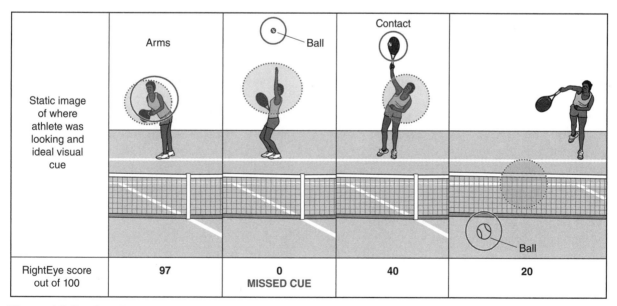

Figure 10.5 Gaze location and important visual cues. Solid circles represent important visual cues. Dotted circles represent the athlete's actual gaze location. Convergence of the two is scored out of a possible 100. Here, the missed cue in the toss phase results in failure to target the contact point and late ball tracking.

A second common error in gaze location is a scattered visual search pattern. Figure 10.4a demonstrates the wider visual search area of a less experienced baseball player. Research demonstrates that experts exhibit fewer fixations of longer duration compared with less skilled performers (Gegenfurtner, Lehtinen, & Säljö, 2011; Mann, Ward, Williams, & Janelle, 2007). Less skilled athletes who display a scattered search pattern end up processing too many cues because they are unsure where to look and what is important.

Late tracking is another common error in gaze location. This occurs especially in fast-moving, open-skilled sports when athletes start late and do not have time to catch up. This can be due to a lack of expertise or a lack of attention or readiness. Late tracking in the beginning of a sequence has negative consequences that multiply further along the biomechanical phases.

Decision Making

In addition to the techniques used in gaze location assessment, the assessment of tactics, strategy, and sequences of play includes showing video (Vickers, 2007) or static images (Bilalic, Langner, Erb, & Grodd, 2010). Alternatively, athletes can be asked to recall certain aspects of what they saw (e.g., the type of play or location of an opponent). Then, athletes are asked to determine what they expect to happen next (event probability) and what would be the best response based on what they perceived (Crognier & Fery, 2005). The assessment includes measured recognition of offense and defense strategies, which guides subsequent training to improve the speed of recognition (Caserta & Abrams, 2007).

Psychological States

Eye-tracking assessment helps us understand the perceptions and thoughts of athletes. Disruptions in visual routines, such as changes in back-and-forth gazes, visual cues, and how fast the eyes move from one cue to another, can be indicators of stress. Inattention, uncertainty, cognitive overload, or rushing can disrupt visual search patterns and reduce the quality of information available for decision making.

With increasing perceptual-cognitive expertise comes the development of visual routines, a subset of preperformance routines (Kim et al., 2008). Visual routines extract salient information from the environment by consistently looking at the same cue at the same time within a biomechanical sequence. For example, eye-tracker research shows that when returning a serve in tennis, the visual routine should follow this sequence: focal attention on the general body position of the opponent, tossing arm, toss, contact point, and then ball tracking (Hunfalvay, 2004). Repetition of the same sequence of visual cues limits the cognitive load required to process the information. The more specific the visual routine, the more effectively information is tracked and processed. Visual search routines can be assessed under various cognitive load conditions, such as at the beginning of practice without fatigue, during drills, and toward the end of practice, when athletes begin to tire and their perceptual-cognitive skills decline.

Part of the perceptual-cognitive preperformance routine is dynamic shifts in visual fixations in which athletes look at a near target and then at a far target for at least one sequence (Hunfalvay et al., in preparation). There may be several reasons for this sequence, including warming up the eye muscles to prepare for fast movement (similar to warming up other muscles before performance) and relaxing and focusing (similar to a preperformance routine). Depending on the task, athletes may dynamically shift between one and three times (Bridgeman, 2007). Performance is poor if the calibration is too short (indicating inattention, rushing, or stress) or too long (indicating indecision or cognitive overload). Changes in perceptual-cognitive psychological states can be measured through a variety of eye-tracking data (see table 10.3).

These states influence each other, and a disruption in one can have a cascading negative effect on performance (see figure 10.6).

Table 10.3 Perceptual-Cognitive Psychological States Measured Through Eye-Tracking Data

Assessment metric	Defined	Possible indicators
Visual routine	Refers to a consistent pattern of gaze location and timing.	Without a routine there is distraction, cognitive overload, lack of skill, and stress.
Gaze fluidity	Movement of the eyes from one location to another. Reduced fluidity resembles stage fright: The eye remains still, looking at one location for several seconds.	Cognitive overload and stress; indicators include reduced reaction time.
Pupil dilation	Indication of stress. Pupil dilation is the size of the pupil, measured in millimeters.	Jomier, Rault, and Aylward (2004) show pupil dilation as an indicator of stress. Difficult to measure unless assessment is conducted in an environment with controlled lighting.
Search rate	Refers to the number of fixations divided by task time.	Increases in fixations with shorter duration could mean information overload or confusion.
Dynamic shifts	Refers to at least one repetition between a near and far target before the initiation of an action.	If absent when previously present, indicates inattention, cognitive overload, or stress.
Quiet eye	A final fixation or tracking gaze on a specific location or object within the visuomotor workspace (Vickers, 2007) allows for information processing (Klostermann, Kredel, & Hossner, 2013).	Absence of quiet eye may be related to indecision and feelings of being rushed, adding to stress levels.

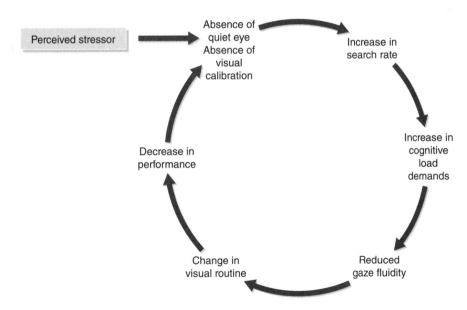

Figure 10.6   Potential downward spiral seen in eye-tracking assessment data.

Eye Tracking and Basketball

A visual search assessment is given to an athlete while shooting free throws. The results reveal an abbreviated quiet-eye period under conditions of fatigue or anxiety. Giving this feedback to the athlete increases awareness of the importance of a steady gaze on the target before movement initiation. Quiet-eye training under stress can make goal-directed visual control more resilient to pressure (Vine et al., 2011, 2014; Wilson, Vine, & Wood, 2009).

Visual and Perceptual-Cognitive Training With Athletes

Effective assessment of perceptual-cognitive skills allows the practitioner to create awareness. Awareness is a precursor to developing strategies for skill enhancement and redirecting what is ineffective.

Phases

There are three phases of training: awareness, association, and automaticity. *Awareness* refers to consciousness of where one should be looking (e.g., looking at the hand placement on a ground stroke in tennis). During the *association* phase, athletes increase their knowledge of what information comes from the cue (e.g., placement of the hand on a tennis racket is an early indicator of spin). *Automaticity* refers to the phase where tracking the cue has been practiced until it requires little conscious thought.

Training should be designed with these three levels in mind. Training for awareness would include calling out a cue word when the hand placement is recognized (e.g., *western* indicating a western grip). Associations would include calling the spin as soon as it is recognized (e.g., *topspin*). Automaticity could include an interception timing drill where the person has to call the spin and then intercept it at the highest point.

Tools

Visual perception is attracted by the size, color, and movement of an object (Karwowski, 2006). Practitioners should use visual attractors such as highlighting, special effects, colored balls, and equipment to attract attention to important areas while reducing irrelevant areas of the visual field. This method engages the recognition and learning loop of visual perception (Braun & Deco, 2013).

A Word of Caution

Psychophysiological assessment is a sophisticated methodology that requires formal education. Supervised training and experience in both the implementation and analysis of biofeedback, neurofeedback, and visual feedback are essential. Due to the sensitivity of the equipment and the measures, improper use can easily compromise data quality and its value (Holmqvist & Nystrom, 2011). Certification in biofeedback and neurofeedback is strongly recommended for consultants who wish to perform psychophysiological assessment. Biofeedback Certification International Alliance (BCIA) is the certifying organization recognized by the Association for Applied Psychophysiology and Biofeedback (AAPB) and the International Society for Neurofeedback and Research (ISNR).

Assessment Tools and Their Availability

Assessment tool	Author	Availability
Optimizing Performance and Health Suite	Vietta "Sue" Wilson	For purchase at https://bfe.org
	Includes three stress assessment scripts (long assessment, short assessment, and simple eyes-open and eyes-closed baseline) and training screens categorized according to modalities.	
Peak Performance Suite	Pierre Beauchamp	For purchase at www.thoughttechnology.com
	Includes 5- and 10-minute HRV Assessments, Psychophysiological Stress Assessment (7 activities), Resonance Frequency Assessment, Best v. Worst Performance, and training protocols designed for athletes.	
ProBaseball Suite	Jane Arave, Wes Sime, Ben Strack, and Pedro Teixeira	For purchase at https://bfe.org
	Includes a stress assessment script (18.5 minutes of baseball-themed stress-inducing tasks and accompanying recoveries), a resonance frequency detector, and reaction-time assessment and progressive focus training screens.	
ProGolf Suite	Jane Arave, Wes Sime, and Harry Van Der Lei	For purchase at https://bfe.org
	Includes stress assessment script using 14 golf-themed tasks (14 minutes), upper trapezius tension assessment, and focus and self-regulation training.	
Reaction Time Suite	Tim Harkness	For purchase at https://bfe.org
	In this suite, SEMG and other types of biofeedback can be combined with reaction-time measures.	
Tennis Performance Suite	Stephanie Nihon	For purchase at https://bfe.org
	Includes three minutes of 1 Hz bins (EEG) assessment, HRV breathing training, SEMG muscle awareness, SC, and Temperature. Beta reduction and SMR increase training in a tennis environment.	
RightEye performance products	Melissa Hunfalvay	For purchase at www.righteye.com
	Remote eye-tracking solutions for assessing and training visual search, visual strength, and visual acuity.	

Chapter Takeaways

- Biofeedback in real time enables athletes to achieve greater awareness of and influence over their psychophysiology.

- An eye tracker is used to examine the location of focal vision (gaze point) within the environment to determine if the athlete is looking at the appropriate cues in a timely manner. Visual attention is the gateway for information processing.

- Psychophysiological monitoring before, during, and after athletic performances reveals optimal states for anticipation, initiation, and recovery.

- HRV training increases the ability to generate emotional responses that are appropriate for the task at hand.

- Muscle activity, palmar sweat activity, respiration, brain wave, and various cardiac indicators are assessment modalities commonly used in biofeedback and neurofeedback.

- Effective visual gaze enhances attention, pattern recognition, and situational awareness, and it leads to improved decision making and performance. Inattention, uncertainty, cognitive overload, and rushing can disrupt visual search patterns and reduce the quality of information available for decision making.

- Athletes progress through incremental levels of training difficulty to improve their awareness and control over their psychophysiology, which in turn transfers to the athletic context as a part of training and competitive routines.

PART THREE

SPECIAL ISSUES IN ASSESSMENT

Part III examines special issues in applied sport psychology in which assessment can be a useful tool. Topics that the chapters address include coaches, parents, and teams; talent identification; sport injury, rehabilitation, and return to sport; concussions; career transitions; consulting within a sport organization; and consultant effectiveness. Assessment of each of these areas is explored in depth, including a rationale for its use, its strengths, and its weaknesses. Additionally, recommended assessments are provided to help you deliver the highest quality and most diverse range of assessment and intervention services to the athletic population.

CHAPTER 11

Coach, Team, and Parent Assessments

Andy Gillham, PhD, CC-AASP, CSCS
Travis Dorsch, PhD
Barbara J. Walker, PhD, CC-AASP
Jim Taylor, PhD, CC-AASP

Athletes' relationships with their coaches, team, and parents are interdependent and dynamic. These relationships can positively reinforce one another and create a nurturing, exciting environment in which athletes can grow. At the same time, these three influences can interact to create a negative environment that leads to poor results and an unsatisfying athletic experience, not to mention unhappiness and unhealthy personal and social development.

The roles coaches, teams, and parents play in the lives of athletes depend on many factors. The impact of these three forces is central to consultants in their work with young athletes, and you may find it beneficial to view this quadrangle of athlete, coach, team, and parent as a system aiming to direct positive efforts toward athletes' healthy athletic and personal development. To that end, a comprehensive assessment of coaches, teams, and parents can help you identify the most significant influences on athletes and fully understand the entire constellation of the athletes' sporting life. Additionally, if you are working with not only athletes but also coaches, teams, and parents, a thorough assessment can assist you in helping them to meet their needs and achieve their goals.

This systems approach may include, for example, asking athletes and parents to be part of a 360-degree assessment of a coaching staff and sport programs (Vidic & Burton, 2011). Or, assessing both coaches and parents can help identify the sources of pressure athletes may be feeling that are hurting their competitive efforts. In sum, as you read this chapter, be cognizant of the forces at play; consider the interconnectedness of athletes, coaches, teams, and parents; and gather as much information as possible about the disparate forces with the goal of using that data to help your clients achieve their athletic goals.

Coach Assessment

There are two critical areas with respect to coach assessment. First, what is the purpose of the assessment? Second, who is in the best position to provide an accurate assessment of coaches? Together, these two areas can be referred to as the *degree of alignment* for the assessment.

With the predominant metric of coach evaluation being wins and losses (Burton & Gillham, 2012; Horn, 2008), it could be argued that coaches are assessed each and every competition.

This notion is certainly true with teams and sports that garner significant media attention, such as professional and Olympic sports. As Bass, Vermillion, and Putz (2014) point out, crowdsourcing a coach's assessment is now possible. A coach's job tasks are so varied (Thelwell, Weston, Greenless, & Hutchings, 2008), however, that assessing various aspects of coaching can be a daunting task. Much of the research on coaching effectiveness has historically focused on identifying effective coaches, whether in terms of wins and losses, athlete development, or character building, and using that data to create models for further examination (e.g., Horn's working model of coaching effectiveness; Horn, 2008) and to build a knowledge base, including a specific definition (e.g., Côté & Gilbert, 2009) of coach effectiveness, in order to improve coaching development programs. There is considerably less information in the literature on precisely how athletic administrators assess coaches, but that is changing (e.g., Gillham, Hansen, & Brady, 2015).

There are many reasons why coaches might be assessed:

- Sport programs are concerned about win–loss record or revenue.

- Programs want to ensure they are offering a quality experience to their athletes.

- Programs want a better understanding of a candidate during the hiring process.

- Programs want metrics on coach strengths and weaknesses to guide development.

- Programs want to offer formative, comprehensive job performance evaluations.

- Parents want to gather information on multiple coaches when deciding whom to hire for their child athlete, particularly in sports with private coaches.

- Areas of disconnect or conflict between coaches and their athletes need to be identified.

Though this list is not exhaustive, it does provide an overview of common reasons for assessing coaches. Note that nearly all of this work has been done with sport coaches, but research is beginning to expand to strength and conditioning coaches (Gilbert & Baldis, 2014; Gillham,

---

Assessment in Action

Conducting Assessments Throughout the Season

Assessments of coaches should occur multiple times throughout a season (Gilbert, 2017). This is critical to developing the relationship between the coach and players, as well as generating valuable information for professional development for the coach. Sport seasons can be long and filled with diverse ups and downs, and a one-shot assessment is not ideal for generating quality information. Ultimately, the objective is to get quality information to design effective consulting interventions, and conducting assessments throughout the season will help gather that quality information.

Doscher, Schofield, Dalrymple, & Bird, 2015; Gillham, Schofield, Doscher, Dalrymple, & Kenn, 2016). Some differences (e.g., the amount coaches are willing to share with others regarding their program, the understanding of training process versus outcome of competitions, and the need for continuing professional development) between strength and conditioning coaches and sport coaches have already been found.

After determining the purpose of the coach assessment, the next step is to identify people with the knowledge, experience, and skills to perform the assessment and collect the relevant data. When purpose and the assessors are aligned, the resulting information will be accurate and meaningful. In contrast, when there is a misalignment, the results of the assessment will be biased or uninformed and as a result have limited value.

Consider the example of an athlete who returns home from practice and tells her father that the training session was boring and she learned nothing. At the next game, where parents gather and talk, this assessment by the athlete can spread quickly among the parents, and the coach may be targeted as unmotivating and ineffective. An overzealous parent might then seek a remedy with the head coach or program director, perhaps lobbying for the coach to be replaced. In this scenario, parents are making a judgment based on secondhand information from a single person and may well be motivated by other reasons than pure coach assessment. As another example, it is not uncommon to place the blame for a botched play on the head coach. Let's say the quarterback attempts a pass to a receiver who runs the incorrect route, and the coach is seen as at fault. Even if it is clear that the receiver blew his route and should have been looking for the ball, it is often assumed the coach should have done more to prepare the team for the game. In this situation, only the coaches and players have direct knowledge of the play, and only they are in a position to accurately assess what transpired and why.

Benefits to Coaches

The primary benefit assessment offers to coaches is the identification of their strengths and weaknesses to help guide their development and improve their coaching efforts. Though coaches are not always open to assessment, some (e.g., Gillham, Doscher, et al., 2015) do recognize the importance of assessment, or at least some form of evaluation, for coach development (e.g., Conroy & Coatsworth, 2006). Consider the aligned example of field reporting that a coach struggles to teach fundamentals during practice sessions. In your consultations with the coach, you could use that assessment information to identify that she needs to improve her communication and teaching practices. That information should then lead the coach to seek out resources (e.g., mentors, experts, books, workshops) for ways to improve her teaching.

Benefits to Athletes

A thorough assessment that includes coaches' skills in the areas of technique, strategy, conditioning, psychology, communication, and team building, just to name a few, will result in information that coaches can use to improve themselves. Athletes will then be beneficiaries of this improved coaching competence. The coach assessment can also help athletes better understand their coaches' personalities, motiva-

tions, intentions, and styles of coaching. Miscommunications, conflicts, and ill feelings can often be relieved simply by providing athletes with an appreciation of where their coaches are coming from. Though coaches may still not interact with the athletes in an ideal way, the athletes' understanding of the coaches enables them to reinterpret the coaches' behavior in a more positive light. This type of assessment situation is an opportunity to work with the coaches and athletes to create a system that functions more effectively and successfully.

Benefits to the Team

An in-depth awareness of coaches' capabilities, gained from an effective assessment protocol, will not only be beneficial to the individual coaches and athletes but also to the team as a unit. Coaches have an immense impact on every aspect of team functioning. This influence occurs at three levels. First, coaches who use an assessment to better themselves are going to be more effective in their work with individual athletes and other coaches on the team. Second, they will be better able to fulfill their designated roles and responsibilities, thus greasing the wheels of the overall team functioning. Third, coaches who improve their capabilities thanks to the assessment will be more effective leaders and managers of their team, thus creating an inspiring environment, more cohesion, better communication, higher performance, and more success.

General Areas of Coach Assessment

Coaches can be assessed in three broad areas: personal characteristics, objective behaviors, and athlete outcomes associated with the coach. Each of these areas has been included in models explaining coach effectiveness (e.g., Horn, 2008).

Coaches are fundamentally people with particular personality characteristics that make them more or less suited for various coaching situations. For example, a figure-skating coach who craves media attention may not be suited for the position of club director in a small community skating club. Similarly, a coach largely focused on results may be best suited to higher levels of competition and may find the demands of working with beginning athletes frustrating. Horn's (2008) model of coach effectiveness indicates that coaches' personal characteristics are a primary antecedent of their coaching behavior.

Observing and rating coach behaviors (e.g., behaviors that increase anxiety among athletes) has been a long-standing part of coach assessment, as evidenced by the phrasing of items on some questionnaires (e.g., Coaching Behavior Questionnaire [CBQ]; Williams et al., 2003) and multiple direct observation tools (e.g., Arizona State University [ASU] Observation Instrument; Lacy & Darst, 1984). Because behavior is the ultimate expression of coaches' capabilities, various assessments of their behavior can provide tangible information about the quality of their work.

Finally, the notion that athlete outcomes—that is, the impact of coaches on athletes' positive sport and personal development—matter most in determining coaches' effectiveness has received considerable attention (Horn, 2008). Côté and Gilbert (2009) included athlete outcomes as a critical component of a coach's expertise. Their argument is grounded in an understanding of positive youth development (Fraser-Thomas, Côté, & Deakin, 2008). Central to the argument is that coaches' primary responsibility involves fostering positive development in their athletes, as opposed to winning competitions, earning awards, or engaging in fund-raising. If this emphasis remains intact, then positive athlete outcomes are more important than the coaching behaviors that prompted the athlete outcomes. However, the focus on athlete outcomes only applies to a segment of the sport population. Côté and Gilbert (2009) include coaching context as part of determining coach effectiveness. So, for example, entry-level and recreational sport participation would place athlete outcomes as a priority in evaluating coach effectiveness, while Olympic and professional sport would place winning as a higher priority.

Specific Assessment Tools

The chapter-ending table Assessment Tools and Their Availability is a comprehensive list-

ing of published assessment tools for coaches that have been shown to have acceptable psychometric qualities. The majority of the quantitative tools are questionnaires, and the majority of the qualitative assessments involve researcher observations. Use the categories in the table to identify the general area you want to assess and then choose the specific assessment tools that best meet your needs. Coach behaviors can be examined by their relation to athlete performance (e.g., CBQ; Williams et al., 2003), creation of a motivational climate (e.g., Motivational Climate Scale for Youth Sports [MCSYS]; Smith et al., 2008), or the overall frequency of certain behaviors (e.g., Coaching Behaviour Scale for Sport [CBS-S]; Côté, Yardley, Hay, Sedgwick, & Baker, 1999; Mallet & Côté, 2006). The Coaching Success Questionnaire-2 (CSQ-2; Gillham, Burton, & Gillham, 2013) was specifically created to assess athlete outcomes.

None of these measures alone will paint a complete portrait of coaches and their relationships with the athletes, team, or parents. Research (i.e., Gillham, Gillham, & Hansen, 2016) has begun to address this notion by using multiple assessments in a single study to show how variables interact and influence each other.

Further Considerations

The greatest concern of coach assessment is alignment, as mentioned throughout this chapter. Misalignment can occur by not being clear about the purpose of the assessment, by selecting raters on the assessment without the appropriate knowledge or experience to provide accurate information, or by modifying a tool in a way that reduces its psychometric qualities. Problems with modifications to instruments can come from the theoretical level, the participants serving as the raters, or the item wordings (Gillham, 2015). Small modifications can make the tool more specific, such as changing *crew* to *team* (Aoyogi, Cox, & McGuire, 2008), while leaving the remaining characteristics of the tool intact. Without training in instrument development, you should use the tool as it was designed in order to reduce measurement error. Viswanathan (2005) details multiple sources of measurement error, and all instruments have some inherent error. The concern is that with each deviation from a published instrument, such as deleting a subscale, using a new group of raters (e.g., parents instead of athletes), or even using a small (e.g., one individual or one team) group, the measurement error increases. These modifications lead to increasingly less valid results that may then be used inaccurately to make staffing or professional development decisions.

Many instruments are best suited to a particular coaching context. For example, the Perceived Motivational Climate in Sport Questionnaire-2 (PMCSQ-2; Newton, Duda, & Yin, 2000) has multiple lower-level variables that are thought to explain the higher-order variables of task and performance (i.e., ego) climates. The PMCSQ-2 is typically regarded as the most widely used measure for coach-created motivational climate, but there are some concerns over reading level for some of the items, which led to the creation of the MCSYS (Smith, Cumming, & Smoll, 2008) to assist in assessing motivational climate with younger athletes or at least those athletes with lower reading ability. Similarly, despite the fact that the Leadership Scale for Sports (LSS; Chelladurai & Saleh, 1980) has been the most frequently used tool to assess coach leadership, questions remain about its validity (Chelladurai, 2007; Chelladurai & Riemer, 1998). Also, research on leadership has expanded to include specific instruments for transformational (e.g., Vella, Oades, & Crowe, 2012) and servant (e.g., Hammermeister et al., 2008) leadership.

Coaches can find assessments uncomfortable because they are being evaluated. Coaches may be resistant to these efforts and may try to sabotage any assessments that are attempted. Consultants must be sensitive to this natural reaction and make an effort to allay any uneasiness by framing it positively in terms of professional development, improved coaching performance, and support for coaching goals. Program administrators and coaches will also need significant justification to commit the time and resources to administer a targeted or comprehensive coach assessment. Providing a compelling rationale that will lay the foundation for buy-in and an organized, goal-driven coach assessment package that includes clear rationale, goals, and benefits will demonstrate how the assessment can be efficiently and effectively administered and the value it will bring to the coaching staff and sport organization.

Team Assessment

Consultants work with sport teams for a variety of reasons. They help individual team members maximize their practice efforts and competitive performances. They also help coaches improve their pedagogical skills, leadership, and other aspects of coaching a team. Finally, they help teams work together effectively, communicate, resolve conflict, and optimize their collective efforts in pursuit of their goals. When working with a team, you need to

- quickly and effectively establish the objectives of your work with the team;
- create common language and understanding among members of the team;
- identify topic areas for creating individual, subteam, and team goals; and
- identify the issues that need to be addressed within the team.

According to Kleinert and colleagues (2012), several group variables are positively associated with team success and thus could be a target for group assessment and intervention. Effective team functioning and the achievement of group psychological outcomes are associated with success, and they rest on the complete, dynamic integration of important intraindividual and interindividual subfactors, processes, and behaviors. Assessments can be used to help develop team cohesion, improve communication, and resolve conflict. Additionally, identifying individual roles, commitment levels, motivation, and leadership preferences, skills, and attributes can all be valuable to team performance.

Approaches to Team Assessment

Within each of the previously mentioned areas (e.g., motivation, leadership preferences), there are simple subjective, or self-rating, assessments, as well as more complex multirater scales that allow for a more comprehensive approach to team assessment. Subjective assessments allow individual athletes to evaluate themselves and are valuable because they help athletes understand themselves better. At the same time, these types of assessments have limitations; for example, their responses may not be accurate or representative of the broader views of the team due to personal past experiences or biases.

Ideally, a team assessment looks at all components (i.e., coaches, athletes, administrators, parents, other stakeholders) as a single entity, or system, rather than as individuals, and it considers the role each component plays in the team's collective efforts. When all members of a team participate in an assessment, the information gained can be more accurate and generalizable across the team. Additionally, this approach mitigates information contaminated by impression management, self-interest, and bias. Using a systems approach to team assessment provides diverse information and offers members of every level of a team useful information that can enhance team performance.

By using a comprehensive package of assessments that meet the needs and goals of a team, all of the stakeholders, including athletes, coaches, administrators, and parents, can gain a more thorough understanding of their roles and impact on the team. The collective output of the assessment can be a powerful catalyst for positive change at all levels. These team assessments can also improve communication between team members, increase self-awareness about the impact members have on team functioning, and foster accountability on the part of team members to contribute to a positive team environment.

Specific Assessment Tools

Team assessments have been studied and used in multiple areas. Those categories include team cohesion, coach and peer assessment, individual and group strengths, personality assessment for team building and teamwork, communication and leadership skills, conflict, and team roles. Examples of specific assessments include the following:

- **Group Environment Questionnaire (GEQ; Carron, Widmeyer, & Brawley, 1985).** The GEQ consists of an 18-item questionnaire that assesses perceived cohesion by individual members and consists of four components. The construct of cohesion is first divided into group and individual factors: group integration and individual attraction to group.
- **Causal Dimension Scale II (CDS-II; McAuley, Duncan, & Russell, 1992).** This scale is a revision of the original Causal Dimension Scale (CDS; Russell, 1982) and takes into consideration the participant as an active agent in the attribution process. The CDS-II assesses causal attributions along four dimensions: locus of causality, stability, personal control, and external control.
- **Collective Efficacy Questionnaire for Sports (CEQS; Short, Sullivan, & Feltz, 2005).** This is a 20-item scale used across various sports. Rather than looking at individual efficacy, it assesses perceived overall team ability, effort, persistence, preparation, and unity.

See the chapter-ending table Assessment Tools and Their Availability for additional constructs and suggestions for assessment.

Debriefing a Team Assessment

A team assessment only has value if the information obtained can be translated into broad understanding of the strengths and weaknesses of a team, tangible change goals, and actionable steps to accomplish those goals. As a consequence, a debriefing with all team members is essential. Not only can a debriefing turn the information from the team assessment into a plan of action, but it can also act as a platform for building cohesion, teaching communication, resolving conflicts, and bringing diverse views and interests into a collective alignment around team goals.

Debriefing an assessment can serve as an opportunity to reflect on members' experience of the team and to make it more meaningful by identifying what they learned about themselves and others from the assessment and how they can use this information constructively. As the consultant, you can shape the debriefing by leading a thought-provoking, open discussion. It can be helpful to establish guidelines to create a supportive, caring environment in which team members feel comfortable and free to express themselves. Suggested guidelines include the following:

- Assessment should create a greater understanding of the team as a whole.
- Everyone has a voice.
- All comments should be constructive and future focused.
- The output of the debriefing should include specific goals and action steps.

The seating arrangements of a debriefing session should be thoughtfully considered. In a traditional classroom-style arrangement, the athletes face the facilitator. This setup is probably the most familiar and most comfortable for the athletes, but it may not result in full participation or deep conversation. This style may be used when you are presenting the results and your observations of the assessment. In a horseshoe or circular arrangement, all team members are at the same level (e.g., sitting in chairs or on the floor), creating a comfortable, open setting for exploration of the team assessment. This style is most conducive to open discussion because team members are facing each other, with no apparent hierarchy. We encourage you to be part of the seating so that you are viewed as an integral part of the group rather than as a separate entity.

The effectiveness of the debriefing depends largely on the attitude that the head coach and staff bring to it. Their receptiveness to the assessment results and willingness to use the information for the betterment of the team will send a powerful message to the athletes. In sum, if the coaches demonstrate buy-in, so will the athletes, and that collective openness will set the tone for a positive, constructive exploration of assessment findings.

Further Considerations

Team assessments have several limitations, and each can lead to a lengthy discussion. The main

reminder is that the quality of the assessment results will only be as good as the quality and objectivity of the input. Problems in this area include a misalignment between the purpose of the assessment and the ability of raters to fulfill that purpose. As you plan a package of assessments, consider how to ensure feedback that will be accurate and useful. You can mitigate this concern to some degree by waiting until you have established rapport and trust with team members. If they know you have their best interests at heart, they are more likely to provide accurate information in the assessment. Additionally, the age, gender, perceived benefits versus costs of the assessment, and overall team attitude (as shaped by the coaches' attitudes) can also influence the value gained from the assessment.

It is also important to recognize the role of team culture on a team assessment. You would be wise to learn about the team's recent history, the attitudes that team members hold, the quality of the relationships among team members, and anything else that might affect their receptivity to team assessment. For example, there may be some bad blood between various team members that might inhibit the willingness to participate openly. The maturity of team members, how long they have been with the team, their potential conflicting motivations and goals, their commitment to the team's future, and their perceived aspirations and hopes for the team, as well as the general team climate, may also influence the value of the assessment.

Parent Assessment

Youth sport is a distinct context for social development (Fraser-Thomas, Côté, & Deakin, 2005; Shields, Bredemeier, LaVoi, & Power, 2005). Accordingly, it is an ecological laboratory for investigating young people's positive and negative developmental outcomes (e.g., Brustad, Babkes, & Smith, 2001). Though children and adolescents often instigate their participation in sport, parents play a vital role in their children's sport involvement. Through this involvement, the potential also exists for parents to undergo changes in their own thoughts, emotions, and behaviors, as well as their relationships with their children, their children's teammates and coaches, and other stakeholders in sport. Collectively, these changes are defined as *parent sport socialization* (Dorsch, Smith, & McDonough, 2009, 2015).

An essential aspect of socialization is learning roles and expectations. People internalize role expectations over time through social learning, cocreating goals with significant others, and adopting behavioral strategies to meet specific demands (Grolnick, Deci, & Ryan, 1997). Given the ubiquity of organized youth sport (AAP, 2000) and the impact of sport on many American families (see Bremer, 2012, for a review), assessing the influence of children's sport participation on parents is important. Achieving this end will foster a deeper understanding of how parents engage in organized youth sport and how their involvement affects children, sport organizations, and communities.

Rationale for Parent Assessment

Assessing parents in organized youth sport is important for three reasons. First, the parental unit, whether containing one or multiple caregivers, forms one-third of the athletic triangle (i.e., athlete, coach, and parent; see Hellstedt, 1987). Therefore, understanding parent experiences is necessary to understanding athlete and coach experiences. Second, the direct impact of parent involvement on child outcomes is substantial. A rich literature in sport highlights the link of parent involvement (e.g., pressure and support behaviors) to key developmental outcomes (e.g., child enjoyment and enthusiasm, autonomy, self-perception of sport skill) for the athletes who participate. Third, parent assessment is fundamental to developing interventions, creating policies, and fostering healthy values and attitudes about sport that promote athletics as a positive experience that supports children's healthy development.

Benefits of Parent Assessment

One essential benefit of assessing parents in youth sport is gaining deeper knowledge of the ways in which parents influence their children's athletic experience. Sport shapes young people

in many ways both within and beyond the athletic arena, and parents have a profound impact on how children

- learn values from their sport experience;
- develop attitudes about competition, success, and failure;
- come to hold beliefs about themselves in terms of motivation, confidence, and resilience; and
- acquire life skills from their sport participation, including persistence, response to setbacks, emotional management, and focus.

A second benefit is that parent assessment allows for a more integrated understanding of the sport system. Sport systems are composed of multiple relationships at multiple levels of the environment (i.e., community, sport organization, family, individual), but the parent–child microsystem is perhaps the most pervasive at the earliest stages of organized youth sport (Atkins, Johnson, Force, & Petrie, 2015; Holt, Tamminen, Black, Sehn, & Wall, 2008; Ullrich-French & Smith, 2006). As suggested earlier, parents are an integral component of the athletic triangle; therefore, in extending the work of Dorsch, Smith, and McDonough (2009, 2015), researchers and consultants who work directly within this triangle can sharpen their collective understanding of young athletes' sport systems by assessing parents' thoughts, emotions, and behaviors in organized youth sport.

A third benefit of assessing parents in organized youth sport is that it allows for a more developmentally informed understanding of the role parents and significant others play in the lives of athletes. An expansive literature highlights the sequential importance placed on information from parents, peers, and adult mentors (e.g., coaches; Harter, 1999) by children and adolescents as they grow. However, researchers have yet to fully integrate the role of parents across salient developmental transitions in organized youth sport. Doing so could provide insight into the mechanisms that drive shifts in the importance athletes place on their parents and specific significant others across development.

A fourth benefit of assessing parents is that it allows for a more nuanced understanding of the impact of parent involvement on specific aspects of the youth sport experience. For example, *motivational climate*, defined as the structure of a social environment that influences individuals' motivation to participate, has been identified as critical to the experiences of young athletes in their sport participation. Research grounded in achievement goal theory (Nicholls, 1984) has focused on the impact of coach-created motivational climates on athletes (Harwood, Keegan, Smith, & Raine, 2015); however, it is plausible that parents also play a significant role in the creation of the motivational climate that envelops their children when they participate in sport (Atkins et al., 2015; Dorsch, Smith, & McDonough, 2015). This influence is both direct and indirect. Parents directly affect their children's motivations by sending messages via their words and actions about what outcomes they most value. For instance, how parents react to victories and defeats can send powerful messages to children about the motivational orientation of their parents, which may then play a significant role in dictating the motivational climate.

Quantitative Parent Assessment

As we have seen, parents influence their children's sport participation in many ways. As a consequence, a major goal of parent assessment is to provide information and insights into the various areas of that influence.

Parent–Child Sport Relationship

According to the recent ecological perspectives of human development (e.g., Bronfenbrenner, 2005), interactions between individuals in an environment result in progressive accommodation (i.e., socialization; Parke & Buriel, 2006) over the life span. As such, the parent–child relationship may be marked by continuous and proximal interactions that evoke subjective feelings such as closeness, struggle, sensitivity, and power (Darling & Steinberg, 1993). Laursen and Collins (2009) argue that researchers may gain a clearer picture of the parent–child relationship by measuring individuals' perceptions of

warmth and conflict simultaneously. Borrowing from this developmental perspective, Dorsch, Smith, and Dotterer (2016) explain warmth in the parent–child sport relationship as "the tendency for the parent–child relationship to be imbued by supportive, affectionate, and sensitive interactions" (p. 133). The authors operationalize conflict in the parent–child sport relationship as "the struggle for agency or power within the [sport] relationship" (p. 133). These definitions build from assessments in the family literature (Child's Report of Parental Behavior Inventory [CRPBI]; Schwarz, Barton-Henry, & Pruzinsky, 1985) and sport literature (Sport Friendship Quality Scale [SFQS]; Ullrich-French & Smith, 2006; Weiss & Smith, 1999).

Despite emerging interest on the part of sport researchers, the parent–child sport relationship is not yet well understood. A promising link has been established in the literature, however, tying parent–child relationship quality to young athletes' sport enjoyment and motivation. Specifically, warm and nurturing parent–child relationships were associated with greater enjoyment and motivation to participate compared with relationships that were perceived as conflictual (Horn & Horn, 2007; Ullrich-French & Smith, 2006). In light of these findings, and the potential for the parent–child relationship to predict child outcomes in sport (Dorsch et al., 2016), assessing parent perceptions of warmth and conflict in the parent–child sport relationship will improve our understanding of the sport parenting experience.

Sport-Related Emotions of Parents

In line with Bronfenbrenner (2005), a host of person-related factors influence how people interact with and are perceived by others in their social environments. One such factor is the experience of *affect*, described as the emotions, feelings, and mood of an individual (Vallerand & Blanchard, 2000). Parent affect in youth sport is understudied, though parents cite it as important to their sport-related experiences (Dorsch et al., 2009). In organized youth sport, a parent's affective experience will affect children's beliefs, emotions, and subsequent behavior related to their sport participation. Additionally, overt expressions of parent emotions, such as excitement and joy after a victory or anger or despondency following a loss, may influence athletes' own perceptions of their performances, as well as their perceptions of the motivational climate. Therefore, assessing parent emotions regarding their children's youth sport participation will not only contribute to the growing body of sport parenting literature, but it will also help develop practical prescriptions that offer insights, information, and tools to help parents become more aware of and use their emotions to their children's benefit during sport participation.

Although dedicated tools for measuring parent affect in organized youth sport do not exist, one widely used instrument is the Positive and Negative Affect Schedule (PANAS-X; Watson & Clark, 1994). The PANAS-X measures general aspects of positive and negative affect, as well as three basic positive emotions (joviality, self-assurance, and attentiveness), four basic negative emotions (fear, hostility, guilt, and sadness), and four more complex emotional states (shyness, fatigue, serenity, and surprise).

Parent Involvement

Parent involvement is a multidimensional construct consisting of parent support and pressure behaviors (Leff & Hoyle, 1995; Stein, Raedeke, & Glenn, 1999). In sport, *parent support* has been operationalized as behaviors or comments (e.g., providing opportunity and materials, attending practices and competitions, demonstrating pleasure, offering praise or performance-contingent feedback) that facilitate sport outcomes that are important to children (Fredricks & Eccles, 2004; Holt et al., 2008; Kidman, McKenzie, & McKenzie, 1999). Parent support has been linked to virtuous outcomes in children such as individuation, enjoyment and enthusiasm, and self-perception of sport skill. *Parent pressure* has been defined as behaviors or comments "designed to prompt athlete responses and outcomes that are important to the parent" (O'Rourke, Smith, Smoll, & Cumming, 2011, p. 400). Parent pressure has been linked to poor outcomes such as dissatisfaction with sport performance, perceptions of an intimidating sport performance environment, and performance anxiety and negative affect.

Again, no dedicated instrument has been developed to measure parent involvement in organized youth sport; however, the Parental Involvement in Activities Scale (PIAS; Anderson, Funk, Elliott, & Smith, 2003) offers an adaptable measure of parental support and pressure in extracurricular settings. A modified version of this measure has also been used in sport-specific settings (Dorsch et al., 2016; Dunn, Dorsch, King, & Rothlisberger, 2016).

Motivational Climate

One of the many salient constructs for parent assessment is the coach-created motivational climate. Indeed, as noted earlier, the climate influences both children's and parents' experiences in sport. Assessing parent perceptions of mastery- and ego-focused motivational climates is essential because these climates may influence the goals parents have for their children and the behaviors they exhibit in the sport setting, both of which may affect their children's participation experiences (Gershgoren, Tenenbaum, Gershgoren, & Eklund, 2011). As parents draw cues from their children's youth sport coaches, they may fortify the motivational climate or attempt to change it. Specifically, a mastery-focused climate may stimulate parent behaviors that seek to enhance children's skill development and enjoyment; however, it could also result in behaviors directed at enhancing ability and outcomes if the parent and coach hold conflicting views regarding the purposes of youth sport. Similarly, an ego-focused climate may stimulate parent behaviors that seek to enhance children's ability and outcomes, yet it could also result in behaviors directed at enhancing skill development and enjoyment. You can refer to the discussion of relevant assessment tools for motivational climate earlier in this chapter for additional insights.

Qualitative Parent Assessment

In addition to quantitative assessments, sport researchers and consultants can use qualitative measures to assess parents in organized youth sport. A number of observation, journaling, and interviewing protocols to assess parent experiences have been successfully designed and implemented.

Kidman and colleagues (1999) examined parents' verbal behavior during selected youth sporting events. A study-designed observation instrument, the Parent Observation Instrument for Sport Events (POISE), was used to observe parent comments during 147 competitions across seven team sports. Frequencies of verbal comments were tabulated by sport and by the nature and target of each comment. Results indicated that, although a high amount of positive comments (47.2 percent) are visible in organized youth sport, a relatively high percentage of negative comments (34.5 percent) also exist.

In extending the conceptualization of parent verbal sideline behavior beyond the simple trichotomy of positive, negative, and neutral, Holt and colleagues (2008) examined parenting styles and associated practices in youth sport. Following a season-long period of observation, data were collected through interviews with parents and children. Interpretation was guided by Grolnick's (2003) theory of parenting styles, and the authors constructed a grounded theory of parenting practices in youth sport. Specifically, parent verbal sideline behaviors were placed on a continuum from more supportive to more controlling. Verbal sideline behaviors were categorized as praise and encouragement (35 percent of parent comments), performance-contingent feedback (5 percent), instruction (35 percent), striking a balance (10 percent), negative comments (10 percent), and derogatory comments (5 percent). Additionally, parents reported demonstrating empathy with their children by experiencing the same emotions they thought their children were experiencing, a finding described as *emotional mirroring* by Dorsch, Smith, and McDonough (2009). Parents also framed their involvement as being directed by their perceived knowledge and experience in sport (e.g., parents who judged themselves as having more insight into sport thought they also had a greater ability to be appropriately involved), as well as by game circumstances (e.g., there were more comments during contests judged to be more important).

Dorsch, Smith, Wilson, and McDonough (2015) conducted follow-up work to examine the alignment of parent goals and verbal sideline behavior at the earliest stage of youth sport. After conducting semistructured interviews and collecting parent journals to identify parent goals for their children's sport participation, in situ audio recordings were collected with parents at competitions over the initial 15 months of their children's organized sport participation. Parent goals were theoretically categorized within the multiple goals framework (see Caughlin, 2010), verbal sideline behaviors were categorized deductively using Holt and colleagues' (2008) framework, and case narratives were constructed to offer an interpretation of the interplay of parent goals and verbal sideline behavior. Dorsch and colleagues articulated 43 goals parents held for their children's youth sport participation, each of which was directed at achieving an instrumental (e.g., improve technical skills), identity (e.g., help child compare well with other athletes), or relational (e.g., learn sportsmanship) goal. In line with Holt and colleagues (2008), parental praise and encouragement ranged from 25 to 48 percent, performance-contingent feedback ranged from 16 to 33 percent, instruction ranged from 13 to 43 percent, striking a balance ranged from 1 to 5 percent, negative comments ranged from 6 to 16 percent, and derogatory comments ranged from 0 to 2 percent.

Further Considerations

Participation in organized sport during childhood and adolescence is nearly ubiquitous in North America (Jellineck & Durant, 2004), and youth participation may affect parents as well as the family unit (Dorsch, Smith, & McDonough, 2009, 2015). Importantly, the value placed on sport by parents appears directly related to the family involvement that stems from the child's participation. Despite this, few studies have taken a family approach in examining socialization into and through sport (see Greendorfer, 2002). Given the popularity and growing competitiveness of organized youth sport programs (AAP, 2000), investigating the effects of youth sport participation on parents represents an important path toward deeper understanding of families in sport and how that information can be used to help parents support rather than undermine their children's athletic participation.

In the interest of achieving this deeper understanding, a number of limitations should be considered. First, although understanding parent involvement in this context benefits from recognizing the perceptions of multiple family members (McHale, Amato, & Booth, 2014), numerous studies show that parents and children have moderate-to-low agreement when reporting on parent behavior, attributions, and values (e.g., Babkes & Weiss, 1999; Kanters, Bocarro, & Casper, 2008; Knafo & Schwartz, 2003). This finding suggests that examining parent and athlete (and perhaps coach) perceptions of relevant constructs should be done with caution as researchers pursue insight into the parallel, but perhaps differentiated, perceptions of parent involvement in organized youth sport. Understanding and amalgamating different stakeholders' perceptions, whether similar or dissimilar, is a vital step toward understanding parent involvement behavior, as well as its antecedents and consequences.

In addition, there are psychometric and measurement concerns related to many of the instruments that are traditionally used to assess parents in organized youth sport. Much of this stems from the fact that many measures have been adapted from the developmental literature. Although the measures have largely demonstrated acceptable reliability in various sport contexts, replication and additional psychometric work are necessary to address potential deficiencies in the use of adapted measures. Additionally, the efficacy of observational, journal, and interview protocols should be corroborated across diverse samples and at various developmental levels. This validation process can be difficult because interpreting data collected using these methods is constrained by the researcher's own experiences, knowledge, and biases, as well as the lens through which the research is designed and executed. In conducting qualitative assessments of parents in organized youth sport, researchers should therefore acknowledge that knowledge is continually constructed through social interaction and is subject to revision as a result of changing circumstances (Schmidt, 2007). Accordingly, qualitative researchers should aim to understand participant narratives while providing context-specific and trustworthy understanding of their experiences (Schweizer, 1998).

A starting point for researchers and practitioners should be viewing socialization as a reciprocal and enduring construct. This belief leans on foundational work conducted by Bell and colleagues examining the reciprocal influences of children on their parents (Bell & Chapman, 1986; Bell & Harper, 1977). In following this road, sport researchers should design studies that investigate the ways parents not only help socialize their children but also are behaviorally and attitudinally influenced by their children and the context of their children's activities (Dix, Ruble, Grusec, & Nixon, 1986; Dorsch, Smith, & McDonough, 2009, 2015; Peters, 1985; Weiss & Hayashi, 1995). Viewing person- and context-related factors in concert can capture a deeper understanding of the processes that characterize parent sport socialization, which can then be used to promote youth sport for the healthy development of the whole child.

Assessment Tools and Their Availability

Assessment tool	Construct	Author and reference	Availability
Leadership Scale for Sports (LSS)	Coach leadership	Chelladurai, P., & Arnott, M. (1985). Decision styles in coaching: Preferences of basketball players. *Research Quarterly for Exercise and Sport, 56*, 15-24. Chelladurai, P., & Riemer, H.A. (1998). In J.L. Duda (Ed.), *Advances in sport and exercise psychology* (pp. 227-253). Morgantown, WV: Fitness Information Technology.	Contact the authors
		The LSS includes areas of coach leadership across five subscales. There are three versions of this instrument in the literature.	
Revised Servant Leadership Profile for Sport	Servant leadership	Page, D., & Wong, P.T.P. (2000). A conceptual framework for measuring servant leadership. In S. Adjiboloos (Ed.), *The human factor in shaping the course of history and development* (pp. 1-28). Lanham, MD: American University Press. Hammermeister, J., Chase, M., Burton, D., Westre, K., Pickering, M., & Baldwin, N. (2008). Servant leadership in sport: A concept whose time has arrived. *Journal of Servant Leadership, 4*, 185-215.	Contact the authors
		This was originally a non-sport-population instrument revised to be used with athletes, who rate their coach's servant leadership behaviors across three subscales.	
Differentiated Transformational Leadership Inventory (DTLI)	Coach leadership	Vella, S.A., Oades, L.G., & Crowe, T.P. (2012). Validation of the differentiated transformational leadership inventory as a measure of coach leadership in youth soccer. *Sport Psychologist, 26*, 207-223.	Contact the authors
		The DTLI assesses coach leadership behaviors congruent with the transformational leadership paradigm.	
Multifactor Leadership Questionnaire (MLQ)	Coach leadership	Avolio, B.J., & Bass, B.M. (2004). *Multifactor Leadership Questionnaire: Manual and sampler set* (3rd ed.). Redwood City, CA: Mind Garden. Rowold, J. (2006). Transformational and transactional leadership in martial arts. *Journal of Applied Sport Psychology, 18*, 312-325.	Contact the authors
		Various versions of the MLQ exist in the literature, and all versions assess leader attributes, behaviors, and leadership styles.	
Decision-style questionnaire	Coach decision making	Chelladurai, P., & Arnott, M. (1985). Decision styles in coaching: Preferences of basketball players. *Research Quarterly for Exercise and Sport, 56*, 15-24. Chelladurai, P., & Quek, C.B. (1991). Decision style choices of high school basketball coaches: The effects of situational and coach characteristics. *Journal of Sport Behavior, 18*, 91-108.	Contact the authors
		Multiple versions of this questionnaire exist in the literature, with one example including both a coach self-report version and a version where the athlete rates the coach.	

(continued)

Assessment Tools and Their Availability *(continued)*

Assessment tool	Construct	Author and reference	Availability
Perceived Motivational Climate in Sport Questionnaire-2 (PMCSQ-2)	Motivational climate	Newton, M.L., Duda, J.L., & Yin, Z. (2000). Examination of the psychometric properties of the Perceived Motivational Climate in Sport Questionnaire-2 in a sample of female athletes. *Journal of Sport Sciences, 18,* 275-290. Duda, J.L., & Whitehead, J. (1998). Measurement of goal perspectives in the physical domain. In J.L. Duda (Ed.), *Advances in sport and exercise psychology measurement* (pp. 21-48). Morgantown, WV: Fitness Information Technology.	Contact the authors
		The PMCSQ-2 assesses the coach-initiated motivational climate across multiple subscales and higher-order factors of task-involving and ego-involving climate.	
Motivational Climate Scale for Youth Sports (MCSYS)	Motivational climate	Smith, R.E., Cumming, S.P., & Smoll, F.L. (2008). Development and validation of the Motivational Climate Scale for Youth Sports. *Journal of Applied Sport Psychology, 20,* 116-136.	Full measure in article; http://dx.doi.org/10.1080/10413200701790558
		The MCSYS assesses the coach-initiated motivational climate for younger athletes. It includes both ego-involving and task-involving subscales.	
Coaches' interpersonal behavior style	Coach interpersonal behaviors	Pelletier, L.G., & Vallerand, R.J. (1996). Supervisors' beliefs and subordinates' intrinsic motivation: A behavioral confirmation analysis. *Journal of Personality and Social Psychology, 71,* 331-341. Pelletier, L.G., Tuson, K.M., & Haddad, N.K. (1997). The Client Motivation for Therapy Scale (CMOTS): A measure of intrinsic motivation, forms of extrinsic motivation, and amotivation for therapy. *Journal of Personality Assessment, 68,* 414-435. Pelletier, L.G., Fortier, M.S., Vallerand, R.J., & Briere, N.M. (2002). Associations among perceived autonomy support, forms of self-regulation, and persistence: A prospective study. *Motivation and Emotion, 25,* 279-306.	Contact the authors
		Athletes rate their coach's interpersonal behaviors around and with them.	
Coaching Behavior Questionnaire (CBQ)	Coach behavior	Kenow, L.J., & Williams, J.M. (1992). Relationship between anxiety, self-confidence, and evaluation of coaching behaviors. *The Sport Psychologist, 6,* 344-357. Kenow, L.J., & Williams, J.M. (1999). Coach-athlete compatibility and athletes' perceptions of coaching behaviors. *Journal of Sport Behavior, 22,* 251-259. Williams, J.M., Jerome, G.J., Kenow, L.J., Rogers, T., Sartain, T.A., & Darland, G. (2003). Factor structure of the Coaching Behavior Questionnaire and its relationship to athlete variables. *The Sport Psychologist, 17,* 16-34.	Contact the authors
		The CBQ includes athlete perceptions and judgments of coach behaviors that are both positive and negatively valenced.	

Assessment tool	Construct	Author and reference	Availability
Coach–Athlete Relationship Questionnaire (CART-Q)	Coach–athlete relationship	Jowett, S., & Ntoumanis, N. (2004). The Coach–Athlete Relationship Questionnaire (CART-Q): Development and initial validation. *Scandinavian Journal of Medicine and Science in Sports, 14*, 245-257.	Full measure in article; http://dx.doi .org/10.1111/ j.1600-0838 .2003.00338.x
	Multiple versions of this instrument exist in the literature, but all include multiple subscales of closeness, commitment, and complementarity.		
Coaching Efficacy Scale (CES)	Coach efficacy	Feltz, D.L., Chase, M.A., Moritz, S.E., & Sullivan, P.J. (1999). A conceptual model of coaching efficacy: Preliminary investigation and instrument development. *Journal of Educational Psychology, 91*, 765-776.	Full measure in article; http://dx.doi .org/10.1037// 0022-0663.91 .4.765
	This multidimensional instrument measures coaching efficacy; it has shown some psychometric concerns.		
Coaching Efficacy Scale II—High School Teams (CES II-HST)	Coach efficacy	Myers, N.D., Feltz, D.L., Chase, M.A., Reckase, M.D., & Hancock, G.R. (2008). The Coaching Efficacy Scale-II: High school teams. *Educational and Psychological Measurement, 68*, 1059-1076.	Full measure in article; http:// dx.doi.org/10 .1177/0013164 408318773
	This updated version of the CES yields improved psychometrics, especially at the high school level, across multiple subscales.		
Coaching Behaviour Scale for Sport (CBS-S)	Coach behavior	Côté, J., Yardley, J., Hay, J., Sedgwick, W., & Baker, J. (1999). An exploratory examination of the Coaching Behavior Scale for Sport. *Avanté, 5*, 82-92.	Contact the authors
		Mallet, C., & Côté, J. (2006). Beyond winning and losing: Guidelines for evaluating high performance coaches. *The Sport Psychologist, 20*, 213-221.	
	Athletes rate their coach's behaviors across training, competition, and organizational context. The CBS-S was designed originally for elite levels.		
Trust in Leader Instrument	Trust in coach	Dirks, K.T. (2000). Trust in leadership and team performance: Evidence from NCAA basketball. *Journal of Applied Psychology, 85*, 1004-1012.	Full measure in article; http:// dx.doi .org/10.1037/ 0021-9010 .85.6.1004
	Athletes rate the coach's behaviors leading to athlete trust.		
Coaching Success Questionnaire-2 (CSQ-2)	Athlete Outcomes	Gillham, A., Burton, D., & Gillham, E. (2013). Going beyond won-loss record to identify successful coaches: Development and preliminary validation of the Coaching Success Questionnaire-2. *International Journal of Sports Science & Coaching, 8*, 115-138.	Full measure in article; http:// dx.doi.org/ 10.1260/ 1747-9541 .8.1.115
	This multidimensional instrument includes 10 four-item subscales across a range of psychosocial athlete development areas. Multiple studies have used the CSQ-2, showing strong psychometric properties in each.		

(continued)

Assessment Tools and Their Availability *(continued)*

Assessment tool	Construct	Author and reference	Availability
Athlete Satisfaction Questionnaire (ASQ)	Athlete satisfaction	Riemer, H.A., & Chelladurai, P. (1998). Development of the Athlete Satisfaction Questionnaire (ASQ). *Journal of Sport & Exercise Psychology, 20,* 127-156.	Full measure in article; http://dx.doi.org/10.1123/jsep.20.2.127
		This multidimensional tool is used to rate coach impact on athlete satisfaction.	
Basic Needs Satisfaction in Relationships Scale (BNSRS)	Athlete satisfaction	La Guardia, J.G., Ryan, R.M., Couchman, C.E., & Deci, E.L. (2000). Within-person variation in security of attachment: A self-determination theory perspective on attachment, need fulfillment, and well-being. *Journal of Personality and Social Psychology, 79,* 367-384. Coatsworth, J.D., & Conroy, D.E. (2009). The effects of autonomy-supportive coaching, need satisfaction, and self-perceptions on initiative and identity in youth swimmers. *Developmental Psychology, 45,* 320-328.	Contact the authors
		The BNSRS is congruent with the SDT perspective on needs satisfaction.	
Coach Evaluation Questionnaire (CEQ)	Coach performance	Rushall, B.S., & Wiznuk, K. (1985). Athletes' assessment of the coach: The Coach Evaluation Questionnaire. *Canadian Journal of Applied Sport Sciences, 10,* 157-161.	Full measure in article
		The CEQ is one of the original coach evaluation tools that outlines basic principles that should be followed, although psychometrics of the instrument itself are largely untested.	
Dimensions of Coaching Performance	Coach Performance	MacLean, J.C., & Chelladurai, P. (1995). Dimensions of coaching performance: Development of a scale. *Journal of Sport Management, 9,* 194-207.	Full measure in article; http://dx.doi.org/10.1123/jsm.9.2.194
		This multidimensional model includes aspects of both coaching process and coaching product variables.	
Coaching Staff Cohesion Scale (CSCS)	Coaching staff	Martin, K. (2002). Development and validation of the Coaching Staff Cohesion Scale. *Measurement in Physical Education and Exercise Science, 6,* 23-42.	Full measure in article; http://dx.doi.org/10.1207/S15327841MPEE0601_2
		The CSCS assesses how well a coaching staff works together.	

Assessment tool	Construct	Author and reference	Availability
Coaching Behavior Assessment System (CBAS)	Coaching behavior	Smith, R.E., Smoll, F.L., & Hunt, E. (1977). A system for the behavioral assessment of athlete coaches. *Research Quarterly, 48*, 401-407.	Contact the authors
		Smith, R.E., & Smoll, F.L. (1990). Self-esteem and children's reactions to youth sport coaching behaviors: A field study of self-enhancement processes. *Developmental Psychology, 26,* 987-993.	
		Smith, R.E., Smoll, F.L., & Christensen, D.S. (1996). Behavioral assessment and interventions in youth sports. *Behavior Modification, 20*, 3-44.	
		Horn, T.S. (1984). Expectancy effects in the interscholastic athletic setting: Methodological considerations. *Journal of Sport Psychology, 7*, 60-76.	
		Horn, T.S. (1985). Coaches' feedback and changes in children's perceptions of their physical competence. *Journal of Educational Psychology, 77*, 174-186.	
		Coatsworth, J.D., & Conroy, D.E. (2006). Enhancing the self-esteem of youth swimmers through coach training: Gender and age effects. *Psychology of Sport and Exercise, 7*, 173-192.	
Multiple versions of this tool can be found in the literature, with options for assessing coaching behaviors broadly or more specific to a single athlete. This is a direct observation tool.			
Arizona State University (ASU) Observation Instrument	Coach instructional practices	Lacy, A.C., & Darst, P.W. (1984). Evolution of a systematic observation instrument: The ASU Observation Instrument. *Journal of Teaching in Physical Education, 3*, 59-66.	Contact the authors
		Cushion, C.J., & Jones, R.L. (2001). A systematic observation of professional top-level youth soccer coaches. *Journal of Sport Behavior, 24*, 354-377.	
		Darst, P.W., Zakrajsek, D.B., & Mancini, V.H. (Eds.). (1989). *Analyzing physical education and sport instruction* (2nd ed.). Champaign, IL: Human Kinetics.	
		Brewer, C.J., & Jones, R.L. (2002). A five-stage process for establishing contextually valid systematic observation instruments: The case of rugby union. *The Sport Psychologist, 16*, 138-159.	
This instrument focuses on coach instructional behaviors during training settings.			

(continued)

Assessment Tools and Their Availability *(continued)*

Assessment tool	Construct	Author and reference	Availability
Coaching Behavior Recording Form (CBRF)	Coaching behavior	Tharp, R.G., & Gallimore, R. (1976). What a coach can teach a teacher. *Psychology Today*, January, 75-78. Darst, P.W., Zakrajsek, D.B., & Mancini, V.H. (Eds.). (1989). *Analyzing physical education and sport instruction* (2nd ed.). Champaign, IL: Human Kinetics. Bloom, G.A., Crumpton, R., & Anderson, J.E. (1999). A systematic observation study of the teaching behaviors of an expert basketball coach. *The Sport Psychologist, 13,* 157-170. Gallimore, R., & Tharp, P. (2004). What a coach can teach a teacher, 1975-2004: Reflections and reanalysis of John Wooden's teaching practices. *The Sport Psychologist, 18,* 119-137.	Contact the authors
		The CBRF is an observational tool for coach behaviors in both training and competitive settings.	
Coaching Analysis Instrument (CAI)	Coach verbal behavior	Franks, I.M., Johnson, R.B., & Sinclair, G.D. (1988). The development of a computerized coaching analysis system for recording behavior in sporting environments. *Journal of Teaching in Physical Education, 8,* 23-32. More, K.G., & Franks, I.M. (1996). Analysis and modification of verbal coaching behaviors. The usefulness of a data-driven intervention strategy. *Journal of Sports Sciences, 14,* 523-543.	Contact the authors
		This observational tool is specific to verbal comments made by the coach.	
DiSC Profile	Personality and behavioral style	Personality Profile Solutions (1997)	For purchase at www.onlinedisc profile.com
		This assessment is based on four behavioral traits: dominance, inducement, submission, and compliance. It profiles how people are likely to react in specific team, management, or leadership situations.	
Myers-Briggs Type Indicator (MBTI)	Personal style preferences	Briggs-Myers, I., & Briggs, K.C. (1985). *Myers-Briggs Type Indicator* (MBTI). Palo Alto, CA: Consulting Psychologists Press.	For purchase at www.cpp.com
		The MBTI provides information on clients' preferences, including where they draw their energy from, how they gather information, how they make decisions, and how they prefer to deal with the outside world.	
Child's Report of Parental Behavior Inventory (CRPBI)	Warmth in the parent–child sport relationship	Schwarz, J.C., Barton-Henry, M.L., & Pruzinsky, T. (1985). Assessing child-rearing behavior: A comparison of ratings made by mother, father, child, and sibling on the CRPBI. *Child Development, 56,* 462-479.	Full measure in article; http://dx.doi.org/10.2307/1129734
		This set of scales is designed to collect children's perceptions of parent global behavior. The warmth subscale was contextualized by Dorsch et al. (2016) to assess children's and parents' self-reports of warmth in the parent–child sport relationship.	

Assessment tool	Construct	Author and reference	Availability
Sport Friendship Quality Scale (SFQS) (modified)	Conflict in the parent–child sport relationship	Weiss, M.R., & Smith, A.L. (1999). Quality of youth sport friendships: Measurement development and validation. *Journal of Sport & Exercise Psychology, 21*, 145-166. Ullrich-French, S., & Smith, A.L. (2006). Perceptions of relationships with parents and peers in youth sport: Independent and combined prediction of motivational outcomes. *Psychology of Sport and Exercise, 7*, 193-214. Dorsch, T.E., Smith, A.L., & Dotterer, A.M. (2016). Individual, relationship, and context factors associated with parent support and pressure in organized youth sport. *Psychology of Sport and Exercise, 23*, 132-141.	Contact the authors
		The original measure was designed to assess friendship quality among peers in youth sport. This measure was adapted by Ullrich-French & Smith to assess perceptions of the parent–child relationship, and a three-item subscale was further contextualized by Dorsch and colleagues to assess conflict in the parent–child sport relationship.	
Positive and Negative Affect Schedule (PANAS-X)	Parent sport-related emotions	Watson, D., & Clark, L.A. (1994). *Manual for the Positive and Negative Affect Schedule (expanded form).* Iowa City, IA: University of Iowa. Dorsch, T.E., Smith, A.L., & Dotterer, A.M. (2016). Individual, relationship, and context factors associated with parent support and pressure in organized youth sport. *Psychology of Sport and Exercise, 23*, 132-141.	Contact the authors
		This measure of affect has been shown to be reliable and valid in multiple settings and with multiple individuals. It was adapted by Dorsch and colleagues to assess parents' sport-related affect in organized youth sport.	
Parental Involvement in Activities Scale (PIAS)	Parent involvement	Anderson, J.C., Funk, J.B., Elliott, R., & Smith, P. (2003). Parental support and pressure and children's extracurricular activities: Relationships with amount of involvement and affective experience of participation. *Journal of Applied Developmental Psychology, 24*, 241-257.	Full measure in article; http://dx.doi.org/10.1016/S0193-3973(03)00046-7
		This study-designed instrument was developed to measure children's perceptions of their parents' involvement in extracurricular activities. It was adapted by Dorsch and colleagues to assess parent support and pressure in organized youth sport.	
Youth Sport Behavior Assessment System (YSBAS)	Parent behavior	Apache, R.R. (2006). The behavioral assessment of parents and coaches at youth sports: Validity and reliability. *The Physical Educator, 63*, 126-133.	Full measure in article
		This behavioral assessment system scores the behaviors of parents and coaches at youth sport games.	
Tool not named	Parent goals	Dorsch, T.E., Smith, A.L., Wilson, S.R., & McDonough, M.H. (2015). Early socialization of parents through organized youth sport. *Sport, Exercise, and Performance Psychology, 4*, 3-18.	Full measure in article; http://dx.doi.org/10.1037/spy0000021
		This qualitatively developed rubric categorizes parent goals for their children in organized youth sport.	

(continued)

ASSESSMENT TOOLS

Assessment Tools and Their Availability *(continued)*

Assessment tool	Construct	Author and reference	Availability
Tool not named	Parent involvement	Holt, N.L., Tamminen, K.A., Black, D.E., Sehn, Z.L., & Wall, M.P. (2008). Parental involvement in competitive youth sport settings. *Psychology of Sport and Exercise, 9,* 663-685.	Full measure in article; http://dx.doi .org/10.1016/ j.psychsport .2007.08.001
	This qualitatively developed rubric codes parental comments on a continuum from more supportive to more controlling.		
Parent Observation Instrument for Sport Events (POISE)	Parent comments	Kidman, L., McKenzie, A., & McKenzie, B. (1999). The nature and target of parents' comments during youth sport competitions. *Journal of Sport Behavior, 22,* 54-68.	Full measure in article
	This systematic observation instrument assesses the nature and target of verbal comments made by parents at youth sport events.		

Chapter Takeaways

- The interconnectedness of athletes, coaches, teams, and parents is vital to maximizing athletes' experiences in sport.

- You should consider the purpose of the assessment, as well as who is in the best position to provide an accurate assessment of the coach to achieve its purpose.

- Coaches' personal characteristics, objective behaviors, and athlete outcomes may be assessed.

- Misalignment can occur by not being clear about the purpose of the assessment, by selecting raters without the appropriate knowledge and experience to provide accurate information on the assessment, or by selecting a tool and modifying it in a way that reduces its psychometric qualities.

- Team assessments can help athletes maximize their practice efforts and competitive performances, help coaches improve their pedagogical skills and leadership, and help teams work together, communicate, and resolve conflict.

- Assessment data should provide an understanding of the strengths and weaknesses of a team, leading to tangible change goals and actionable steps to accomplish those goals.

- Debriefing after an assessment is a critical component of the process.

- Youth sport is a powerful setting for investigating developmental outcomes in youth.

- As a result of children's participation in sport, parents become observers and participants, creating the potential for parents to undergo changes in their own thoughts, emotions, and behaviors, as well as their relationships with others.

- Parent assessment is fundamental to developing interventions and creating policies that promote athletics as a positive experience.

- Parent assessment affords a deeper knowledge of parents' influence on their children's athletic experience, allowing for a more integrated understanding of the sport system.

CHAPTER 12
Talent Identification

Barbara B. Meyer, PhD, CC-AASP

Stacy L. Gnacinski, PhD

Teresa B. Fletcher, PhD, LPC

It is increasingly common for professional sport organizations and elite sport teams to include sport psychology consultants in the talent identification (TID), or drafting, of players. Sport psychology consultants may be involved throughout the entire draft process, participating in dissemination and interpretation of psychological assessments, one-on-one or group interviews with athletes, and draft-day decisions. Consultants may also be involved on an intermittent or as-needed basis, answering questions from front-office personnel (e.g., general managers [GMs], coaches, scouts) about the reliability and validity of psychological assessments or facilitating discussions among front-office personnel on how to interpret and act upon disparate data (e.g., performance metrics, scouting reports, psychological assessments).

Despite recognizing the importance of psychological factors in performance achievement, the inclusion of psychological data in TID processes has generated concerns among GMs and coaches as well as sport psychology scholars and practitioners (Anshel & Lidor, 2012). Regardless of scholarly concerns about the inclusion of psychology in the TID process, the reality is that psychological data will be available to elite sport organizations whether consultants are involved in the process or not. Contrary to explanations typically provided for opting out of TID (Anshel & Lidor, 2012), we have observed that a complete lack of consultant engagement in TID often proves detrimental to the athletes, the sport organization, and the reputation of the sport psychology profession itself. As such, we assert that sport psychology consultants must look beyond the concerns that preclude our involvement in TID practices and look toward solutions that facilitate our ethical involvement. We further contend that using appropriately collected and interpreted psychological data as part of an integrated TID process puts athletes at no greater risk of deselection than other types of data typically used (e.g., medical history, performance metrics, physical attributes). To demonstrate how sport psychology generally and consultants specifically can contribute to the integrated TID process, this chapter explores an overview of TID models and research; the assessment of psychosocial factors linked to TID; and implications for consultants working with athletes, teams, and sport organizations.

Talent Identification Models and Research

Over the past 30 years, there has been considerable debate about the definition of TID (Anshel & Lidor, 2012). Consistent with currently recognized talent models (Abbott & Collins,

2004), this chapter operationally defines *TID* as the identification of athletes with "the greatest potential to excel in sport" by coaches and affiliate sport organizations (Abbott & Collins, 2004, p. 395).

In the earliest TID programs, sport organizations and national governing bodies embraced myopic, unidimensional, and reductionistic perspectives on sport talent, whereby young athletes were evaluated once on a few characteristics (e.g., anthropometrics, physical attributes, current performance) and subsequently labeled as talented or not (Bar-Or, 1975; Gimbel, 1976). Within these early TID programs, and even within early talent development (TDE) programs, psychology was rarely if ever included in any capacity (e.g., assessment, development). Given the complexity of sport performance, as well as the limitations associated with attempting to predict future elite-level performance among young children, these early perspectives and one-off approaches were met with theoretical and empirical concern among TID scholars (Abbott & Collins, 2004; Durand-Bush & Salmela, 2001; Vaeyens, Güllich, Warr, & Philippaerts, 2009). Sport psychologists also were criticized during this time for their insensitivity to the nature versus nurture debate and for their lack of consideration of developmental processes in talent acquisition (Régnier, Salmela, & Russell, 1993, as cited in Durand-Bush & Salmela, 2001).

Underpinned by the seminal TDE work of Bloom (1985) and Côté (1999), Abbott and Collins broke new theoretical ground in 2004 by proposing that TID models be adapted to embrace a multidimensional, constructivist perspective of sport talent that includes psychobehavioral (e.g., goal setting, monitoring and evaluation) factors of performance. Abbott and Collins further suggested that including psychobehavioral factors in TID models was necessary in order to bridge the gap between TID and TDE in practice. Though this theoretical contention was well received by TID scholars and practitioners in sport psychology, the most recently proposed models of elite sport TID (Talent Identification and Talent Promotion, United Kingdom [Vaeyens et al. 2009]; Foundations, Talent, Elite and Mastery [FTEM; Gulbin,

Croser, Morley, & Weissensteiner, 2013]) lack theoretical and empirical support for application in research and practice settings (Collins & MacNamara, 2011; MacNamara & Collins, 2014; Pinder, Renshaw, & Davids, 2013). As such, TID programs in sport remain minimally effective, with research pointing toward low to moderate program efficacy (Vaeyens et al., 2009), along with talent wastage or athlete harm during TDE (MacNamara & Collins, 2015). Taken together, the criticisms of existing TID models and low efficacy of TID programs highlight the ongoing challenges associated with the selection, assessment, and interpretation of all TID variables in sport.

Consistent with these challenges, and despite the fact that psychological characteristics and psychosocial behaviors are widely accepted as mechanisms that facilitate progression across stages of sport TDE (Abbott & Collins, 2004; Durand-Bush & Salmela, 2001; MacNamara & Collins, 2015), the selection, assessment, and interpretation of psychological variables in a TID context continue to spark controversy among consultants. Stemming from the work of sport psychology pioneers Coleman Griffith, Bruce Ogilvie, and Thomas Tutko, and fueled by ethical concerns about psychological measurement and profiling (Anshel & Lidor, 2012), many consultants remain hesitant to participate in TID. Reservations aside, and consistent with the preceding suggestion that psychological variables will play a role in the TID process whether consultants like it or not, current thoughts in the field are that sport psychology professionals should take a seat at the TID table and facilitate a scientifically sound process of psychological assessment. According to MacNamara and Collins (2015), the appropriate use of psychological data in TID is long overdue, and "future work in TID must begin to consider the full range of factors underpinning both successful progression along the talent pathway as well as those that may negatively impact on development leading to talent wastage or, more seriously, human damage" (p. 77). By including psychological data in TID, we may be able to bridge the gap between TID and TDE in a way that benefits the athletes and enhances the efficacy of TID programs (Abbott & Collins, 2004). With this in mind, the following section outlines a process by which consultants can ethically and effectively participate in the selection, assessment, and interpretation of psychological variables in TID.

Assessment of Psychosocial Factors Linked to Talent in Sport

In light of the ethical concerns around the assessment of psychosocial factors for TID purposes, we preface this section with our professional and philosophical beliefs about how psychological data should be used by sport teams and organizations in TID contexts. First and foremost, we believe that psychological TID assessment must be linked to the TDE process and must not be used in isolation to select or deselect athletes from draft or team consideration. Much the same way that a National Basketball Association (NBA) team will assign a staff member to work with the first-round draft selection on his technical weaknesses (e.g., free throws, hook shots), similar resources must be in place to facilitate the development of any identified psychological weaknesses in TDE environments.

Second, we do not support the use of clinical assessments for TID purposes under any circumstances. In addition to the fact that many consultants are not qualified to engage in mental health assessment, it would be unethical and perhaps illegal to include information about an athlete's mental health status in the TID process. Should a sport team or organization wish to engage in mental health assessment in a genuine effort to identify appropriate support systems (e.g., licensed counselors), the assessment should be conducted by a clinically trained and certified professional after athlete selection procedures have been finalized (see chapter 5).

Finally, we believe that consultant involvement in the TID process should be preceded by a comprehensive needs assessment with the team or sport organization so as to understand their goals for and expectations of the engagement (see chapter 16). For example, if the team is interested in knowing how athletes respond to stress, we would select specific psychological inventories and behavioral observation protocols to meet that goal. The needs assessment provides an opportunity to educate other professionals on the team about the type of information that can be gleaned from psychological inventories and to discuss best practices for integrating these psychological data with physical and technical data to create a comprehensive performance profile and development plan for each athlete.

Informed by these philosophical underpinnings, we now describe a sample of widely accepted methods for the scientifically sound assessment of psychological and psychosocial factors that are relevant for TID. The purpose of this section is not to provide an all-encompassing review of assessment methods, nor is it to provide a rigorous psychometric evaluation of any specific tool; rather, its purpose is to provide a foundation of knowledge and a set of tools for consultants attempting to navigate the TID process. In addition to matching your selection of assessments to the criteria outlined in the preliminary needs assessment of a team, we recommend that you consider including multiple and related assessment methods in TID so as to provide the most complete representation possible of the athlete's psychological strengths and areas for development. What follows is an overview of inventories (i.e., general trait, sport specific, psychological skills use, comprehensive), behavioral observation methods, and qualitative interview methods that can be used in TID. Unless otherwise indicated, all assessments in this chapter have sound psychometric properties, including acceptable validity, reliability, and internal consistency.

General Trait Inventories

Some of the controversy about consultant involvement in TID stems from the fact that the inclusion of personality or trait assessments in the selection process has typically been viewed as unethical and unfair to athletes (Abbott & Collins, 2004; Anshel & Lidor, 2012). We agree that general trait assessments are unethical and unfair when administered alone; however, they can provide valuable psychological context for interpreting the physical and technical data collected by other professionals involved in TID and for informing the development of performance interventions delivered by consultants (Harmison, 2011). With this in mind, a sample of general trait assessments (i.e., personality, anxiety, mood) is discussed next.

Personality

Two of the most common inventories for assessment of personality in sport and other domains are the Mini-Markers (Saucier, 1994) and the 16 Personality Factors Questionnaire (16PF; Cattell, Cattell, & Cattell, 1993). Though the reliability and validity of both inventories have been established across populations and cultures (Cattell, 1996; Palmer & Loveland, 2004), Saucier's Mini-Markers may be preferred by consultants given the relative ease of administration and scoring, length, simplicity, and availability (Palmer & Loveland, 2004). Depending on the specific population or athlete characteristics, the 16PF may be a more viable option for administration, such as among individuals with a lower level of education or reading comprehension (e.g., fifth grade) (Cattell & Mead, 2008).

It is important to remind others involved in the TID process (e.g., coaches, scouts) that personality alone is a poor predictor of future performance outcomes (Abbott & Collins, 2004; Anshel & Lidor, 2012). That said, research suggests knowledge of an athlete's personality can inform individualized strategies to enhance TDE processes (Harmison, 2011), predict potential training or performance behaviors (Woodman, Zourbanos, Hardy, Beattie, & McQuillan, 2010), and provide insight into the athlete–coach relationship (Kenow & Williams, 1999). With that in mind, it would be advantageous for athletes to have their sport-specific psychological, physical, and technical data evaluated in the context of their personality scores, thereby facilitating holistic TID and TDE processes. Similarly, it would be beneficial for team management and staff to take each athlete's personality characteristics into account when designing and implementing individualized development plans.

General Anxiety

The two most common inventories for assessment of general anxiety in sport are the State-Trait Anxiety Inventory (STAI; Spielberger, 1983) and the State-Trait Inventory for Cognitive and Somatic Anxiety (STICSA; Ree, French, MacLeod, & Locke, 2008). Although the STAI has been referenced in more than 3,500 publications and has long been considered the gold standard in anxiety research, the STICSA may be more appropriate for measuring cognitive and somatic anxiety in adult populations (Grös, Antony, Simms, & McCabe, 2007; Roberts, Hart, & Eastwood, 2015).

It is known that trait, cognitive, and somatic anxiety can influence training behaviors and performance (Hayslip, Petrie, MacIntire, & Jones, 2010; Woodman & Hardy, 2003). Because of the well-established link between anxiety and performance, an athlete with anxious tendencies should be encouraged to implement psychological strategies in an effort to mitigate any undesired effect of anxiety on performance. From a TID perspective, athletes demonstrating high levels of anxiety and high scores in psychological skills use (e.g., relaxation, imagery) maintain psychological profile strength and the potential for TDE as compared with athletes demonstrating high levels of anxiety and low scores in psychological skills use, who may present with more areas for psychological development prior to and during the transition into elite sport.

Mood

Two of the most common mood assessments in sport are the Profile of Mood States (POMS; McNair, Lorr, & Droppleman, 1971) and the Brunel Mood Scale (BRUMS; Terry, Lane, Lane, & Keohane, 1999). Though both inventories are psychometrically sound, the POMS has been the inventory of choice in much of the sport psychology literature, as well as in recent literature examining the link between psychological recovery and performance (Bresciani et al., 2011).

In the context of TID, weak links between mood profile and sport performance have been identified (Beedie, Terry, & Lane, 2000; Rowley, Landers, Kyllo, & Etnier, 1995). Regardless of which inventory is selected, the transient nature of mood means that the timing of mood assessment should be considered during administration (Terry, 1995). A single assessment of mood in a cross-sectional collection format (e.g., sport combine or draft scenario) will be of minimal value in predicting performance in the months or years ahead. Rather, it will be more valuable to assess mood longitudinally (e.g., across a competitive season, in conjunction with yearly scouting reports) in order to understand mood tendencies and variation during particularly challenging or successful phases of sport participation. This recommendation to monitor psychological data longitudinally is consistent with those of TID scholars (Abbott & Collins, 2004) and likely holds for other psychological assessment inventories as well.

Sport-Specific Inventories

To complement general trait assessments, which provide psychological context to other performance-related data (Harmison, 2011), sport-specific assessments provide information about how an athlete may think or behave during competitive situations. Sport-specific psychological characteristics, unlike general trait characteristics, demonstrate stronger and more direct links to sport performance, thereby providing information closely related to athlete thoughts, emotions, and behaviors before, during, and after competition. The following paragraphs discuss assessments of achievement goal orientation, mental toughness, competitive anxiety, confidence, and psychological skills.

Achievement Goal Orientation

The most common and appropriate way to assess achievement goal orientation (i.e., the extent to which one is motivated to master a task and demonstrate improvement or the extent to which one is motivated to win and demonstrate superiority over others) is the Task and Ego Orientation in Sport Questionnaire (TEOSQ; Duda, 1989; see chapter 7 for more details). In the context of TID, a task or mastery orientation has been associated with persistence, positive affect, challenge seeking, achievement-related behaviors, self-worth, confidence, enjoyment, and perceptions of competence (Duda, 2005), all indirect correlates of performance.

By contrast, the role of an ego or outcome orientation in the acquisition and maintenance of skills related to elite sport performance is less apparent. Some literature demonstrates that ego orientation is necessary at the most elite levels of sport to match the competitive environment, while other literature demonstrates that high levels of ego orientation alone may be linked to low levels of perceived competence and maladaptive achievement-related behaviors (Duda, 2005). Given the orthogonal nature of the two orientations, it would be optimal for an athlete to display high levels of task orientation with or without accompanying high levels of ego orientation (Duda, 2005). Due to the importance of a task orientation in the pursuit of performance excellence in sport (Williams, 1998), use of the TEOSQ during TID may provide valuable information for identifying athletes who already embrace a task orientation, as well as identifying athletes who would benefit from strategies aimed at shifting from ego to task orientation.

Mental Toughness

Two common inventories for the assessment of mental toughness in sport are the Sports Mental Toughness Questionnaire (SMTQ; Sheard, Golby, & van Wersch, 2009) and the Mental Toughness Questionnaire (MTQ48; Perry, Clough, Crust, Earle, & Nicholls, 2013) (see the chapter-ending table Assessment Tools and Their Availability for more details). For consultants who want to compare the ease of administration and psychometric properties of these two inventories for TID purposes, we refer you to two papers (Crust & Swann, 2011; Gucciardi, Mallet, Hanrahan, & Gordon, 2011) that contain in-depth comparisons and critical analyses of the inventories. Although some links between mental toughness and sport performance have been identified (Crust & Clough, 2005; Jones, Hanton, & Connaughton, 2002), the literature is inconclusive given the ongoing debate around the operational definition of mental toughness within our profession (Jones et al., 2002; Loehr, 1986; Perry et al., 2013; Sheard et al., 2009). Due to the absence of a theoretically sound mental toughness construct, and despite the popular use of the term by the lay public, consultants should be mindful of the challenges associated with interpreting and disseminating data from mental toughness assessments to coaches and other team personnel.

Competitive Anxiety

Two of the more common assessments for competitive anxiety in sport are the Competitive State Anxiety Inventory-2 (CSAI-2; Martens, Burton, Vealey, Bump, & Smith, 1990) and the Sport Competition Anxiety Test (SCAT; Martens, 1977). That said, research findings linking CSAI-2 and SCAT results to sport performance are equivocal at best (Martens, Burton, Vealey, Bump, & Smith, 2002; Martens, Gill, Scanlan, & Simon, 2002; see chapter 7 for more details). When interpreted alongside results of trait anxiety measures (e.g., STAI, STICSA) in a TID context, competitive anxiety assessments may provide valuable information about the potential for self-handicapping behaviors and achievement avoidance behaviors often associated with excessive anxiety and fear of failure (MacNamara & Collins, 2015), thereby illuminating the need for an athlete to engage in training for intensity regulation (e.g., relaxation, mindfulness, imagery). These competitive anxiety assessments may also help distinguish athletes with particularly high thresholds for anxiety in challenging situations, a potential advantage when paired with other desirable characteristics (e.g., confidence, task orientation) necessary for optimal TDE (MacNamara & Collins, 2015).

Confidence

The most common assessment for sport-specific confidence is the State Sport-Confidence Inventory (SSCI; Vealey, 1986). Unique to the constructs and assessments discussed thus far, strong links have been identified between sport confidence and performance (Craft, Magyar, Becker, & Feltz, 2003; Woodman & Hardy, 2003). As a result of the strong link between sport confidence and performance, the inclusion of sport confidence assessments in TID is appropriate. Given the susceptibility of self-confidence measures to social desirability bias generally (Vealey, 2002) and TID assessment specifically, consultants might consider including a Marlowe-Crowne Social Desirability Scale (Crowne & Marlowe, 1960) or other method

during administration, triangulating quantitative data with behavioral observation of the athlete, and triangulating quantitative data with qualitative interviews of those who know the athlete well.

Psychological Skills Use

The three most common inventories for assessment of psychological skills use in sport are the Test of Performance Strategies 2 (TOPS-2; Hardy, Roberts, Thomas, & Murphy, 2010), Athletic Coping Skills Inventory (ACSI-28; Smith, Schultz, Smoll, & Ptacek, 1995), and Ottawa Mental Skills Assessment Tool (OMSAT-3*; Durand-Bush, Salmela, & Greens-Demers, 2001). A distinct advantage of the TOPS-2 is that psychological skills use is assessed in both training and performance contexts (Hardy et al., 2010), a point of consideration for TID given that successful elite athletes report the use of psychological skills more effectively and consistently than their less successful counterparts (MacNamara, Button, & Collins, 2010; Taylor, Gould, & Rolo, 2008). Consultants involved in TID should focus on the identification of athletes who already report psychological skills use in training and competition or those who may benefit from integrating psychological skills into their existing training or performance routines. In other words, assessment of psychological skills use during TID is important because results may protect athletes with strong psychological skills use from being deselected for physical or technical deficiencies alone, while also revealing psychological skills to target for development among prospects with top physical ratings.

Comprehensive Inventories

Rather than constructing a comprehensive TID assessment by combining multiple instruments, an alternative approach may be to administer an instrument such as the Psychological Characteristics of Developing Excellence Questionnaire (PCDEQ; MacNamara & Collins, 2011). The PCDEQ was developed to assess both the possession of psychological traits and skills (i.e., psychological characteristics of developing excellence) and the ability to deploy these

PCDEs when needed. Though the authors of the instrument "are *not* suggesting the use of this questionnaire as a crude selection tool" (p. 1283), we believe it would be appropriate to use the PCDEQ alongside physical and technical skill assessments in environments that link TID to TDE processes.

Assessment in Action

Standardizing Assessment Procedures for Maximum Benefit

To obtain the most accurate understanding of the psychosocial makeup of each prospective draft choice and thereby make meaningful comparisons across prospective draft choices to facilitate TID, sport psychology consultants should ensure that assessment inventories are administered in a standardized and supervised manner. Specifically, each athlete should complete the inventory or battery of inventories in the same format (i.e., paper and pencil, electronic), in the same environment (e.g., quiet office or meeting room), and under the supervision of someone trained in psychological assessment who can answer questions and provide clarification. The results can then serve as one source of reliable and valid data, among many, in the TID process.

Behavioral Observation

In addition to psychological inventories, behavioral observation may be a useful type of assessment in TID. Traditionally, behavioral observation in TID is conducted by front-office and scouting staff for the purpose of assessing technical skill development across time. Although scouts and other team personnel may monitor psychological behaviors (e.g., frequent outbursts of aggression or frustration), they are unlikely to be trained in behavioral observation or analysis the way a consultant would be. In the experience of the first author, observation of psychological behavior is frequently used to augment TID data in both the physical and technical domains (where it is triangulated within and between these domains), but it is less frequently used in triangulation with other assessments (e.g., inventories) in the psychological domain. To facilitate behavioral observation within the psychological domain, consultants should consider a process such as the following.

In their book on single-subject research methods in sport, Barker, McCarthy, Jones, and Moran (2011) outline a process for observation that may be appropriate in a TID context. First, consultants and associated TID professionals should select and operationally define behaviors critical to TDE and sport performance. Behaviors of interest might include those associated with PCDEs or behaviors specific to the culture of the sport organization. Second, methods of behavioral observation should be determined. These might include direct observations (e.g., frequency of behaviors observed, rates of behaviors elicited), interval recordings (e.g., data collection during specific intervals across time), self-report measures of behavior (e.g., questionnaires), performance profiling (Butler & Hardy, 1992), videotaping, and psychophysiological assessment (e.g., biofeedback). A selection of these methods (e.g., direct observations, videotaping) can be easily integrated within current scouting practices. Third, consideration should be given to measures of agreement or reliability across observers (e.g., GM and consultant) and observation time points (e.g., the athlete in a game and the athlete in the weight room). Calculations of percent agreement are simple to conduct in the field, are easily interpreted by members of the TID staff, and provide a level of confidence in the precision of psychologically oriented interpretations of behavior. For additional information on behavioral observations and methods, we refer you to chapter 9 of this book.

As mentioned previously, results of behavioral observation assessments should be triangulated with physical and technical data, as well as with other types of psychological data (e.g., inventory responses). Although inventories and qualitative interviews are effective means of collecting psychological data, it is our belief that behavioral observation is invaluable for confirming or refuting previous interpretations of desirable or undesirable psychological characteristics in TID. For example, if commitment to sport was identified as an important psychological characteristic during the needs analysis, the consultant might recommend that the MTQ48 (Perry et al., 2013) be administered and behavioral observation of practice attendance, consistency of effort, independent preparation, early arrivals to practice, and resilience after setbacks be used to confirm or refute MTQ48 responses.

Qualitative Interviews

Another mode of assessment often used in the TID process is the qualitative interview. Although qualitative interviews have long been used in nonsport domains to collect and assess information that may be predictive of employee performance (Goho & Blackman, 2006; Huffcutt, 2010; Roulin, Bangerter, & Yerly, 2011), this method of assessment is rarely maximized in sport draft or TID processes. This may be due to the fact that, historically, interviews have been conducted by team scouts, GMs, and coaches who do not have professional training in qualitative data collection or analysis. Consequently, much of the time allocated to the actual interview is wasted asking nondistinguishing questions for which the team already has answers (e.g., anthropometric data, business details) and engaging in aimless small talk. An opportunity clearly exists to maximize formal and informal interviews so as to triangulate data collected via psychological inventories and behavioral observations. By standardizing the interview protocol using empirically grounded methods, interviewers may be able to gather trustworthy information regarding how, for example, athletes respond to challenging or anxiety-inducing evaluative situations (for which they have not been prepped by an agent or adviser), as well as how their interpersonal style or leadership skills will fit within an established team culture.

To the best of our knowledge, there are few exemplars in the sport psychology literature for developing and then conducting a structured or established interview protocol. Those that do exist represent an interview protocol most appropriate for intake sessions or initial client evaluations (Andersen, 2000; Gardner & Moore, 2005; Taylor & Schneider, 1992). That said, Côté, Ericsson, and Law (2005) suggest that interview procedures can be used to assess deliberate practice behaviors (i.e., expert-performance framework; Ericsson & Smith, 1991), as well as to trace developmental processes to expert performance (Côté, Baker, & Abernethy, 2003). Côté et al. (2005) then delineate a standardized method for eliciting reliable, discriminant, and verifiable historical information relevant to training- and practice-related behaviors that may be pertinent to long-term talent development.

With Côté's (2005) suggestion in mind, general interview methods for qualitative research have been used to glean information regarding constructs such as those outlined in the General Trait Inventories and Sport-Specific Inventories sections of this chapter. For instance, qualitative researchers have been able to explain both process- and performance-related psychological phenomena such as intensity regulation (i.e., choking; Hill & Shaw, 2013), resilience (Fletcher & Sarkar, 2012), and imagery use (Driediger, Hall, & Callow, 2006), as well as psychosocial competencies and environmental conditions of sport success (Holt & Dunn, 2004). Over the past decade, qualitative research experts in sport psychology have refined methodologies and articulated clear guidelines to ensure the utmost quality of data collected (Holt & Tamminen, 2010; Smith & Caddick, 2012; Sparks & Smith, 2014). In the absence of existing TID interview protocols, it is recommended that consultants review the general interview literature as well as the sport-specific literature on qualitative research methodology before engaging in TID interviews.

In addition to reviewing the literature, consultants should be mindful of classic interview response errors and biases that may reduce the objectivity of interviews. Although the most effective way to minimize response errors and bias is to ensure you are well-trained in interview procedures (Chapman & Zweig, 2005; Van Iddekinge, Raymark, Eidson, & Attenweiler, 2004), you might also consider planning for other factors (e.g., eye contact, postural changes, facial expressions, social desirability effect) that can influence the objectivity of the interview (Martin, Bowen, & Hunt, 2002; Roulin et al., 2011). We also remind consultants involved in draft or similar lengthy TID processes that interview objectivity is greatly influenced by the number of interviews conducted back to back, as well as the total time spent interviewing during an assessment day (Simonsohn & Gino, 2013). For those seeking more information on the sport-specific interview process, see chapter 8 of this book.

Implications for Consultants

The introductory section of this chapter exposed several concerns about the meaningful inclusion of psychological assessment in sport TID. We acknowledge that engagement in TID is not easy and holds risks for consultants, and it requires a significant amount of preparation and collaboration with sport teams and organizations to uphold a high standard of ethics (refer to chapter 3) and scientific rigor throughout the process. However, psychological data will continue to be collected and interpreted regardless of consultant involvement, often to the detriment of both the athletes assessed and the team using the data. The ethical and practical consequences of consultant nonengagement in TID may prove more detrimental than any consequences that occur as a result of consultant engagement. With that in mind, we identify additional implications for professional practice to assist you in preparing for ethical engagement in elite sport TID.

First, ownership of psychological data must be considered and agreed upon before data collection begins. Though this may not be possible in all TID environments, we recommend that consultants retain ownership of the data; removal of consultant involvement from the organization would leave sensitive data with teams and organizations that may be unable or unqualified to work with it.

Second, psychological assessment and interpretation should only be conducted by consultants or similarly trained professionals. Just as a sport psychology consultant would not conduct bench press evaluations or evaluate baseball-throwing mechanics, neither should strength and conditioning personnel, coaches, or other staff members conduct and interpret psychological assessments. The fact that commercialized psychological assessments with automated response systems are becoming increasingly available to teams (e.g., Flippen Profile, Pondera Virtual Coach) makes this admonition even more salient. The ease of obtaining psychological data of unknown quality prompts our suggestion for consultants to conduct preassessment conversations with front-office staff to educate them about collecting psychological data in the most scientifically sound and ethical manner possible.

Third, we must remain mindful that some professional sport organizations (e.g., FIFA) and teams are attempting to select and contract athletes as early as nine years of age. Most of the data collection methods suggested in this chapter have been validated in adult populations. Thus, just as we have observed with the effects of physical maturity on TID selections, the effects of psychological maturity on TID selections must also be considered as they relate to psychological assessment. To account for effects of maturity across domains, longitudinal and interdisciplinary approaches (i.e., collaboration between disciplines) are far more effective in TID than cross-sectional and multidisciplinary approaches (i.e., discrete assessments by each discipline).

Finally, we want to make clear that we are not proposing that any of the inventories, behavioral observation, or interview methods described in this chapter were developed for the rudimentary selection or deselection of athletes in TID. Rather, we are suggesting that administering combinations of psychometrically sound assessments may facilitate comprehensive psychological profile interpretations that can be included in the holistic assessment of sport talent (i.e., physical, technical, psychological). In facilitating scientifically sound methods of psychological data collection and interpretation, we can begin to bridge the gap between TID and TDE practices for the optimization of athlete health and performance.

Assessment Tools and Their Availability

Assessment tool	Construct	Author and reference	Availability
Mini-Markers	Personality	Saucier, G. (1994). Mini-Markers: A brief version of Goldberg's unipolar big-five markers. *Journal of Personality Assessment, 63*, 506-516.	Full measure in article; http://dx.doi.org/10.1207/s15327752jpa6303_8
		This 40-item tool assesses the Big Five personality traits. It has been used in various adult populations and cultures and is relatively easy to administer and score.	
16 Personality Factors Questionnaire (16PF)	Personality	Cattell, R.B., Cattell, A.K., & Cattell, H.E.P. (1993). *16PF Fifth Edition questionnaire*. Champaign, IL: Institute for Personality and Ability Testing.	For purchase at www.pearsonclinical.com
		This 185-item tool assesses 16 primary personality traits. It has been used in various youth and adult populations and cultures. It takes approximately 30-50 minutes to administer, and responses can be scored by hand or by submission to the publisher for automatic computer scoring. This tool is suitable for populations with lower levels of education or reading comprehension.	
State-Trait Anxiety Inventory (STAI)	Anxiety	Spielberger, C.D., Gorsuch, R.L., & Lushene, R. (1970). *STAI manual*. Palo Alto, CA: Consulting Psychologists Press.	For purchase at www.mindgarden.com
		The STAI assesses state and trait levels of general anxiety. It has been used in various populations and cultures and is relatively easy to administer and score. Recent criticisms have emerged around its construct validity, specifically as it relates to the depression symptomatology of anxiety being measured.	
State-Trait Inventory for Cognitive and Somatic Anxiety (STICSA)	Anxiety	Ree, M.J., French, D., MacLeod, C., & Locke, V. (2008). Distinguishing cognitive and somatic dimensions of state and trait anxiety: Development and validation of the State-Trait Inventory for Cognitive and Somatic Anxiety (STICSA). *Behavioral and Cognitive Psychotherapy, 36*, 313-332.	Full measure in article; http://dx.doi.org/10.1017/S1352465808004232
		The STICSA assesses both state and trait symptoms of cognitive and somatic anxiety. It has been used in various populations and cultures and is relatively easy to administer and score.	
Profile of Mood States 2nd Edition (POMS 2)	Mood	McNair, D.M., Lorr, M., & Droppleman, L.F. (1971). *ETIS manual for the Profile of Mood States*. San Diego: Educational and Industrial Testing Service.	For purchase at www.mhs.com
		This 65-item tool assesses mood states. It has been used in various adult populations and cultures and is relatively easy to administer and score. Short forms (e.g., 30 items, 35 items) have been validated.	
Brunel Mood Scale (BRUMS)	Mood	Lane, A.M., & Lane, H.J. (2002). Predictive effectiveness of mood measures. *Perceptual and Motor Skills, 94*, 785-791.	Request a copy at www.moodprofiling.com
		This 24-item tool assesses mood states. It has been used in various adolescent and adult populations and cultures and is relatively easy to administer and score.	

Assessment tool	Construct	Author and reference	Availability
Task and Ego Orientation in Sport Questionnaire (TEOSQ)	Achievement goal orientation	Duda, J.L. (1989). The relationship between task and ego orientation and the perceived purpose of sport among male and female high school athletes. *Journal of Sport and Exercise Psychology, 11*, 318-335.	Full measure in article; http://dx.doi.org/10.1123/jsep.11.3.318
This 13-item tool assesses levels of task and ego orientation. It has been used in various youth and adult athlete populations and cultures and is relatively easy to administer and score.			
Sports Mental Toughness Questionnaire (SMTQ)	Mental toughness	Sheard, M., Golby, J., & van Wersch, A. (2009). Progress toward construct validation of the Sports Mental Toughness Questionnaire (SMTQ). *European Journal of Psychological Assessment, 25*, 186-193.	Full measure in article; http://dx.doi.org/10.1027/1015-5759.25.3.186
This 14-item tool assesses levels of mental toughness. It has been used in various adult athlete populations and is relatively easy to administer and score.			
Mental Toughness Questionnaire (MTQ48)	Mental toughness	Perry, J.L., Clough, P.J., Crust, L., Earle, K., & Nicholls, A.R. (2013). Factorial validity of the Mental Toughness Questionnaire 48. *Personality and Individual Differences, 54*, 587-592.	For purchase at http://aqrinternational.co.uk/mtq48-mental-toughness-questionnaire
This 48-item tool assesses four facets of mental toughness (i.e., control, commitment, challenge, confidence). It has been used in various adult athlete populations and cultures.			
State Sport-Confidence Inventory (SSCI)	Confidence	Vealey, R.S. (1986). Conceptualization of sport-confidence and competitive orientation: Preliminary investigation and instrument development. *Journal of Sport Psychology, 8*, 221-246.	Full measure in article; http://dx.doi.org/10.1123/jsp.8.3.221
This 13-item tool assesses state sport confidence. It has been used in various adolescent and adult athlete populations and is relatively easy to administer and score.			
Test of Performance Strategies (TOPS 2)	Psychological skills use	Hardy, L., Roberts, R., Thomas, P.R., & Murphy, S.M. (2010). Test of Performance Strategies (TOPS): Instrument refinement using confirmatory factor analysis. *Psychology of Sport and Exercise, 11*, 27-35.	Full measure in article; http://dx.doi.org/10.1016/j.psychsport.2009.04.007
This 64-item measure assesses ability and frequency of using psychological skills in practice and competition environments. It has been used in various adolescent and adult athlete populations and is relatively easy to administer and score.			
Athletic Coping Skills Inventory-28 (ACSI-28)	Psychological skills use	Smith, R.E., Schultz, R.W., Smoll, F.L., & Ptacek, J.T. (1995). Development and validation of a multidimensional measure of sport-specific psychological skills: The Athletic Coping Skills Inventory-28. *Journal of Sport & Exercise Psychology, 17*, 379-398.	Full measure in article; http://dx.doi.org/10.1123/jsep.17.4.379
This 28-item measure assesses classes of psychological coping. It has been used in various adolescent and adult athlete populations and is relatively easy to administer and score.			

(continued)

Assessment Tools and Their Availability *(continued)*

Assessment tool	Construct	Author and reference	Availability
Ottawa Mental Skills Assessment Tool (OMSAT-3*)	Psychological skills use	Durand-Bush, N., Salmela, J.H., & Greens-Demers, I. (2001). The Ottawa Mental Skills Assessment Tool (OMSAT-3*). *The Sport Psychologist, 15,* 1-19.	For purchase at www.mindeval.com/en/
	This 48-item tool assesses mental strengths and weaknesses of athletes. It has been used in various youth and adult athlete populations and cultures.		
Psychological Characteristics of Developing Excellence Questionnaire (PCDEQ)	Psychological traits, skills, and skills use	MacNamara, Á., & Collins, D. (2011). Development and initial validation of the Psychological Characteristics of Developing Excellence Questionnaire. *Journal of Sport Sciences, 29,* 1273-1286.	Full measure in article; http://dx.doi.org/10.1080/02640414.2011.589468
	This 59-item tool assesses the possession and deployment of characteristics necessary for developing sport excellence. It has been validated in adolescent athlete populations. Given its recent emergence in sport research, few studies have involved this tool to date. It is relatively easy to administer and score.		

Chapter Takeaways

- Consultants can and should play an important and ethically appropriate role in the selection, assessment, and interpretation of psychological variables in a TID context.

- By including psychological data in TID, we may be able to bridge the gap between TID and TDE in a way that benefits the athletes and enhances the efficacy of TID programs.

- Psychological inventories, behavioral observation, and qualitative interviews can be used to triangulate with TID data in the physical and technical domains, as well as with other sources of data in the psychological domain.

- Assessment of psychological traits, such as personality, provides valuable psychological context for interpreting the physical and technical data collected by other professionals involved in TID and for informing the development of performance interventions delivered by consultants.

- Sport-specific psychological inventories provide information about how an athlete may think, behave, or react during competitive situations.

- Observation of psychological behaviors can augment TID data in both the physical and technical domains, as well as in other types of psychological assessments (i.e., psychological inventories, qualitative interviews).

- Opportunities exist to develop (or modify preexisting) interview protocols for use in TID contexts.

- Psychological TID assessment must not be used in isolation to select or deselect athletes from team consideration.

- In the context of TID, it is ideal to triangulate psychological data within (e.g., quantitative, behavioral, qualitative) and between (e.g., physical assessments, technical assessments) sources of collected data.

- To facilitate best practices in the TID process, consultants should maintain ongoing communication with the sport team or organization, from structuring the nature of the engagement to participating in postdraft discussions on translating TID data into individual and comprehensive player development plans (i.e., TDE).

CHAPTER 13

Sport Injury, Rehabilitation, and Return to Sport

Monna Arvinen-Barrow, PhD, CPsychol AFBPsS, UPV Sert

Jordan Hamson-Utley, PhD, LAT, ATC

J.D. DeFreese, PhD

An injury sustained in sport is much more than a damaged body part, such as a torn ligament or a broken wrist. Instead, the injury belongs to an athlete with aspirations, hopes, and fears powerfully affected by the injury. The injury is the beginning of a potentially long and arduous rehabilitation, recovery, and return to sport, best described as a complex process that poses an interconnected array of physical and psychosocial challenges for the athlete.

What makes injury rehabilitation challenging is that athletes' reactions are influenced by a wide range of individual and situational differences (Brewer, Andersen, & Van Raalte, 2002), resulting in an unpredictable experience for the injured athlete. For consultants working with injured athletes and collaborating with a sports medicine team, understanding those reactions, as well as assessing, identifying, and implementing appropriate psychosocial interventions that complement the physical rehabilitation, may improve both the rehabilitation experience and the outcome of the recovery process.

This chapter explores the role of assessment in sport injury and rehabilitation by focusing on musculoskeletal injuries. The chapter first provides an overview of the assessment of psychosocial factors linked to sport injury. This exploration is then followed by sections related to assessment for musculoskeletal sport injury.

Assessment of Psychosocial Factors Linked to Sport Injury

The biopsychosocial model of sport injury rehabilitation (Brewer et al., 2002) presumes that an athlete's responses to injury are best understood as an interaction of biological (e.g., metabolism, tissue repair, sleep), psychological (e.g., personality, cognition, affect, behavior), and social (e.g., life stress, social support, rehabilitation environment) factors. These factors are influenced by characteristics of the injury (e.g., type, cause, severity) and a range of sociodemographic factors (e.g., age, gender). This interaction is proposed to be bidirectional and is said to affect intermediate rehabilitation and recovery outcomes (e.g., range of motion, pain reduction, rate of recovery). These intermediate outcomes also have a bidirectional relationship with overall rehabilitation outcomes (e.g., functional performance, quality of life, treatment satisfaction, readiness to return to sport).

Psychosocial responses to sport injuries are typically connected to a range of preinjury factors (Wiese-Bjornstal, Smith, Shaffer, & Morrey, 1998), and preinjury factors can affect the ways in which an athlete thinks, feels, behaves, and performs after the injury. Cognitive appraisals and emotional and behavioral responses postinjury will evolve in a bidirectional, cyclical manner (Wiese-Bjornstal et al., 1998), ultimately affecting a range of physical and psychosocial rehabilitation outcomes. These interactions are also influenced by personal and situational factors (Wiese-Bjornstal et al., 1998) and can vary depending on the stage of the recovery process (e.g., Clement, Arvinen-Barrow, & Fetty, 2015).

Assessing athletes' thoughts, emotions, and behaviors during injury rehabilitation can help formulate the initial needs analysis, act as markers of recovery progress, indicate distress and other mood disturbances, and help evaluate athletes' readiness to return to sport (Taylor & Taylor, 1997). Assessments can be used in a myriad of ways during the rehabilitation of sport injury, including at the beginning and end of rehabilitation (pre- and posttest), during each phase of rehabilitation, and across the rehabilitation process to sample a target of interest (e.g., mood). Moreover, if injured athletes have previously been through a rehabilitation progression, past assessments can aid in improving the current rehabilitation plan. Assessments also allow a critical element of the recovery process—namely, educating injured athletes on what to expect during rehabilitation, including pain, progress, setbacks, and recovery.

Psychosocial assessment after an injury should be conducted with the following considerations. First, injured athletes' psychosocial health and well-being should be central in determining the assessment needs. For example, if an athlete does not display any signs of reinjury anxiety, administering a reinjury anxiety inventory may not be warranted. Second, the consultant should be qualified to administer the chosen assessment; some mental health assessments

require clinical training or licensure. Third, if mental health assessments are used during sport injury rehabilitation, and the athlete displays signs of psychopathology, it is important to have an appropriate referral network in place. Finally, given that sport injury rehabilitation is often stressful for athletes (Arvinen-Barrow, Hemmings, Weigand, Becker, & Booth, 2007; Clement, Granquist, & Arvinen-Barrow, 2013), consultants should be aware of all physical assessments being conducted and be careful not to overassess at the time of injury. To ensure successful physical and psychosocial sport injury rehabilitation, consultants should therefore work in close collaboration with an interprofessional sports medicine team (Arvinen-Barrow & Clement, 2015, 2017; Clement & Arvinen-Barrow, 2013).

Injured athletes confront different physical and psychosocial stressors at different stages of recovery (Kamphoff, Thomae, & Hamson-Utley, 2013). Therefore when choosing assessments, the phase of rehabilitation is an important consideration. The phases are grounded in the physical benchmarks of progress within rehabilitation, but the psychosocial elements of each stage are equally important to ensure successful recovery (Kamphoff et al., 2013). Phase 1, the athlete's reaction to injury, includes the physical elements of pain, deformity, swelling, and lack of range of motion and the psychosocial elements of anxiety, pain tolerance, and social support. Phase 2 is characterized by the physical markers of improved strength and moving toward full function of the injured body, as well as the psychosocial elements of confidence, efficacy, motivation, and social support. Phase 3, the return-to-sport phase, is noted for on-field physical assessments evaluating sport-specific movements at full speed; psychosocially, this final stage includes concerns such as confidence, fear of reinjury, malingering, and readiness to return to sport. Each phase includes assessment opportunities for immediate intervention, and assessing athletes across the three phases can provide a wealth of knowledge of the athletes' progress throughout the recovery process.

Assessment for Musculoskeletal Sport Injury

With the preceding considerations in mind, the following sections provide a general overview of assessment areas during the rehabilitation of musculoskeletal sport injuries. It also introduces selected psychosocial inventories (see the chapter-ending table Assessment Tools and Their Availability) that we have found to be useful during various phases of rehabilitation. Unless otherwise noted, all of the assessment tools presented have sound psychometric properties, including acceptable validity, reliability, and internal consistency.

Initial Needs

To ensure successful rehabilitation and safe and timely return to sport, understanding athlete needs is of primary importance (Kamphoff et al., 2013; Taylor & Taylor, 1997). In addition to any systematic evaluations pertaining to physical characteristics of the injury, we recommend that you work with athletes to assess their self-rated perceptions of physical and psychosocial factors that will influence the time and quality of the rehabilitation process. Albeit not a psychometrically validated tool, rehabilitation profiling is an effective way to assess this (Taylor & Taylor, 1997). Rehabilitation profiling allows athletes to become a central part of the process and develop awareness of their psychosocial and physical needs (Kamphoff et al., 2013). Rehabilitation profiling can also be beneficial for you as a consultant by building rapport and trust, facilitating communication between you and the athlete, providing a graphic depiction of the athlete's self-perceptions in relation to the injury, and facilitating the development of meaningful physical, psychological, performance, and lifestyle goals during the rehabilitation and recovery process (Arvinen-Barrow & Hemmings, 2013).

Rehabilitation Team Needs

Injured athletes should have appropriate medical and psychosocial support systems in place where all members of the support team have a clear understanding of their role in the rehabilitation process (Clement & Arvinen-Barrow, 2013). One way to systematically assess this is to develop a rehabilitation team sociogram (i.e., a visual tool to identify affiliations between members of the group). Through a rehabilitation sociogram, relevant team members can be identified, roles and responsibilities clarified, and potential gaps in athlete needs highlighted and addressed. Preliminary research appears to support a dual-layered rehabilitation team (Arvinen-Barrow & Clement, 2015, in press), where those involved in the medical diagnosis and treatment form the primary treatment team around the athlete. The secondary rehabilitation team consists of professionals (e.g., coach, sport nutritionist, sport psychology consultant, strength and conditioning coach) and individuals (e.g., family, friends, spouses, teammates) who are important for recovery but may not have a significant role in the day-to-day medical treatment of the injury.

Social Support

Athlete perceptions of and interactions with their primary and secondary rehabilitation team members are a key coping resource for their initial injury and rehabilitation responses (Udry, Gould, Bridges, & Tuffey, 1997). Social support has been shown to be negatively associated with postinjury state anxiety, as well as symptoms of anxiety and depression at the return-to-play phase (Yang et al., 2014). Consultants and sports medicine professionals should therefore facilitate injured athletes' actual and perceived social support within the rehabilitation environment to promote more adaptive postinjury outcomes (Granquist & Stadden, 2015). One brief measure of athlete satisfaction with social support is the short form of the Social Support Questionnaire

Sources of and Satisfaction With Social Support

Injured athletes' social support levels have been shown to be negatively associated with postinjury state anxiety, as well as symptoms of anxiety and depression at the return-to-play phase (Yang et al., 2014). This exercise can help you understand the social support your athlete feels is currently available postinjury and throughout rehabilitation. Assess the athlete's current satisfaction with her social support by using the SSQ6 or by simply having a conversation with the athlete about her sources of support and how satisfied she is with that support. Discuss options for maintaining or improving this level of social support by considering additional sources and support behaviors from these sources. Have the athlete process things she can do to improve her satisfaction with her social support. Actively thinking about sources of support and highlighting the importance of different types of support can help clients better understand their own social support needs and people they can turn to in times of doubt.

(SSQ6; Sarason, Sarason, Shearin, & Pierce, 1987). Although use of specific measures might be appealing, having a conversation with athletes about their support might be even more beneficial. Ultimately, you should make it a priority to understand athletes' perceived amount and sources of social support to enhance coping skills postinjury. Assessment of social support may be particularly beneficial after the initial postinjury evaluation and immediately before returning to play.

Readiness for Rehabilitation

As a consultant, you should be aware of athletes' readiness to engage in the rehabilitation process. When entering rehabilitation, injured athletes may experience new and potentially uncomfortable changes in their lifestyle, including restricted mobility, limitations on activities, reliance on others, and time demands of rehabilitation. They may also need to make significant changes in their behavior to ensure a complete and timely recovery, such as engaging in a difficult rehabilitation regimen, following a pain management protocol, and modifying their eating habits. To date, few measures exist that are specifically aimed at assessing athletes' readiness for rehabilitation. Current measures include the Stages of Psychological Readiness for Injury Rehabilitation (SRP-IR; Clement, 2008), Processes of Change Questionnaire for Injury Rehabilitation (POCQ-IR; Wong, 1998), Decisional Balance in Injury Rehabilitation (DB-IR; Clement, 2008), and Self-Efficacy-Injury Rehabilitation (SE-IR; Wong, 1998). Although research evidence in support of assessing readiness for rehabilitation is limited, psychological readiness has been linked to athletes' self-efficacy (Clement, 2008), which has been found to predict rehabilitation attendance (Levy, Polman, & Clough, 2008), which in turn has an effect on physical and psychosocial rehabilitation outcomes.

Personality

A myriad of personality, or dispositional, factors may affect injured athletes' psychosocial responses both immediately after sustaining an injury and throughout the rehabilitation process. Given the wide range of personality factors that influence thinking, emotions, behavior, and performance, deciding which personality factors to include in a rehabilitation assessment program can be a daunting task. To provide guidance, we highlight anxiety and locus of control as personality factors with unique relevance to rehabilitation outcomes. Understanding the role these factors play in recovery from injury and how to assess them will help you have a positive impact on the psychosocial health of injured athletes.

Anxiety

Anxiety is defined as an emotional reaction to a situation characterized by feelings of apprehension, tension or nervousness, worries or unpleasant thoughts, and physiological changes (Spielberger, 1988). It is conceptualized as both a trait (generalized) and state (context-specific) response to situations of uncertainty (e.g., the severity of an injury or the probability of a full recovery and return to sport). It is important for consultants to understand the impact of anxiety on the injury rehabilitation process. Research has shown that athletes higher in trait anxiety exhibit more frequent injury and reinjury occurrence (Lavallee & Flint, 1996). Anxiety also may influence how prepared an athlete is to return to competition (Podlog & Eklund, 2006). The State-Trait Anxiety Inventory (STAI; Spielberger, 1983) is the most commonly used measure of trait and state anxiety among athlete populations. Implementing interventions to help athletes cope with anxiety can facilitate optimal athlete responses during the rehabilitation protocol.

Locus of Control

Locus of control, or one's tendency to perceive the degree to which the cause of achievement (rehabilitation) outcomes is under one's control (Weiner, 1985), represents another key personality factor influencing athletes' psychosocial responses postinjury. Driven by trait tendencies and state expressions of locus of control, athletes endorsing an internal locus of control exhibit higher rates of rehabilitation adherence (Murphy, Foreman, Molloy, & Molley, 1999) and higher levels of postinjury sport involvement (Nyland, Cottell, Harreld, & Caborn, 2013). Consultants should assess athletes' trait locus of control at the start of the rehabilitation, so they can introduce interventions to help athletes have an internal locus of control to facilitate rehabilitation and return to sport. The Condition-Specific Measure of Locus of Control in the Multidimensional Health Locus of Control (MHLC) scales (Wallston, Stein, & Smith, 1994) and Sports Rehabilitation Locus of Control (SRLC) scale (Murphy et al., 1999) are suitable assessment tools for this purpose.

Cognitions

The ways in which athletes think about their injuries, rehabilitation, and return to sport play a significant role in all phases and aspects of their recovery. Athletes' thinking directly influences a range of psychological factors, such as confidence, focus, and motivation. The content of their thoughts also affects their emotions, with negative thinking leading to negative emotions and positive thinking leading to positive emotions. Finally, thinking influences rehabilitation-related behaviors, such as rehabilitation adherence and effort. Having an understanding of athletes' thought processes can help consultants recognize problems before or shortly after they arise and take action to help athletes change their thinking if needed.

Attitudes and Expectations

Understanding athlete attitudes toward and expectations of rehabilitation is an emergent area of assessment within sports medicine. Typically when entering rehabilitation, athletes have expectations about the rehabilitation process and outcomes, and these expectations are often influenced by their attitudes toward the injury, the rehabilitation process and outcomes, and the primary treatment provider (Arvinen-Barrow, Clement, & Bayes, 2012). These attitudes and expectations can influence whether athletes are willing to actively engage in the rehabilitation process, highlighting the importance of ensuring that the attitudes and expectations of injured athletes align with both their own needs and those held by the sports medicine team.

Research suggests that gender, geographic location, sport type (e.g., physical contact versus nonphysical contact), and previous sport medical experience influence athlete attitudes toward and expectations of sports medicine professionals (e.g., Arvinen-Barrow et al., 2012; Arvinen-Barrow et al., 2015; Clement et al., 2012). A few assessment tools measure injured athletes' attitudes toward and expectations of rehabilitation, namely the Attitudes Toward Physiotherapist Form (ATP-F; Arvinen-Barrow et al., 2012) and Expectations about Athletic Training (EAAT; Clement et al., 2012). Both of these assessments are relatively long and thus may not be appropriate in all clinical settings.

Motivation

Motivation is crucial to effective rehabilitation and return to sport. Without the motivation to overcome the immense physical and psychosocial hurdles that are an inevitable part of recovery from a serious injury, athletes will not expend the effort necessary to surmount those challenges for a complete and timely recovery and a successful return to sport. Thus, initial and ongoing motivational assessment is essential in order to customize the chosen interventions to better meet the needs and goals of the injured athlete.

It is also important to recognize how motivation plays a different role in each of the three phases of injury rehabilitation. Early on, the injury may have a shocking, unsettling effect on athletes, potentially leading to feelings of denial and avoidance behaviors at a time when high motivation and immediate rehabilitative action are essential. Motivation is also vital as athletes progress through rehabilitation, particularly when recovery is a long and slow process back to activity.

The return-to-sport time frame can produce conflicting motivations. Motivation often increases as athletes regain near-full functionality and see the light at the end of the tunnel; however, as the return to sport approaches, they may also experience fears related to their return, resulting in a decline in motivation and increase in malingering behavior (e.g., complaints of pain; statements about lack of readiness; missed, shortened, or poor-quality rehabilitation sessions). Consistent assessment of athletes' motivation will allow you to note any red flags that arise and provide early, effective interventions that will keep motivation high throughout the return-to-sport process (Hamson-Utley, Arvinen-Barrow, & Granquist, 2014).

Motivational assessments can also be used to identify specific types of motivation that catalyze athletes' efforts to adhere to the rehabilitation regimen. Simply put, the type of motivation that drives the athlete can help you create a motivational environment that best meets his motivational needs. We believe the revised 18-item Sport Motivation Scale (SMS-II; Pelletier, Rocchi, Vallerand, Deci, & Ryan, 2013) that measures intrinsic, extrinsic, and amotivation in sport is useful for assessing potential changes in motivation across the recovery period. The Sports Injury Rehabilitation Beliefs Survey (SIRBS; Taylor & May, 1996) is another useful tool to assess motivation, particularly when behavioral changes are noticed in rehabilitation (e.g., nonadherence), because it can provide insight into potential causes of the change in motivation and rehabilitation-related behavior.

Self-Efficacy

Self-efficacy (i.e., belief in one's capabilities to organize and execute actions required to produce a desired result; Bandura, 1977), merits consideration for athletes undergoing rehabilitation. Research has shown positive associations between higher rehabilitation efficacy and compliance with treatment protocols (e.g., Taylor & May, 1996). Higher self-efficacy during rehabilitation has also been associated with higher reported function and fewer subjective symptoms during rehabilitation (Thomeé et al., 2007). Accordingly, assessment of self-efficacy and interventions to build self-efficacy can enhance rehabilitation performance. Several sport-specific self-efficacy measures for athletes can aid such work. We recommend the Athletic Injury Self-Efficacy Questionnaire (AISEQ; Sordoni, Hall, & Forwell, 2002) because it measures athletes' perceptions of their ability to complete their assigned rehabilitation exercises.

Return-to-Sport Confidence

Confidence also merits assessment at the time of injury, particularly during the rehabilitation and return-to-sport phases. Like self-efficacy, confidence in one's ability to execute behaviors and movements facilitates more positive behaviors (e.g., performance) and cognitive and affective outcomes for athletes. Understanding individual athlete confidence can help in the selection of interventions to enhance postinjury psychological and physical responses. Specifically, confidence assessment in the return-to-sport phase can provide a crucial baseline for psychological skills training moving forward. Return-to-sport confidence may be effectively assessed using the Injury-Psychological Readiness to Return to Sport scale (I-PRRS; Glazer, 2009) or the Return to Sport After Serious Injury Questionnaire (RSSIQ; Podlog & Eklund, 2005).

Perceived Injury Susceptibility

A new area of assessment within the injury and rehabilitation context is athletes' perceptions of injury susceptibility (Deroche, Yannick, Brewer, & Le Scanff, 2007). We know that previous injury occurrence influences an individual's perceived susceptibility to sport injury (Deroche et al., 2007; Gnasinski, Arvinen-Barrow, Brewer, & Meyer, 2016) and that previous injury plays a role in future injury risk perceptions (Kontos, 2004). Thus, addressing such perceptions during rehabilitation, particularly in phase 3, is of primary importance to ensure safe return to sport and to minimize the risk of future injury. Given its brevity and ease of administration, the Perceived Susceptibility to Sport Injury (PSSI) scale (Deroche et al., 2007) can be useful when athletes return to sport.

Emotions

Emotions play a powerful role in many aspects of athletes' rehabilitation, recovery, and return to sport. They have a significant impact on athletes' thinking and behavior, which in turn influence the athletes' ability to tolerate pain and their adherence, motivation, confidence, and readiness to return to sport. Systematic use of instruments that assess emotions can help consultants monitor athletes' emotional states during recovery and provide intervention as needed to help the athletes cope with the emotional challenges of rehabilitation and return to sport.

Mood

When athletes sustain a serious injury, they experience a myriad of moods. These are mostly distressing initially, then increasingly positive as the recovery progresses, and are likely to fluctuate throughout the phases of rehabilitation (e.g., Clement et al., 2015). Assessing mood states periodically during the course of rehabilitation is important, particularly to ensure early detection of mental health issues that may emerge (Andersen, 2004). Often, mood-related difficulties remain hidden during rehabilitation because athletes may not articulate their thoughts and feelings effectively to their treatment providers. The two most common mood assessments are the Brunel Mood Scale (BRUMS; Terry, Lane, Lane, & Keohane, 1999) and the Profile of Mood States (POMS; McNair, Lorr, & Droppleman, 1971). We recommend the use of the BRUMS in sport injury settings because it is shorter and more user friendly.

Depression

Depression is one of the mood constructs that may require attention beyond the use of the BRUMS or POMS. Many athletes experience depressive episodes during sport injury rehabilitation (Arvinen-Barrow et al., 2007), and depression is a risk factor for noncompliance with medical treatment (DiMatteo, Lepper, & Croghan, 2000). It is important to recognize depressive symptoms in the injured athletes you work with and to understand the appropriate course of action to address these symptoms quickly and effectively.

Depending on your professional background and competencies, we recommend that you assess injured athletes for depression yourself or refer injured athletes to a mental health professional with the appropriate training to assess the athlete (see chapter 5 for more on mental health screening). Two commonly used and recommended measures of depression are the Beck Depression Inventory (BDI; Beck, Ward, Mendelson, Mock, & Erbaugh, 1961) and the Hamilton Rating Scale for Depression (HRSD; Hamilton, 1960). Both measures are widely used and publically available, and both should be administered and scored by a trained professional with knowledge of and experience with clinical depression management.

Anger

Anger is another mood state that may become evident during rehabilitation, as determined by data from the BRUMS and POMS, self-reports from the injured athletes, observed behavior, or reports from the sports medicine team, family, or others. Anger is one of the most common psychological reactions to sport injuries (Clement et al., 2013), and if not addressed, it can lead to increased frustration, lack of motivation, and problems with treatment compliance. The State-Trait Anger Expression Inventory-2 (STAXI-2; Spielberger, 1999) is considered the gold standard for anger assessment. Although not specific to sport injury, the STAXI-2 is easy to administer to adolescent and adult athletes at all levels, and it can facilitate conversations with athletes that raise their awareness of their anger, help identify the sources of anger, and lead to the development of strategies to alleviate the anger.

Stress

Sports medicine professionals have identified stress as the most common emotion present in injured athletes during rehabilitation, and the inability to cope with the stress is one reason why rehabilitation may not lead to a successful outcome (Arvinen-Barrow et al., 2007; Clement et al., 2013). To date, there is no known stress measure specific to sport injury rehabilitation; however, we recommend the Brief COPE (Carver, 1997) to help gain insight into how an athlete is coping with the stressors associated with sport injury. These results can then help you identify a personalized plan of action for the athlete.

Reinjury Anxiety and Fear

A specific form of anxiety that might warrant further evaluation, particularly during the latter stages of the rehabilitation process, is reinjury anxiety. An athlete who faces pressure to return to play before being psychologically ready may experience reinjury anxiety. Due to its relatively short form, the Re-Injury Anxiety Inventory (RIAI; Walker, Thatcher, & Lavallee, 2010) is an easily administered measure that offers useful information about reinjury anxiety, particularly if conversations with the athlete warrant further evaluation of apprehension about returning to activity. Additionally, the Tampa Scale for Kinesiophobia (TSK) can be used for evaluating fear of reinjury (Miller, Kori, & Todd, 1991). Originally developed to measure fear of movement related to chronic back pain, the TSK assesses the subjective rating of kinesiophobia, or fear of movement. This can be useful when athletes display signs of fear of reinjury, particularly as the return to sport nears.

Pain

Assessments of pain type (e.g., acute versus chronic), characteristics (e.g., sharp, shooting), and level (e.g., 1-10) can inform you about the physical healing process, the relationship injured athletes have with pain (e.g., high versus low tolerance), and the need for a referral back to the treating physician (Granquist & Stiller-Ostrowski, 2014). Pain is a complex biopsychosocial experience that has significant ramifications for injured athletes in their rehabilitation and return to sport. One aspect that can be moderated is the athlete's subjective perceptions of pain. These subjective perceptions to an injury or surgical repair are often influenced by prior injury, visual representation of the injury (i.e., how the injury looks), and education (e.g., knowledge about what has happened and what will happen). Injured athletes may report that they're in so much pain they can't do rehab. Because of its significant presence during rehabilitation, consistent assessment of pain can help injured athletes develop and use effective coping skills to mitigate their pain; ensure their rehabilitation stays on track; and make pain more objective and tangible, thus enabling injured athletes to better understand and learn to control their pain perceptions (Granquist & Stiller-Ostrowski, 2014).

Pain assessments can also capture the quality or characteristics and location of the pain. Used at the beginning of rehabilitation (phase 1), an indication of extreme pain with a less severe injury may suggest a lower pain threshold, which can guide pain management throughout the rehabilitation. Used during rehabilitation (phase 2) and return to sport (phase 3), pain assessments can monitor pain levels and correlations with setbacks in progress. In phase 3, an athlete with a fear of reinjury or a perceived lack of readiness or return-to-play confidence may report a resurgence of pain as a means of delaying the return. In this situation, pain assessments can create opportunities for athletes to reveal concerns about origins of their current pain.

Sport-specific pain instruments can assess injured athletes' coping abilities as they relate to pain. We recommend the Sports Inventory for Pain (SIP; Meyers, Bourgeois, Stewart, &

LeUnes, 1992) because it assesses athletes' pain tolerance, pain coping, and compliance with medical treatment. The Athletic Coping Skills Inventory (ACSI-28; Smith, Schutz, Smoll, & Ptacek, 1995) can also be beneficial because it assesses athletes' coping skills for prolonged serious injury and reveals psychological resources (or lack thereof) to assist in recovery.

Adherence

Though thinking and emotions play a vital role in rehabilitation and return to sport, athletes' behavior is where the rubber meets the road. In other words, it is what injured athletes do that ultimately dictates the quality of their recovery. Their behavior in every aspect of their rehabilitation and return to sport, including adherence to their rehabilitation regimen, sleep, and nutrition, must be maximized. As a consequence, assessing rehabilitation-related behavior is essential to ensure injured athletes are doing everything required for timely and complete recovery.

Injured athletes receive the most benefit from the expertise of their sports medicine team when they diligently follow the prescribed rehabilitation protocol. Thus, adherence (i.e., completing all relevant behaviors aimed at recovery from injury; Granquist & Brewer, 2013) is an important behavioral outcome. Because under- or overadherence to rehabilitation is particularly troubling, adherence should be assessed continually (i.e., daily or weekly based on expected injury duration) during rehabilitation until return to sport has been achieved. Two measures of rehabilitation adherence are the Sport Injury Rehabilitation Adherence Scale (SIRAS; Brewer et al., 2000) and the Rehabilitation Adherence Measure for Athletic Training (RAdMAT; Granquist, Gill, & Appaneal, 2010), both developed to record sports medicine professionals' observations of athletes' rehabilitation in clinical settings. Given that adherence is usually related to the treatment modalities prescribed by the sports medicine professionals, the consultant should work with said professionals to gain better understanding of the adherence responses of injured athletes. Such information can then be used to promote positive biopsychosocial responses during rehabilitation.

Understanding Adherence

Adherence is completing all relevant behaviors aimed at recovery from injury (Granquist & Brewer, 2013). This exercise can help you to determine your client's level of adherence and work with him to better adhere to his individual rehabilitation protocol. Working in collaboration with the client's primary treatment provider (e.g., sports medicine professional), assess your client's level of adherence to the treatment protocol. Next, discuss with the client ways to maintain or improve this level of adherence. Consider both environmental and personal factors that could promote adherence. Monitoring adherence through communication with the clinical care provider enables a holistic approach to care and affords the patient an understanding of the mind–body connection during injury rehabilitation.

Physical Progress

Assessing physical progress has valuable biopsychosocial implications for injured athletes. Consistent progress can build confidence and self-efficacy, reduce negative thoughts and emotions, and promote motivation and adherence to the rehabilitation regimen. Conversely, the absence of steady progress or the occurrence of setbacks during the recovery can have detrimental effects on these psychosocial responses. To measure physical progress during injury rehabilitation, sports medicine professionals reference existing anatomical norms against physical parameters of healing and recovery. In a collaborative rehabilitation team, recovery indicators can be shared with consultants within legal guidelines for the benefit of the injured athlete. If the athlete's physical progress exceeds expected recovery norms, this knowledge can have a positive effect on the athlete. However, physical testing can also decrease motivation and adherence if recovering athletes fail to meet individual or standardized norms for physical progress.

Assessment Tools and Their Availability

Assessment tool	Construct	Author and reference	Availability
Rehabilitation profiling	Initial needs assessment	Taylor, J., & Taylor, S. (1997). *Psychological approaches to sports injury rehabilitation*. Gaithersburg, MD: Aspen.	Full measure in chapter 1
	This self-report measure is used to assess personal and physical factors that have a significant impact on the quality and duration of rehabilitation. It is useful for all populations.		
Rehabilitation sociogram	Rehabilitation team needs assessment	Clement, D., & Arvinen-Barrow, M. (2013). Sport medicine team influences in psychological rehabilitation: A multidisciplinary approach. In M. Arvinen-Barrow & N. Walker (Eds.), *The psychology of sport injury and rehabilitation* (pp. 156-170). Abingdon, UK: Routledge.	Full measure in chapter
	This tool is used to identify composition of the rehabilitation team and to gain clarity of the roles, relationships, and interactions among members involved. It is useful for all populations.		
Social Support Questionnaire (short form) (SSQ6)	Social support	Sarason, I.G., Sarason, B.R., Shearin, E.N., & Pierce, G.R. (1987). A brief measure of social support: Practical and theoretical implications. *Journal of Social and Personal Relationships, 4,* 497-510.	Full measure in article; http://dx.doi.org/10.1177/0265407587044007
	This self-report measure is used to identify sources of social support and to measure satisfaction with the support. It is thus far validated to be used with adult populations only.		
Stages of Psychological Readiness for Rehabilitation (SRP-IR)	Psychological readiness for rehabilitation: stages of change	Clement, D. (2008). The transtheoretical model: An exploratory look at its applicability to injury rehabilitation. *Journal of Sport Rehabilitation, 17,* 269-282.	Contact the author
	This self-report measure is used to identify individuals' stage of psychological readiness for sport injury rehabilitation. It should be used in conjunction with other measures of psychological readiness for rehabilitation. It is thus far validated to be used with adult populations only.		
Processes of Change Questionnaire for Injury Rehabilitation (POCQ-IR)	Psychological readiness for rehabilitation: processes of change	Wong, I. (1998). *Injury rehabilitation behavior: An investigation of stages and processes of change in the athletic-therapist relationship.* (Unpublished master's thesis). University of Oregon, Eugene, OR.	Full measure in thesis
	This self-report measure is used to identify individuals' cognitive and behavioral processes related to their psychological readiness for sport injury rehabilitation. It should be used in conjunction with other measures of psychological readiness for rehabilitation. It is thus far validated to be used with adult populations only.		
Decisional Balance in Injury Rehabilitation (DB-IR)	Psychological readiness for rehabilitation: decisional balance	Clement, D. (2008). The transtheoretical model: An exploratory look at its applicability to injury rehabilitation. *Journal of Sport Rehabilitation, 17,* 269-282.	Contact the author
	This self-report measure is used to identify individuals' pros and cons related to sport injury rehabilitation. It should be used in conjunction with other measures of psychological readiness for rehabilitation. It is thus far validated to be used with adult populations only.		

Assessment tool	Construct	Author and reference	Availability
Self-Efficacy-Injury Rehabilitation (SE-IR)	Psychological readiness for rehabilitation: self-efficacy	Wong, I. (1998). *Injury rehabilitation behavior: An investigation of stages and processes of change in the athletic-therapist relationship.* (Unpublished master's thesis). University of Oregon, Eugene, OR.	Full measure in thesis
	This self-report measure is used to identify individuals' perceptions about their self-efficacy related to sport injury rehabilitation. It should be used in conjunction with other measures of psychological readiness for rehabilitation. It is thus far validated to be used with adult populations only.		
State-Trait Anxiety Inventory (STAI)	Trait and state anxiety	Spielberger, C.D., Gorsuch, R.L., & Lushene, R. (1970). *STAI manual.* Palo Alto, CA: Consulting Psychologists Press.	For purchase at www.mindgarden.com
	This introspective self-report measure is used to measure both trait and state anxiety. It should only be given by a person trained to use and interpret it. There are different versions of this measure for different populations and in different languages.		
Condition-Specific Measure of Locus of Control (MHLC)	Locus of control	Wallston, K.A., Stein, M.J., & Smith, C.A. (1994). Form C of the MHLC scales: A condition-specific measure of locus of control. *Journal of Personality Assessment, 63*, 534-553.	Individual assessment items can be found at http://dx.doi.org/ 10.1207/s153277 52jpa6303_10; contact the authors for full version
	This self-report measure assesses patients' locus of control relative to any medical or health-related condition (e.g., athletic injury). Reliability and validity have been established in adult patient populations.		
Sports Rehabilitation Locus of Control (SRLC) scale	Locus of control	Murphy, G.C., Foreman, P.E, Simpson, C.A., Molloy, G.N., & Molley, E.K. (1999). The development of a locus of control measure predictive of injured athletes' adherence to treatment. *Journal of Science and Medicine in Sport, 2*, 145-152.	Full measure in article; http://dx.doi.org/ 10.1016/S1440-2440(99)80194-7
	This self-report measure assesses locus of control in injured athletes via dimensions of internal, powerful others, and chance items. It has exhibited acceptable reliability and validity with adult athletes.		
Attitudes Toward Physiotherapist Form (ATP-F)	Rehabilitation attitudes	Arvinen-Barrow, M., Clement, D., & Bayes, N. (2012). Athletes' attitudes toward physiotherapist. *International Journal of Multi-Disciplinary Studies and Sports Research, 2*(July), 324-334.	Contact the authors
	This self-report measure assesses athletes' attitudes toward their medical professional on four constructs: stigma tolerance, confidence in medical professional, personal openness, and cultural preference. It is thus far validated to be used with adult populations only.		

(continued)

Assessment Tools and Their Availability *(continued)*

Assessment tool	Construct	Author and reference	Availability
Expectations About Athletic Training (EAAT)	Rehabilitation expectations	Clement, D., Hamson-Utley, J.J., Arvinen-Barrow, M., Kamphoff, C., Zakrajsek, R.A., & Martin, S.B. (2012). College athletes' expectations about injury rehabilitation with an athletic trainer. *International Journal of Athletic Therapy & Training, 17*(4), 18-27.	Contact the authors
		This self-report measure of athletes' expectations about the rehabilitation services measures four constructs: personal commitment, facilitative conditions, sports medicine professional expertise, and realism. It is thus far validated to be used with adult populations only.			
Sport Motivation Scale-II (SMS-II)	Motivation	Pelletier, L., Rocchi, M., Vallerand, R.J., Deci, E.L., & Ryan, R.E. (2013). Validation of the revised Sport Motivation Scale (SMS-II). *Psychology of Sport & Exercise, 14*, 329-341.	Full measure in article; http://dx.doi.org/10.1016/j.psychsport.2012.12.002
		This self-report measure of athletes' behavioral regulation in sport measures intrinsic and extrinsic motivation in sport as defined by SDT. The revised version (2013) is validated to be used with adult populations only.			
Sports Injury Rehabilitation Beliefs Survey (SIRBS)	Motivation	Taylor, A.H., & May, S. (1996). Threat and coping appraisal as determinants of compliance with sports injury rehabilitation: An application of protection motivation theory. *Journal of Sports Sciences, 14*, 471-482.	Full measure in article; http://dx.doi.org/10.1080/02640419608727734
		This self-report measure of athletes' beliefs about rehabilitation measures five scales: susceptibility, treatment efficacy, self-efficacy, rehabilitation value, and severity. It is thus far validated to be used with adult populations only.			
Athletic Injury Self-Efficacy Questionnaire (AISEQ)	Self-efficacy	Sordoni, C., Hall, C., & Forwell, L. (2002). The use of imagery in athletic injury rehabilitation and its relationship to self-efficacy. *Physiology Canada, 54*, 177-185.	Contact the authors
		This self-report measure of athlete efficacy during rehabilitation can be used with adult athlete populations.			
Injury-Psychological Readiness to Return to Sport (I-PRRS)	Confidence	Glazer, D.D. (2009). Development and preliminary validation and the injury-psychological readiness to return to sport scale (I-PRRS). *Journal of Athletic Training, 44*, 185-189.	Full measure in article; http://natajournals.org/doi/full/10.4085/1062-6050-44.2.185
		This self-report measure is used to assess an athlete's psychological readiness to return to full sport participation after sport injury. It is thus far validated to be used with adult populations only.			

Assessment tool	Construct	Author and reference	Availability
Return to Sport After Serious Injury Questionnaire (RSSIQ)	Confidence	Podlog, L., & Eklund, R.C. (2005). Return to sport after serious injury: A retrospective examination of motivation and psychological outcomes. *Journal of Sport Rehabilitation, 14,* 20-34.	Full measure in article; http://dx.doi.org/ 10.1123/jsr.14.1.20
	This self-report measure is used to assess an athlete's perceived psychological outcomes of returning to sport. It measures cognitive, affective, and behavioral aspects of return to sport and is thus far validated to be used with adult populations only.		
Perceived Susceptibility to Sport Injury (PSSI)	Perceived susceptibility to sport injury	Deroche, T., Yannick, S., Brewer, B.W., & Le Scanff, C. (2007). Predictors of perceived susceptibility to sport-related injury. *Personality and Individual Differences, 43,* 2218-2228.	Details of measure in article; http://dx.doi.org/ 10.1016/j.paid.2007 .06.031
	This self-report measure is used to assess individuals' perceptions about their absolute and comparative sport injury risk. It is thus far validated to be used with adult populations only.		
Brunel Mood Scale (BRUMS)	Mood states	Lane, A.M., & Lane, H.J. (2002). Predictive effectiveness of mood measures. *Perceptual and Motor Skills, 94,* 785-791.	Visit www.moodprofiling. com to request a copy
	The BRUMS is a brief self-report measure of mood states among adolescents and adults.		
Profile of Mood States (POMS)	Mood states	McNair, D.M., Lorr, M., & Droppleman, L.F. (1971). *ETIS manual for the Profile of Mood States.* San Diego: Educational and Industrial Testing Services.	For purchase at www.mhs.com
	This self-report measure is used to assess the mood states of people 13 years of age and older.		
Beck Depression Inventory (BDI)	Depression	Beck, A.T., Ward, C.H., Mendelson, M., Mock, J., & Erbaugh, J. (1961). An inventory for measuring depression. *Archives of General Psychiatry, 4,* 561-571.	For purchase at www.pearsonclinical.com
	The BDI is a self-report measure of core depressive symptoms. Licensed mental health providers can use the BDI-II in conjunction with a diagnostic interview to aid in depression diagnosis and treatment. It can be used with adults.		
Hamilton Rating Scale for Depression (HRSD)	Depression	Hamilton, M. (1960). A rating scale for depression. *Journal of Neurological Neurosurgical Psychiatry, 23,* 56-62.	Free at http://healthnet .umassmed.edu/mhealth/ HAMD.pdf
	This self-report measure of depression severity should be administered only to adults who have previously been diagnosed with depression by a physician or licensed mental health practitioner.		

(continued)

Assessment Tools and Their Availability *(continued)*

Assessment tool	Construct	Author and reference	Availability
State-Trait Anger Expression Inventory-2 (STAXI-2)	Anger	Spielberger, C.D. (1999). *State-Trait Anger Expression Inventory-2 (STAXI-2): Professional manual.* Tampa, FL: Psychological Assessment Resources.	For purchase at www4.parinc.com
	This self-report measure is used to assess individuals' experience, expression, and control of anger.		
Brief COPE	Coping with stressors	Carver, C.S. (1997). You want to measure coping but your protocol's too long: Consider the Brief COPE. *International Journal of Behavioral Medicine, 4*, 92-100.	Free at www.psy.miami .edu/faculty/ccarver/ sclBrCOPE.html
	This self-report measure assesses common adaptive and maladaptive coping behaviors. Validity and reliability have been established for adult populations.		
Re-Injury Anxiety Inventory (RIAI)	Reinjury anxiety	Walker, N., Thatcher, J., & Lavallee, D. (2010). A preliminary development of the Re-Injury Anxiety Inventory (RIAI). *Physical Therapy in Sport, 11*(1), 23-29.	Contact the authors
	This self-report measure is used to assess individuals' affect about reinjury at the moment they are completing the measure. It is thus far validated to be used with adult populations only.		
Tampa Scale for Kinesiophobia (TSK)	Fear of reinjury	Miller, R.P., Kori, S.H., & Todd, D.D. (1991). The Tampa Scale: A measure of kinesiophobia. *Clinical Journal of Pain, 7*(1), 51-52.	Free at www.tac.vic.gov .au/__data/assets/ pdf_file/0004/ 27454/tampa_scale_ kinesiophobia.pdf
	This self-report measure is used to assess individuals' fear of movement or reinjury. It can be used to measure unhelpful thoughts and beliefs about pain in chronic pain populations.		
Sports Inventory for Pain (SIP)	Pain	Meyers, M.C., Bourgeois, A.E., Stewart, S., & LeUnes, A. (1992). Predicting pain response in athletes: Development and assessment of the sports inventory for pain. *Journal of Sport & Exercise Psychology, 14*(3), 249-261.	Contact the authors
	This self-report measure is used to assess how athletes respond psychologically when in pain. It measures five constructs: coping through direct action (COP), cognitively mediated coping (COG), catastrophizing (CAT), avoidance (AVD), and somatic awareness (SOM). It is used with adult populations only.		
Athletic Coping Skills Inventory-28 (ACSI-28)	Coping skills	Smith, R.E., Schutz, R.W., Smoll, F.L., & Ptacek, J.T. (1995). Sport psychology development and validation of a multidimensional measure of sport-specific psychological skills: The Athletic Coping Skills Inventory-28. *Journal of Sport & Exercise Psychology, 17*(4), 379-398.	Contact the authors
	This self-report measure of coping skills includes dimensions of coping with adversity, peaking under pressure, goal setting and mental preparation, concentration, freedom from worry, confidence, achievement motivation, and coachability. A personal resources score can be created by summing all dimensional scores. It is normed for use with adult athletes.		

Assessment tool	Construct	Author and reference	Availability
Sport Injury Rehabilitation Adherence Scale (SIRAS)	Adherence	Kolt, G.S., Brewer, B.W., Pizzari, T., Schoo, A.M.M., & Garrett, N. (2007). The Sport Injury Rehabilitation Adherence Scale: A reliable scale for use in clinical physiotherapy. *Physiotherapy, 93*, 17-22.	Full measure in article; http://dx.doi.org/10.1016/j.physio.2006.07.002
	This sports medicine clinician–rated measure is used to assess adherence to clinic-based activities. It measures intensity of rehabilitation completion, frequency of following instructions and advice, and receptivity to changes in rehabilitation. It is used worldwide in adult populations.		
Rehabilitation Adherence Measure for Athletic Training (RAdMAT)	Adherence	Granquist, M.D., Gill, D.L., & Appaneal, R.N. (2010). Development of a measure of rehabilitation adherence for athletic training. *Journal of Sport Rehabilitation, 19*, 249-267.	Full measure in article; http://dx.doi.org/10.1123/jsr.19.3.249
	This sports medicine clinician–rated measure is used to assess adherence to clinic-based activities. It measures attendance and participation, communication, and attitude and effort. It is used worldwide in adult populations.		

Chapter Takeaways

- The sport injury recovery process is far more than a physical experience, encompassing a complex, interconnected array of physical and psychosocial challenges.
- Existing literature has highlighted the importance of assessing athletes' thoughts, emotions, and behaviors during sport injury rehabilitation to help formulate initial needs analysis, act as markers of progress toward recovery, indicate distress and other mood disturbances, and evaluate athletes' readiness to return to sport.
- Initial assessment of the injury and the athlete's associated psychological responses to the injury are key to the long-term success of an injured athlete who is working with a consultant.
- Consultants should consider the phase of rehabilitation; injured athletes are confronted with different physical and psychosocial stressors at different stages of recovery.
- Pain and other stressors associated with the rehabilitation process should be assessed because they can present barriers to recovery.
- When choosing assessments, be careful not to overassess the athlete, and make sure administering said assessments is within your professional competencies.
- The social support resources available to athletes are important to facilitate their motivation and adherence and to minimize their stress throughout the rehabilitation process. Knowing an athlete's current sources and levels of social support can aid you in facilitating their rehab experience.
- Inventories in this chapter are suggested for use only with the populations noted; further research is needed to expand the application range.
- Effective patient care involves communication between practitioners, a team approach that includes sharing results of inventories and making suggestions to improve care as the athlete progresses.

CHAPTER 14

Assessment and Management of Sport-Related Concussions

Robert Conder, PsyD, ABPP

Alanna Adler Conder, PsyD

The U.S. Centers for Disease Control and Prevention (CDC) estimates that 45 million children and adolescents and 15 million adults participate in organized recreational sport (Gilchrist, Thomas, Xu, McGuire, & Coronado, 2011). At the college level, there are 450,000 players participating in all sports and over 160,000 participating in sports identified as concussion generating. At the professional level, there are an estimated 1,600 players in the NFL and roughly the same number in the National Hockey League (NHL), and many are at risk for concussions during play. Though sport provides opportunities for positive physical, intellectual, and social development (Weiss, Kipp, & Bolter, 2012), it also poses the risk of injury, including orthopedic injury and sport-related concussions (SRCs). Unfortunately, SRCs are a common experience at all levels of sport and recreational activity (Guskiewicz, 2015). The CDC estimates that each year there are 1.4 to 3.8 million instances of mild traumatic brain injury (TBI; a term formerly used for concussions) from all causes, with an estimated 17 percent coming from sport (Gilchrist et al., 2011). These figures are estimates based on emergency room admissions and probably underestimate the true prevalence of SRC injuries because many go unrecognized or do not receive medical care, especially at the level of an emergency room visit.

Given the force and biomechanics of contact and collision sports, SRC risk cannot be eliminated. Rather, the goal is to minimize concussions and their impact through clean play, equipment advances, timely concussion identification, and proper management. These interventions reduce the negative sequelae of concussions and help the athlete return to competitive play as quickly and safely as possible.

The issue of SRC has gained prominence in recent years, both in the medical field and the popular media, for several reasons. First, many high-profile athletes in sports such as boxing, football, hockey, and soccer have sustained SRCs that have either required extended recovery time or have been career ending, including Sidney Crosby of the Penguins, Ben Roethlisberger of the Steelers, and Cam Newton of the Panthers. Second, there is growing awareness of the long-term ramifications of SRC injuries, as evidenced by the 2015 legal judgment against the NFL (*Turner & Wooden v. National Football League & NFL Properties*, 2015), which may include long-term neurocognitive dysfunction and the emergence of neurologic illness later in life. Third, SRC education and assessment have increased in youth and collegiate sport due to state legislation mandates by all 50 states and the District of Columbia, as well as rulings by the NCAA. Consequently, medical professionals, sport administrators, coaches, and parents have become acutely aware of the dangers of concussion for young athletes.

Because of this mounting concern for the health and well-being of athletes in SRC-prone sports, it is incumbent on consultants who work in these high-risk sports to become educated about SRC identification, risk, and management; gain the means to assess SRCs; and be capable of working with and making timely referrals to appropriately trained health care professionals (Conder & Conder, 2015a). This chapter provides an overview of SRCs for the sport psychology consultant, whether you are involved in direct assessment and treatment of the concussed athlete or are providing supportive services or coordination of services to the athlete. Knowledge of the essential components of concussion assessment and treatment is critical for all consultants working with athletes.

SRC Consultation Essentials

A critical first step in concussion management is accurate detection and diagnosis. Among several diagnostic schema for SRCs, the most comprehensive currently accepted diagnostic criteria were formulated in the consensus statement from the 4th International Conference on Concussion in Sport, generally referred to as the *Zurich Conference* (McCrory et al., 2013). According to this document, "Concussion is a brain injury and is defined as a complex pathophysiological process affecting the brain, induced by biomechanical forces" (p. 250). The statement further elaborates that the force may be from a direct blow to the head or may come from physical forces elsewhere on the body transmitted to the head; that the concussion results in

time-limited neurologic impairment (although there may be a longer time course); that the immediate symptoms are due to a functional neurometabolic process rather than a structural injury that can be imaged using traditional neuroimaging techniques; and that concussion symptoms have a typical clinical presentation and should resolve in a typical sequential course. A majority of single, uncomplicated concussions resolve within 7 to 10 days; however, a longer recovery time may be needed in children and adolescents (McCrory et al., 2013).

SRC Symptoms and Course of Recovery

As shown in table 14.1, SRC symptoms are grouped into four clusters: physical, cognitive, emotional, and sleep.

Though a majority of collegiate and professional athletes with single, uncomplicated SRCs recover within 7 to 10 days, emerging data from a multiclinical assessment approach suggest it often takes three to four weeks for a complete recovery, especially for younger athletes (Henry, Elbin, Collins, Marchetti, & Kontos, 2015). This parallels the work of McCrea and colleagues, which supports a longer period of physiologic vulnerability even after traditional post-SRC assessment suggests symptom resolution (Nelson, Janecek, & McCrea, 2013). Growing consensus suggests that SRCs are best managed within a comprehensive education, prevention, and management program based in a clinic, school, or team or league. This program should provide resources and information geared toward all stakeholders involved, including athletes, parents, coaches, teachers, consultants, and sports medicine profession-

Table 14.1   Core Concussion Symptom Clusters

Physical	Cognitive	Emotional	Sleep
Headache	Difficulty concentrating	Irritability	Drowsiness
Balance problems and dizziness	Difficulty remembering	Sadness	Sleeping more than usual
Visual problems	Feeling mentally foggy	More emotional	Sleeping less than usual
Fatigue	Feeling slowed down	Nervousness	Difficulty falling asleep
Sensitivity to light and noise	Answers questions slowly	Lability	Difficulty staying asleep

Data from Centers for Disease Control and Prevention 2013.

als. As a consultant working with athletes with SRCs, you are likely mandated by your state law and professional organization to know the fundamentals of SRC injury to ensure you can play an active role in helping athletes receive the best possible care.

Concussion Education Resources

Several resources for concussion education are available to consultants. The CDC's Heads Up Concussion in Youth Sports website (www.cdc.gov/HeadsUp/youthsports) provides free downloadable educational handouts for players, coaches, sport officials, and parents. It is particularly suitable for K–12 sport programs. Collegiate and professional sport organizations have specific SRC training programs for their health care personnel that are based on material from the Zurich Conference (McCrory et al., 2013). The NCAA program addresses the special needs of the collegiate student-athlete (www.ncaa.org/health-and-safety/concussion-guidelines). The NHL, the NFL, and Major League Soccer (MLS) use a neuropsychological concussion evaluation model (Lovell, 2006). Finally, many professional organizations have developed concussion guidelines for their disciplines, such as the American Medical Society for Sports Medicine (AMSSM), the American Academy of Neurology (AAN), and NATA (Echemendia, Giza, & Kutcher, 2015). Of these guidelines, the NATA position statement is one of the most comprehensive and pragmatic documents available. It is useful for all disciplines (Broglio et al., 2014), and therefore consultants working with concussed athletes should be familiar with it regardless of their discipline.

Components of SRC Assessment

With the preceding SRC education and management guidelines in mind, this section provides an overview of essential components of SRC assessment. Integrating data obtained from each assessment component during the postconcussion period is critical to maximize safe SRC recovery and expedite return to play (RTP) and return to learn (RTL) baseline assessment.

Preseason baseline neurocognitive assessment is essential, providing an individualized reference point for comparison in the event of an SRC, especially if the athlete has a preexisting academic learning disability, ADHD, or chronic medical or psychological condition. No athlete is perfect, and many have preexisting symptoms when not injured that can confound postinjury assessment and symptom management, necessitating the need for baseline assessment. Serial postinjury evaluations can be compared against the baseline to establish that an SRC has occurred, to quantify the initial degree of impairment and graduated improvement with rehabilitation and intervention, and to document final recovery. Some argue that this testing is too expensive to be practical and does not prevent concussions (Randolph, 2011); however, the consensus among sports medicine professionals is that it is essential when used within an integrated management program.

The Post-Concussion Symptom Scale (PCSS) is an established self-report tool for assessing preinjury baseline symptoms and for assessing and monitoring postinjury concussion symptoms

Assessment in Action

Using the PCSS in a Guided Interview Format

Consultants should complete this assessment tool in an interview format with concussed clients to better understand their SRC experience. The athlete rates each current SRC symptom on a scale from 0 to 6, and the consultant's interview elucidates activity and setting triggers and patterns in symptom clusters while encouraging the athlete to identify coping behaviors that reduce symptoms. Though only the PCSS total symptom score reliably predicts symptoms lasting longer than 28 days postinjury (Meehan et al., 2013), this recommended approach provides the consultant with valuable information for tailoring interventions and making appropriate, timely referrals to speed up SRC recovery.

(Pardini et al., 2004). When administered soon after SRC injury, PCSS scores can measure the extent of the injury compared with baseline functioning and may help predict which athletes may have a longer or more complicated recovery (Meehan, Mannix, Straccioloni, Elbin, & Collins, 2013). As with any psychometric instrument, education and training for using the PCSS instrument is necessary. The PCSS is widely used by both athletic trainers and consultants alike, provided that they have the education required to assess and monitor SRC injuries.

The Sport Concussion Assessment Tool-3 (SCAT3; McCrory et al., 2013) is another useful comprehensive instrument that can be administered both at baseline and field-side after a suspected SRC injury by the sports medicine professional responsible for immediate postinjury care. It assesses levels of consciousness, learning and memory, orientation, balance, range of motion, and coordination. A child version of the SCAT3 is available for athletes aged 5 to 12 years. The NHL has used the X2 iPad app version of the SCAT3 for baseline assessment. Due to the complexity of this instrument, advanced training in assessment and interpretation may be needed. However, athletic trainers, physicians, and psychologists with appropriate training can administer the SCAT3. If the consultant responsible for immediate care does not have such training, it is recommended that you use the Sport Concussion Recognition Tool, which relies more on observation of the athlete and a brief game-specific memory questionnaire (McCrory et al., 2013).

Administration of computerized neurocognitive assessment at preinjury baseline is a well-established protocol for assessing large numbers of athletes at one time (e.g., team level). However, although computerized assessment offers ease of administration, concerns remain about reliable and valid psychometrics and valid data interpretation. Appropriate personnel can supervise administration of computerized testing, but test results must be interpreted by consultants with appropriate training in psychometric theory and concussion management. It is recommended that neuropsychologists provide such test interpretation or be available for consultation (Echemendia et al., 2013). Two commonly used computerized instruments for SRC assessment include ImPACT (ImPACT Applications, 2015) and Cogstate CCAT. Core neurocognitive functions assessed by computer programs include attention, reaction time and processing speed, and memory. Scores are compared against general athletic groups. Postinjury reevaluation with the computerized instrument used at baseline can identify specific neurocognitive concussion sequelae and help track the course of recovery from the SRC. The computer program chosen should provide statistics indicating if the change in performance is truly significant and greater than changes due to practice effects, and it should have sound psychometrics that support the statistical reliability and validity of the instrument. Otherwise, the obtained results could be inaccurate (Alsalaheen, Stockdale, Pechumer, & Broglio, 2015; Nelson et al., 2016).

In summary, assessment tools used at baseline assist in establishing critical preinjury baseline functioning and preexisting symptoms necessary for comparison when assessing the presence and extent of postinjury concussion. Assessing a concussed athlete without an appropriate preinjury baseline can be done, but results must be interpreted with greater caution.

Monitoring and Assessment of Physical and Neurocognitive Recovery

Monitoring physical recovery from SRC is easier when preinjury baseline data are available for comparison and when it involves collaboration with sports medicine professionals. Such monitoring is usually based on assessing the target symptoms that are most often present in general and in the specific athlete, separate from any acute orthopedic injury. Headaches and balance problems are the most common physical problems noted. Headaches can persist long after other physical symptoms, such as fatigue and painful sensitivity to light and sound, subside. Readministering the PCSS done at baseline targets core SRC symptoms to monitor postinjury and during recovery, and it helps tailor an individualized rehabilitation intervention plan. Similarly, readministering computerized neurocognitive assessments postinjury can be used to establish postinjury depreciation in memory, processing speed, reaction time, and concentration and to monitor recovery of these neurocognitive functions over time. Athletic trainers most often monitor physical recovery related to sport performance, whereas sport psychology consultants can monitor neurocognitive and physiologic symptoms hindering recovery, as well as the athlete's psychological reaction to these symptoms.

Monitoring and Assessment of Psychological Recovery

Traditional SRC recovery models have focused primarily on physical and neurocognitive recovery, often missing the role psychosocial factors play in exacerbating SRC symptoms and prolonging the recovery process. Typical psychological reactions include anxiety, irritability, and depression, but a variety of other emotional reactions can be expressed, such as anger or rage, originating both from psychological and neurophysiological etiologies (Broshek, DeMarco, & Freeman, 2015). What follows is a brief review of psychological domains and accompanying assessment measures that provide useful information for the sport psychology consultant when monitoring psychological and psychosocial recovery from SRC.

Motivation

The issue of motivation for recovery during SRC is somewhat unique among athletes, particularly at the elite level. As opposed to nonathletic clinical patients (especially patients in litigation), athletes tend to be highly motivated to return to their sport after injury. Concussed athletes are more likely to deny rather than exaggerate the extent of their injuries. Usually the sports medicine professional working with the athlete has intimate knowledge of an athlete's motivation and reactions to injury; thus, the professional's input can be critical in determining if a player may be minimizing or exaggerating concerns. In formal sport neuropsychological evaluations, standard tests of motivation and effort, symptom exaggeration, or malingering should be included.

Tests for assessing motivation can include the Reliable Digit Span (RDS), Computerized Assessment of Response Bias (CARB; Conder, Allen, & Cox, 1992), Rey Fifteen-Item Test (FIT; Reznek, 2005), and the Dot Counting Test (DCT; Boone, Lu, & Hertzberg, 2002). The concept behind all motivation measures is that they are usually passed by motivated people even with neurologic injury or intellectual disability because they measure effort, not ability. Overall, the verification of adequate motivation is essential to establishing the validity of all other SRC assessment results (Millis, 2015).

Depression

The Beck Depression Inventory (BDI; Beck, Ward, Mendelson, Mock, & Erbaugh, 1961) and the Hamilton Rating Scale for Depression (HRDE; Hamilton, 1960) can be used to measure depressive symptoms after an SRC (Kontos, Covassin, Elbin, & Parker, 2012). Some athletes may have mild to moderate mood changes, irritability, or sadness that clinically subsides after one to two weeks. These psychological problems may not meet full criteria for a mood disorder diagnosis, but the BDI can help identify at-risk athletes, including those with prior mental health problems. Though one would hope that a past history of depression or anxiety would have been reported to the sports medicine professionals, elevations on the BDI or similar scales can prompt a conversation addressing past or current psychological factors. The FastScreen modification of the BDI (Vargas, Rabinowitz, Meyer, & Arnett, 2015) is useful for athletes with comorbid physical injuries. The value of the BDI-FastScreen is that it removes the somatic section from the longer version because it may lead to false-positive diagnosis of depression in patients with valid pathophysiology due to physical injury or illness.

Anxiety

Anxiety is another serious psychological factor that can prolong SRC recovery. Covassin et al. (2014) found increases in both state and trait anxiety after an SRC when compared against orthopedic injury controls. Though the classic anxiety measure used in sport is the State-Trait Anxiety Inventory (STAI; Spielberger, 1988), more specific sport anxiety measures include the Sport Anxiety Scale-2 (SAS-2; Smith, Smoll, & Cumming, 2007) and the Competitive State Anxiety Inventory-2 Revised (CSAI-2R; Cox, Martens, & Russell, 2003).

Mood

A useful assessment to assess athletes' mood following an SRC is the Profile of Mood States (POMS; McNair, Lorr, & Dropplemen, 1971). Mainwaring, Hutchison, Bisschop, Comper, and Richards (2010) used the POMS with concussed athletes and found that the athletes exhibited a concussion crevice. This crevice reflected depleted vigor, increased fatigue, and lack of physical and mental stamina. Additionally, traditional psychological instruments such as the adult and adolescent versions of the Minnesota Multiphasic Personality Inventory-2 (MMPI-2; Butcher, Graham, Tellegen, & Kaemmer, 1989) remain extremely useful in psychologically complex cases. However, though pathological findings on psychometric instruments provide useful information, a comprehensive clinical mental status examination by a qualified mental health professional can be invaluable to identify common problematic psychological and emotional reactions often experienced by concussed athletes, leading to appropriate intervention early in the recovery process.

Social Support

Another important area to assess is the level of social support available to the concussed athlete. Research suggests that concussed university student-athletes experience lower levels of perceived support from all sources (e.g., family, friends, teammates, athletic trainers) in comparison to student-athletes with orthopedic injuries (Covassin et al., 2014). Two measures that can be useful with concussed athletes (depending on their age) are the modified version of the Social Support Questionnaire (SSQ6; Covassin et al., 2014) and the Child and Adolescent Social Support Scale for Healthy Behaviors (CASSS-HB; Cullum & Mayo, 2015).

Quality-of-Life Assessment

Health-related quality of life (HRQOL) is an important construct in the physical and emotional health of athletes of all ages and levels of competition. Research has found that athletes tend to have higher levels of HRQOL in comparison to nonathlete peers, especially in emotional functioning (Lam, Valier, Bay, & McLeod, 2013). However, athletes with prolonged recovery or postconcussion syndrome (PCS) have reported lower levels of HRQOL, especially in physical and school functioning. The instruments frequently used in HRQOL studies include the Pediatric Quality of Life Inventory (PedsQL; Varni & Limbers, 2009), SF-36 Health Survey (Ware, Snow, Kosinski, & Gandek, 1993), and SF-12 Health Survey (Jenkinson et al., 1997), all of which can be useful, particularly if SRC recovery is substantially prolonged due to concussion severity.

RTP Assessment

The recommended RTP protocol promulgated by the Zurich Conference states that, to support the natural healing process, concussed athletes should go into a shutdown stage with no physical exertion and minimal cognitive exertion immediately after the injury (McCrory et al., 2013). However, extended shutdown has been shown to prolong symptoms (Schneider et al., 2013). As such, a timely juxtaposition of rest and activity optimizes recovery. After a shutdown of a few days, an exertional trial lead by a member of the sports medicine team can be attempted, usually on an ergometer or stationary bike. When athletes are asymptomatic both at rest and during exertion, they can be cleared by a physician to begin the five-day graduated RTP protocol supervised by their sports medicine professional. If athletes become symptomatic at any of the five stages, they are to stop the protocol for that day, and the next day they should return to the stage in which they previously were not reporting symptoms. A sample graduated RTP protocol is detailed in McCrory et al. (2013) and presented in table 14.2. Usually, the RTP protocol is initiated by the athletic trainer and supervised by the team physician. However, the sport psychology consultant needs to be aware of the RTP protocol, monitor the athlete's psychological reactions during RTP, report any new symptoms to the trainer or physician, and assist the athlete when the RTP protocol is not progressing as planned,

Table 14.2   RTP Exercise Progression

Stage	Exercise
1	No activity
2	20-30 minutes of cardio activity: walking, stationary bike Weightlifting at light intensity (no bench, no squat; low weight, high reps) Goal: 30-40 percent of maximum heart rate
3	30 minutes of cardio activity: jogging at a medium pace Sit-ups, push-ups, and lunge walks, 25 reps each Weightlifting at moderate intensity Goal: 40-60 percent of maximum heart rate
4	30 minutes of cardio activity: running at a fast pace Sit-ups, push-ups, and lunge walks, 50 reps each Sport-specific agility drills in three planes of movement Resume regular weightlifting routine Goal: 60-80 percent of maximum heart rate
5	Noncontact practice drills, warm-up and stretch 10 minutes Intense noncontact, sport-specific agility drill for 60 minutes Goal: 80-100 percent of maximum heart rate
6	Full-contact practice
7	Full participation in competition

Adapted from McCrory et al. 2013.

either due to the emergence of new symptoms or psychological reactions slowing the recovery progression.

Refractory Sport-Related PCS Assessment

In cases of prolonged recovery or complex pre-existing risk factors for refractory PCS, the sport psychologist consultant will typically refer the athlete for a comprehensive but focused neuro-cognitive evaluation with personality assessment instruments and symptom validity measures. These evaluations are best administered by a neuropsychologist trained in SRCs. Neurocognitive domains to be assessed include attention and concentration (auditory and visual), learning and memory (auditory and visual), executive functioning, and working memory (Echemendia, Putukian, Mackin, Julian, & Shoss, 2001). Suggested neurocognitive assessment instruments are listed in the chapter-ending table Assessment Tools and Their Availability.

Additional advanced measures such as psychophysiologic and neurophysiologic assessment can help elucidate the biopsychological etiology of the refractory experience (Conder & Conder, 2014). Such comprehensive assessments can help delineate the refractory nature of the injury, identify personal strengths to guide rehabilitation, detect factors that inhibit recovery, and generate an effective treatment plan to facilitate recovery (Conder & Conder, 2015b). This comprehensive evaluation is usually beyond the scope of training of sport psychology consultants, but consultants should know when to make a referral to an appropriate professional and how to integrate the results of the assessment into their rehabilitation of the concussed athlete.

Role of Assessment in RTL

As athletes with persistent physical or neurocognitive symptoms return to their daily lives (e.g., school, university, work), many require a range of alternative reentry options and temporary accommodations. School reentry is a particular challenge given its rigorous demands for processing and output speed, sustained or concentrated focus, memory storage and retrieval, and oculomotor scanning and tracking. RTL supports are individually tailored depending on the residual SRC symptoms identified in postinjury assessment measures. An essential component of RTL planning is the pairing of residual SRC symptoms identified on serial assessment with specific school supports and accommodations. Targeted RTL accommodations might include a modified schedule, rest breaks, extended time on tests, modified assignments, copies of class notes, and reduced computer time. RTL accommodations can be conceptualized along a continuum, as shown in table 14.3. Concussed student-athletes can return to school at any level and progress through more or less supports as dictated by their recovery course.

Individualized RTL supports are gradually reduced as serial assessments or classroom performance show progressive SRC recovery. Consultants should work with available sport

neuropsychologists and educational personnel to ensure that accommodations help the concussed student-athlete function academically and psychologically at this phase of the recovery.

Currently, most states do not have formal RTL protocols in place following SRCs, but several states are in the process of establishing guidelines, policies, and procedures. In North Carolina, RTL procedures developed by the Wake County and Charlotte-Mecklenburg School Districts served as a guide for statewide implementation (Conder, 2013; Newlin & Hooper, 2015). Recently, the North Carolina State Board of Education implemented an education policy titled Return-to-Learn After Concussion (HRS-E-001) mandating that all public and charter schools in the state "develop a plan for addressing the needs of students preschool through twelfth grade suffering concussions." The policy requires that school plans include "guidelines for removal of the student from physical and mental activity when there is suspicion of concussion," as well as "delineation of requirements for safe return-to-learn or play following concussion" (North Carolina State Board of Education, 2016). The need for RTL supports following SRC has been endorsed by the American Academy of Pediatrics (AAP; Halstead et al., 2013) and the NCAA (2014), both of which highlight the need for an interdisciplinary team approach involving all academic, health care, and sport personnel as an essential part of the RTL process.

Table 14.3 RTL Accommodation Progression

Stage	RTL progression
1	Homebound with or without instruction
2	Modified school day with accommodations
3	Full school day with accommodations
4	Full school day with graduated tapering of accommodations
5	Full school day without accommodations

Assessment Tools and Their Availability

Assessment tool	Construct	Author and reference	Availability
Post-Concussion Symptom Scale (PCSS)	Concussion symptoms	Pardini, D., Stump, J.E., Lovell, M.R., Collins, M.W., Moritz, K., & Fu, F.H. (2004). The Post-Concussion Symptom Scale (PCSS): A factor analysis. *British Journal of Sports Medicine, 38*, 661-662.	Free at www. globalconcussions .org/resources/Post-Concussion-Symptom-Scale.pdf
	This classic athlete self-rating scale on physical and cognitive dimensions of concussion is used at preinjury baseline and for tracking recovery.		
Rivermead Post Concussion Symptoms Questionnaire (RPQ)	Concussion symptoms	King, N.S., Crawford, S., Wenden, F. J.,Moss, N.E.G., & Wade, D. T. (1995). The Rivermead Post Concussion Symptom Questionnaire. *Journal of Neurology, 242*(9), 587-592.	Free at http:// www.tbi-impact.org/ cde/mod_templates/ 12_F_06_ Rivermead.pdf
	This self-rating scale for subjective dimensions of concussion is used more in nonathletic settings but is considered a classic instrument.		
Sport Concussion Assessment Tool-3 (SCAT3), adult and child versions	Concussion baseline assessment	McCrory, P., Meeuwisse, W., Aubry, M., Cantu, B., Dvorak, J., Echemendia, R.J., . . . Turner, M. (2013). Consensus statement on concussion in sport: The 4th International Conference on Concussion in Sport held in Zurich, November 2012. *Clinical Journal of Sport Medicine, 23*(2), 89-117.	Free at http:// bjsm.bmj.com/ content/47/5/ 259.full.pdf
	This pencil-and-paper sport concussion assessment tool can be used at preinjury baseline and postinjury to assess possible concussions. It is for health care professionals with training in concussion assessment.		
Sport Concussion Recognition Tool	Concussion baseline assessment	McCrory, P., Meeuwisse, W., Aubry, M., Cantu, B., Dvorak, J., Echemendia, R.J., . . . Turner, M. (2013). Consensus statement on concussion in sport: The 4th International Conference on Concussion in Sport held in Zurich, November 2012. *Clinical Journal of Sport Medicine, 23*(2), 89-117.	Free at http:// bjsm.bmj.com/ content/47/5/ 267.full.pdf
	This tool for evaluating possible sport concussion is designed for use by health care professionals who do not have specific training in sport concussion.		
King-Devick Test	Concussion baseline assessment	Leong, D.F., Balcer, L.J., Galetta, S.L, Evans, G., Gimre, M., & Watt, D. (2015). The King–Devick test for sideline concussion screening in collegiate football. *Journal of Optometry, 8*(2), 131-139.	For purchase at www.kingdevick test.com
	This short concussion assessment tool can be used for preinjury baseline assessment and as a sideline assessment tool postinjury.		

(continued)

Assessment Tools and Their Availability *(continued)*

Assessment tool	Construct	Author and reference	Availability
Cogstate CCAT	Computerized baseline assessment	Cogstate CCAT (2016). Manual for Cogstate Computerized Cognitive Assessment Tool. Melbourne, Australia: Cogstate.	For purchase at www.cogstate.com
	This computerized neurocognitive task is used for preinjury baselines and postinjury concussion assessment. Note reliability concerns for all computerized measures.		
ImPACT	Computerized baseline assessment	ImPACT Applications. (2015). *Immediate Post-Concussion Assessment and Cognitive Testing (ImPACT)*. Pittsburgh: ImPACT Applications. Retrieved from www.impacttest.com.	For purchase at www.impacttest.com
	This computerized neurocognitive task is used for preinjury baselines and postinjury concussion assessment. Note reliability concerns for all computerized measures.		
Reliable Digit Span (RDS)	Symptom validity in concussions (if needed)	Schroeder, R.W., Twumasi-Ankrah, P., Baade, L.E., & Marshall, P. (2011). Reliable digit span: A systemic review and cross-validation study. *Assessment, 19*(1), 21-30.	Contact the authors
	The RDS establishes the validity of the player's effort in concussion assessment.		
Computerized Assessment of Response Bias (CARB)	Symptom validity in concussions (if needed)	Allen, L.M., Conder, R.L., Green, P., & Cox, D.R. (1997). *CARB 97 manual for the Computerized Assessment of Response Bias*. Durham, NC: CogniSyst.	Contact the authors
	This tool establishes the validity of the player's effort in concussion assessment.		
Word Choice	Symptom validity in concussions (if needed)	Wechsler, D. (2009). *Advanced clinical solutions for the WAIS-IV and WMS-IV*. San Antonio: Pearson.	For purchase at www.pearson clinical.com
	This tool establishes the validity of the player's effort in concussion assessment.		
Rey 15-Item Test (FIT)	Symptom validity in concussions (if needed)	Reznek, L.I. (2005). The Rey 15-item measure for malingering: A meta-analysis. *Brain Injury, 19*(7), 539-543.	Available in Strauss, E., Sherman, E.M.S., & Spreen, O. (2006). *A Compendium of neuropsychological tests: Administration, norms, and commentary* (2nd ed.). New York: Oxford.
	This tool establishes the validity of a player's effort in concussion assessment.		
Dot Counting Test (DCT)	Symptom validity in concussions (if needed)	Boone, K.B., Lu, P., & Hertzberg, D.S. (2002). *The Dot Counting Test manual*. Los Angeles: Western Psychological Services.	For purchase at www.wpspublish.com
	The DCT establishes the validity of a player's effort in concussion assessment.		

Assessment tool	Construct	Author and reference	Availability
Digits Forward/ Digits Backward Test	Concussion cognitive tests: attention and concentration (auditory)	Iverson, G.L., Brooks, B.L., White, T., & Stern, R.A. (2008). Neuropsychological Assessment Battery (NAB): Introduction and advanced interpretation. In A.M. Horton Jr. & D. Wedding (Eds.), *The neuropsychology handbook* (pp. 279-343). New York: Springer.	For purchase at www.parinc.com
	This brief task measures auditory attention and concentration.		
Brief Test of Attention (BTA)	Concussion cognitive tests: attention and concentration (auditory)	Schretlen, D. (1989). *Brief Test of Attention*. Baltimore: Psychological Assessment Resources.	For purchase at www.parinc.com
	This sustained auditory concentration task measures auditory working memory.		
Penn State University Symbol Cancellation Task (PSUSCT)	Concussion cognitive tests: attention and concentration (visual)	Conder, R., Conder, A., Register-Mihalik, J., Conder, L., & Newton, S. (2015). Preliminary normative data on the Penn State University symbol cancellation task with nonconcussed adolescents. *Applied Neuropsychology: Child, 4*(3), 141-147.	Contact the authors
	This pencil-and-paper visual symbol cancellation task measures speeded visual target recognition; it is also useful for assessment of vestibulo-ocular problems.		
Hopkins Verbal Learning Test–Revised (HVLT-R)	Learning and memory (auditory)	Brandt, J., & Benedict, R.H. (2001). *Hopkins Verbal Learning Test–Revised: Professional manual*. Baltimore: Psychological Assessment Resources.	For purchase at www.parinc.com
	This auditory-verbal learning test is sensitive to memory loss from concussions.		
Brief Visuospatial Memory Test–Revised (BVMT-R)	Learning and memory (visual)	Benedict, R.H., Schretlen, D., Groninger, L., Dobraski, M., & Shpritz, B. (1996). Revision of the Brief Visuospatial Memory Test: Studies of normal performance, reliability, and validity. *Psychological Assessment, 8*(2), 145.	For purchase at www.parinc.com
	Visual-spatial learning test, sensitive to memory loss from concussions.		
Symbol Digit Modalities Test (SDMT)	Learning and memory (visual)	Smith, A. (2002). *Symbol Digit Modalities Test*. Torrance, CA: Western Psychological Services.	For purchase at www.wpspublish.com
	This short visual learning task is sensitive to concussions and brain dysfunction.		
Controlled Oral Word Association (COWA)	Executive abilities and fluency (auditory)	Benton, A.L., Hamsher, S.K., & Sivan, A.B. (1983). *Multilingual aplasia examination* (2nd ed.). Iowa City, IA: AJA Associates.	For purchase at www.parinc.com
	This word generation task involves executive abilities and is sensitive to the effects of concussion.		

(continued)

Assessment Tools and Their Availability *(continued)*

Assessment tool	Construct	Author and reference	Availability
Color Trails Test (CTT)	Executive abilities and fluency (visual)	D'Elia, L., & Satz, P. (1996). *Color Trails Test*. Baltimore: Psychological Assessment Resources.	For purchase at www.parinc.com
	This visual-spatial motor task requiring cognitive flexibility and executive abilities is sensitive to the effects of concussion.		
Beck Depression Inventory-II (BDI-II)	Depression	Beck, A.T., Ward, C.H., Mendelson, M., Mock, J., & Erbaugh, J. (1961). An inventory for measuring depression. *Archives of General Psychiatry, 4*, 561-571.	For purchase at www.pearson clinical.com
	The BDI-II is a classic self-report measure of depression. It has been used in some studies of depression after concussion.		
BDI-FastScreen	Depression	Vargas, G., Rabinowitz, A., Meyer, J., & Arnett, P.A. (2015). Predictors and prevalence of postconcussion depression symptoms in collegiate athletes. *Journal of Athletic Training, 50*(3), 250-255.	For purchase at www.pearson clinical.com
	This version of the BDI may be better for athletes with physical injuries because it omits the items that measure valid physical malfunction that could lead to a false-positive diagnosis of depression.		
Center for Epidemiologic Studies Depression Scale (CESD)	Depression	Radloff, L.S. (1991). The use of the Center for Epidemiologic Studies Depression Scale in adolescents and young adults. *Journal of Youth and Adolescence, 20*(2), 149-166.	Free at www.cesd-r.com
	This depression scale is used in studies of mood disorders after concussion in athletes.		
State-Trait Anxiety Inventory (STAI)	Trait and state anxiety	Spielberger, C.D., Gorsuch, R.L., & Lushene, R. (1970). *STAI manual*. Palo Alto, CA: Consulting Psychologists Press.	For purchase at www.mind garden.com
	The STAI is the classic state-trait anxiety scale; used in studies of mood disorders after sport concussions.		
Sport Anxiety Scale-2 (SAS-2)	Anxiety	Smith, R.E., Smoll, F.L., Cumming, S.P., & Grossbard, J.R. (2006). Measurement of multidimensional sport performance anxiety in children and adults: The Sport Anxiety Scale-2. *Journal of Sport & Exercise Psychology, 28*, 479-501.	Full measure in article; http://dx.doi .org/10.1123/ jsep.28.4.479
	The SAS-2 assesses anxiety before and after SRC.		
Competitive State Anxiety Inventory-2 Revised (CSAI-2R)	Anxiety	Cox, R.H., Martens, M.P., & Russell, W.D. (2003). Measuring anxiety in athletics: The Revised Competitive State Anxiety Inventory-2. *Journal of Sport & Exercise Psychology, 25*, 519-533.	Contact the authors
	The CSAI-2R assesses anxiety before and after SRC.		
Profile of Mood States 2nd Edition (POMS 2)	Mood states	McNair, D., Lorr, M., & Dropplemen, L. (1971). *Profile of Mood States*. San Diego: Educational and Industrial Testing Services.	For purchase at www.mhs.com
	The POMS 2 is used in studies of elite athletic performance and for assessing psychological reactions to sport concussions.		

Assessment tool	Construct	Author and reference	Availability
Minnesota Multiphase Personality Inventory-2 (MMPI-2)	Mood states	Butcher, J.N., Dahlstrom, W.G., Graham, J.R., Tellegen, A., & Kaemmer, B. (1989). *The Minnesota Multiphasic Personality Inventory-2 (MMPI-2): Manual for administration and scoring*. Minneapolis: University of Minnesota Press.	For purchase at www.pearson clinical.com
	This complex psychological inventory is useful for complicated or prolonged psychological reactions to concussions. It requires specialized clinical training for administration and interpretation.		
Social Support Questionnaire (SSQ6)	Social support	Covassin, T., Crutcher, B., Bleecker, A., Heiden, E.O., Daily, A., & Yang, J.Z. (2014). Postinjury anxiety and social support among collegiate athletes: A comparison between orthopedic injuries and concussions. *Journal of Athletic Training*, 49(4), 462-468.	Contact the authors
	This inventory is useful for measuring degree and sources of support after a sport concussion.		
Child and Adolescent Social Support Scale for Healthy Behaviors (CASSS-HB)	Social support	Cullum, K.G., & Mayo, A.M. (2015). A review of the Child and Adolescent Social Support Scale for Healthy Behaviors. *Clinical Nurse Specialist*, 29(4), 198-202.	Contact the authors
	This inventory is useful for measuring degree and sources of support after a sport concussion.		
Pediatric Quality of Life Inventory (PedsQL)	Health-related quality of life	Varni, J.W., & Limbers, C.A. (2009). The Pediatric Quality of Life Inventory: Measuring pediatric health-related quality of life from the perspective of children and their parents. *Pediatric Clinics*, 56(4), 843-863.	Free at www.proqolid.org
	This inventory is useful for measuring perceived quality of life after physical illness and is used in sport concussion studies.		
SF-36 Health Survey	Health-related quality of life	Ware, J.E., Snow, K.K., Kosinski, M., & Gandek, B. (1993). *SF-36 Health Survey manual and interpretation guide*. Boston: The Health Institute.	Free at www.rand .org/health/surveys_ tools/mos/36-item-short-form/survey-instrument.html
	This respected self-report inventory measures well-being and functional health in adults. It is not a disease-specific survey but has been used in various studies of injured athletes, including sport concussions.		
SF-12 Health Survey	Health-related quality of life	Jenkinson, C., Layte, R., Jenkinson, D., Lawrence, K., Petersen, S., Paice, C., & Stradling, J. (1997). A shorter form health survey: Can the SF-12 replicate results from the SF-36 in longitudinal studies? *Journal of Public Health Medicine*, 19(2), 179-186.	Free at campaign .optum.com/ optum-outcomes/ what-we-do/health-surveys/sf-12v2-health-survey.html
	This shorter version of the SF-36 measures perceived functional health and well-being. It is limited but useful when several inventories are being administered to athletes with sport concussions.		

Chapter Takeaways

- Knowledge of the components of concussion assessment and treatment is critical for all consultants working with athletes.

- SRCs are common at all levels of sport and recreational activity. The CDC estimates there are 1.4 to 3.8 million concussions per year from all causes, with an estimated 17 percent coming from sport.

- Public awareness is growing about the ramifications of untreated SRC injuries, as evidenced by legal judgments against the NFL, state legislation mandates for SRC education and identification in youth and high school sport, and similar rulings by the NCAA.

- Preseason baseline neurocognitive assessment provides an individualized reference point for comparison in the event an SRC occurs.

- Athletes with problematic preinjury medical, academic, or emotional conditions are at higher risk for having a protracted SRC recovery.

- Postinjury assessments help identify and monitor physical, neurocognitive, and psychological SRC sequelae in order to target individualized treatment to maximize recovery.

- Traditional SRC recovery models have focused primarily on physical and neurocognitive recovery, often missing the role psychosocial factors play in exacerbating symptoms and prolonging the recovery process.

- RTP protocols guide sport reentry by progressing the concussed athlete from removal from sport and physical shutdown through graduated, structured stages of physical exertion. Athletes are monitored to ensure there is no symptom reemergence at each stage until the protocol is complete and the athlete can resume full sport participation.

- RTL protocols guide school reentry by identifying concussed student-athletes with residual physical, neurocognitive, and behavioral SRC symptoms that may compromise academic progress and by providing supports and accommodations that are gradually tapered until SRC symptoms resolve and the student-athlete can resume full academic demands.

- In cases of prolonged recovery or when the athlete has complex preexisting risk factors that suggest PCS, the sport psychologist consultant will typically refer the athlete for a comprehensive but focused neurocognitive evaluation by a sport neuropsychologist.

CHAPTER 15
Career Transition

Claire-Marie Roberts, PhD

Marisa O. Davis, MEd

In the past two decades, interest in the career transitions of athletes has gained momentum. The evolution of research in this field has helped us understand that athletic careers are not discrete occurrences composed of participation, termination, and retirement but rather a sequence of "different stages and transitions" (Wylleman, Lavallee, & Alfermann, 1999, p. 11) that present idiosyncratic challenges. Each athlete has different ways of coping with these demands. Our aim in this chapter is to provide information, insights, and practical assessment tools to help you guide transitioning athletes in a way that is positive, constructive, and life affirming during a time that is often experienced as negative, unpredictable, and stressful.

To meet this goal, it is essential to view athletes and their careers from a holistic perspective, and we use the concept of life career development as an overarching theme throughout this chapter. *Life career development* is defined as self-development over the life span through the interaction and integration of the roles, settings, and events of a person's life (Gysbers & Moore, 1975). It uses a holistic approach to understand career development throughout one's lifetime and takes the perspective that career decisions are informed by the roles people assume (e.g., student, sibling, athlete), the environments they participate in (e.g., school, training facility), and the events that occur during their lifetime (e.g., graduation, the birth of a child, athletic injury). All aspects of a person's identity and life circumstances work together to inform voca-

tional choices. Thus, a life career comprises all the jobs, occupations, careers, and experiences individuals have over the course of their lifetime. Ultimately, by viewing athletes holistically, you acknowledge that their career as an athlete is one part of their existence and one chapter of many that comprise their life story.

The athletic career is an important chapter in an athlete's life career, containing its own set of transitions to navigate. In hopes of providing resources for assisting athletes at various points in their athletic career and thus their overall life career, we have structured this chapter to first discuss career transitions within an athletic career and then move to the transition out of sport, or athletic career retirement.

Though each athlete's transition process is different, using standardized assessment tools at various points of the transition is beneficial because they provide structure and direction for services and assist in quantifying improvements in coping and other psychosocial skills (Nideffer & Sagal, 2001). However, the process-driven nature of transitions can make certain constructs difficult to measure, especially as the transition evolves. Therefore, we recommend using a combination of quantitative and qualitative assessments that are both informative and readily adaptable to the needs and goals of the transitioning athlete. Ultimately, your understanding of the client should guide your choice of assessment tools, and, as with any assessment, you must understand the psychometric properties of the measure used and explain its limitations to your client.

In this chapter, we explain the theoretical and empirical foundations of the body of knowledge surrounding athletic career transitions, the key issues for consideration when consulting with athletes in transition, and useful assessment tools. We will discuss key issues and related assessments for athletes experiencing within-career transitions and for those retiring from their athletic career.

Athletic Career Transitions

An athletic career is a significant chapter of an athlete's life career and one that contains its own set of transitions. In sport psychology literature, *athletic career* is commonly defined as "a multi-year sport activity, voluntarily chosen by the person, and aimed at achieving his/her individual peak in athletic performance in one or several sport events" (Alfermann & Stambulova, 2007, p. 713). Shifts in our perceptions of athletes' careers have led us to conclude that, in the athletic sense, *career* refers to all levels of competitive sport (e.g., local, regional, national, international amateur, professional) and involves the successful negotiation of turning phases through a series of stages (Stambulova, 2014), also known as *career transitions*. Alfermann and Stambulova (2007) therefore have conceptualized the athletic career transition as "a set of specific demands related to practice, competitions, communication, and lifestyle that athletes have to cope with in order to continue successfully in sport or to adjust to the post-career" (p. 713).

Normative athletic career transitions are foreseeable turning phases within an athletic career, such as the need for athletes to move into sport specialization or an amateur athlete turning professional. In these types of experiences, preparation to negotiate the next career phase helps the individual cope with the challenge of the transition. Conversely, nonnormative athletic career transitions reflect nonstandard and less foreseeable events, such as deselection, transferring to a new team, or serious injury. The likelihood of being able to prepare for a nonnormative transition is low and therefore may explain why some athletes experience difficulties in completing such a transition.

Research has identified two types of career transitions within an athletic career: within-career transitions and athletic career termination. These transitions can either be normative or nonnormative experiences (Stambulova, 2014). Regardless of whether athletes encounter a normative or a nonnormative transition, the way in which they cope with the transition demands can lead them to experience a healthy career transition, reflecting successful coping with the transition process (Alfermann & Stambulova, 2007); a crisis transition, indicating the athlete is not coping with the challenges presented; or a reaction that lies somewhere on a continuum between these two extremes (Roberts, Mullen, Evans, & Hall, 2015). For athletes experiencing transition crises, two potential secondary outcomes have been identified: a delayed successful transition, which comes after successful interventions, and an unsuccessful transition for those who are without access to effective interventions (Stambulova, 2012).

Within-Career Transitions

Within-career transitions are periods of normative and nonnormative events that occur throughout the developmental life cycle of an athletic career (Jones, Mahoney, & Gucciardi, 2014). They describe the changes athletes experience as they move through the stages of their career. Career stages are consecutive time periods of an athlete's sport career and development (Alfermann & Stambulova, 2007), with each stage representing different levels of performance requirements, training loads, and psychosocial demands. To conceptualize the course of athlete development, Stambulova (1994), Salmela (1994), and Durand-Bush and Salmela (2002) proposed a career stage framework for athletic careers, the tenets of which are summarized in table 15.1.

These definitions and frameworks are a useful developmental guide when working with athletes. At the same time, we need to remember that the progress of an athletic career occurs alongside the development of the individual in other areas of life (e.g., psychological, psychosocial, academic, vocational, financial). This interplay between an athletic career and other areas of life forms the basis for important contributions to a person's overall life career development.

Table 15.1   Athletic Career Stage Frameworks

	Stambulova's general (normative) stages of an athletic career	Salmela and Durand-Bush's general (normative) stages of an athletic career
Stage 1	Beginning of sport specialization	Initiation
Stage 2	Transition to more intensive training in the chosen sport	
Stage 3	Transition from junior to senior or high achievement sport	Development
Stage 4	Amateur to professional sport	Perfection
Stage 5	Peak to the final stage	Maintenance
Stage 6	Transition to the postcareer	Discontinuation

Table 15.2   Conceptual Models of the Athletic Career

	Athletic career descriptive models	Career explanatory transition models
What do they depict?	The development and life cycle of an athletic career	The process of transition through an athletic career, including reasons for, demands of, coping with, outcomes of, and consequences of the transition
What are the key features?	A set of stages ranging from the preparation or initiation stage of an athletic career through to development and specialization, investment and culmination, maintenance, and finally discontinuation	The process of coping with the demands presented by the transition; outcomes are categorized as either successful or crisis transitions
Who developed them?	Bloom, 1985; Côté, 1999; Salmela, 1994; Stambulova, 1994; Wylleman & Lavallee, 2004	Schlossberg, 1981; Stambulova, 2003; Taylor & Ogilvie, 1994

To illustrate the range, complexities, and potential timing of transitions within an athlete's life, Wylleman and Lavallee (2004) proposed a conceptual developmental model representing those normative movements from one phase of an athlete's life to the next. Their model illustrates how each within-career transition in the athlete's sporting life may occur in conjunction with progression in other aspects of the athlete's life, such as psychological, psychosocial, and academic development. The model was updated to include vocational and financial development and was subsequently renamed the *holistic athletic career model* (Wylleman, Reints, & DeKnop, 2013).

Conceptual Models

To conceptualize athletic career transitions, two categories of theoretical models attempt to capture the life cycle and processes involved. First, athletic career descriptive models detail the life cycle of an athletic career as a miniature life-span course covering the changes in athletes and in their social environment across stages (Alfermann & Stambulova, 2007) and predicting the existence and order of normative career transitions. Second, career explanatory models focus on reasons for demands, coping, outcomes, and consequences related to a transition. Coping processes are central to both types of models and include methods used by athletes to adjust to transition demands (Alfermann & Stambulova, 2007). A summary of these models and their tenets can be found in table 15.2.

These definitions and conceptual models provide us with a starting point in understanding the key stages and features of athletic career transitions. At the same time, research has led us away from attempting to shoehorn athletic careers into general frameworks of careers and transitions (see an overview in Alfermann & Stambulova, 2007), moving instead toward a more culturally informed understanding of the nuances of the individual sport career (Stambulova & Ryba, 2013).

Key Issues in Consultation and Recommendations for Assessment

The theoretical and conceptual information covered so far serves as a foundation for your work in supporting athletes through athletic career transitions. In this section, we discuss some of the key issues that mediate the transitional experience, and we offer brief descriptions of assessments that may be helpful in designing and delivering appropriate individualized interventions for athletes preparing for or in transition. Unless otherwise noted, the assessment tools in this chapter have sound psychometric properties, including acceptable validity, reliability, and internal consistency.

Coping

Coping is part of a complex cycle of stress and adaptation (Nicholls, 2010). Effective coping in any domain of life is determined by the balance between perceived resources and barriers (Stambulova, 2003). Therefore, if someone lacks the necessary resources and faces too many or insurmountable barriers, a crisis may ensue. The ability to cope with uncertainty and a wide range of new demands is central to the outcome of all athletic career transitions. Popular coping strategies used by athletes in transition include acceptance, positive reinterpretation and growth, planning, active coping, mental disengagement, and seeking of social support for emotional reasons (Grove, Lavallee, & Gordon, 1997). Of course, not all coping strategies are effective, and some athletes engage in denial or turn to alcohol or drug use in an effort to cope with their current circumstances. The ability to assess coping is fundamental to predicting those at risk of crisis transitions and to informing an intervention plan that focuses on building effective coping skills and resilience.

Coping strategies within the athletic population have principally been measured using a sport-specific version of Folkman and Lazarus' (1988) Ways of Coping Questionnaire (WCQ) and Carver, Scheier, and Weintraub's (1989) COPE Inventory. Both of these instruments require athletes to recall stressful situations and how they managed them, including coping strategies and the extent to which they were used. The coping questionnaires recommended may be:

- **Ways of Coping Questionnaire (WCQ; Folkman & Lazarus, 1988).** The WCQ measures coping processes as opposed to coping dispositions or styles. It is designed to identify and assess thoughts and actions that people use to cope with stressful situations such as transitions. The WCQ consists of 50 items (plus 16 fill items) within eight subscales that are measured on a 4-point Likert scale, including confrontive coping (6 items), distancing (6 items), self-controlling (7 items), seeking social support (6 items), accepting responsibility (4 items), escape and avoidance (8 items), planful problem solving (6 items), and positive reappraisal (7 items). Athletes are asked to identify a recent stressful experience to anchor their responses to the items on the questionnaire. The issue with this measure is that the internal consistencies are often unsatisfactory, and test–retest reliabilities are unreported (e.g., Schwarzer & Schwarzer, 1996). This is a common issue with coping measures. The authors of the scale urge users to adjust the WCQ to make its coping statements context specific to enhance validity and reliability. This measure may be of use when you are working with athletes experiencing a wide range of within-career transitions in order to identify their typical style of coping.

- **COPE Inventory (Carver et al., 1989).** Because people may engage in a wide range of coping responses during a given period, the COPE Inventory, a 60-item questionnaire, was designed to assess a broad range of such responses, both functional and dysfunctional. There are 15 scales, each consisting of 4 items: positive reinterpretation and growth, mental disengagement, focus on and venting of emotions, use of instrumental social support, active coping, denial, religious coping, humor, behavioral disengagement, restraint, use of emotional social support, substance use, acceptance, suppression of competing activities, and planning.

- **Brief COPE (Carver, 1997).** The Brief COPE is a 28-item version of the COPE Inventory that measures self-distraction, active coping, denial, substance use, use of emotional support, instrumental support, behavioral disengagement, venting, positive reframing, planning, humor, acceptance, religion, and self-blame. The Brief COPE was developed specifically for situations in which participant response burden is a considering factor.

- **Coping Function Questionnaire (CFQ; Kowalski & Crocker, 2001).** The CFQ was developed to assess problem-focused, emotion-focused, and avoidance coping in sport participants. It is recommended for use in situations where you are seeking to measure the function of coping rather than the coping strategies employed. Coping serves three functions: Problem-focused coping aims to change the person–situation relationship, emotion-focused coping relates to the management of emotion and physiological reactions generated by stressful situations and environments, and avoidance coping is where the person actively leaves the stressful situation or environment. The CFQ measures these three subscales of coping function using 18 items, scored on a 5-point scale, that ask how much the individual uses each coping function to handle a self-indicated stressful situation. This assessment is of particular use with adolescent athletes because it has been specifically validated with this population.

Self-Identity

People's identity is composed of their self-identity and social identity and is based on the mix of talents they possess, roles they hold, groups of which they are a member, and character traits they display. Athletic identity is a subset of overall identity and is the degree to which people perceive themselves to be an athlete as opposed to other roles, such as student, friend, or parent. It can also be described as how big a piece of the pie, so to speak, their athletic role is in relation to other aspects of their self-identity.

Athletic identity plays a central role in athletic career transitions. For athletes whose self-identity consists predominantly of their athletic identity, attributes such as commitment in training and sport-related goals, persistence, motivation, and discipline predict the likelihood of successful within-career transitions. However, there is a strong positive correlation between high levels of athletic identity and low levels of career maturity, delayed career development, difficulties adjusting to injury, and identity crises. Athletes who are disproportionately invested in their sport often forgo the exploration and development of other roles, interests, skills, and abilities that could result in a more balanced and adaptable self-identity. The focus on and commitment to one identity at the expense of exploring other areas is referred to as *identity foreclosure*. As previously discussed, an athletic career should be one part of an athlete's life career, not the entire life career. Yet, if athletic identity predominates athletes' self-identity, they will be less likely to develop the attitudes and competencies necessary to make realistic career decisions, and a crisis transition will be a more likely outcome as they transition out of sport. Identifying those athletes at risk of identity foreclosure is critical to bringing about preemptive change during the course of an athletic career.

Athletic identity as a construct has been studied widely over the past 20 years. Thus, a number of standardized assessments are available. However, standardized assessments are not always appropriate to use with every client. The Measuring Possible Selves (MPS) exercise described in the Thinking About the Future sidebar is an excellent task to use with clients who may benefit from a more informal exercise rather than a standardized assessment. Some of the most common standardized assessments for athletic identity include the following:

- **Sport Identity Index (SII; Curry & Weaner, 1987).** The 37-item SII measures the degree to which an individual identifies with the sport role. It collects a score (out of 100) of sport importance to the individual and a ranking of its importance against other areas of life (e.g., peer, kinship, academic, vocational). The SII comprises three subscales: reasons for participating in sport (15 items), personal evaluation of sport involvement (11 items), and other expectations of sport involvement (7 items). We recommend this measure to help assess athletes experiencing high levels of role conflict during their athletic career. Although limited in its application, the SII is a valuable tool because it measures the hierarchy of the sport identity within the context of other identities.

- **Athletic Identity Measurement Scale (AIMS; Brewer, Van Raalte, & Linder, 1990, 1993).** The AIMS is the most popular assessment of athletic identity in athletes and is used widely by consultants. It is a seven-item scale consisting of three subscales: social identity (three items), exclusivity (two items), and negative affectivity (two items). The subscales are measured with a 7-point Likert scale and responses are summed to produce a total athletic identity score.

- **Athletic Identity Measurement Scale–Plus (AIMS-Plus; Cieslak, 2004).** The AIMS-Plus questionnaire was based on the original AIMS (Brewer & Cornelius, 2001), SII (Curry & Weaner, 1987), identity structural theory (Stryker, 1980), and cognitive identity theory (Burke, 1991). The AIMS-Plus is a self-report questionnaire with 22 items and a Likert-scale model of response ranging from 0 to 100 (0 = totally disagree; 100 = totally agree). Cieslack (2004) claimed that the AIMS did not examine the significance of one's internal identity and external role and the relationship of athletic identity to other identities. To address the criticisms of the AIMS, he developed the AIMS-Plus, which he reports has satisfactory validity and reliability.

The AIMS-Plus measures two major categories of identity: internal and external identity components. The internal subscales are self-identity, positive affectivity, and negative affectivity. The external subscales are social identity and exclusivity. The athletic identity score is obtained by calculating the average score between the sum of the internal components and the sum of the external components.

Assessment in Action

Thinking About the Future

In cases where a formal assessment tool is not appropriate, the Measuring Possible Selves (MPS) exercise may be useful. Possible selves are a central concept in identity and career transition research. They refer to images people have about who they might become, who they would like to become, who they should become, or who they fear becoming in the future (Markus & Nurius, 1986). These images are central to successful career transitions because successful transitions are fueled by modification of an individual's set of possible selves, which leads to successful identity growth and ultimately aids a successful career transition.

In the MPS exercise, people write down their hoped-for selves, which are their visions of where they want to be in the future and might include personal, physical, educational, lifestyle, family, occupational, and leisure interests. Separately, they list their feared possible selves, or visions of where they do not want to be in the future (e.g., in a job with no prospects). During consultations, you can examine both lists as points for discussion, or you can use them as part of a goal-setting exercise where you create action plans for how the athlete might move toward the hoped-for selves and away from the feared selves. The goal of this exercise is to help clients gain clarity about their desired future, which can help determine appropriate next steps to move toward their desired future. It also provides insight into undesired futures, possible consequences of inaction, and ways to avoid the undesired futures.

- **Public-Private Athletic Identity Scale (PPAIS; Nasco & Webb, 2006).** The PPAIS is a 10-item questionnaire that measures both the public and private dimensions of athletic identity. There have been suggestions that it measures similar constructs to the AIMS, yet the AIMS may be more heavily weighted with items that evaluate the private dimension of athletic identity. This scale is valuable because it helps distinguish between the behavioral effects of private and public athletic identity, which in turn enhances our ability to design appropriate and effective interventions.

Support

An athlete's identity, both self and social, is influenced by social support networks. Family, friends, teammates, coaches, agents, trainers, consultants, and even the media (Cosh, Crabb, & LeCouter, 2013) can function as forms of social support. According to Stambulova, Alfermann, Statler, and Côté (2009), "Athletes perceive social support from significant others as the most important resource at the beginning and at the end of the career" (p. 408). At the same time, support is not always positive. Negative support can include doubt, skepticism, pigeonholing, fixating on the athlete's athletic identity and achievements, or problematizing the athlete's transition within or out of sport. Athletes also must be mindful of whether the support they receive is real or perceived. *Perceived support* refers to the belief that one's network can or will offer effective support in times of need. Though perceptions of support have been shown to be beneficial in predicting adjustment to stressful life events (Wethington & Kessler, 1986), athletes must be aware that their perceptions do not always translate into receiving actual support. It is not uncommon

---

Assessment in Action

Identifying Sources of Support

This exercise can help identify people and organizations in your clients' social support systems and the types of support that are present or lacking in order to assist with goal setting or action planning. Social support can be organized into four types of behaviors: emotional (expressions of love, trust, empathy, and caring), instrumental (tangible aid and service), informational (advice, suggestions, and information), and appraisal (information that can be used for self-evaluation and esteem) (House, 1981). For this exercise, first discuss these types of support with your clients to ensure they understand them. Then have the client draw an image similar to the one shown here, with each box representing a type of support and the circle representing an unknown type of support. In each box, the client lists all the people and organizations that provide that type of support, and in the circle, the client lists people and organizations that provide support that they are unable to classify. The key to this exercise is processing it with the clients in order to gain a better understanding of what types of support are present and what types they may need to seek out and to identify appropriate places to turn to for support in various situations.

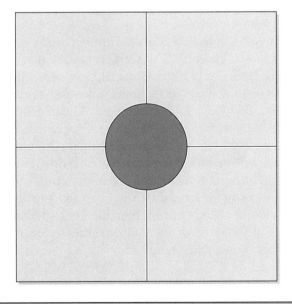

for athletes to experience positive social support from their coaches and organization while they are playing, only to find that once they have exited their sport, the support disappears. Social support can affect self-identity either positively or negatively. As a result, the type of social support or perceptions about social support can influence athletes' self-identity, their attitude toward and approach to transition, and their ability to embrace new identities and roles.

Several assessments and exercises can identify and measure an athlete's social support and quality of interpersonal relationships. We recommend two standardized measures that may provide insight into the quality and availability of these resources for your clients:

- **Sport Interpersonal Relationships Questionnaire (SIRQ; Wylleman, Vanden Auweele, De Knop, Sloore, & De Martelaer, 1995).** The SIRQ assesses the quality of athletes' relationships in their social network. It comes in three versions, one for each relationship in the athletic triangle: athlete–coach (SIRQ-AC), athlete–parent (SIRQ-AP), and parent–coach (SIRQ-PC). The SIRQ can be used to evaluate the quality of athletes' relationships as a means to generate self-awareness of and expectations for the best sources of social support during their transition. Apart from the benefits of examining the best sources of social support in detail, feedback can be generated as a result of completing the questionnaires and used to inform behavioral modifications.

- **Perceived Available Support in Sport Questionnaire (PASS-Q; Freeman, Coffee, & Rees, 2011).** *Perceived support* typically refers to a person's belief that assistance would be available if required. The PASS-Q is a 16-item measure that assesses four types of perceived support: emotional, esteem, informational, and tangible. Using this questionnaire with athletes in transition can help you understand if there are any gaps in support that need to be addressed so that athletes perceive that they can access relevant assistance when required.

Retirement

The final career transition in sport is athletic retirement, and there is a great deal of research interest surrounding the topic. The frequent associations with dysfunctional reactions such as depression, addiction, financial difficulties, and suicidal ideation (Roberts, Mullen, Evans, & Hall, 2015) may account for this research interest. Researchers suggest that, although this transition is the most normative because every athlete will face retirement, it is often the most difficult to navigate without challenges. Successful negotiation of athletic career termination is considered a smooth path to adjustment to life after an athletic career. However, a smooth transition can be difficult to achieve because athletes coming to the end of their career may face a barrage of challenges, including relinquishing the structure of physical training and competition, contending with bodily changes, missing the people with whom they had been working, foregoing their primary identity and establishing a new one, trying to carve out a new social status within society, and starting a new occupation. A number of notable factors can have significant bearing on the transition out of sport, including the reasons for retirement, athletic identity, career or preretirement planning, and availability and type of support available.

Reasons for Retirement

The causes of athletic career retirement may influence how athletes approach their transition out of sport and, ultimately, its outcome. It has been suggested that when athletes choose to retire from their sport, their perception of control over this decision means they are more likely to successfully meet the challenges of athletic retirement and have a relatively smooth transition (McKnight et al., 2009; Petitpas, Champagne, Chartrand, Danish, & Murphy, 1997). In contrast, athletes who have been forced to exit their sport due to deselection or injury, for example, may feel little control over the transition and perceive that they had no choice in the decision. In these types of situations, athletes often feel there are still goals to accomplish and enjoyment to be gained, so they cling to their athletic role (Petitpas et al., 1997). However, research by Roberts et al. (2015) suggests that rather than focusing on dichotomizing reactions to retirement (healthy versus crisis transitions), the reality may exist on a continuum somewhere between retirement crises and uncomplicated adaptation.

In terms of effective adaptation to athletic career retirement, experience has shown that retiring through injury is one of the most concerning scenarios for athletes. Not only is injury-induced retirement a nonnormative transition, but contending with the physical complications of an injury often means athletes' life satisfaction is negatively affected, and hence their adjustment to postsport life may be slow and challenging.

Likewise, athletes who are deselected experience difficulties associated with a nonnormative transition, and as a consequence adapting to life after sport may be challenging. Additionally, research has suggested that burnout may play a role in the decision to retire from sport (Roberts et al., 2015). For further details on burnout, please refer to chapter 7.

Assessment of Retirement Decisions

A number of assessments can help you identify the reasons for athletic career retirement, providing knowledge you can use to design appropriate interventions for athletes in career transition. Two examples follow:

- **Athletes' Retirement Decision Inventory (ARDI; Fernandez, Stephan, & Fouquereau, 2006).** The ARDI is a self-report tool that assesses the pattern of reasons for athletic retirement. It is based on the push pull anti-push anti-pull framework, within which athletes may fluctuate when their athletic careers are coming to an end. There are 39 items that assess four subscales: push (6), pull (12), anti-push (6), and anti-pull (15). This assessment may help you and the athlete understand how the pull to retirement

also exists against concerns of a life without sport (anti-pull) and how a deselected athlete (push) might feel it was too early to retire (anti-push). This assessment helps identify the most prominent factor in the ending of the athletic career and form the basis for career transition interventions or counseling.

- **Revised Causal Dimension Scale (CDSII; McAuley, Duncan, & Russell, 1992).** The CDSII is used to identify the reasons for athletic career retirement. The measure employs a combination of qualitative and quantitative methods and starts by asking athletes to state the most important reason for retiring from their highest level of competitive sport. They are then asked to rate this causal attribution (reason for retirement) along four dimensions, each of which consists of three items rated on 9-point Likert-type scales: locus of causality, causal stability, personal control, and external control.

Postsport Career Planning and Development

In this section, we discuss key topics in career development, including career planning, barriers to career decision making, values, interests, skills and aptitudes, and personality. We suggest assessments that raise awareness of these factors for the purpose of developing bespoke interventions to support preretirement planning.

Career Development Theories

As athletes begin to move toward athletic career retirement, planning for life after sport becomes increasingly important. Career development theories can be useful for conceptualizing the transition process because they help us understand how and why people make career-related decisions, which can aid in developing career transition interventions.

Social cognitive career theory (SCCT; Lent, Brown, & Hackett, 1994), grounded in Bandura's social cognitive theory (1986), suggests that career choices are developed and actioned through self-efficacy, outcome expectations, and goals. For example, people who experience competency and positive outcomes from certain activities form lasting interests in them, such as athletes moving through a long-term athletic career. The model of career self-management is Lent and Brown's (2013) extension of the SCCT that helps explain a variety of career decisions made over the course of an individual's life span. This model suggests that outcome expectations and self-efficacy work together to predict career goals, actions, and outcomes. Happenstance learning theory (HLT; Krumboltz, 2009) explains that we have no way of predicting who will follow what career path, but a person's learning experiences, whether occurring in a planned or unplanned fashion, present opportunities for career action.

Understanding these career development theories can help you assist clients with integrating the unique experiences in their athletic career into their overall life career development as they prepare for and negotiate the transition from an athletic career to a postsport career. They also provide theoretical context to the career planning and development assessments included in this chapter and are recommended for use with transitioning athletes.

Career Planning and Development Assessments

Preretirement planning is a challenge many athletes face. It can be difficult to manage the immediate priority of excelling in their current career while balancing the need to plan for a postsport career. As a result, career-assistance programs, which provide targeted resources and guidance on a range of life skills and personal management topics, are becoming increasingly popular and more readily available. Career maturity is also a helpful area to assess when working with athletes on career-related issues. It involves people's readiness to make career decisions and takes into account their attitudes toward and knowledge of career decision making. Understanding your client's level of career maturity can help you design and implement effective interventions for career development.

This section reviews common career development assessments that can help clients plan and prepare for life after sport. We include five categories of assessments based on the construct they are designed to assess: barriers to career decision making, values, interests, personalities, and skills and aptitudes.

Research (Roberts et al., 2015; Stambulova & Ryba, 2013) and our own consulting experiences suggest that introducing preretirement planning as early as possible helps prepare athletes for life after sport. These instruments can also be used during or after athletes' exit from an athletic career, especially if they are experiencing difficulties adjusting to their retirement. As with all assessments, deciding if and when to introduce these measures should be based on your knowledge of your clients and their needs.

Barriers to Career Decision Making

As athletes approach athletic retirement, it is essential to assess their readiness to begin the transition process. Identifying barriers to transition is critical because, as we have previously stated, if a person lacks the necessary resources and faces too many or insurmountable barriers, a crisis transition may ensue. The assessments that follow will help you assist your clients with identifying barriers that may hinder their transition process and help you with providing interventions to help your clients overcome those barriers.

- **My Vocational Situation (MVS; Holland, Daiger, & Power, 1980).** The MVS is designed to assess a person's readiness for career decision making and to identify unclear vocational goals. It consists of 18 true–false questions, 8 yes–no questions, and space for open-ended answers. There are three subscales: lack of vocational identity, lack of information or training, and emotional and personal barriers. It is helpful for identifying areas hindering a client's forward progress.

- **Career Beliefs Inventory (CBI; Krumboltz & Vosvick, 1996).** The CBI can be used to explore generalizations, assumptions, and beliefs that your clients hold about themselves and the work world that may hinder them from taking career-related actions. It is designed to stimulate conversation with the goal of discovering new possibilities. The CBI has 96 items and five subscales: my current career situation, what seems necessary for my happiness, factors that influence my decisions, changes I am willing to make, and effort I am willing to initiate.

- **Motivational Appraisal of Personal Potential (MAPP).** The MAPP assessment is a popular and comprehensive career assessment tool that helps identify future career directions. It consists of 71 items that assess career interests, values, personality, aptitudes, and work activities. Each item is presented as a triad in which athletes select one they most prefer, select one they least prefer, and leave one blank.

- **Career Decision-Making Self-Efficacy Scale (CDSE; Taylor & Betz, 1983).** The CDSE assesses the degree to which people believe they are capable of completing tasks necessary to make career-related decisions. The CDSE is based on the premise that career decisions, achievements, and adjustment behaviors are subject to the influence of self-efficacy beliefs. It is available in a 50-item or 25-item format (Betz, Klein, & Taylor, 1996) and has five subscales: self-appraisal, occupational information, goal selection, planning, and problem solving.

- **Career Maturity Inventory—Form C (CMI Form C; Savickas & Porfeli, 2012).** *Career maturity* refers to a person's attitudes toward and knowledge of career decision making and is a prerequisite for the ability to make sound and realistic occupational choices. The CMI Form C assesses aspects of career adaptability. The assessment comprises 24 items across four subscales (concern, curiosity, confidence, and consultation) that respondents answer in an agree–disagree format. Responses are scored using an answer key that calculates scores for each subscale and a total summed score to indicate career choice readiness. This score can be compared with established percentile ranks located in the *CMI Administration and Use Manual*

(Crites, 1978). We have found the CMI to be a useful screening tool to address areas of concern where athletes may not have enough information about themselves or the world in order to make a realistic career decision.

Values

Values inventories help people identify, clarify, understand, and prioritize the relative importance of values, activities, and work conditions. Some inventories measure work-related values, some measure personal values, and some measure a combination of the two. Understanding personal and work values is important to career development because work values have been shown to be valid predictors of job satisfaction.

An example of a value inventory is the O*NET Work Importance Profiler (WIP; National Center for O*NET Development, n.d.). The WIP helps clients understand what is important to them in a job and identify potential occupations that possess similar characteristics. The clients sort cards that describe various aspects of work based on how important those aspects are to their ideal job. The tool is offered

---

Assessment in Action

Identifying and Prioritizing Values for Exploring Future Careers

For clients who prefer an informal assessment, an exercise such as the Values Auction or Values Pie may be appropriate. In these exercises, clients determine their own values and rank them according to importance. In the Values Auction, clients rank their values by determining how much money they would spend on each at an auction. In the Values Pie, clients draw a pie where each slice represents one of their values, its size corresponding to its importance. The goal of these exercises is to help clients identify and prioritize values, activities, and work conditions that may be present in their future occupation in order to recognize potential matches for future occupations.

in computerized format (WIP) or paper-and-pencil format (Work Importance Locator [WIL]) and can be self-scored and self-interpreted. However, processing the results with your clients increases their self-awareness and reflection. The tool measures six predetermined work values (achievement, independence, recognition, relationships, support, and working conditions) rather than allowing clients to determine their own values. Using predetermined values may be beneficial with clients struggling to identify their own work-related values. The WIP is one of the career exploration tools available in the O*NET Resource Center and links directly to occupations in O*NET OnLine, a free online database of detailed information on over 800 occupations.

Interests

Interest inventories help people clarify their likes and dislikes of various activities and then summarize their interests into patterns. These tools create awareness of possibilities, confirm tentative choices, and align interests with occupational areas. Many interest inventories are based on Holland's theory of vocational personalities and work environments (1997). He theorized that people and work environments can be classified into six types: realistic (R), investigative (I), artistic (A), social (S), enterprising (E), and conventional (C), or RIASEC. When people work in environments that are similar to their interest or personality type, they are more likely to be satisfied and successful at work.

• **Self-Directed Search (SDS; Holland, 1985).** The SDS was created by Holland (1985) and is based on his RIASEC theory. Clients respond to questions about their activities, interests, competencies, and aspirations, and a three-letter Holland Code is developed based on the three types (R, I A, S, E, or C) that best describe the client's work personality. The reports include a list of occupations (with required level of education), leisure activities, and fields of study that have three-letter codes similar to the client's. This tool helps establish work interests and hence potential suitable jobs, and it has

been reported to be both valid and reliable. The SDS is one of the most widely used career interest inventories, and the three-letter Holland Code can be used with many other tools. Several free adaptations of this assessment are available online; however, many of the free adaptations have limitations. For example, they are often shortened, are not adequately tested for validity and reliability, and offer an incomplete picture of work interests due to the limited number of items.

• **O*NET My Next Move: Interest Profiler (National Center for O*NET Development, n.d.).** The Interest Profiler at My Next Move is another free online tool that links to O*NET OnLine, and it also follows the RIASEC theory. The tool contains 60 questions about feelings toward common work activities and is structured on a 5-point Likert scale. The results provide insight into work activities and occupations that are similar to the client's indicated interests.

Skills and Aptitudes

Identifying and articulating skills are an essential part of career development because people are more likely to thrive in careers for which they possess relevant skills. These assessments can help athletes make decisions about pursuing career options that may require strengthening their skills or shifting their energies into finding a career more closely aligned with the skills they already possess.

One such assessment is the Campbell Interest and Skill Survey (CISS; Campbell, 1995). The CISS measures people's interests ("How much do you like an activity?") and skills ("How confident do you feel performing the activity?"). It rates people on seven orientation scales: influencing, organizing, helping, creating, analyzing, producing, and adventuring. The results provide insight into the interplay between a client's interests and skills using the following ratings: pursue (both skill and interest are high), develop (interest is high, skill is lower), explore (skill is high, interest is lower), and avoid (both skill and interest are low). This instrument, which has 320 multiple-choice items, focuses on occupations that require postsecondary education and may not be appropriate for all clients. It is based on Campbell's model for occupational orientations (Campbell, 1995) and also loosely corresponds to the RIASEC themes. Certain educational levels or certification are required to purchase and administer it.

Personality Inventories

Personality inventories assess personal, emotional, and social traits and behaviors, strengths, and communication styles (see chapter 6). It can be particularly helpful because the results can be applied to clients' behavior in their athletic career. These assessments are often based on the work of Carl Jung, who theorized that all people fall into four categories based on personality patterns: extroversion versus introversion, sensing versus intuition, thinking versus feeling, and judging versus perceiving. According to Jung, each person's personality type is composed of a combination of these four trait categories. Thus, personality inventories provide insights into how people prefer to function and how they might typically respond to certain work environments or situations. Note that some clients may feel pressure to provide socially desirable answers on personality inventories.

However, some inventories contain built-in lie scales to counteract this deliberate attempt to distort the results.

One example of a personality inventory is the Myers-Briggs Type Indicator (MBTI; Briggs-Myers & Briggs, 1985). The MBTI is perhaps the best-known and most widely used career self-assessment; however, it requires certification and must be purchased in order to administer and interpret it. A four-letter personality type, patterned after Jung's taxonomy, is developed based on clients' preferences for where they draw their energy from, how they gather information, how they make decisions, and how they prefer to deal with the outside world. Table 15.3 illustrates the basic preferences of the four dichotomous personality types that combine to create the 16 four-letter personality types. This assessment is useful because many tools use the MBTI four-letter personality type. There are also many adaptations of this instrument that are free and do not require certification that can be used in conjunction with other assessment tools that use the MBTI personality types. This tool has good validity and reliability; however, its constructs have been questioned because of the absolute classification scheme, which makes it possible for people with relatively similar scores to be labeled with much different personalities (Pittenger, 1993).

Table 15.3   MBTI Personality Type and Preferences

Favorite world		Information gathering		Decision making		Structure	
Extraversion (E)	Draws energy from action	Sensing (S)	Prefers details and facts Trusts information that is tangible and concrete	Thinking (T)	Prefers to first look for logic and consistency	Judging (J)	Prefers things to be decided
Introversion (I)	Draws energy from quiet time spent alone	Intuition (N)	Prefers to interpret and add meaning Interested in theory, context, or patterns	Feeling (F)	Prefers to first look at individuals and special circumstances	Perceiving (P)	Prefers to stay open to new information and options

Based on Briggs-Myers and Briggs 1985.

• **MBTI Step II Interpretive Report Form Q (MBTI Step II; Quenk, Hammer, & Majors, 2001).** The MBTI Step II expands on the MBTI by addressing individual differences within each type. The MBTI Step II breaks down the four MBTI types into five detailed subcategories called *facets*, with dichotomous poles and a midzone that provides additional information about specific behavioral preferences. This tool requires certification to administer, score, and interpret.

• **Clifton StrengthsFinder (Clifton & Anderson, 2001).** Clifton StrengthsFinder is an online tool designed to help people uncover their talents and discover their natural strengths. The client has 20 seconds to respond to a statement, and there are 180 Likert-scaled statements total. There are 34 signature strengths, and the resulting report highlights the client's top 5 strengths. A report with the client's remaining strengths is available for an additional fee. The online portal provides access to several additional reports, including an individualized explanation of the unique interplay of the client's top strengths. There are also action items to help clients continue to develop their strengths, and suggestions are offered on ways to use their talents in everyday life. StrengthsQuest is a version of StrengthsFinder that is adapted for use with student populations.

• **Values In Action Inventory of Strengths (VIA-IS; Peterson & Seligman, 2004).** The VIA-IS is a free online tool based on the principles of positive psychology. It is designed to help people understand and develop their particular character strengths, which fall under six virtue categories: wisdom, courage, humanity, justice, temperance, and transcendence. The assessment and resulting list of character strengths with descriptions are free; however, additional in-depth reports are available for a fee. Though the authors state that the VIA-IS is valid and reliable, they offer no evidence to support their claim. As a consequence, any conclusions you draw should be made with caution, and the results of the VIA-IS are best used in conjunction with other data to strengthen its accuracy.

Adjusting to Retirement

A number of assessments have been developed to identify the career transition needs and experiences of athletes and can help determine their level of adjustment to athletic retirement. For the most part, these assessments have been developed to shed light on the experience of retirement from sport, although some may be used with athletes undergoing within-career transitions.

• **Career Transitions Inventory (CTI; Heppner, 1998).** The CTI is a 40-item, 6-point Likert-scale assessment designed to assess the psychological resources and barriers that athletes may have when contending with retirement from their sport careers. The five subscales measure motivation to move forward (readiness), confidence in the ability to make a successful career change (confidence), feelings of personal control over the career transition process (control), perceived social support (perceived support), and the degree to which the individual perceives the career transition to be independent and autonomous (decision independence). The CTI can raise awareness of internal barriers that prevent athletes from experiencing an effective transition into retirement and can be used to design strategies to overcome those barriers.

• **Professional Athletes Career Transition Inventory (PACTI; Blann, 1984, as cited in Blann & Zaichkowsky, 1989).** The PACTI assesses the career transition needs of professional athletes. The assessment itself comprises four components. The Career Planning Scale (CPS) indicates the extent to which athletes are involved in career planning. The Career Needs Scale (CNS) measures individuals' financial needs and the role of spouses or partners in the planning process. The Life Satisfaction Scale (LSS) assesses how satisfied athletes are with their life at the present moment, and the Career Awareness Scale (CAS) establishes the level of the athletes' career awareness. Using this measure with athletes during the course of their professional career may provide insight into who is at risk for difficulties in retirement and what interventions may be beneficial for building resources to cope with transitions during the sport career.

• **Athlete Retirement Questionnaire (ARQ; Sinclair & Orlick, 1993).** The ARQ was designed to measure the transitional experience of high-performance athletes. This 35-item self-report instrument gathers data on athletes' careers and their athletic retirement transition. Three subscales are measured: reasons for retirement (11 items), difficulties encountered during transition (11 items), and coping strategies (13 items). Athletes respond to the items using a 5-point Likert scale. This questionnaire helps generate an understanding of how to help athletes during their transition by identifying areas of support needed.

• **British Athlete Lifestyle Assessment Needs in Career and Education Scale (BALANCE Scale; Lavallee & Wylleman, 1999).** The BALANCE scale identifies athletes at risk of experiencing difficulties in their transition out of sport. Its 12 subscales assess the potential for adjustment difficulties resulting from mediators of the retirement experience: the perception of control over athletic retirement, athletic identity, identity foreclosure, social support and mentoring, previous experience in transitions, continued involvement in sport, occupational planning, socioeconomic status, transferrable skills, achievement of sport-related goals, access to transition support services, and having a new focus after sport. A score above 65 on this scale indicates considerable adjustment difficulties to career termination (Lavallee & Wylleman, 1999). This instrument has been shown to accurately predict career termination difficulties, and as a result its strengths lie in administration during the course of an athletic career. It can also be used with current athletes or those already transitioning out of sport.

Limitations and Concerns

This chapter has provided a deeper understanding of career transitions and practical information about assessments that can complement and enhance your consultations with athletes in transition. We have attempted to ensure that the purpose of each assessment tool is clear, whether there is a cost associated with its use, and whether it requires special training or certification to administer.

However, before using any of the assessments recommended in this chapter, it is important to acknowledge their limitations. First, these assessments are not diagnostic tools but rather measures of characteristics, traits, states, susceptibilities, and needs within the context of athletic transition. Recall from chapter 4 that many assessments have an inherent cultural bias because they were developed in Western Europe and North America, and thus caution should be exercised when deciding whether they will be a valuable addition to your work with diverse clients (see chapter 4 for more on diversity as it relates to sport psychology assessment). Furthermore, caution should be exercised when deciding whether to administer these tools to adolescent athletes; the majority have been developed and validated with adult populations. Finally, we strongly recommend that you complete any assessment yourself that you intend to use with clients. Familiarity with wording of assessment items, scoring, results, and feedback is paramount to maximizing the effectiveness of these tools.

Assessment Tools and Their Availability

Assessment tool	Construct	Author and reference	Availability
Ways of Coping Questionnaire (WCQ)	Coping	Folkman, S., & Lazarus, R.S. (1988). *Manual for the Ways of Coping Questionnaire*. Palo Alto, CA: Consulting Psychologists Press.	For purchase at www.mindgarden.com
	The WCQ measures coping processes as opposed to coping dispositions or styles. It is designed to assess and identify thoughts and actions that people use to cope with stressful situations such as transitions. As with many of the coping measures, the internal consistencies are not satisfactory, and test–retest reliabilities are unreported (e.g., Schwarzer & Schwarzer, 1996).		
COPE Inventory	Coping	Carver, C.S., Scheier, M.F., & Weintraub, J.K. (1989). Assessing coping strategies: A theoretically based approach. *Journal of Personality and Social Psychology, 56*, 267-283.	Free at www.psy.miami .edu/faculty/ccarver/ sclCOPEF.html
	Given that people engage in a wide range of coping responses, the COPE Inventory, a 60-item questionnaire, assesses a broad range of coping responses, both functional and dysfunctional. The length of this questionnaire makes response burden a factor, thereby affecting questionnaire completion and consequently data quality.		
Brief COPE	Coping	Carver, C.S. (1997). You want to measure coping but your protocol's too long: Consider the Brief COPE. *International Journal of Behavioral Medicine, 4*, 92-100.	Free at www.psy.miami .edu/faculty/ccarver/ sclBrCOPE.html
	The Brief COPE is a 28-item version of the COPE Inventory, developed specifically for situations in which participant response burden is a considering factor.		
Coping Function Questionnaire (CFQ)	Coping	Kowalski, K.C., & Crocker, P.R.E. (2001). Development and validation of the Coping Function Questionnaire for adolescents in sport. *Journal of Sport and Exercise Psychology, 23*, 136-155.	Contact the authors
	This questionnaire was developed to assess coping function in adolescent athletes.		
Sport Identity Index (SII)	Athletic identity	Curry, T.J., & Weaner, J.S. (1987). Sport identity salience, commitment, and the involvement of self in role: Measurement issues. *Sociology of Sport Journal, 4*, 280-288.	Contact the authors
	This questionnaire measures the degree to which a person identifies with the sport role. We recommend this measure to help assess athletes experiencing high levels of role conflict in their athletic career. Although limited in its application, the SII is valuable because it measures the hierarchy of the sport identity within the context of other identities (whereas other measures do not).		
Athletic Identity Measurement Scale (AIMS)	Athletic identity	Brewer, B.W., Van Raalte, J.L., & Linder, D.E. (1993). Athletic identity: Hercules' muscles or Achilles heel? *International Journal of Sport Psychology, 24*, 237-254.	Contact the authors
	The AIMS is the most popular unidimensional assessment of athletic identity and is used widely by consultants. However, it does not consider the multidimensionality of athletic identity, including the relationship between athletic identity and other identities.		

Assessment tool	Construct	Author and reference	Availability
Athletic Identity Measurement Scale–Plus (AIMS-Plus)	Athletic identity	Cieslak, T. (2004). *Describing and measuring the athletic identity construct: Scale development and validation.* (Unpublished doctoral dissertation). Ohio State University, Columbus, OH.	Contact the author
	The AIMS-Plus was developed in response to criticisms of the original AIMS and measures two major categories of identity: internal and external components. The athletic identity score is obtained by calculating the average score between the sum of the internal components and the sum of the external components.		
Public-Private Athletic Identity Scale (PPAIS)	Athletic identity	Nasco, S.A., & Webb. W.M. (2006). Towards an expanded measure of athletic identity: The inclusion of public and private dimensions. *Journal of Sport and Exercise Psychology, 28,* 434-453.	Contact the authors
	The PPAIS is a 10-item questionnaire that measures both the public and private dimensions of athletic identity. It helps distinguish between the behavioral effects of private and public athletic identity, which enhances the ability to design appropriate interventions.		
Sport Interpersonal Relationships Questionnaire (SIRQ)	Support	Wylleman, P., De Knop, P., Vanden Auweele, Y., Sloore, H., & De Martelaer, K. (1996). Sport Interpersonal Relationships Questionnaires (SIRQ). In A. Ostrow (Ed.), *Directory of psychological tests in the sport and exercise sciences* (pp. 162-164). Morgantown, WV: Fitness Information Technology.	Contact the authors
	The SIRQ assesses the quality of athletes' relationships in their social network. It can be used to evaluate the quality of athletes' relationships as a means to generate self-awareness and expectations for the best sources of social support during their transition.		
Perceived Available Support in Sport Questionnaire (PASS-Q)	Support	Freeman, P., Coffee, P., & Rees, T. (2011). The PASS-Q: The Perceived Available Support in Sport Questionnaire. *Journal of Sport & Exercise Psychology, 33,* 54-74.	Contact the authors
	The PASS-Q is a 16-item measure that assesses four types of perceived support: emotional, esteem, informational, and tangible. It can help you understand if there are any gaps in support provision that need to be addressed so athletes perceive that they can access relevant assistance when required.		
My Vocational Situation (MVS)	General career assessment	Holland, J.L., Daiger, D.C., & Power, P.G. (1980). *My Vocational Situation.* Palo Alto, CA: Consulting Psychologists Press.	Free at www.education .umd.edu/CHSE/ resources/Assessment/ schoolassess/Tools/ MVS/MVS.pdf
	The MVS assesses readiness for career decision making and helps identify unclear vocational goals.		
Career Beliefs Inventory (CBI)	General career assessment	Krumboltz, J.D., & Vosvick, M.A. (1996). Career assessment and the career beliefs inventory. *Journal of Career Assessment, 4,* 345-361.	For purchase at www.mindgarden.com
	The CBI is a 96-item assessment that can be used to explore generalizations, assumptions, and beliefs that clients hold about themselves and the work world that may hinder them from taking career-related actions.		

(continued)

Assessment Tools and Their Availability *(continued)*

Assessment tool	Construct	Author and reference	Availability
Motivational Appraisal of Personal Potential (MAPP)	General career assessment	Retrieved from www.assessment.com	Free truncated results and paid additional reports at www.assessment.com
		The MAPP consists of 71 items that assess career interests, values, personality, aptitudes, and work activities. It is a comprehensive career assessment tool that helps identify future career directions.	
Career Decision-Making Self-Efficacy Scale (CDSE)	General career assessment	Taylor, K.M., & Betz, N.E. (1983). Applications of self-efficacy theory to the understanding and treatment of career indecision. *Journal of Vocational Behavior, 22,* 63-81.	For purchase at www.mindgarden.com/79-career-decision-self-efficacy-scale
		The CDSE assesses the degree to which people believe they are capable of completing tasks necessary to make career-related decisions.	
Career Maturity Inventory—Form C (CMI Form C)	General career assessment	Savickas, M.L., & Porfeli, E.J. (2012). Career adaptabilities scale: Construction, reliability, and measurement equivalence across 13 countries. *Journal of Vocational Behavior, 80,* 661-673.	Contact the authors
		The CMI Form C comprises 24 items that assess aspects of career adaptability.	
O*Net Work Importance Profiler (WIP) and Work Importance Locator (WIL)	Values inventory	National Center for O*NET Development. (n.d.). *Work Importance Profiler (WIP).* O*NET Resource Center. Retrieved from www.onetcenter.org/WIP.html.	Free at www.onetcenter.org
		These tools help clients understand what is important to them in a job and identify occupations that may possess similar characteristics.	
Self-Directed Search (SDS)	Interests inventory	Holland, J.L. (1985). *Making vocational choices: A theory of vocational personalities and work environments.* Englewood Cliffs, NJ: Prentice Hall.	Free at www.self-directed-search.com
		The SDS is one of the most widely used career interest inventories. It identifies an individual's three-letter Holland Code that can be used with many other tools to establish work interests and suitable job roles.	
O*NET My Next Move: Interest Profiler	Interests inventory	National Center for O*NET Development. (n.d.). *My Next Move: Interest Profiler.* Retrieved from www.mynextmove.org.	Free at www.mynextmove.org
		The O*NET Interest Profiler contains 60 questions about feelings toward common work activities. The results provide insight into work activities and occupations that are similar to the client's indicated interests.	
Campbell Interest and Skill Survey (CISS)	Skills and aptitude tests	Campbell, D.P. (1995). The Campbell Interest and Skill Survey (CISS): A product of ninety years of psychometric evolution. *Journal of Career Assessment, 3,* 391-410.	Free at www.pearson assessments.com/tests/ciss.htm
		The CISS measures an individual's interests and skills and provides insights into the interplay between the client's interests and skills	
Myers-Briggs Type Indicator (MBTI)	Personality inventories	Briggs-Myers, I., & Briggs, K.C. (1985). *Myers-Briggs Type Indicator (MBTI).* Palo Alto, CA: Consulting Psychologists Press.	For purchase at www.myersbriggs.org
		The MBTI provides information on clients' preferences for where they draw their energy, how they gather information, how they make decisions, and how they prefer to deal with the outside world.	

Assessment tool	Construct	Author and reference	Availability
MBTI Step II Interpretive Report Form Q (MBTI Step II)	Personality inventories	Quenk, N.L., Hammer, A.L., & Majors, M.S. (2001). *MBTI Step II manual: Exploring the next level of type with the Myers-Briggs Type Indicator Form Q.* Palo Alto, CA: Consulting Psychologists Press.	For purchase at http://career assessmentsite.com
	The MBTI Step II expands on the MBTI by addressing individual differences within each type.		
Clifton StrengthsFinder	Personality inventories	Clifton, D.O., & Anderson, E. (2001). *StrengthsQuest: Discover and develop your strengths in academics, career, and beyond.* Washington, DC: Gallup Organization.	For purchase at www.gallupstrengths center.com
	The StrengthsFinder helps people uncover their talents and discover their natural strengths.		
Values In Action Inventory of Strenghts (VIA-IS)	Personality inventories	Peterson, C., & Seligman, M.E.P. (2004). *Character strengths and virtues: A handbook and classification.* New York and Washington, DC: Oxford University Press and American Psychological Association.	Free list of character strengths and paid additional reports at www.viacharacter.org
	The VIA is designed to help people understand and develop their particular character strengths.		
Athletes' Retirement Decision Inventory (ARDI)	Reasons for retirement	Fernandez, A., Stephan, Y., & Fouquereau, E. (2006). Assessing reasons for sport career termination: Development of Athletes' Retirement Decision Inventory (ARDI). *Psychology of Sport and Exercise, 7,* 407-421.	Contact the authors
	The ARDI is a self-report tool that assesses the pattern of reasons for athletic retirement. It helps identify the most prominent factor in the ending of the athletic career and forms the basis for career transition interventions or counseling.		
Revised Causal Dimension Scale (CDSII)	Reasons for retirement	McAuley, E., Duncan, T., & Russell, D. (1992). Measuring causal attributions: The revised Causal Dimension Scale (CDSII). *Personality and Social Psychology Bulletin, 18,* 566-573.	Free at www.epl.illinois .edu/measures/pdf/CDS .pdf
	The CDSII identifies the reasons for athletic career retirement. It employs a combination of qualitative and quantitative methods and starts by asking athletes to state the most important reason for retiring from their highest level of competitive sport.		
Career Transitions Inventory (CTI)	Assessing adjustment to athletic retirement	Heppner, M.J. (1998). The Career Transitions Inventory: Measuring internal resources in adulthood. *Journal of Career Assessment, 6,* 135-145.	Free at qtrial2014az1 .az1.qualtrics.com/ SE/?SID=SV_0qCiuS2 ubjr6pkV&Q_JFE=0
	The CTI assesses the psychological resources and barriers that athletes may have when contending with retirement from their sport career. The CTI can raise awareness of internal barriers that prevent athletes from experiencing an effective transition into retirement and can be used to design strategies to overcome those barriers.		

(continued)

Assessment Tools and Their Availability *(continued)*

Assessment tool	Construct	Author and reference	Availability
Professional Athletes Career Transition Inventory (PACTI)	Assessing adjustment to athletic retirement	Blann, F.W., & Zaichkowsky, L. (1989). *National Hockey League and Major League Baseball players' post-sport career transition surveys*. Final report prepared for the National Hockey League Players' Association, USA.	Contact the authors
	The PACTI assesses the career transition needs of professional athletes. Using this measure with athletes during the course of their professional career may provide insight into who is at risk for difficulties in retirement and what interventions may help build resources to cope with transitions during the sport career.		
Athlete Retirement Questionnaire (ARQ)	Assessing adjustment to athletic retirement	Sinclair, D.A., & Orlick, T. (1993). Positive transitions from high-performance sport. *The Sport Psychologist*, 7, 138-150.	Contact the authors
	The ARQ measures the transitional experience of high-performance athletes. This 35-item self-report instrument gathers data on the athlete's career and athletic retirement transition. It helps generate an understanding of how to help athletes during their transition by identifying areas of support needed.		
British Athlete Lifestyle Assessment Needs in Career and Education (BALANCE) Scale	Assessing adjustment to athletic retirement	Lavallee, D., & Wylleman, P. (1999). Toward an instrument to assess the quality of adjustment to career transitions in sport: The British Athlete Lifestyle Assessment Needs in Career and Education (BALANCE) Scale. In V. Hosek, P. Tilinger, & L. Bilek (Eds.), *Psychology of sport and exercise: Enhancing the quality of life: Proceedings of the 10th European Congress of Sport Psychology, Prague: Charles University* (pp. 322-324). Prague: The 10th European Congress of Sport Psychology.	Contact the authors
	The BALANCE scale identifies athletes at risk of experiencing difficulties in their transition out of sport. It has been shown to accurately predict career termination difficulties, and as a result its strengths lie in administration during the course of an athletic career.		

Chapter Takeaways

- A person's life career often involves various jobs, occupations, careers, and vocations.

- A significant chapter of athletes' life careers will be dedicated to their athletic career, yet in many cases, they will require a second career once they have retired from sport.

- Developing within an athletic career involves the negotiation of several stages in order to reach the highest levels of representation. Movement from one stage to the next is referred to as a *career transition*.

- There are two types of athletic career transitions: Within-career transitions involve the development of the athletic career, and athletic retirement is the final transition into a postsport life.

- Athletic career transitions can be normative (predictable) or nonnormative (unpredictable).

- Athletic career transitions may result in a healthy and successful transition, a crisis transition, or an experience somewhere in between.

- Consultants can play a vital role in helping athletes maximize their chances of experiencing a successful transition.

- Coping, identity, support, and preretirement planning all mediate the quality of the transition experience, and all can be assessed in various ways to determine if athletes require individualized interventions to increase their chances of a successful transition.

- The assessments available for use with athletes experiencing career transitions form the foundation for interventions used by consultants and are designed to raise awareness, determine preferences, and measure needs.

- Although there are many advantages to using assessments in consultation with athletes in transition, caution should be exercised in using measures with a distinct cultural bias or with specific populations that the tools have not been validated with (e.g., adolescents).

- Take care to fully understand the needs of the client before deciding whether to use an assessment and determining the most suitable tool for the individual.

CHAPTER 16

Systems Approach to Consulting in Sport Organizations

Charles A. Maher, PsyD, CC-AASP

Jim Taylor, PhD, CC-AASP

Assessment is an evidence-based process (AERA, APA, & NCME, 2014; Wright, 2010) used by consultants as a professional service for a range of people in sport organizations. This chapter explores how to conceptualize, design, and implement a comprehensive assessment program within a sport organization. It describes how assessment services and programs, when purposefully designed and systematically implemented, can provide valuable information to every level of a sport organization—including athletes, coaches, athletic directors, and GMs—as a means of better understanding and maximizing individual and team performance.

Assessment services in sport psychology can inform and guide sport organizations about the following:

- Psychological functioning of athletes
- Evaluation of mental skills and performance enhancement programs
- Enhancement of team development
- Analysis of policies and procedures for fostering the psychological well-being of athletes
- Planning for the professional education and training of staff

- Organizational development
- Other programming decisions having to do with sport organizations

Sport organizations that can benefit from assessment services in sport psychology are diverse in nature and scope and include youth sport, high school sport, intercollegiate athletics, professional sport, sports medicine facilities, and private performance centers. For all these organizations, assessment services can provide a treasure trove of valuable information if they are delivered in a systematic manner within relevant organizational, social, and cultural contexts (Hoymand & Gillespie, 2010).

You may be most familiar with assessment as an evidence-based process for the individual athlete, as has been discussed in many other chapters of this book. However, you may not have considered how assessment services can be designed and implemented with some of your clients. Specifically, you may not have thought about assessment services as a distinct professional offering in your consulting or how such professional services can allow you to provide more value to your clients and expand your consulting practice with a range of sport organizations.

Assessment services can contribute to many professional decisions and activities in sport organizations. The scope of assessment as an essential offering is limited only by the needs and goals of a sport organization and by your ability to identify opportunities for using assessment at the individual, team, and organizational levels.

Assessment services can provide value to a sport organization in a variety of areas. First, assessment services can take the form of needs assessment, identifying areas for mental and emotional development of athletes. Also, assessment services can help clients set goals for player development for teams and departments. Furthermore, assessment services can assist in the design, implementation, and evaluation of sport psychology programs at group, team, and organizational levels. Finally, and most importantly, assessment services can provide information for comprehensive strategic planning of the operations of a sport organization.

To illustrate the wide range of ways in which assessment services can benefit sport organizations, here are some real-life examples of decisions and activities that have been used by the authors to enhance the operations and development of a sport organization:

- Identifying the psychological and emotional needs of athletes as a basis for formulating individualized development plans within a professional sport franchise
- Monitoring the extent to which a collegiate team is making progress toward its performance goals
- Assisting GMs, scouts, and coaches in identifying and selecting players as part of the annual draft for a professional hockey team
- Assessing the psychological and emotional needs of injured athletes within a sports medicine unit of a university athletic department
- Determining the effectiveness of a mental skills program that has been used by teenage athletes in a private performance institute
- Evaluating a team-building program administered to varsity teams in a high school athletic department

- Assessing the professional development needs of a coaching staff for a professional sport franchise
- Reviewing the policies and procedures of a collegiate athletic program

In developing a comprehensive assessment program that is targeted and will produce the desired results for a sport organization, you must consider several key aspects of organizational structure (Groth-Marnat, 2009), including the (a) client (e.g., athletes, coaches, administrators, support staff; Maher, 2012); (b) level of service (e.g., individuals, teams, organizational units; Salmon, Stanton, Gibbons, Jenkins, & Walker 2013); (c) service setting (e.g., field or court, training room, classroom, community; Boehm-Davis, Durso, & Lee, 2014); (d) focus of service (e.g., mental preparation, substance abuse education, staff training, team development; Mertens 2005); and (e) methods of service (e.g., rating scale, self-assessment questionnaire, interview protocol; Tennenbaum, Eklund, & Kamata, 2012).

These kinds of assessment services are particularly relevant for your work with coaches and administrators, who need as much information as they can gather to help them in their decision making for programs, athletes, and other personnel and who want to take a systematic approach to all aspects of organizational functioning and performance (Kaufman, 2000; Miller, 1978). Particularly with the emergence of data as a powerful tool in sport, organization-wide assessment services can be one more arrow in the quiver of sport organizations.

In this chapter, we cover how assessment services can be an important component of the professional continuum of services, programs, and products that are part of your consulting practice. This coverage will occur within the framework of a systems approach. More specifically, we will highlight how assessment services and programs can become an integral part of your consulting work. We will explore how assessment services can help clients make informed decisions about athletes' performance as well as about related areas such as program evaluation and planning, staff evaluation and development, and broad-based organizational functioning (Maher, 2012).

Systems Approach

A systems approach to consulting in sport organizations allows you to consider a range of factors related to service delivery (Maher, 2012; Miller, 1978). We offer this perspective for several reasons. First, this approach enables you to offer a structured, cohesive program of services that clearly delineates the value you can bring to sport organizations at every level of functioning and performance. Second, we have found it the most effective means of integrating sport psychology services into a sport organization with many levels and many stakeholders. Third, it allows you to more efficiently and effectively administer consulting services to an audience with different needs and goals that require cooperation and collaboration (Boehm-Davis et al., 2014).

Identifying Assessment Needs

The first step in offering assessment services is to identify the levels at which an assessment program would provide value to a sport organization. In this regard, the organization is reflected in all the policies, programs, and services of the particular organizational unit. This process begins by considering what consulting services you might provide to meet its needs and goals. From this analysis, you can determine how assessments may allow you to optimize the value of your consulting services. This two-step procedure is best administered in a structured way, guided by a set of questions that demonstrate the benefits of an assessment at the various levels of an organization (e.g., athlete, coaching staff, team, overall organization).

Athlete

In many areas of applied professional psychology, including sport psychology, assessment is best recognized and used at the individual level (Wright, 2010). In this regard, individual assessment of the athlete in terms of performance enhancement and personal development is the most common form of assessment. Individual assessment is also facilitated by the fact that the assessment methods, procedures, and instruments for individuals are the most developed empirically and that the focus of much of sport psychology has been on individual performance.

At the level of individual assessment, there will be many opportunities to assist a sport organization in the design and implementation of assessment services and programs based on its needs and goals. Here are some examples, drawn from our own consulting experiences, in which the design and implementation of assessment services at the individual level have proven to be valuable to both the individual athletes and the organization as a whole:

- As part of talent identification and athlete selection
- As the basis for a performance-enhancement program aimed at maximizing competitive performances followed by periodic assessment for evaluating progress toward performance goals
- As a means of gathering the ratings of coaches and others about the priority developmental goals of individual athletes
- As a way to assess mental health status for the purpose of clinical referral and treatment
- As a way to evaluate concussions
- As a way to assess psychological and emotional states following a serious injury and as part of the subsequent rehabilitation and return-to-sport program
- As part of a comprehensive career-planning and transition program

Coaching Staff

Coaching is a difficult job, whether it is for a high school or junior program, at the college level, or at the Olympic or professional ranks and whether you are a coaching intern or a head coach. Coaches have to fulfill so many roles and responsibilities that it can be a challenge to do all of them well. Consequently, you can provide immense value to a sport organization by working with its coaches to ensure they are performing at their highest level possible both individually and collectively. A well-designed coach assessment program can be a valuable means of helping coaches, individually and as a staff, get the most out of their efforts. Essential areas of coaching performance that are highly amenable to assessment (and intervention) include pedagogy, leadership development, communication, conflict resolution, team dynamics, stress management, and professional development, among others.

Team

Our experiences have shown that consulting services in sport organizations, including assessment, are not appreciated, valued, or used at the team level as much as they should be. Resistance to assessment is usually due to the potential financial costs, time involved, receptivity of the athletes and coaching staff, and worry about the unintended consequences of attempting to alter the current team environment. However, given that maximizing team functioning and performance are the ultimate goals of a sport organization, team consulting that includes assessment seems a natural opportunity for you to make a significant contribution.

Here are some examples of team assessment services that could be offered to a sport organization:

- Needs assessment as a basis for team development
- Motivational climate
- Role definitions and satisfaction
- Team functioning and cohesion
- Team goal setting
- Communication and conflict resolution
- Pregame routines of team units
- Performance feedback to coaches and team members

Organization

What happens in the offices of a sport organization can be as important to success as what happens on the field. The functioning and performance of the executive team and various departments, including human resources, sales, marketing, community relations, and technol-

ogy, play a vital role in the long-term success and viability of a sport organization. Additionally, the ability of the leadership team and its support staff to assess and understand organizational needs, current capabilities, and goals and then use this information to plan for the future can't be understated.

Because the focus of a sport organization is the field of play, the impact a consultant can make, from the corner office down to the mailroom, is not fully appreciated. You can bring even more value to your work with a sport organization by offering assessment and consulting services to the front office (Hoymand & Gillespie, 2010). Assessment at the organizational level can allow you to identify and develop real, often hidden opportunities to improve performance not only to the field of play but also in other key areas of a sport organization (Maher, 2012).

In this respect, the value of an assessment program at the organizational level is reflected by the extent that it provides practical decision-making information. This kind of information allows the client (e.g., coach, athletic administrator) to make informed decisions concerning, for example, the need for programs, the extent to which programs are being implemented, and the degree to which programs have attained their goals.

Here are some examples, drawn from our professional experiences, of how assessment programs have been perceived as valuable at the organizational level of a sport entity:

- Provision of information for a strategic plan for a division of collegiate athletics
- Generation of information for making decisions about professional staffing needs in an NFL organization
- Determination of a staff leadership development program for an NBA organization
- Analysis and synthesis of information about amateur draft prospects and free agents as part of a professional baseball scouting process
- Evaluation of performance services (i.e., strength and conditioning, athletic train-

ing, mental skills training) in an NHL franchise

- Identification of athlete needs (e.g., sport psychology, career transition, education)

Determining Readiness for Assessment Services

Though every sport organization shares common structures and processes, each has unique values, visions, missions, needs, and goals. Not all are ready to gain the benefits of an assessment program. As a consequence, it can be helpful for you to work with an interested organization to determine its readiness to embark on a comprehensive assessment program and build such services into its operational routines (Weiner, 2009).

When you make this determination in collaboration with key stakeholders in the sport organization, you allow them to make choices as to what kind of assessment services and programs can best meet their needs and goals. This judgment will also enable you to target the areas most and least suitable for the design and implementation of an organization-wide assessment program.

From our professional experiences in providing assessment services to sport organizations, and within the systems approach, we have formulated guidelines to use in helping sport organizations make immediate strategic decisions about if and how to incorporate assessment services into their operations. These guidelines encompass a range of human and organizational factors that influence the effectiveness of consulting services (Kilbourne, Neumann, Pincus, Bauer, & Stall, 2007):

- **Organizational history:** Explore the organizational history of using sport psychology services and conducting data-driven activities for athletes, coaching staff, teams, and organizational units. It would be useful to know the extent to which assessment has been perceived as a valuable professional activity by those who coach and work with athletes. For example, have there been previous assessment programs, and have these initiatives been valued or dismissed?

- **Identification of the champion:** Determine who in the organization is championing the assessment program, and learn their motives and intentions.

- **Organizational circumstances:** Consider the stability of the sport organization in terms of leadership and support to sustain assessment. Will the members who want the assessment program still be part of the organization when the assessment program is being implemented?

- **Understanding of assessment:** Explore what the decision makers in the organization understand about assessment, what it involves, and the value it can bring. Are their perceptions and expectations realistic? Are you setting yourself up for success or failure?

- **Gauging of benefits:** Ask the stakeholders what they believe will be the benefits of an assessment program for the organization.

- **Timing of the initiative:** Evaluate whether the timing is right for an assessment program based on the history of the organization, the season the team is in, the current status of the team, and future goals.

- **Resistance to assessment:** Identify anyone within the organization who may resist or undermine your efforts in administering the assessment program, thus placing the program in jeopardy.

- **Resource availability:** In conjunction with the organization, make sure that necessary resources are available to administer the agreed-upon assessment program. This guideline ensures that there is adequate funding, personnel are trained and available to provide the services, and necessary space is available to conduct assessment activities.

By following these guidelines when considering the implementation of an assessment program in a sport organization, you can ensure that all stakeholders, including yourself, are making informed decisions that will result in the support you need to do the best job possible and allow the organization to gain the greatest value possible from its investment of time, money, and resources.

Questions to Ask

The following questions can guide you in determining concerns that should be explored in evaluating the viability and value of an assessment program at each level of a sport organization:

- Has the sport organization been involved in assessment before? If so, for what purposes, and what value emerged? If not, why not?

- How could an assessment program be beneficial to the organization?

- What areas of the organization would be most useful to assess?

- What methods, procedures, and instruments would be used in an organization-wide assessment program?

- Can an assessment program be realistically implemented given the time constraints of the organization?

- Who is qualified to administer an assessment program based on the needs and goals of the sport organization?

- What would an organization-wide assessment cost?

Dimensions of Assessment Services

In creating the most value for sport organizations, there are nine dimensions of assessment services that you need to consider:

1. **Levels:** Identify the potential assessment opportunities that exist within a sport organization, including athletes, coaching staff, team, and organization.
2. **Needs:** Perform a structured exploration of the needs and goals of every level of

---

Assessment in Action

Assessment Needs and Goals Assessment

This exercise helps consultants identify the areas on which a decision to use assessments will be based. An assessment regimen can be used in many ways and with many stakeholders within a sport organization. Have your clients indicate the following: the level at which the assessment will be administered; the needs and goals that the assessment protocols are based on; the logistics of the assessments, including who, what, when, and where; how the assessment program will be implemented; and how the data from the assessments will be analyzed, evaluated, and used to fulfill the original goals of the assessment regimen.

---

a sport organization. A key question to ask is, "What part of your organization would you like to know more about?"

3. **Agreement:** Come to an agreement on what assessment services will be provided, who will provide them, when and where they will be administered, the fee you will charge the sport organization, and what deliverables you will provide from the assessment program.

4. **Design:** Design the assessment program in collaboration with relevant stakeholders in the sport organization. Steps may include identifying the needs and goals of the assessment program, selecting the appropriate assessments, formulating a structured assessment protocol, and training personnel (if necessary).

5. **Preparation:** Prepare the sport organization for implementation of the assessment program by announcing the program at all levels, describing its purpose and goals, encouraging stakeholder buy-in, and explaining the nuts and bolts of the process.

6. **Implementation:** Administer the assessment program to the target levels of the sport organization. This includes providing an assessment location, inviting the indicated people, and conducting the assessment.

7. **Evaluation:** Collect and analyze the assessment data and create reports for each target group within the sport organization that describe the purpose, goals, findings, conclusions, and actionable steps that emerge from the information.

8. **Dissemination:** Provide reports to the various stakeholders and schedule meetings with each target group to explain the findings and their meaning, receive feedback about the administration and results of the assessment, and discuss how to put the findings into action.

9. **Effectiveness:** Evaluate the effectiveness of the assessment program in terms of how practical it was (e.g., didn't disrupt organizational functioning), how useful the resulting information was, what the value it brought to the sport organization, and whether it is worth continuing on an ongoing basis.

Determining the readiness of a sport organization is important. This evaluation will dictate the kinds of assessment consulting assistance that can be provided to the client. Figure 16.1 has been used by the first author in consulting with collegiate and professional sport organizations to make sure a systematic approach is taken to planning an assessment service and evaluating its implementation and benefits.

Assessment Service Planning and Evaluation Inventory

Assessment service: _____

Sports organization: _____

Date: _____

Use this inventory to guide you in the planning and evaluation of the assessment service. Apply the scale to each item. Then use the ratings for the development and improvement of the assessment service.

Scale

Yes (Y)   Somewhat (SW)

No (N)   Not Applicable (NA)

Planning

1. ____ The assessment has been designed based on the needs and goals of the organization.

2. ____ The assessment regimen has been selected based on the essential questions that the organization wants answered.

3. ____ The purpose of the assessment has been made known to and has been agreed upon by administrators, coaches, and other relevant stakeholders.

4. ____ Sufficient steps have been taken to ensure appropriate confidentiality and other safeguards intended to protect the recipients of the assessment.

5. ____ Necessary informed consent forms have been completed by those participating in the assessment.

6. ____ A schedule of administering the assessment has been established with input from relevant stakeholders.

7. ____ Procedures for analysis and interpretation of assessment data have been developed and described.

8. ____ A system for the communication of assessment information to relevant stakeholders has been created.

Evaluation

1. ____ Practicality: The assessment occurred in a way that was not disruptive to the normal functioning of the organization.

2. ____ Utility: The assessment information has been perceived as being useful for decision making by the administrators, coaches, team members, or other relevant stakeholders.

3. ____ Propriety: The assessment occurred in ways that adhered to accepted ethical standards.

4. ____ Technical adequacy: The assessment involved methods and procedures that were valid and reliable for the purpose of the assessment.

5. ____ Value to organization: The completed assessment and its accompanying results proved to be beneficial to organizational needs and goals by the relevant stakeholders.

Figure 16.1   This inventory allows consultants to make sure they are taking all essential dimensions into account in the planning and evaluation of a service.

From J. Taylor, 2018, *Assessment in applied sport psychology* (Champaign, IL: Human Kinetics).

Chapter Takeaways

- Assessment is an evidence-based process used by consultants as a professional service for a range of individuals in sport organizations.

- Assessment services, when systematically designed and implemented, can provide valuable information to athletes, coaches, and administrators in sport organizations.

- Assessment services can be used at every level of sport to maximize individual and team functioning and performance.

- Assessment services can provide benefits to many areas within a sport organization, including needs, goals, development, programs, personnel selection, staff development, and organizational effectiveness.

- Assessment programs can be developed at every level of a sport organization, including athlete, coaching staff, team, and organization.

- A systems approach to assessment services allows you to identify various consulting opportunities at individual, team, and organizational levels.

- In a systems approach, you are guided in considering many important areas when deciding what kinds of assessment services to provide, including the level of service, client needs, nature and scope of the agreement for services provision, and design, implementation, evaluation, and dissemination of an assessment program.

- Assessment programs can offer value to a sport organization with departmental evaluations, staffing needs, program evaluations, and athlete needs.

- You can work with an interested organization to determine its readiness to embark on a comprehensive assessment program and build such services into its operational routines.

CHAPTER 17
Consultant Effectiveness

Stephen P. Gonzalez, PhD, CC-AASP

Ian Connole, PhD, CC-AASP

Angus Mugford, PhD, CC-AASP

Jim Taylor, PhD, CC-AASP

The term *consultant effectiveness* refers to the quality of the services that consultants deliver to their clients (Anderson, Miles, Mahoney, & Robinson, 2002). The benchmark for measuring your effectiveness is how well your clients are able to use the knowledge, insights, and tools you provide them with to improve their mental capabilities, maximize their competitive performances, and achieve their athletic goals.

Although being effective is a matter of common sense, the idea of assessing consultants' effectiveness is neither common nor well documented in the field. A challenge in exploring consultant effectiveness is identifying what determines effectiveness. The field of applied sport psychology has an obligation to its consumers to provide the best possible services to meet their needs and goals. Moreover, determining which services, programs, and products are effective requires engaging in regular, comprehensive self-assessment.

Without specific knowledge of what makes a consultant effective, how can our field be accountable to clients and the public? The age of accountability was a charge by a former president of the AASP to the field of applied sport psychology to better assess competence and effectiveness

(Smith, 1989). For the last three decades following this charge, the discussion of effectiveness has been addressed in numerous ways, but neither the rigor of investigation nor implementation in applied settings has advanced a great deal. The field of applied sport psychology must examine consultant effectiveness to help researchers, educators, and practitioners make needed gains in this important area of the profession.

The purpose of this chapter is to provide an in-depth exploration into how to evaluate your effectiveness as a consultant. In this chapter, we discuss the benefits of evaluating consultant effectiveness, general areas of assessing consultant effectiveness, and available assessment methods, as well as limitations, concerns, and recommendations for future work and assessment of effectiveness.

Benefits of Assessing Consultant Effectiveness

Applied sport psychology is based on the application of theoretically driven and evidence-based practices with the goal of helping athletes maximize their mental preparation, optimize their performance, and achieve their sport goals. Over the past three decades, there has been an increased awareness and acceptance of sport psychology throughout sport, from youth sport programs and NCAA athletics to national governing bodies and professional organizations. With this steady rise in both visibility and impact, many have called for increased accountability and evaluation of applied practitioners (Anderson et al., 2002; Grove, Norton, Van Raalte, & Brewer, 1999; Rowell, 1998; Smith, 1989; Strean, 1998). Specifically, Anderson et al. (2002) identified four key stakeholders to whom consultants should be accountable: the athlete, the secondary client (the coach, organization, or individual who funds the services), the consultant, and the field. Effective evaluation of your services can provide direct benefits to each of these stakeholders. However, the dearth of research literature and conspicuous absence of coursework in graduate programs in sport psychology suggest that the practice of consultant evaluation is not receiving the attention it deserves.

When considering the reasons for evaluating consultant effectiveness, the following benefits have been offered: "rendering judgment, facilitating improvement, generating knowledge, being accountable, documenting effectiveness (Anderson et al., 2002; Anderson, Miles, Robinson, & Mahoney, 2004; Gould, Murphy, Tammen, & May, 1991), and striving for personal excellence (Orlick & Partington, 1987a; Partington & Orlick, 1987)" (Haberl & McCann, 2012, p. 66). Haberl and McCann also proposed two additional benefits that had not been previously addressed in the literature: enhancing the status of sport psychology within an organization and reconnecting with your sense of purpose (i.e., by hearing how you have made a difference in your clients' lives). Taken together, these benefits are centered on the desire to improve your performance and thus your ability to positively affect those you serve and the profession you represent (i.e., all stakeholders).

The athletes you work with will benefit from the opportunity to evaluate you and from your ongoing improvement from that feedback. Many forms of consultant evaluation involve direct qualitative or quantitative feedback from athletes. These opportunities to offer feedback provide athletes with many benefits associated with reflection (cf. Kolb, 1984), such as improved self-awareness, increased understanding, and better retention of what they learned from you through the examination of their experiences learning and applying mental skills. Additionally, learning theories and educational research suggest that reflective practices are critical in the process of applying past knowledge to new situations, metacognition (i.e., thinking about thinking), and ongoing learning (Costa & Kallick, 2008).

Another way athletes can benefit from providing evaluations is by seeing you model the desire to achieve personal excellence in your own work (Haberl & McCann, 2012; Orlick & Partington, 1987a). This modeling can promote an environment where vulnerability is acceptable, and growth, rather than perfection, is the expectation. Moreover, your ability to learn from client feedback and tailor future services allows you to further meet their needs and goals (Anderson et al., 2002; Haberl & McCann, 2012). Consequently, the evaluation of your consulting can result in more effective collaboration in your work with clients and improvements to your services, both essential to the effective practice of applied sport psychology (Anderson et al., 2002; Halliwell, 1990).

As data-driven statistics and performance metrics evolve and integrate into more sport settings, the push to quantify results increases in sport psychology services. An additional benefit to both you and the field is the ability to provide data and feedback from athletes, coaches, and other critical stakeholders regarding your effectiveness. In their work with the United States Olympic Committee (USOC), Haberl and McCann (2012) addressed how ongoing reporting of effectiveness measures to their superiors informed them of current perceptions, demonstrated accountability, modeled their pursuit of excellence, and demonstrated the return on investment for their secondary client (the USOC). Therefore, evaluation may provide justification for maintaining sport psychology positions, developing future positions, or increasing roles within organizations, while also providing secondary clients with evidence of the impact you are making.

Understanding what makes consultants effective in delivering interventions is also critical to establishing, developing, and improving graduate education and professional training programs. Information gathered from research on consultant effectiveness can shape curricular decisions in several areas, including the selection of course requirements, the types of practicum experiences available to graduate students, and the ways in which faculty supervise those training experiences. This information can also help prospective graduate students make informed decisions about which programs offer the best training and the best fit for their professional goals.

Finally, you are also a key beneficiary of evaluating your effectiveness as a consultant. There is no doubt that receiving direct, honest feedback can be both threatening and uncomfortable; none of us one wants to feel our services are less than exceptional (Haberl & McCann, 2012). Yet, practicing what you preach often involves challenging your comfort zone for continued growth. Your ability to practice meaningful self-reflection, assessment, and evaluation is at the core of your ability to grow as a sport psychology professional.

Deep reflection on feedback has proven to be a valuable tool for self-evaluation. Cropley, Hanton, Miles, and Niven (2002) described reflection as an introspective and exploratory experience by which you can identify and cultivate knowledge-in-action (cf. Schön, 1983), which is the ability to synthesize theory and professional knowledge to be applied intuitively in the moment in order to best meet the demands of a complex situation—an essential skill for sport psychology services. Much as athletes benefit from reflecting on their application of mental skills in competition, you can benefit from reflective practices in regard to your own performance. Supporting this notion, research has demonstrated that reflection plays a valuable role in enhancing self-awareness, improving effectiveness of services, and adding to the knowledge of best practices (Andersen, 2000; Anderson, Knowles, & Gilbourne, 2004). At a practical level, rigorous, consistent evaluation can improve the quality of your services, maximizing the value you bring to your current clients and attracting new clients.

Given the many stakeholders involved in your sport psychology services, the impact of evaluating yourself is multiplied as you influence others directly through the process and results of evaluating your effectiveness and indirectly through your own professional growth. As a consequence, your ability to continually improve your craft not only benefits yourself and the individuals, teams, and organizations you work with but also the profession of sport psychology as a whole.

Considerations for Assessing Consultant Effectiveness

Despite the clear benefits and need to assess consultant effectiveness, professionals in our field have recognized a lack of appropriate methods to assess that effectiveness (Smith, 1989; Strean, 1998). Over time, some scholarship regarding consultant effectiveness has emerged (Anderson et al., 2002; Dunn & Holt, 2003; Halliwell, 1990; Hankes, 1996; Lubker, Visek, Watson, & Singpurwalla, 2012; Martindale & Collins, 2007; Mugford, Hesse, & Morgan, 2014; Sharpe & Hodge, 2011), but research has been sporadic and unsystematic. Consultant effectiveness has largely been examined in two ways: studying the characteristics and behaviors of successful consultants and studying whether outcomes of services or interventions were successful (i.e., improved competitive performance). This section offers a comprehensive overview of the literature regarding consultant effectiveness. We will first address the literature on what characteristics make a consultant effective, and then we will review outcome approaches to evaluating consultant effectiveness.

Characteristics of Effective Consultants

The predominant approach to evaluating consultant effectiveness is qualitative-based research examining characteristics of effective consultants. We use the term *characteristics* broadly to include both consultant and client perspectives of what qualities and behaviors make the deliverer of applied sport psychology effective.

Table 17.1 is a simple, organized resource providing effective consultant characteristics, complete with definitions and citations. All

Table 17.1 Characteristics of Consultant Effectiveness Across Personal, Social, and Professional Dimensions

Effectiveness factor	Description
Dimension 1: personal characteristics	
Likeable	Being perceived as having something applied and concrete to offer (Orlick & Partington, 1987a)
	Having a generally positive disposition
	Being sensitive to client needs (Orlick & Partington, 1987a)
Respect for others	Having respect for the coaches, staff, and team history; treating all members of the team equally; and earning respect from the client rather than demanding it (Dunn & Holt, 2003)
Communication and inter-personal skills	Being able to speak and use words that clearly convey messages and information to clients (Orlick & Partington, 1987b)
	Being approachable and supportive of clients (Lubker et al., 2012)
	Having skills, such as reading body language and tone when communicating, that enable a practitioner to connect better with a client (Dunn & Holt, 2003; Hankes, 1996)
Effectiveness factor	**Description**
Dimension 2: social characteristics	
Working relationship and rapport with client	Developing a relationship with the client based on the following (Anderson et al., 2002): · Trust · Openness
	Collaboration (i.e., working with the client and not merely providing one-way communication)
	Helping the client have confidence in the practitioner's ability and skill (Halliwell, 1990)
	Helping the client feel cared for by the practitioner (Orlick & Partington, 1987a)
	Building connections to create positive change and meet the athlete's needs (Sharpe & Hodge, 2011)
	Connecting with the many stakeholders involved on a team or in an organization; being seen as part of the team (Mugford, Hesse, & Morgan, 2014)
Fitting into the environment	Being able to read situations and provide sport psychology support without interrupting the flow of the training or competition environment (Halliwell, 1990)
	Appropriately applying consulting at training sites (Orlick & Partington, 1987a)
	Having the ability to adapt to multiple environments, such as competition and practice environments (Mugford et al., 2014)
Serving multiple roles	Being perceived by clients as the following (Dunn & Holt, 2003): · Being a co-coach on the team or a liaison for the clients to coaching staff · Having ample social involvement to feel part of the team · Being emotionally involved in clients' well-being and goals
	Having the ability to handle days of variety, including the following (Mugford et al., 2014): · Mentoring other consultants (if applicable) · Doing workshops for team staff members · Working with individual and group clients · Preparing presentations · Helping with research
Limited visibility	Not broadcasting one's presence to athletes or the public (Halliwell, 1990)

Effectiveness factor	Description
Dimension 3: professional characteristics	
Flexibility in delivery and decision making	Being able to meet individual needs by providing person-specific input, being flexible with goals and objectives of sessions, and not having a standard agenda for providing services (Orlick & Partington, 1987a)
	Being able to process information from a client about an issue and make an appropriate decision that best addresses the clients' needs, such as applying the most appropriate theory of motivation to guide an intervention (Martindale & Collins, 2007)
Accessibility	Being available for follow-up sessions before and during the competitive season (Orlick & Partington, 1987a)
	Being available to build relationships
	Having multiple contacts with individuals and not just groups of people (Orlick & Partington, 1987a)
Knowledge	Having mental training knowledge, including theories, best practices, and application of mental skills training (Anderson et al., 2002)
	Having at least a basic understanding of a client's sport or performance (Lubker et al., 2012)
	Integrating theory and practice to put learned knowledge to work for a client (Mugford et al., 2014)
Delivery style	Delivering sport psychology and mental training that is well received by the target audience, such as using appropriate humor or using metaphors that are easy to understand (Anderson et al., 2002)
	Being able to deliver a simple, concrete message that is connected to the performance of the client (Mugford et al., 2014)
Professional status	Having a certification or a license to practice backed by the APA or AASP (Lubker et al., 2012)
Experience	Having nine months of experience working with athletes and two to three years of experience studying sport psychology (Orlick & Partington, 1987a)
	Moving beyond simply delivering sessions to clients and being able to plan, organize, document, and have situational awareness (Mugford et al., 2014)
	Having experience participating in or competing in a sport (Lubker et al., 2012)

Note: All studies in this table directly evaluated what athletes and coaches preferred and found to be effective in a consultant.

studies in this overview involved interviewing athletes, coaches, or other consultants to understand what attributes make a consultant effective, as well as preferences for characteristics in a consultant.

In our review of the literature, three primary dimensions of effectiveness emerge: personal characteristics, which are individual qualities and behaviors that are dispositional in nature; social characteristics, which are behaviors that create rapport with a client and integrate well into a client's environment; and educational and technical characteristics, which are acquired skills and competencies from academic training and professional experiences. Within each of these dimensions are factors that contribute to consultant effectiveness.

Personal Characteristics

Personal characteristics are consultants' dispositions and behaviors that enable them to be approachable, open to client needs and goals, and effective in communicating useful information, insights, and tools. In reviewing the literature, three factors appear to contribute most to effective personal characteristics.

Likeability The first factor is being likeable, which Orlick and Partington (1987a) described as having a positive disposition, having something concrete and practical to offer, and having sensitivity to a client's needs. Having a positive disposition can help consultants appear relaxed and welcoming, particularly if a client is feeling uncomfortable, anxious, or emotionally distressed. If consultants are perceived as likeable, they are more likely to be remembered positively and be retained for future work.

Respect for Others The second factor is having respect for others, which Dunn and Holt (2003) have described as demonstrating respect for athletes, coaches, staff, and team history rather than demanding respect. Showing respect for others can also contribute to likeability and help build rapport with clients. Additionally, respecting others enables consultants to empower all stakeholders in a performance environment rather than appearing overpowering or restrictive.

Communication and Interpersonal Skills Communication and interpersonal skills are the third personal factor contributing to consultant effectiveness. Several researchers have defined *communication* and *interpersonal skills* as using understandable language (Lubker et al., 2012; Orlick & Partington, 1987a), being approachable and supportive (Dunn & Holt, 2003), and being able to read body language and tone to best meet the needs of the client (Hankes, 1996). Communication is vital to consulting and encompasses verbal and nonverbal communication to track a client's comfort and understanding of the services provided.

Social Characteristics

Social characteristics are factors that contribute to consultants' ability to build rapport with clients and integrate into team, practice, and competitive environments. Previous research has identified four factors that contribute to effective social characteristics.

Rapport Rapport and developing a working relationship with the client involves having a relationship between client and practitioner based on trust, openness, and collaboration (Anderson et al., 2002); the client having confidence in the practitioner's ability (Halliwell, 1990); the client feeling cared for by the practitioner (Orlick & Partington, 1987a); the practitioner building a connection to meet the client's needs (Sharpe & Hodge, 2011); and the practitioner connecting with all members of a team (Mugford et al., 2014). In essence, a working relationship and rapport are developed through transparency, confidence, and trust while collaborating with a client and important stakeholders to create positive change and meet the client's needs. Rapport is one of the most important factors related to successful consulting; without it, the knowledge and skill of a practitioner has little practical value (Orlick & Partington, 1987a).

Multiple Roles Consultants must be capable of fulfilling multiple roles. This characteristic is most relevant to consultants who work with entire teams rather than individual athletes. It is also helpful for consultants who collaborate with colleagues to provide services to a team (e.g., at a training center, academy, or university). Serving multiple roles when working with a team means being perceived by clients as emotionally involved in the goals and well-being of the team, being socially involved with the team, and acting as a liaison between the athletes and their coach (Dunn & Holt, 2003). Serving multiple roles when working on a team with other consultants means being able to handle a variety of responsibilities, such as working with teams and individuals, mentoring other consultants, and helping with research and presentations (Mugford et al., 2014).

In team settings, it is rare for effective consultants to simply deliver mental skills training and be done. To be helpful, especially with teams that have limited staff due to budget constraints, consultants may need to fill many roles, contribute to the team in any way that is necessary and appropriate, and provide value to their clients beyond what they are contractually obliged to do. For example, many consultants speak of running equipment to athletes, carrying team supplies, helping pick up after training sessions, driving team vans, and picking up food for athletes when necessary. These tasks may appear menial but are highly valued by a team's stakeholders.

Fitting In   This attribute involves integrating smoothly into a client's practice and competition environments without being perceived as an outsider or getting in the way. More specifically, it has been described as being able to read situations and client needs to effectively deliver sport psychology services without disturbing training or competition (Halliwell, 1990; Mugford et al., 2014; Orlick & Partington, 1987a). Delivering services to clients outside a classroom or office setting can be challenging even for experienced consultants. Not creating discomfort or interfering with coaches and athletes while being accessible and delivering on-the-spot feedback to clients is vital for consultants to be effective.

Low Profile   The last social characteristic involves the ability to maintain a low profile in your work with athletes and teams. Halliwell (1990) describes this quality as not broadcasting your presence to other athletes, teams, or the public. It is important that consultants are quiet allies to their clients and not walking billboards for their own services. Accordingly, confidentiality is important to maintain and enhance consultants' relationships with athletes and coaches. This is a crucial balance to strike when working with an athlete and reporting to a GM, coach, or administrator. Maintaining a low profile while being clear about the limits of what is shared and what is confidential is a tightrope that consultants must walk regularly.

Professional Characteristics

Professional characteristics are the final dimension of what makes consultants effective. These attributes are developed through formal education and training experiences. In total, seven factors contribute to this dimension.

Flexibility   The first factor is having flexibility in delivering mental skills. *Flexibility* is defined as the ability to put aside predetermined goals and session agendas to meet a client's needs at a given time (Orlick & Partington, 1987a). It also involves being responsive to the constantly changing schedules of stakeholders and being

able to adapt to how, when, and where you deliver sport psychology services.

Decision Making   *Decision making* refers to processing information and making sound decisions based on the needs and goals of clients, particularly when faced with competing options (Martindale & Collins, 2007). This ability is essential at every level of the consulting process, including choosing assessments, conducting evaluations, interpreting and integrating relevant information, and designing and implementing interventions.

Accessibility   *Accessibility* refers to consultants not only being present but being available when needed and following up with clients (Orlick & Partington, 1987a). It also refers to having a clearly defined consulting process and an organized client management system to systematically meet clients' needs.

Knowledge   *Knowledge* is defined as having an understanding of sport psychology theories, research, best practices, and applications (Anderson et al., 2002); having an understanding of a client's sport and performance (Lubker et al., 2012); and having the ability to integrate theory and practice into evaluation and intervention to best help a client (Mugford et al., 2014). Knowledge is necessary to be ethically competent in practicing sport psychology and implementing mental training, but mere content knowledge is not sufficient. An effective consultant is able to apply knowledge and understanding to a client's sport in a contextually appropriate manner.

Delivery Style   *Delivery style* refers to how you present the information aimed at helping clients meet their needs and achieve their goals. Simply put, it involves presenting sport psychology information and tools with clear, concrete messages (Mugford et al., 2014) in a way that clients can understand and readily use (Anderson et al., 2002). For example, using relatable metaphors to explain a complex mental skill, such as imagery, is an effective delivery style. As with many of these educational and technical characteristics, having supervised experiences as well as observing seasoned consultants can help young consultants develop an effective delivery style.

Experience   This attribute differs from the previous characteristics in that it cannot be acquired through coursework or supervision alone. Instead, experience can only be gained through time spent doing the work of sport psychology consulting. Elements of experience that have been addressed in the literature include having a minimum of nine months of experience working with athletes and at least two to three years of studying sport psychology (Orlick & Partington, 1987a), doing more than delivering mental skills (Mugford et al., 2014), and having athletic experience (Lubker et al., 2012).

Effective consultants have years of relevant study and direct consulting experience in the development, planning, organization, and implementation of services that meet client needs and goals and that produce tangible improvements in performance. Moreover, this experience is broad, involving every aspect of sport psychology service delivery, including relationship building, assessment, goal identification, intervention planning, implementation, evaluation, client management, and more.

Professional Status   Professional status begins with an earned degree (master's or doctorate in sport psychology or related field), licensure (for those trained in clinical or counseling psychology or related mental health fields), or certification (e.g., Certified Consultant of the AASP) demonstrating a minimal level of competence. In a consumer market analysis of preferred characteristics of consultants, Lubker et al. (2012) found that both male and female athletes ranked professional status as the most important attribute of a consultant. In their work, Lubker et al. defined *professional status* as having a certification or license backed by either the AASP or the APA.

As consultants gain experience, their professional status is enhanced in a variety of ways. A résumé filled with consulting work with diverse and perhaps notable athletes and teams adds to professional status. Conference presentations and awards by professional organizations also highlight status. Additionally, blogs, newsletters, social media presence, exposure in traditional media (e.g., radio, television, newspaper, and magazine interviews), and especially authorship of books add to professional status that prospective clients may find appealing.

Methods of Assessment

Consultant effectiveness can be evaluated in several ways. Anderson et al. (2002) identified three such indicators: the acquisition of mental skills by athletes that increase their well-being, athlete responses to services (e.g., attitude, perceptions, buy-in), and enhanced competitive performance (based on both subjective and objective measures).

The first two measures mentioned are the best means of judging consultant effectiveness. Anderson et al. (2002) comment that psychometrically standardized measures (e.g., Athletic Coping Skills Inventory-28 [ACSI-28]; Smith, Schultz, Smoll, & Ptacek, 1995) and performance profiling (e.g., Test of Performance Strategies [TOPS]; Thomas, Murphy, & Hardy, 1999) are typical ways consultants can evaluate an athlete's acquisition of mental skills (see chapter 7 for more details). In terms of well-being, tests such as the Profile of Mood States (POMS; McNair, Lorr, & Droppleman, 1971) are useful for evaluating life satisfaction and overall mood. When evaluating a client's response to the support provided by a consultant, rather than simply asking athletes about their attitude toward consultants and the services they provide (which may be biased due to social desirability), Anderson et al. (2002) recommend measuring adherence to mental training. For example, using journals, diaries, or log books to record when athletes are practicing mental training techniques would provide consultants with insight into how much a client adheres to and values the training. This method is helpful in assessing consultant effectiveness because it indicates athletes' attitudes toward, belief in, and commitment to the sport psychology work.

Perhaps the most obvious way to evaluate consultant effectiveness is the degree to which clients improve their athletic performances and better achieve their goals. However, though athletes and teams often hire consultants to help achieve competitive success, such results are not a reliable measure of consultant effectiveness. The reality of sport is that there are many contributors to improved performance and results. For example, personnel, physical maturity, physical fitness, technical and tactical progress, understanding of the sport, and equipment may all influence performance and competitive success. Additionally, if consultants are going to take credit for their clients' successes, they must be willing to accept responsibility for their clients' failures, both of which are unfair to the consultant, the athlete or team, and the many others who contribute to athletes' efforts.

There is no single gold standard in assessing consultant effectiveness, partly due to the complexity and diversity of consulting situations. Historically in sport psychology consulting, assessment has focused on the impact of interventions and client success as indicators of successful consultation rather than on the consultants themselves (Anderson, 2000; Sharp & Hodge, 2011). It is likely true that many clients care more about their bottom-line success (i.e., their competitive results) than about evaluating the consultants themselves. However, both consultants and the field as a whole can gain significant insight into the quality of the interaction and the impact of the consultant–client relationship on client success. Having an understanding of the context, role, and purpose of assessing consultant effectiveness is also essential in this process.

Consultant Effectiveness Form

The Sport Psychology Consultant Effectiveness Form (CEF) is an evaluation inventory designed to measure consultants' field services for quality assessment and improvement. Despite being developed almost 30 years ago, Partington and Orlick's work on measuring consultant effectiveness remains some of the seminal work in this area. Based on their consulting experience and two intensive qualitative studies they conducted with Olympic athletes (Orlick & Partington, 1987a) and Olympic coaches (Orlick & Partington, 1987b), they were able to validate the CEF with an Olympic population. The CEF is displayed in figure 17.1.

The CEF includes 10 items about consultant characteristics (e.g., "Seemed willing to provide an individualized mental training program based on my input and needs," "Proved to be trustworthy"). Each item is rated on an 11-point numerical scale ranging from 0 ("Not at all") to 10 ("Yes, definitely"). Six additional items concern the duration of several types of contact

between the athlete and consultant (e.g., "How many contact hours in a team setting and in individual sessions"). Though the initial focus is on the consultant and accessibility, perhaps the most important dimension is perceived consultant effectiveness. This third area is assessed by two rating criteria, the consultant's "effect on you" and "effect on team." The 11-point numerical scales for effectiveness range from "Hindered or interfered" (–5), to "No effect" (0), through to "Helped a lot" (+5).

Benefits of the CEF include simplicity, ease of administration, and depth of feedback. The norms and validation it offers also make it valuable. At the same time, these data were collected three decades ago, which may call into question the validity and generalizability to athletes, coaches, and consultants in the 21st century (though the CEF certainly maintains high face validity). Attempts to rectify this weakness of the CEF include modifications made by USOC sport psychologists to assess consultant effectiveness during several recent Olympic cycles (see Haberl & McCann, 2012, for more information).

Customized Athlete Self-Report Surveys

In some respects, the CEF is an example of a consumer satisfaction survey. However, by creating your own athlete self-report survey, you increase the ability to customize contextually relevant information and engage athletes in a deeper, more specific way. For 21st-century athletes, this personalized approach may include an online assessment using web-based survey software. This standardized format enables you to not only receive feedback at the conclusion of a consulting relationship, performance cycle, or contract but also throughout a consulting relationship, thus providing ongoing feedback that allows you to continually update and improve your service delivery.

Direct Athlete Feedback

Though a high-tech approach to evaluating your effectiveness, such as using smartphone applications or online surveys, is efficient, a more high-touch method may provide a different sort of value. Sitting down with your

Sport Psychology Consultant Evaluation Form

Name _____   Consultant's name _____

Sport _____

Please rate your sport psychology consultant on each of the following characteristics by using a number from 0 to 10, as seen on the following scale.

Not at all   Yes, definitely
| 0 | 1 | 2 | 3 | 4 | 5 | 6 | 7 | 8 | 9 | 10 |

1. Consultant characteristics   Ratings

Has useful knowledge about mental training that seemed to apply directly to my sport.   _____

Seemed willing to provide an individual mental training program based on my input and needs.   _____

Seemed open, flexible, and ready to collaborate and cooperate with me.   _____

Proved to be trustworthy.   _____

Was easy for me to relate to (e.g., I felt comfortable and that he or she understood me).   _____

Fitted in with others connected to the team.   _____

Tried to help me draw upon my strengths (e.g., the things that already worked for me)
in order to make my best performance more consistent.   _____

Tried to help me overcome possible problems, or weaknesses, in order to make my
best performance even better and more consistent.   _____

Provided clear, practical, concrete strategies for me to try out in an attempt to solve problems
or improve the level and consistency of my performance.   _____

2. How effective was this consultant?

	Hindered or interfered									Helped a lot
Effect on you	-5	-4	-3	-2	-1	0	+1	+2	+3	+4	+5
Effect on team	-5	-4	-3	-2	-1	0	+1	+2	+3	+4	+5

3. Do you have any recommendations to improve the quality or effectiveness of the sport psychology consultation service being offered?

_____

_____

Figure 17.1   Assessing consultant effectiveness with an established measure.

From J. Taylor, 2018, *Assessment in applied sport psychology* (Champaign, IL: Human Kinetics). Adapted, by permission, from J. Partington and T. Orlick, 1987, "The consultant evaluation form," *The Sport Psychologist* 1(4): 309-317.

clients and asking for feedback periodically has several benefits. First, you are able to have an open-ended conversation about how things are going in your work, thus allowing clients to frame the discussion in their own way. Second, you can use the interaction to probe further issues that come to your attention about your effectiveness. Third, by being open to feedback, you model a healthy vulnerability and receptiveness to growth, sending a powerful message to your clients. Admittedly, by asking for feedback from your clients, you may put them in a position of offering information that may be critical of you. This new role may make them uncomfortable and reluctant to be open and honest with you. At the same time, assuming you have a trusting relationship with your clients, your genuine interest in receiving honest feedback about how you are doing would seem to provide an opportunity to strengthen your connection with them.

In this process of evaluating your effectiveness with your clients, there is the risk that you may not like what you hear. If this situation arises, you can again model openness to all types of feedback as growth opportunities. You can also use these opportunities to discuss any incongruence that exists between your perceptions of what you are delivering and clients' perceptions of what they are receiving and to explore your clients' expectations about your work.

Collegial Feedback

Client documentation (i.e., case notes) is a potential vehicle for assessing consultant effectiveness through peer mentoring, supervision, and feedback. Case notes offer a great opportunity to receive feedback from peers, mentors, and supervisors. Regardless of your education and training, you can use client conceptualizations, intervention development and planning, and ongoing records of your client work as a way to gain collegial feedback from those you trust. The ability to critically reflect on the work you are doing with clients in collaboration with a colleague can be a powerful tool for professional development.

Another form of peer feedback often used in graduate education involves video recording and analyzing client sessions. Video has long provided a way to gain self-awareness of interpersonal and professional service delivery, as well as valuable feedback from colleagues who review the recordings. It also allows for observation of a wide variety of client situations. Fukkink, Trienekens, and Kramer (2011) conducted a meta-analysis of 217 studies that used video for professional training in the helping professions and found significant benefits of its use. This evidence suggests that consultants can improve their professional skills through video feedback. Therefore, many supervision programs continue to use video as a cornerstone of training (Goldman, Pea, Barron, & Derry, 2014). Whether consultants continue to use it as a tool for professional development once in practice is another question. Clearly, there are still many opportunities to use video recordings of clients' sessions as a development tool throughout your career.

Though video analysis of professional service delivery is clearly valuable, there are ethical considerations related to the use, storage, and destruction of the recordings. Obtaining informed consent and handling the recordings in an ethical way should be paramount concerns.

Critically evaluating your work with colleagues, through both case notes and video, has two other benefits. First, you can better identify what is not working. Ineffective strategies and approaches may be missed if consultants are so consumed with the process of working with clients that they fail to find a new perspective from which to view their work. By closely examining your practices with clients, whether relational or tangible, you are able to see more clearly those aspects of your consulting that may not be bringing value to your clients. Second, you can identify your best practices, meaning those methods that are well received by and effective with clients.

Self-Reflection

Whether a neophyte in the field or an experienced veteran, at the heart of this chapter lies the ability to critically self-reflect on your capabilities as a consultant. Woodcock, Humphries, and Mugford (2008) used a nine-week intensive supervisory experience as an example of the leverage that reflective practice can create in professional service delivery. The neophyte in this case highlighted the value of self-reflection by stating that those new to the field

> invariably operate in situations that are daunting and complex . . . [and] quality supervision can maximize developmental opportunities through organizing appropriate self-reflection, fostering a developmental approach through optimal supervisory relationships, and responding to perceived failings and anxiety in a way that is supportive that also stimulates learning and development. (p. 15)

Accordingly, initial supervisory relationships can help consultants develop an ongoing process of self-reflection long after formal supervision concludes. How you process consulting experiences allows you to balance appraisals, heighten your objectivity and self-awareness, and see challenges rather than threats, much like a client may experience from your assistance in facilitating reflection. In other words, this process of self-reflection enables us to practice what we preach to our clients.

Reflective practice has received a great deal of support in sport psychology literature (Anderson, Knowles, & Gilbourne, 2004; Cropley, Miles, Hanton, & Anderson, 2007; Knowles, Gilbourne, Tomlinson, & Anderson, 2007), particularly for its ability to improve self-awareness and generate new knowledge, understanding, and skills. Much of this exploration has centered on inexperienced practitioners, but self-reflection for consultants at any level is highly relevant given that professional development is an ongoing process in which value can be gained at any point in a career trajectory. Though there are many approaches and methodologies for self-reflection, one example was shared by Gibbs (1988) and the British education system as a six-stage reflective cycle:

1. Description of an event
2. Thoughts and feelings
3. Evaluation
4. Analysis
5. Conclusion
6. Action plan

Simplicity and clarity are key dimensions in the self-reflective experience. Additionally, the goal of any self-reflection is to enhance learning, mastery, and development as a consultant. However, without theoretical foundation, empirical rigor, or deliberate checks and balances to avoid personal biases, the practical value of self-reflection can be deceptive and limited (Cropley & Hanton, 2011; Martindale & Collins, 2007).

Process Approaches

The complexity of sport psychology consulting means that providing a clear definition of *effective practice* has been elusive (Cropley et al., 2007). A case-study approach has been recommended as a way to collect evaluative information that will increase consultants' accountability to stakeholders, including athletes, coaches, parents, and administers (Anderson et al., 2002). Client satisfaction is often a key indicator of consultant effectiveness; however, it may not always be the most accurate measure. Specifically, research has found that students who learn the most tend to evaluate their instructors the least favorably (Parker & Thomas, 1980). By adopting a case-study approach, you can have the flexibility of collecting feedback from individuals or teams for a specific intervention or a general service and do it in a real-life context. This approach allows you to incorporate multiple datasets for various stakeholders rather than relying on one particular source of feedback that may or may not be accurate. In the context of measuring consultant effectiveness, this method may involve using client satisfaction surveys, postsession and postseason evaluations, objective performance measures, and coach and parent ratings to provide a more comprehensive, nuanced assessment of your effectiveness with your clients.

Chapter Takeaways

- All consultants should make it a priority to evaluate their effectiveness by the means that best fits both the contexts in which they work and the goals of their evaluation.

- Assessing consultant effectiveness, though highly desirable, is neither common nor well documented in the field.

- Identifying what composes consultant effectiveness remains a challenge.

- Assessing effectiveness is important for the key stakeholders to whom consultants are accountable: the athletes, the secondary client (i.e., the coach, organization, or individual who funds the services), the consultants themselves, and the field of sport psychology.

- Research investigating effective characteristics of consultants can be organized into three dimensions: personal characteristics, social characteristics, and professional characteristics.

- Indicators of consultant effectiveness include athletes' acquisition of mental skills and increased well-being, athletes' responses to services, and enhanced competitive performance.

- Though there is no single gold standard in assessing consultant effectiveness, consultants can use objective inventories, customized self-report surveys, direct athlete feedback, collegial feedback, and self-reflection.

EPILOGUE

The preface described how assessment is similar to a precompetitive routine in which athletes can incorporate a multitude of strategies to ensure their total preparation and maximize their competitive performances. These strategies might include various forms of physical, mental, equipment, and team readiness. But it wouldn't be realistic or helpful for athletes to include too many of these techniques; that would require far too much time and energy. In fact, they would feel overwhelmed by so many options. Instead, through experimentation, athletes select those strategies that are most effective and efficient in their preparations to build a routine that meets their needs and goals and that is most comfortable and beneficial to them.

You may feel similarly overwhelmed by the breadth of assessment options that have been provided in this book. But, just as athletes do, you should base your assessment routine on several factors. First, examine what your assessment needs and goals are with your clientele and, based on that evaluation, choose the assessments that are the best fit. Second, consider your personality and style of interaction with your clients and then select assessments that are most in sync with who you are and how you like to interact with your clients. Third, just because an assessment doesn't seem right based on face value, you shouldn't disqualify it outright. You never know what is right for you until you try it out. So, experiment with assessments before you pass judgment; you may surprise yourself, finding that an assessment you didn't initially feel was a good fit ends up being a valuable tool in helping your athletes achieve their goals.

Again, much like athletes, what begins as a large, unstructured swath of strategies that may or may not seem beneficial is progressively whittled down to a quiver of assessments that become part of your assessment routine. Through this process, you not only further develop your ability to understand your clients, but you also increase your ability to help them achieve their athletic goals.

REFERENCES

Chapter 1

American Psychological Association (APA). Glossary of psychology terms. www.apa.org/research/action/glossary.aspx?tab=10.

Cone, J.D. (1995). Assessment practice standards. In S.C. Hayes, V.M. Follette, R.M. Dawes, & K. Grady (Eds.), *Scientific standards for psychological practice: Issues and Recommendations* (pp. 201-224). Reno, NV: Context Press.

Kahneman, D. (2013). *Thinking, fast and slow.* New York: Farrar, Straus & Giroux.

Kaheman, D., Lovallo, D., & Sibony, O. (2011). The big idea: Before you make that big decision . . . *Harvard Business Review.* Retrieved from https://hbr.org/2011/06/the-big-idea-before-you-make-that-big-decision.

Kahneman, D., & Tversky, A. (1974). Judgment under uncertainty: Heuristics and biases. *Science, 185,* 1125-1131.

Chapter 2

Albrecht, R.R., & Feltz, D.L. (1987). Generality and specificity of attention related to competitive anxiety and sport performance. *Journal of Sport Psychology, 9,* 231-248.

American Educational Research Association (AERA), American Psychological Association (APA), National Council on Measurement in Education (NCME), & Joint Committee on Standards for Educational and Psychological Testing (JCSEPT). (2014). *Standards for educational and psychological testing.* Washington, DC: Authors.

Bakker, F.C., van Diesen, R.J.A., Spekreijse, M.C., & Pijpers, J.R. (1993). Cognitive strategies of elite and non-elite triathlon participants. *Proceedings of the Eighth World Congress of Sport Psychology* (pp. 332-336). Lisbon, Portugal.

Baumgartner, T.A., Mahar, M.T., Jackson, A.S., & Rowe, D.A. (2016). *Measurement for evaluation in kinesiology* (9th ed.). Burlington, MA: Jones and Bartlett.

Bergandi, T.A., Shryock, M.G., & Titus, T.G. (1990). The Basketball Concentration Survey: Preliminary development and validation. *The Sport Psychologist, 4,* 119-129.

Boutcher, S.H. (1990). The role of performance routines in sport. In G. Jones & L. Hardy (Eds.), *Stress and performance in sport* (pp. 231-245). London: Wiley.

Carron, A.V., Widmeyer, W.N., & Brawley, L.R. (1985). The development of an instrument to assess cohesion in sport teams: The Group Environment Questionnaire. *Journal of Sport Psychology, 7,* 244-266.

Cone, J.D. (1995). Assessment practice standards. In S.C. Hayes, V.M. Follette, R.M. Dawes, & K. Grady (Eds.), *Scientific standards for psychological practice: Issues and recommendations* (pp. 201-224). Reno, NV: Context Press.

Craft, L.L., Magyar, T.M., Becker, B.J., & Feltz, D.L. (2003). The relationship between the Competitive State Anxiety Inventory-2 and sport performance: A meta-analysis. *Journal of Sport and Exercise Psychology, 25,* 44-65.

Cronbach, L.J. (1951). Coefficient alpha and the internal structure of tests. *Psychometrika, 16*(3), 297-334.

Duda, J.L. (1989). Relationship between task and ego orientation and the perceived purpose of sport among high school athletes. *Journal of Sport and Exercise Psychology, 11,* 318-335.

Duda, J.L., & Nicholls, J.G. (1992). Dimensions of achievement motivation in schoolwork and sport. *Journal of Educational Psychology, 84*(3), 290-299.

Gardner, F., & Moore, Z. (2006). *Clinical sport psychology.* Champaign, IL: Human Kinetics.

Gardner, F.L., & Moore, Z.E. (2007). *The psychology of enhancing human performance: The Mindfulness-Acceptance-Commitment (MAC) Approach.* New York: Springer.

George, D., & Mallery, P. (2003). *SPSS for Windows step by step: A simple guide and reference, 11.0 update* (4th ed.). Boston: Allyn & Bacon. .

Gerrig, R.J., & Zimbardo, P.G. (2002a). *Psychology and life* (16th ed.). Boston: Allyn and Bacon. Retrieved from www.apa.org/research/action/glossary.aspx?tab=20.

Gerrig, R.J., & Zimbardo, P. G. (2002b). *Psychology and life* (16th ed.). Boston: Allyn and Bacon. Retrieved from www.apa.org/research/action/glossary.aspx?tab=17.

Gould, D., Greenleaf, C., Chung, Y., & Guinan, D. (2002). A survey of U.S. Atlanta and Nagano Olympians: Variables perceived to influence performance. *Research Quarterly for Exercise & Sport, 73*(2), 175-186.

Hanin, Y.L. (1980). A study of anxiety in sports. In W.F. Straub (Ed.), *Sport psychology: An analysis of athlete behavior* (pp. 236-249). Ithaca, NY: Mouvement.

Hanin, Y.L. (1986). State and trait anxiety research on sports in the USSR. In C.D. Spielberger & R. Diaz-Guerreo

(Eds.), *Cross-cultural anxiety* (Vol. 3, pp. 45-64). Washington, DC: Hemisphere.

Hanin, Y.L. (1997). Emotions and athletic performance: Individual zones of optimal functioning. *European Yearbook of Sport Psychology, 1,* 29-72.

Hardy, L. (1990). A catastrophe model of performance in sport. In G. Jones & L. Hardy (Eds.), *Stress and performance in sport* (pp. 81-106). Chichester, UK: Wiley.

Hardy, L. (1996). Testing the predictions of the cusp catastrophe model of anxiety and performance. *The Sport Psychologist, 10,* 140-156.

Highlen, P.S., & Bennett, B.B. (1983). Elite divers and wrestlers: A comparison between open- and closed-skilled athletes. *Journal of Sport Psychology, 5,* 390-409.

Jones, G., & Hardy, L. (1990). Stress in sport: Experiences of some elite performers. In G. Jones & L. Hardy (Eds.), *Stress and performance in sport* (pp. 247-277). Chichester, UK: Wiley.

Likert, R. (1932). A technique for the measurement of attitudes. *Archives of Psychology, 22*(140), 1-55.

Losby, J., & Wetmore, A. (2012, February). *Using Likert scales in evaluation survey work.* Slideshow presented at the Coffee Break, Evaluation and Program Effectiveness Team, Division for Heart Disease and Stroke Prevention, Centers for Disease Control and Prevention. Retrieved from www.cdc.gov/dhdsp/pubs/docs/cb_february_14_2012.pdf.

Malhotra, N.K. (2006). Questionnaire design and scale development. In R. Grover & M. Vriens, (Eds.), *The handbook of marketing research: Uses, misuses, and future advances* (pp. 83-94). Thousand Oaks, CA: Sage. doi:10.4135/9781412973380.n5

Martens, R., Burton, D., Vealey, R.S., Bump, L.A., & Smith, D.E. (1990). Development and validation of the Competitive State Anxiety Inventory-2 (CSAI-2). In R. Martens, R.S. Vealey, & D. Burton (Eds.), *Competitive anxiety in sport* (pp. 193-208). Champaign, IL: Human Kinetics.

Martin, J.J., & Gill, D.L. (1991). The relationships among competitive orientation, sport-confidence, self-efficacy, anxiety, and performance. *Journal of Sport and Exercise Psychology, 13*(2), 149-159.

Matell, M.S., & Jacoby, J. (1971). Is there an optimal number of alternatives for Likert scale items? Study I: Reliability and validity. *Educational and Psychological Measurement, 31,* 657-674.

McGrath, J.E. (1970). Major methodology issues. In J.E. McGrath (Ed.), *Social and psychological factors in stress* (pp. 19-49). New York: Holt, Rinehart & Winston.

Moran, A. (1996). *The psychology of concentration in sport performers.* Hove, UK: Psychology Press.

Newton, M., Duda, J.L., & Yin, Z. (2000). Examination of the psychometric properties of the Perceived Motivational Climate in Sport Questionnaire-2 in a sample

of female athletes. *Journal of Sports Sciences, 18*(4), 275-290. doi:10.1080/026404100365018

Nideffer, R.M. (1976). Test of Attentional and Interpersonal Style. *Journal of Personality and Social Psychology, 34*(3), 394-404.

Nideffer, R.M. (1990). Use of the Test of Attentional and Interpersonal Style in Sport. *The Sport Psychologist, 4,* 285-300.

Nideffer, R.M. (1992). *The Attentional and Interpersonal Style Inventory: Theory and applications.* New Berlin, WI: Assessment Systems International.

Nideffer, R.M. (1995). *Test of Attentional and Interpersonal Style: Revised.* New Berlin, WI: Assessment Systems International.

Nunnally, J.C. (1967). *Psychometric theory.* New York: McGraw-Hill.

Nunnally, J.C. (1978). *Psychometric theory* (2nd ed.). New York: McGraw-Hill.

Osgood, C.E. (1952). The nature and measurement of meaning. *Psychological Bulletin, 49*(3), 197-237. http://dx.doi.org/10.1037/h0055737

Osgood, C.E. (1960). The cross-cultural generality of visual-verbal synesthetic tendencies. *Behavioral Science, 5*(2), 146-169. doi:10.1002/bs.3830050204

Osgood, C.E. (1964). Semantic differential technique in the comparative study of cultures. *American Anthropologist, 66*(3), 171-200. doi:10.1525/aa.1964.66.3.02a00880

Osgood, C.E., Saporta, S., & Nunnally, J.C. (1956). Evaluative assertion analysis. *Litera, 3,* 47-102.

Spence, J.T., & Spence, K.W. (1966). The motivational components of manifest anxiety: Drive and drive stimuli. In C.D. Spielberger (Ed.), *Anxiety and behavior* (pp. 291-326). New York: Academic Press.

Thomas, P.R., & Over, R. (1994). Psychological and psychomotor skills associated with performance in golf. *The Sport Psychologist, 8,* 73-86.

Van Schoyck, S.R., & Grasha, A.F. (1981). Attentional style variations and athletic ability: The advantages of a sports-specific test. *Journal of Sport Psychology, 3,* 149-165.

Vealey, R. (1986a). Conceptualization of sport-confidence and competitive orientation: Preliminary investigation and instrument development. *Journal of Sport Psychology, 8,* 221-246.

Vealey, R. (1986b). Sport personality: A paradigmatic and methodological analysis. *Journal of Sport and Exercise Psychology, 11,* 216-235.

Vealey, R. (2001). Understanding and enhancing self-confidence in athletes. In R. Singer, H. Hausenblas, & C. Janelle (Eds.), *Handbook of sport psychology* (2nd ed., pp. 550-565). New York: Wiley.

Wulf, G. (2007). *Attention and motor skill learning.* Champaign, IL: Human Kinetics.

Chapter 3

Adams, A.J., & Kuzmits, F.E. (2008). Testing the relationship between a cognitive ability test and player success: the National Football League case. *Athletic Insight, 10*(1), 1-14.

American Educational Research Association (AERA), American Psychological Association (APA), & National Council on Measurement in Education (NCME). (2014). *Standards for educational and psychological testing* (5th ed.). Washington, DC: AERA.

American Psychological Association (APA). (2002). *Ethical principles of psychologists and code of conduct.* Retrieved from www.apa.org/ethics/code2002.html.

Association for Applied Sport Psychology (AASP). (n.d.). *AASP ethical principles and standards.* Retrieved from www.appliedsportpsych.org/about/ethics/ethics-code/.

Bersoff, D.N., & Hofer, P.T. (1990). The legal regulation of school psychology. In C.R. Reynolds & T.B. Gutkin (Eds.), *The handbook of school psychology*, 2nd ed., 937-961. New York: Wiley.

Comer, R. (2014). *Abnormal psychology* (8th ed.). New York: Worth.

Dana, R.H. (1994). Testing and assessment ethics for all persons: Beginning and agenda. *Professional Psychology: Research and Practice, 25*(4), 349-354.

Etzel, E.F., Yura, M., Perna, F., & Vosloo, J. (2014). Ethics in assessment and testing in sport and exercise psychology. In E.F. Etzel & J.C. Watson (Eds.), *Ethical issues in sport exercise and performance psychology* (pp. 189-204). Morgantown, WV: Fitness Information Technology.

Hankes, D.M. (2012). Sport and performance psychology: Ethical issues. In S.M. Murphy (Ed.), *The Oxford handbook of sport and performance psychology* (pp. 328-342). New York: Oxford University Press.

Kahneman, D., & Tversky, A. (1974). Judgment under uncertainty: Heuristics and biases. *Science, 185,* 1125-1131.

Knauss, L.K. (2001). Ethical issues in psychological assessment in school settings. *Journal of Personality Assessment, 77*(2), 231-241.

Mirabile, M.P. (2005). Intelligence and football: Testing for differentials in collegiate quarterback passing performance and NFL compensation. *Sport Journal, 8*(2). Retrieved from http://thesportjournal.org/article/intelligence-and-football-testing-for-differentials-in-collegiate-quarterback-passing-performance-and-nfl-compensation/

Moore, Z.E. (2003). Ethical dilemmas in sport psychology: Discussion and recommendations for practice. *Professional Psychology: Research and Practice, 34*(6), 601-610.

O'Connor, E.A. (2004). Which questionnaire? Assessment practices of sport psychology consultants. *Sport Psychologist, 18,* 464-468.

Tymins, A., & Fraga, A. (2014). Wondering about the Wonderlic: Does it predict quarterback performance? Retrieved from http://harvardsportsanalysis.org/2014/04/.

Zito, M., Herzog, T., & Shipherd, A. (2013). What's in a name: Some ins and outs of representing yourself. *AASP Spring Newsletter, 28*(1), 17-18. Retrieved from www.appliedsportpsych.org/site/assets/newsletter/2013/spring/.

Chapter 4

Acquadro, C., Conway, K., Hareendran, A., Aaronson, N., & European Regulatory Issues and Quality of Life Assessment (ERIQA) Group. (2008). Literature review of methods to translate health-related quality of life questionnaires for use in multinational clinical trials. *Value Health, 11*(3), 509-521.

Albani, C., Blaser, G., Geyer, M., Schmutzer, G., Brähler, E., Bailer, H., & Grulke, N. (2005). [The German short version of "Profile of Mood States" (POMS): Psychometric evaluation in a representative sample]. *Psychotherapie, Psychosomatik, Medizinische Psychologie, 55*(7), 324-330.

Altahayneh, Z.L. (2003). *The effects of coaches' behaviors and burnout on the satisfaction and burnout of athletes* (Doctoral dissertation). Retrieved from the Florida State University Database. (FSU_migr_etd-0005 [IID]).

American Counseling Association (ACA). (2014). *2014 ACA code of ethics.* Alexandria, VA: Author.

American Psychological Association (APA). (2002). *Ethical principles of psychologists and code of conduct.* Washington, DC: Author.

American Psychological Association (APA). (2010). *Publication manual of the American Psychological Association* (6th ed.). Washington, DC: Author.

American Psychological Association (APA). (2016). *Guidelines for assessment of and intervention with persons with disabilities.* Retrieved from www.apa.org/pi/Disability/resources/assessment-disabilities.aspx.

Andrade, E., Arce, C., Torrado, J., Garrido, J., De Francisco, C., & Arce, I. (2010). Factor structure and invariance of the POMS mood state questionnaire in Spanish. *Spanish Journal of Psychology, 13*(01), 444-452.

Andrade, F.E., Lois, R.G., & Arce, F.C. (2007). [Psychometric properties of the Spanish version of the Revised Competitive State Anxiety Inventory-2 with athletes]. *Psicothema, 19*(1), 150-155.

Arce, C., De Francisco, C., Andrade, E., Seoane, G., & Raedeke, T. (2012). Adaptation of the Athlete Burnout Questionnaire in a Spanish sample of athletes. *Spanish Journal of Psychology, 15*(3), 1529-1536.

Aroian, K.J., Kulwicki, A., Kaskiri, E.A., Templin, T.N., & Wells, C.L. (2007). Psychometric evaluation of the Arabic language version of the Profile of Mood States. *Research in Nursing & Health, 30*(5), 531-541.

Asghar, E. (2011). *A comparative study of multidimensional talent in field hockey at development stage between the players of Germany and Pakistan* (Unpublished dissertation). University of Leipzig, Germany.

Association for Spiritual, Ethical, and Religious Values in Counseling (ASERVIC). (2015). *Spiritual competencies*. Retrieved from www.aservic.org/resources/spiritual-competencies/.

Azevedo, M.H., Silva, C.F., & Dias, M.R. (1991). O Perfil de Estados de Humor. Adaptação à população Portuguesa. *Psiquiatria Clínica, 12*, 187-193.

Bagherpour, T., Hashim, H.A., Saha, S., & Ghosh, A.K. (2012). Effects of progressive muscle relaxation and internal imagery on Competitive State Anxiety Inventory-2R among taekwondo athletes. *International Proceedings of Economics Development & Research, 30*, 218.

Balaguer, I., Castillo, I., & Tomas, I. (1996). Analysis of the psychometric properties of the Task and Ego Orientation in Sport Questionnaire (TEOSQ) in its Spanish version. *Psicologica, 17*, 71-81.

Baldwin, J.A. (1980). The psychology of oppression. In M. Asante & A.S. Vandi (Eds.), *Contemporary black thought* (pp. 85-110). Beverly Hills, CA: Sage.

Bara Filho, M., Andrade, D., Miranda, R., Núñez, J.L., Martín-Albó, J., & Ribas, P.R. (2011). Preliminary validation of a Brazilian version of the Sport Motivation Scale. *Universitas Psychologica, 10*(2), 557-566.

Bayyat, M.M., Almoghrabi, A.H., & Ay, K.M. (2016). Preliminary validation of an Arabic version of the Sport Motivation Scale (SMS-28). *Asian Social Science, 12*(7), 186-196.

Bertoldi, R. (2014). *Fatores preditores do burnout em atletas: Um estudo com atletas brasileiros profissionais de futsal* (Unpublished dissertation). Universidade Federal do Rio Grande do Sul, Brazil.

Bickenbach, J E. (2012). The International Classification of Functioning, Disability and Health and its relationship to disability studies. In N. Watson, A. Roulstone, & C. Thomas (Eds.), *Routledge handbook of disability studies* (pp. 51-66). Abingdon, UK: Routledge.

Bortoli, L., & Robazza, C. (2003). Orientamento motivazionale nello sport. *Giornale Italiano di Psicologia dello Sport, 3*, 63-67.

Brière, N.M., Vallerand, R.J., Blais, M.R., & Pelletier, L.G. (1995). Développement et validation d'une mesure de motivation intrinsèque, extrinsèque et d'amotivation en contexte sportif: L'Échelle de Motivation dans les Sports (EMS). *International Journal of Sport Psychology, 26*, 465-489.

Brooks, D., & Althouse, R. (2000). *Racism in college athletics* (2nd ed.). Morgantown, WV: Fitness Information Technology.

Burtscher, J., Furtner, M., Sachse, P., & Burtscher, M. (2011). Validation of a German version of the Sport Motivation Scale (SMS28) and motivation analysis in competitive mountain runners. *Perceptual and Motor Skills, 112*(3), 807-820.

Candela, F., Zucchetti, G., & Villosio, C. (2014). Preliminary validation of the Italian version of the original Sport Motivation Scale. *Journal of Human Sport and Exercise, 9*(1), 136-147.

Captain, G. (1991). Enter ladies and gentleman of color: Gender, sport, and the ideal of African American manhood and womanhood during the late nineteenth and early twentieth centuries. *Journal of Sport History, 18*(1), 81-102.

Cashwell, C.S., & Young, J.S. (2011). *Integrating spirituality and religion into counseling: A guide to competent practice* (2nd ed.). Alexandria, VA: American Counseling Association.

Chen, L.H., Kee, Y.H., & Tsai, Y.M. (2008). Relation of dispositional optimism with burnout among athletes. *Perceptual and Motor Skills, 106*(3), 693-698.

Chen, K.M., Snyder, M., & Krichbaum, K. (2002). Translation and equivalence: The Profile of Mood States short form in English and Chinese. *International Journal of Nursing Studies, 39*(6), 619-624.

Cho, S. (2014). *A self-determination theory perspective on burnout among Korean athletes: Perceived coaching behaviors and satisfaction/thwarting of psychological needs* (Unpublished dissertation). Florida State University, Tallahassee, FL.

Chung, P.K., & Dong Liu, J. (2012). Examination of the psychometric properties of the Chinese translated Behavioral Regulation in Exercise Questionnaire-2. *Measurement in Physical Education and Exercise Science, 16*(4), 300-315.

Coakley, J.J. (2007). *Sport in society: Issues and controversies* (9th ed.). New York: McGraw-Hill.

Coelho, E.M., Vasconcelos-Raposo, J., & Mahl, Á.C. (2010). Confirmatory factorial analysis of the Brazilian version of the Competitive State Anxiety Inventory-2 (CSAI-2). *Spanish Journal of Psychology, 13*(01), 453-460.

Cole, K.W., & Tinsley, T.M. (2009). Sports counseling. In American Counseling Association (Ed.), *The ACA encyclopedia of counseling* (pp. 522-524). Alexandria, VA: American Counseling Association.

Daly, A., Jennings, J., Beckett, J.O., Leashore, B.R. (1995). Effective coping strategies of African Americans. *Social Work, 40*(2), 240-248.

Dieffenbach, K & Statler, T. (2012). More similar than different: The psychological environment of Paralympic sport. Journal of Sport Psychology in Action, 3(2), 109-118.

Dillon, K.M., & Tait, J.L. (2000). Spirituality and being in the zone in team sports: A relationship? *Journal of Sport Behavior, 23*(2), 91-100.

Ellison, C.W. (1983). Spiritual well-being: Conceptualization and measurement. *Journal of Psychology and Theology, 11*(4), 330-340.

Fillion, L., & Gagnon, P. (1999). French adaptation of the shortened version of the Profile of Mood States. *Psychological Reports, 84,* 188-190.

Fonseca, A.M., & de Paula Brito, A. (2005). The issue of the cross-cultural adjustment of instruments for psychological evaluation in national sport contexts—The case of the Task and Ego Orientation in Sport Questionnaire (TEOSQ). *Psychologica, 39,* 95-118.

Forster-Scott, L. (2005). *The creation of the saliency of race in sport questionnaire: Exploring issues of Black racial identity development in sport.* (Unpublished doctoral dissertation). Philadelphia: Temple University.

Fuentes, M.A., & Adames, H.Y. (2014). Theories, models, and practices for understanding gender, race and ethnicity in clinical assessment. In M.L. Miville & A.D. Ferguson (Eds.), *The handbook of race-ethnicity and gender in psychology* (pp. 313-328). New York: Springer.

Gill, D.L. (2007). Gender and cultural diversity. In G. Tenenbaum & R.C. Eklund (Eds.), *Handbook of sport psychology* (3rd ed., pp. 821-844). New York: Wiley.

Gill, D.L., & Deeter, T.E. (1988). Development of the sport orientation questionnaire. Research Quarterly for Exercise and Sport, 59(3), 191-202.

Gill, D.L., & Kamphoff, C. (2010). Gender in sport and exercise psychology. In D.R. McCreary & J.C. Chrisler (Eds.), *Handbook of gender research in psychology, Volume 2: Gender research in social and applied psychology* (pp. 565-585). New York: Springer.

Granero-Gallegos, A., Baena-Extremera, A., Gómez-López, M., Sánchez-Fuentes, J.A., & Abraldes, J.A. (2014). Psychometric properties of the "Sport Motivation Scale (SMS)" adapted to physical education. *Journal of Sports Science & Medicine, 13*(4), 801.

Guillemin, F., Bombardier, C., & Beaton, D. (1993). Cross-cultural adaptation of health-related quality of life measures: Literature review and proposed guidelines. *Journal of Clinical Epidemiology, 46,* 1417-1432.

Hall, T.W., & Edwards, K.J. (2002). The Spiritual Assessment Inventory: A theistic model and measure for assessing spiritual development. *Journal for the Scientific Study of Religion, 41*(2), 341-357.

Hanrahan, S.J. (2005). Able athletes with disabilities: Issues and group work. In M.B. Andersen (Ed.), *Sport psychology in practice* (pp. 223-247). Champaign, IL: Human Kinetics.

Helms, J.E. (1995). An update of Helm's white and people of color racial identity models. In J.G. Ponterotto, J.M. Cassas, L.A. Suzuki, & C.M. Alexander (Eds.), *Handbook of multicultural counseling* (pp. 181-198). Thousand Oaks, CA: Sage.

Hettler, B. (1976). *The six dimensions of wellness model.* Stevens Point, WI: National Wellness Institute. Retrieved from http://c.ymcdn.com/sites/www.nationalwellness.org/resource/resmgr/docs/sixdimensionsfactsheet.pdf.

Howe, P.D. (2008). *The cultural politics of the Paralympic movement through an anthropological lens.* New York: Routledge.

Hyde, J.S. (2005). The gender similarities hypothesis. *American Psychologist, 60*(6), 581-592.

Isoard-Gautheur, S., Oger, M., Guillet, E., & Martin-Krumm, C. (2010). Validation of a French version of the Athlete Burnout Questionnaire (ABQ): In competitive sport and physical education context. *European Journal of Psychological Assessment, 26*(3), 203.

Jobling, A. (2012). The Paralympic Games. *International Journal of Disability, Development and Education, 59*(3), 225-229. doi:10.1080/1034912X.2012.697710

Jones, J.M. (1997). *Prejudice and racism* (2nd ed.). New York: McGraw-Hill.

Khalaf, S.B.H. (2014). *Arabic women's participation in sport: Barriers and motivation among Egyptian and Kuwaiti athletes.* Unpublished doctoral dissertation. University of Wales, Bangor, UK.

Khalil, N.L.B.M. (2015). *The influence of reward and leadership style on the extrinsic motivation among royal Malaysian police officers* (Unpublished doctoral dissertation). Universiti Utara Malaysia.

Kim, B.J., & Gill, D.L. (1997). A cross-cultural extension of goal perspective theory to Korean youth sport. *Journal of Sport and Exercise Psychology, 19,* 142-155.

Koenig, H.G., Parkerson, G.R., & Meador, K.G. (1997). Religion index for psychiatric research. *American Journal of Psychiatry, 153,* 885-886.

Landrine, H., & Klonoff, E.A. (1994). The African American acculturation scale: Development, reliability, and validity. *Journal of Black Psychology, 20*(2), 104-127.

Lapchick, R.E. (2015). *The Racial and Gender Report Card.* Retrieved from www.tidesport.org/reports.html.

Li, C., Kawabata, M., & Zhang, L. (2016). Validity and reliability of the Sport Motivation Scale-II for Chinese athletes. *International Journal of Sport and Exercise Psychology,* March, 1-14.

Linn, M.C., & Kessel, C. (2006). Assessment and gender. In J. Worell & C.D. Goodheart (Eds.), *Handbook of girls' and women's psychological health: Gender and wellbeing across the lifespan* (pp. 40-50). New York: Oxford University Press.

Lonsdale, C., Hodge, K., & Rose, E.A. (2008). The Behavioral Regulation in Sport Questionnaire (BRSQ): Instrument development and initial validity evidence. *Journal of Sport & Exercise Psychology, 30*(3), 323.

Martinent, G., Ferrand, C., Guillet, E., & Gautheur, S. (2010). Validation of the French version of the Competitive State Anxiety Inventory-2 Revised (CSAI-2R) including frequency and direction scales. *Psychology of Sport and Exercise, 11*(1), 51-57.

Matsumoto, D., & Juang, L. (2008). *Culture and psychology* (4th ed.). Belmont, CA: Wadsworth Cengage Learning.

McNair, D.M., Lorr, M., & Droppleman, L.F. (1971). *EITS manual for the Profile of Mood States.* San Diego: Educational and Industrial Testing Service.

Monteiro, D., Moutão, J., & Cid, L. Validation of the Behavioral Regulation Sport Questionnaire (BRSQ) in a sample of Portuguese athletes. *Revista de Paicologia del deporte.* Submitted for publication.

Nasta, M.T., Grussu, P., Quatraro, R.M., Cerutti, R., & Grella, P.V. (2002). Cholesterol and mood states at 3 days after delivery. *Journal of Psychosomatic Research, 52*(2), 61-63.

Nejedlo, R.J., Arredondo, P., & Benjamin, L. (1985). *Imagine: A visionary model for the counselors of tomorrow.* Dekalb, IL: George's Printing.

Nideffer, R.M. (2007). Reliability and validity of The Attentional and Interpersonal Style (TAIS) inventory concentration scales. In D. Smith & M. Bar-Eli (Eds.), *Essential readings in sport and exercise psychology* (pp. 265-277). Champaign, IL: Human Kinetics.

Oomen, T.K. (1994). Race, ethnicity and class: An analysis of interrelations. *International Social Science Journal, 139,* 83-93.

Peers, D., Spencer-Cavaliere, N, & Eales, L. (2014). Say what you mean: Rethinking disability language in Adapted Physical Activity Quarterly. *Adapted Physical Activity Quarterly, 31*(3), 265-282.

Peili, Z. (1994). The revised Chinese norm of the Competitive State Anxiety Inventory (CSAI-2). *Psychological Science,* 6.

Pelletier, L.G., Fortier, M.S., Vallerand, R.J., Tuson, K.M., Briere, N.M., & Blais, M.R. (1995). Toward a new measure of intrinsic motivation, extrinsic motivation, and amotivation in sports: The Sport Motivation Scale (SMS). *Journal of Sport and Exercise Psychology, 17,* 35-53.

Perrier, M., Smith, B., Strachan, S.M., & Latimer-Cheung, A. (2014). Narratives of athletic identity after acquiring a permanent physical disability. *Adapted Physical Activity Quarterly, 31*(2), 106-124.

Peters, D., & Kohe, G. (2016). Introduction to high performance disability sport coaching. In G. Kohe & D. Peters (Eds.), *High performance disability sport coaching.* Abingdon, UK: Routledge.

Ponterotto, J.G., Utsey, B.O., Pederson, P.B. (2006). *Preventing prejudice: A guide for counselors, educators, and parents* (2nd ed.). Thousand Oaks, CA: Sage.

Ram, N., Starek, J., Johnson, J. (2004). Race, ethnicity, and sexual orientation: Still a void in sport and exercise psychology? *Journal of Sport & Exercise Psychology, 26*(2), 250-268.

Ridnour, H., & Hammermeister, J. (2008). Spiritual well-being and its influence on athletic coping profiles. *Journal of Sport Behavior, 31*(1), 81-92.

Ryba, T.V., Schinke, R.J., & Tenenbaum, G. (2009). *The cultural turn in sport psychology.* Morgantown, WV: Fitness Information Technology.

Schinke, R., & Hanranhan, S. (2009). *Cultural sport psychology.* Champaign, IL: Human Kinetics.

Scholz, U., Doña, B.G., Sud, S., & Schwarzer, R. (2002). Is general self-efficacy a universal construct? Psychometric findings from 25 countries. *European Journal of Psychological Assessment, 18*(3), 242-251.

Sellers, R.M., Rowley, S.A.J., Chavous, T.M., Shelton, N.J., & Smith, M.A. (1997). Multidimensional inventory of Black identity: A preliminary investigation of reliability and construct validity. Journal of Personality and Social Psychology, 73(4), 805-815.

Semerjian, T.Z. (2009). Disability in sport and exercise psychology. In T.V. Ryba, R.J. Schinke, & G. Tenenbaum (Eds.), *The cultural turn in sport psychology* (pp. 259-284). Morgantown, WV: Fitness Information Technology.

Silva, C.F., & Howe, P.D. (2012). The (in)validity of supercrip representation of Paralympian athletes. *Journal of Sport and Social Issues, 36*(2), 174-194. doi:10.1177/0193723511433865

Simons, H.D., Bosworth, C., Fujita, S., & Jensen, M. (2007). The athlete stigma in higher education. *College Student Journal, 41*(2), 251-273.

Steinfeldt, J., Reed, C., & Steinfeldt, M.C. (2010). Racial and athletic identity of African American football players at historically black colleges and universities and predominantly white institutions. *Journal of Black Psychology, 36*(3), 3-24.

Stöber, J., Otto, K., Pescheck, E., Becker, C., & Stoll, O. (2007). Perfectionism and competitive anxiety in athletes: Differentiating striving for perfection and negative reactions to imperfection. *Personality and Individual Differences, 42*(6), 959-969.

Storch, E.A., Kolsky, A.R., Silvestri, S.M., & Storch, J.B. (2001). Religiosity of elite college athletes. *The Sport Psychologist, 15,* 346-351.

Tatum, B.D. (2003). *Why are the black kids sitting together in the cafeteria? And other conversations about race* (revised). New York: Plenum.

Teo, E.W., Khoo, S., Wong, R., Wee, E.H., Lim, B.H., & Rengasamy, S.S. (2015). Intrinsic and extrinsic motivation among adolescent ten-pin bowlers in Kuala Lumpur, Malaysia. *Journal of Human Kinetics, 45*(1), 241-251.

Tinsley, T. (2005). The self-reported multicultural sports counseling competencies among professional school counselors and Play It Smart academic coaches. *Dissertation Abstracts International, 66*(11), 3942.

Tweedy, S.M., & Vanlandewijck, Y.C. (2009). International Paralympic Committee position stand—Background and scientific principles of classification in Paralympic sport. *British Journal of Sports Medicine*, *45*(4), 259-269. doi:10.1136/bjsm.2009.065060

United Nations (UN). Convention on the Rights of Persons with Disabilities, 13 December 2006, A/RES/61/106.

Vallerand, R.J., Blais, M.R., Brière, N.M., & Pelletier, L.G. (1989). Construction et validation de l'échelle de motivation en éducation (EME). *Canadian Journal of Behavioural Science/Revue Canadienne des Sciences du Comportement*, *21*(3), 323-349.

Vallerand, R.J., Pelletier, L.G., Blais, M.R., Brière, N.M., Senecal, C., & Vallieres, E.F. (1992). The Academic Motivation Scale: A measure of intrinsic, extrinsic, and amotivation in education. *Educational and Psychological Measurement*, *52*(4), 1003-1017.

van de Vijver, F.J.R., & Poortinga, Y.H. (1997). Towards an integrated analysis of bias in cross-cultural assessment. *European Journal of Psychological Assessment*, *13*(1), 29-37.

Vandiver, B.J., Cross, W.E., Jr., Worrell, F.C., & Fhagen-Smith, P.E. (2002). Validating the Cross Racial Identity Scale. *Journal of Counseling Psychology*, *49*(1), 71-85.

Viladrich, C., Appleton, P.R., Quested, E., Duda, J.L., Alcaraz, S., Heuzé, J.P., et al. (2013). Measurement invariance of the Behavioural Regulation in Sport Questionnaire when completed by young athletes across five European countries. *International Journal of Sport and Exercise Psychology*, *11*(4), 384-394.

Vitali, F., Bortoli, L., Bertinato, L., Robazza, C., & Schena, F. (2014). Motivational climate, resilience, and burnout in youth sport. *Sport Sciences for Health*, *11*(1), 103-108.

Walker, J. (2012). Meet the superhumans. Retrieved from www.channel4.com/info/press/news/channel-4-takes-over-tv-with-meet-the-superhumans-campaign.

Ward, D.G., Sandstedt, S.D., Cox, R.H., & Beck, N.C. (2005). Athlete-counseling competencies for U.S. psychologists working with athletes. *The Sport Psychologist*, *19*, 318-334.

Watson, N.J., & Nesti, M. (2005). The role of spirituality in sport psychology consulting: An analysis and integrative review of literature. *Journal of Applied Sport Psychology*, *17*, 228-239.

Williams, J.E., Satterwhite, R.C., & Best, D.L. (1999). Pancultural gender stereotypes revisited: The five factor model. *Sex Roles*, *40*(7/8), 513-525.

World Health Organization (WHO). (2001). *International Classification of Functioning, Disability and Health (ICF)*. Geneva: Author.

Yamada, Y., & Hirosawa, M. (2009). Does Typus Melancholicus determine characteristics of athlete burnout symptom and its process among Japanese university athletes? *Journal of Human Ergology*, *38*(2), 67-79.

Yokoyama, K., Araki, S., Kawakami, N., & Tkakeshita, T. (1990). [Production of the Japanese edition of profile of mood states (POMS): Assessment of reliability and validity]. *Nihon Koshu Eisei Zasshi*, *37*(11), 913-918.

Yeun, E.J., & Shin-Park, K.K. (2006). Verification of the Profile of Mood States-Brief: Cross-cultural analysis. *Journal of Clinical Psychology*, *62*(9), 1173-1180.

Ziemainz, H., Abu-Omar, K., Raedeke, T.D., & Krause, K. (2004). *Zur Prävalenz von Burnout aus bedingungsbezogener Perspektive* [Burnout in sports The prevalence of burnout from an environmental perspective]. *Leistungssport*, *34*, 12-17.

Chapter 5

American Psychiatric Association (APA). (2013). *Diagnostic and statistical manual of mental disorders* (5th ed.). Washington, DC: Author.

Andersen, M.B., & Williams, J.M. (1988). A model of stress and athletic injury: Prediction and prevention. *Journal of Sport and Exercise Psychology*, *10*, 294-306.

Anshel, M.H., & Sutarso, T. (2007). Relationships between sources of acute stress and athletes' coping style in competitive sport as a function of gender. *Psychology of Sport and Exercise*, *8*, 1-24.

Babor, T.F., Higgins-Biddle, J.C., Saunders, J.B., & Monteiro, M.G. (2001). *The Alcohol Use Disorders Identification Test: Guidelines for use in primary care* (2nd ed.). World Health Organization (WHO). Retrieved from www.talkingalcohol.com/files/pdfs/WHO_audit.pdf.

Berger, B.G., Pargman, D., & Weinberg, R.S. (2007). *Foundations of exercise psychology* (2nd ed.). Morgantown, WV: Fitness Information Technology.

Bonci, C.M., Bonci, L.J., Granger, L.R., Johnson, C.L., Malina, R.M., Milne, L.W., . . . & Vanderbunt, E.M. (2008). National Athletic Trainers' Association position statement: Preventing, detecting, and managing disordered eating in athletes. *Journal of Athletic Training*, *43*, 80-108.

Burton, R.W. (2000). Mental illness in athletes. In D. Begel & R. Burton (Eds.), *Sport psychiatry: Theory and practice* (pp. 61-81). New York: Norton.

Cohen, S., & Williamson, G. (1988). Perceived stress in a probability study of the United States. In S. Spacapan & S. Oscamp (Eds.), *The social psychology of health* (pp. 31-67). Newbury Park, CA: Sage.

Conners, C.K., Erhardt, D., & Sparrow, E. (1999). *CAARS Adult ADHD Rating Scales: Technical manual*. New York: Multi-Health Systems.

Dhalla, S., & Kopec, J.A. (2007). The CAGE questionnaire for alcohol misuse: A review of reliability and validity studies. *Clinical & Investigative Medicine*, *30*, 33-41.

Eaton, W.W., Muntaner, C., Smith, C., Tien, A., & Ybarra, M. (2004). Center for Epidemiologic Studies Depression Scale: Review and revision (CESD and CESD-R). In M.E. Maruish (Ed.), *The use of psychological testing for treatment planning and outcomes assessment* (3rd ed., pp. 363-377). Mahwah, NJ: Erlbaum.

Fairburn, C.G., & Beglin, S.J. (1994). Assessment of eating disorder psychopathology: Interview or self-report questionnaire? *International Journal of Eating Disorders, 16,* 363-370.

Galambos, S.A., Terry, P.C., Moyle, G.M., & Locke, S.A. (2005). Psychological predictors of injury among elite athletes. *British Journal of Sports Medicine, 39,* 351-354.

Garner, D.M., Olmsted, M.P., Bohr, Y., & Garfinkel, P.E. (1982). The Eating Attitudes Test: Psychometric features and clinical correlates. *Psychological Medicine, 12,* 871-878.

Gil-Monte, P.R., & Peiró, J.M. (1998). A model of burnout process development: An alternative from appraisal models of stress. *Comportamento Organizacional E Gestão, 4,* 165-179.

Gold, P.W., & Chrousos, G.P. (2002). Organization of the stress system and its dysregulation in melancholic and atypical depression: High vs. low CRH/NE states. *Molecular Psychiatry, 7,* 254-275.

Green, G.A., Uryasz, F.D., Petr, T.A., & Bray, C.D. (2001). NCAA study of substance use and abuse habits of college student-athletes. *Clinical Journal of Sport Medicine, 11,* 51-56.

Gulliver, A., Griffiths, K.M., Mackinnon, A., Batterham, P.J., & Stanimirovic, R. (2015). The mental health of Australian elite athletes. Journal of Science and Medicine in Sport, 18, 255-261.

Hainline, B., Bell, L., & Willfert, M. (2014). Substance use and abuse. In G.T. Brown (Ed.), *Mind, body and sport: Understanding and supporting student-athlete mental wellness* (pp. 61-64). Indianapolis: National Collegiate Athletic Association. Retrieved from www.ncaapublications.com.

Hammond, T., Gialloreto, C., Kubas, H., & Davis, H.H. (2013). The prevalence of failure-based depression among elite athletes. *Clinical Journal of Sports Medicine, 23,* 273-277.

Houck, P.R., Spiegel, D.A., Shear, M.K., & Rucci, D. (2002). Reliability of the self-report version of the Panic Disorder Severity Scale. *Depression and Anxiety, 15,* 183-185.

International Olympic Committee (IOC). (2009). *The International Olympic Committee (IOC) consensus statement on periodic health evaluation of elite athletes.* Lausanne, Switzerland: Author.

Johnson, F., & Wardle, J. (2005). Dietary restraint, body dissatisfaction, and psychological distress: A prospective analysis. *Journal of Abnormal Psychology, 114,* 119-125.

Kellman, M., & Kallus, K.W. (2001). *Recovery-Stress Questionnaire for athletes: User manual.* Champaign, IL: Human Kinetics.

Kellmann, M., & Kallus, K.W. (2016). The Recovery-Stress Questionnaire for Athletes. In K.W. Kallus & M. Kellmann (Eds.), *The Recovery-Stress Questionnaires: User manual* (pp. 86-131). Frankfurt am Main: Pearson Assessment & Information GmbH.

Kerr, Z., Marshall, S.W., Harding, H.P., & Guskiewicz, K.M. (2012). Nine-year risk of depression diagnosis increases with increasing self-reported concussions in retired professional football players. *The American Journal of Sports Medicine, 40,* 2206-2212.

Kessler, R.C., Adler, L., Ames, M., Demler, O., Faraone, S., Hiripi, E., . . . Walters, E.E. (2005). The World Health Organization Adult ADHD Self-Report Scale (ASRS). *Psychological Medicine, 35,* 245-256.

Knapp, J., Aerni, G., & Anderson, J. (2014). Eating disorders in female athletes: Use of screening tools. *Current Sports Medicine Reports, 13,* 214-218.

Knight, J.R., Sherritt, L., Harris, S.K., Gates, E.C., & Chang, G. (2003). Validity of brief alcohol screening tests among adolescents: A Comparison of the AUDIT, POSIT, CAGE, and CRAFFT. *Alcoholism: Clinical and Experimental Research, 27,* 67-73.

Kokotalio, P.K., Henry, B.C., Koscik, R.E., Fleming, M.F., & Landry, G.L. (1996). Substance use and other health risk behaviors in collegiate athletes. *Clinical Journal of Sport Medicine, 6,* 183-189.

Markser, V.Z. (2011). Sport psychiatry and psychotherapy. Mental strains and disorders in professional sports. Challenges and answer to societal changes. *European Archives of Psychiatry and Clinical Neuroscience, 261,* S182-S185.

Maron, B.J., & Pelliccia, A. (2006). The heart of trained athletes: Cardiac remodeling and the risks of sports, including sudden death. *Circulation, 114,* 1633-1644.

Martinent, G., Decree, J.C., Isoard-Gauthier, S., Wired, E., & Ferrand, C. (2014). Evaluations of the psychometric properties of the Recovery-Stress Questionnaire for Athletes among a sample of young French table tennis players. *Psychological Reports, 114,* 326-340.

Matheny, K.B., Aycock, D.W., Curlette, W.L., & Junker, G.N. (2003). The Coping Resources Inventory for Stress: A measure of perceived resourcefulness. *Journal of Clinical Psychology, 59,* 1261-1277. http://dx.doi.org/10.1002/jclp.10219

McEwen, B.S. (2008). Central effects of stress hormones in health and disease: Understanding the protective and damaging effects of stress and stress mediators. *European Journal of Pharmacology, 583,* 174-185.

McNulty, K.Y., Adams, C.H., Anderson, J.M., & Affenito, S.G. (2001). Development and validation of a screening tool to identify eating disorders in female athletes. *Journal of the American Dietetic Association*, *101*, 886-892.

Mitchell, J.J., & Robert-McComb, J.J. (2014). Screening for disordered eating and eating disorders in female athletes. In J.J. Robert-McComb, R.L. Norman, & M. Zumwalt (Eds.), *The active female: Health issues across the lifespan* (pp. 191-206). New York: Springer.

National Collegiate Athletic Association (NCAA). (2014). NCAA student-athlete substance use study: Executive summary August 2014. Retrieved from www.ncaa.org/about/resources/research/ncaa-student-athlete-substance-use-study-executive-summary-august-2014.

Nattiv, A., Loucks, A.B., Manore, M.M., Sanborn, C.F., Sundgot-Borgen, J., & Waren, M.P. (2007). American College of Sports Medicine position stand. The female athlete triad. *Medicine and Science in Sports and Exercise*, *39*, 1867-1882.

Nixdorf, I., Frank, R., Hautzinger, M., & Beckmann, J. (2013). Prevalence of depressive symptoms and correlating variables among German elite athletes. *Journal of Clinical Sport Psychology*, *7*, 313-326.

Osman, A., Bagge, C.L., Gutierrez, P.M., Konick, L.C., Kopper, B.A., & Barrios, F.X. (2001). The Suicidal Behaviors Questionnaire-Revised (SBQ-R): Validation with clinical and nonclinical samples. *Assessment*, *5*, 443-454.

Parr, J.W. (2011). Attention-deficit hyperactivity disorder and the athlete: New advances and understanding. *Clinics in Sports Medicine*, *30*, 591-610.

Perna, F.M., & McDowell, S.L. (1995). Role of psychological stress in cortisol recovery from exhaustive exercise among elite athletes. *International Journal of Behavioral Medicine*, *2*, 13-26.

Peters, L., Sunderland, M., Andrews, G., Rapee, R.M., & Mattick, R.P. (2012). Development of a short form Social Interaction Anxiety Scale (SIAS) and Social Phobia Scale (SPS) using nonparametric item response theory: The SIAS-6 and SPS-6. *Psychological Assessment*, *24*, 66-76.

Pope, Z., Gao, Y., Bolter, N., & Pritchard, M. (2014). Validity and reliability of eating disorder assessments used with athletes: A review. *Journal of Sport and Health Science*, 1-11.

Proctor, S.L., & Boan-Lenzo, C. (2010). Prevalence of depressive symptoms in male intercollegiate student-athletes and nonathletes. *Journal of Clinical Sport Psychology*, *4*, 204-220.

Putukian, M. (2014). How being injured affects mental health. In G.T. Brown (Ed.), *Mind, body and sport: Understanding and supporting student-athlete mental wellness* (pp. 61-64). Indianapolis: National Collegiate Athletic Association. Retrieved from www.ncaapublications.com.

Rao, A.L., Asif, I.M., Drezner, J.A., Toresdahl, B.G., & Harmon, K.G. (2015). Suicide in National Collegiate Athletic Association (NCAA) athletes: A 9-year analysis of the NCAA resolutions database. *Sports Health*, *7*, 452-457.

Reardon, C.L., & Factor, R.M. (2010). Sport psychiatry: A systematic review of diagnosis and medical treatment of mental illness in athletes. *Sports Medicine*, *40*, 961-980.

Robert-McComb, J.J., & Mitchell, J.J. (2014). Menstrual dysfunction screening and management for active females. In J.J. Robert-McComb, R.L. Norman, & M. Zumwalt (Eds.), *The active female: Health issues across the lifespan* (pp. 93-109). New York: Springer.

Sabo, D., Miller, K.E., Melnick, M.J., Farrell, M.P., & Barnes, G.M. (2005). High school athletic participation and adolescent suicide: A nationwide US study. *International Review for the Sociology of Sport*, *40*, 5-23.

Scanlan, T.K. (1982). Social evaluation: A key developmental element in the competition process. In R.A. Magil, M.J. Ashe, & F.L. Smoll (Eds.), *Children in sport* (2nd ed., pp. 128-152). Champaign, IL: Human Kinetics.

Schaal, K., Tafflet, M., Nassif, H., Thibault, V., Pichard, C., Alcotte, M., . . . Toussaint, J.-F. (2011). Psychological balance in high-level athletes: Gender-based differences and sport-specific patterns. *PLoS ONE*, *6*, 1-9.

Skinner, H.A. (1982). The Drug Abuse Screening Test. *Addict Behavior*, *7*, 363-367.

Smith, A.M., & Milliner, E.K. (1994). Injured athletes and the risk of suicide. *Journal of Athletic Training*, *29*, 337-341.

Spitzer, R.L, Kroenke, K., Williams, J.B.W., & Lowe, B. (2006). A brief measure for assessing generalized anxiety disorder. *Archives of Internal Medicine*, *166*, 1092-1097.

Sullivan, B.K., May, K., & Galbally, L. (2007). Symptom exaggeration by college adults in attention-deficit hyperactivity disorder and learning disorder assessments. *Applied Neuropsychology*, *14*, 189-207.

Sundgot-Borgen, J., & Torstveit, M.K. (2004). Prevalence of eating disorders in elite athletes is higher than in the general population. *Clinical Journal of Sport Medicine*, *14*, 25-32.

Thome, J., & Espelage, D. (2004). Relations among exercise, coping, disordered eating, and psychological health among college students. *Eating Behaviors*, *4*, 337-351.

Thompson, R.A., & Sherman, R. (1999). "Good athlete" traits and characteristics of anorexia nervosa: Are they similar? *Eating Disorders*, *7*, 181-190.

Thompson, R.A., & Sherman, R. (2014). Reflections on athletes and eating disorders. *Psychology of Sport and Exercise*, *15*, 729-734.

Torstveit, M.K., Rosenvinge, J.H., & Sundgot-Borgen, J. (2008). Prevalence of eating disorders and the predictive power of risk models in female elite athletes: A controlled study. *Scandinavian Journal of Medicine and Science in Sports*, 18, 108-118.

Vargas, G., Rabinowitz, A., Meyer, J., & Arnett, P.A. (2015). Predictors and prevalence of postconcussion depression symptoms in collegiate athletes. *Journal of Athletic Training*, 50, 250-255.

Weigand, S., Cohen, J., & Merenstein, D. (2013). Susceptibility for depression in current and retired student athletes. *Sports Health*, 5, 263-266.

White, R.D., Harris, G.D., & Gibson, M.E. (2014). Attention deficit hyperactivity disorder and athletes. *Sports Health*, 6, 149-156.

Wiggins, M.S., Lai, C., & Deiters, J.A. (2005). Anxiety and burnout in female collegiate ice hockey and soccer athletes. *Perceptual & Motor Skills*, 101, 519-524.

Yang, J., Peek-Asa, C., Corlette, J.D., Cheng, G., Foster, D.T., & Albright, J. (2007). Prevalence of and risk factors associated with symptoms of depression in competitive college student athletes. *Clinical Journal of Sports Medicine*, 17, 481-487.

Chapter 6

Ahmetoglu, G., & Chamorro-Premuzic, T. (2013). *Personality 101*. New York: Springer.

Alessandri, G., Vecchione, M., Eisenberg, N., & Łaguna, M. (2015). On the factor structure of the Rosenberg (1965) General Self-Esteem Scale. *Psychological Assessment*, 27(2), 621-635. doi:10.1037/pas0000073

Armstrong, S., & Oomen-Early, J. (2009). Social connectedness, self-esteem, and depression symptomatology among collegiate athletes versus nonathletes. *Journal of American College Health*, 57(5), 521-526. doi:10.3200/JACH.57.5.521-526

Atkinson, J.W. (1957). Motivational determinants of risk-taking behavior. *Psychological Review*, 64(6, Pt. 1), 359-372. http://dx.doi.org/10.1037/h0043445

Baumeister, R.F., Campbell, J.D., Krueger, J.I., & Vohs, K.D. (2003). Does high self-esteem cause better performance, interpersonal success, happiness, or healthier lifestyles? *Psychological Science in the Public Interest*, 4, 1-44.

Brewer, B. (2008). Fear of failure in the context of competitive sport: A commentary. *International Journal of Sports Science and Coaching*, 3(2), 199-200. doi:10.1260/17479508785100761

Burger, J.M., & Cooper, H.M. (1979). The desirability of control. *Motivation and Emotion*, 3(4), 381-393. http://dx.doi.org/10.1007/bf00994052

Cattell, R.B., & Eber, H.W. (1966). *The Sixteen Personality Factor Questionnaire manual*. Champaign, IL: Institute for Personality and Ability Testing.

Conroy, D.E. (2001). Fear of failure: An exemplar for social development research in sports. *Quest*, 53(2), 165-183. doi:10.1080/00336297.2001.10491736

Conroy, D.E., & Elliot, A.J. (2004). Fear of failure and achievement goals in sport: Addressing the issue of the chicken and the egg. *Anxiety, Stress, and Coping*, 17, 271-285.

Conroy, D.E., Elliot, A.J., & Pincus, A.L. (2009). The expression of achievement motives in interpersonal problems. *Journal of Personality*, 77, 495-526.

Conroy, D.E., Poczwardowski, A., & Henschen, K.P. (2001). Evaluative criteria and consequences associated with failure and success for elite athletes and performing artists. *Journal of Applied Sport Psychology*, 13(3), 300-322. doi:10.1080/104132001753144428

Conroy, D.E., Willow, J.P., & Metzler, J.N. (2002). Multidimensional fear of failure measurement: The Performance Failure Appraisal Inventory. *Journal of Applied Sport Psychology*, 14(2), 76-90. http://dx.doi.org/10.1080/104132002522907752

Coopersmith, S. (1959). A method for determining types of self-esteem. *The Journal of Abnormal and Social Psychology*, 59(1), 87-94. http://dx.doi.org/10.1037/h0048001

Coopersmith, S. (1967). *The antecedents of self-esteem*. San Francisco: W.H. Freeman.

Coopersmith, S. (1981). *Self-esteem inventories*. Menlo Park, CA: Mind Garden. http://dx.doi.org/10,1037/t06456-000

Crocker, J., & Knight, K.M. (2005). Contingencies of self-worth. *Current Directions in Psychological Science*, 14(4), 200-203. doi:10.1111/j.0963-7214.2005.00364.x

Crocker, J., & Park, L.E. (2004). The costly pursuit of self-esteem. *Psychological Bulletin*, 130(3), 392-414. doi:10.1037/0033-2909.130.3.392

Deci, E.L. (1972). *Intrinsic motivation*. New York: Plenium Press.

Diseth, Å., & Kobbeltvedt, T. (2010). A mediation analysis of achievement motives, goals, learning strategies, and academic achievement. *British Journal of Educational Psychology*, 80, 671-687. doi:10.1348/000709910X492432

Dunn, J.G.H., Causgrove Dunn, J., Gamache, V., & Holt, N.L. (2014). A person-oriented examination of perfectionism and slump-related coping in female intercollegiate volleyball players. *International Journal of Sport Psychology*, 45, 298-324.

Dvash, A., & Mannheim, B. (2001). Technological coupling, job characteristics and operators' well-being as moderated by desirability of control. *Behaviour & Information Technology*, 20, 225-236.

Elliot, A.J., & Church, M.A. (2003). A motivational analysis of defensive pessimism and self-handicapping. *Journal of Personality*, 71, 369-396.

Elliot, A.J., & McGregor, H.A. (1999). Test anxiety and the hierarchical model of approach and avoidance achievement motivation. *Journal of Personality and Social Psychology*, 76, 628-644.

Ewan, R. (1998). *Personality: A topical approach: Theories, research, major controversies, and emerging findings*. Mahwah, NJ: Erlbaum.

Eysenck, H.J., Nais, D.K., & Cox, D.N. (1982). *Sports and personality, 4*(1), 1-56. doi:10.1016/0146-6402(82)90004-2

Flett, G.L., and Hewitt, P.L. (2005). The perils of perfectionism in sports and exercise. *Current Directions in Psychological Science, 14*(1), 14-18. doi: 10.1111/j.0963-7214.2005.00326

Flett, G.L., & Hewitt, P.L. (2014). 'The perils of perfectionism in sports' revisited: Toward a broader understanding of the pressure to be perfect and its impact on athletes and dancers. *International Journal of Sport Psychology, 45*(4), 395-407.

Fox, A. (2003). Fear of failure in the context of competitive sports. *International Journal of Sports Science and Coaching, 3*(2), 173 -177. http://dx.doi.org/10.1260/174795408785100789

Frost, R.O., and Henderson, K.J. (1991). Perfectionism and reactions to athletic competition. *Journal of Sport and Exercise Psychology, 13*(4), 323-335.

Frost, R.O., Martens, P., Lahart, C., and Rosenblate, R. (1990). The dimensions of perfectionism. *Cognitive Research and Therapy, 14*(5), 449-468. doi:10.1037/t05500-000

Gaudreau, P., & Thompson, A. (2010). Testing a 2 × 2 model of dispositional perfectionism. *Personality and Individual Differences, 48*, 532-537.

Gotwals, J.K., Dunn, J.G.H., & Wayment, H.A. (2003). An examination of perfectionism and self-esteem in intercollegiate athletes. *Journal of Sport Behavior, 26*(1), 17-38.

Gotwals, J.K., Stoeber, J., Dunn, J.H., & Stoll, O. (2012). Are perfectionistic strivings in sport adaptive? A systematic review of confirmatory, contradictory, and mixed evidence. *Canadian Psychology/Psychologie Canadienne, 53*(4), 263-279. doi:10.1037/a0030288

Gucciardi, D.F., Mahoney, J., Jalleh, G, Donovan, R.J., & Parkes, J. (2012). Perfectionist profiles among elite athletes and differences in their motivational orientations. *Journal of Sport & Exercise Psychology, 34*(2), 159-183. doi: http://dx.doi.org/10.1037/t20394-000

Hewitt, P.L., & Flett, G.L. (1991). Perfectionism in the self and social contexts: Conceptualization, assessment, and association with psychopathology. *Journal of Personality and Social Psychology, 60*(3), 456-470. doi:10.1037/0022-3514.60.3.456

Hewitt, P.L., & Flett, G.L. (2004). *Multidimensional Perfectionism Scale*. North Tonawanda, NY: Multi-Health Systems. Retrieved from www.mhs.com/product.aspx?gr=cli&prod=mps&id=overview.

Hill, A.P., Witcher, C.G., Gotwals, J.K., & Leyland, A.F. (2015). A qualitative study of perfectionism among self-identified perfectionists in sport and the performing arts. *Sport, Exercise, and Performance Psychology, 4*(4), 237-253. doi:10.1037/spy0000041

Hogan, R. (1976). *Personality theory*. Englewood Cliffs, NJ: Prentice Hall.

John, O.P., Donahue, E.M., & Kentle, R.L. (1991). *Big Five Inventory (BFI)*. PsycTESTS. doi:10.1037/t07550-000

Kelly, G.A. (1955). *The psychology of personality constructs*. New York: Norton.

Kerr, G.A., & Goss, J.D. (1997). Personal control in elite gymnasts: The relationships between locus of control, self-esteem, and trait anxiety. *Journal of Sport Behavior, 20*(1), 69-82.

Kolt, G.S., & Roberts, P.D. (1998). Self-esteem and injury in competitive field hockey players. *Perceptual and Motor Skills, 13*(49), 353-354.

Lazarus, R.S. (1991). Progress on a cognitive-motivational-relational theory of emotion. American Psychologist, 46(8), 819.

Leotti, L., Iyengar, S., & Ochsner, K. (2010). Born to choose: The origins and value of the need for control. *Trends in Cognitive Sciences, 14*(10), 457-467. doi:10.1016/j.tics.2010.08.001

Leary, M.R., & Baumeister, R.F. (2000). The nature and function of self-esteem: Sociometer theory. In M.P. Zanna (Ed.), *Advances in experimental social psychology* (Vol. 32, pp. 1-62). San Diego: Academic Press.

Martin, A.J., & Marsh, H.W. (2003). Fear of failure: Friend or foe? *Australian Psychologist, 38*, 31-38.

Maslow, A.H. (1968). *Motivation and personality*. New York: Harper & Row.

McCrae, R.R., & Costa, P.T. (1999). A 5-factors theory of personality. In O.P. John, R.W. Robins, & L.A. Pervin (Eds.), *Handbook of personality theory and research* (Vol. 2, pp. 139-153). New York: Guilford Press.

Morizot, J. (2014). *Big Five Personality Trait Short Questionnaire (BFPTSQ)*. PsycTESTS. doi:10.1037/t36090-000

Nideffer, R.M., & Sagal, M. (2001). *Assessment in sport psychology*. Morgantown, WV: Fitness Information.

Rainey, D.W. (1995). Stress, burnout, and intention to terminate among umpires. *Journal of Sport Behavior, 18*, 312-323.

Rapalyea, L.L. (2010). Does sports involvement influence character? Profiling character traits for different sports. *Dissertation Abstracts International, Section B, 71*(4-B), 2736.

Rasquinha, A., Dunn, J.G., and Causgrove Dunn, J. (2014). Relationships between perfectionistic strivings, perfectionistic concerns, and competitive sport level. *Psychology of Sport and Exercise, 15*(6), 659-667.

Razon, R., & Tenenbaum, G. (2014). Measurement in sport and exercise psychology. In J.L.Van Raalte & B.W Brewer (Eds.), *Exploring sport and exercise psychology*

(3rd ed., pp. 279-309). Washington, DC: American Psychological Association.

Rebar, A.L., & Conroy, D.E. (2013). Experimentally manipulated achievement goal state fluctuations regulate self-conscious emotional responses to feedback. *Sport, Exercise, and Performance Psychology, 2*(4), 233-249. doi:10.1037/a0034645

Rosenberg, M. (1965). *Society and the adolescent self-image.* Princeton, NJ: Princeton University Press.

Sagar, S.S., Busch, B.K., & Jowett, S. (2010). Success and failure, fear of failure, and coping responses of adolescent academy football players. *Journal of Applied Sport Psychology, 22,* 213-230. doi:10.1080/10413201003664962

Sagar, S.S., & Stoeber, J. (2009). Perfectionism, fear of failure, and affective responses to success and failure: The central role of fear of experiencing shame and embarrassment. *Journal of Sport & Exercise Psychology, 31,* 602-627.

Seligman, M.E.P. (1975). *Helplessness.* San Francisco: Freeman.

Sowislo, J.F., & Orth, U. (2013). Does low self-esteem predict depression and anxiety? A meta-analysis of longitudinal studies. *Psychological Bulletin, 139,* 213-240. doi:10.1037/a0028931

Sowislo, J.F., Orth, U., & Meier, L.L. (2014). What constitutes vulnerable self-esteem? Comparing the prospective effects of low, unstable, and contingent self-esteem on depressive symptoms. *Journal of Abnormal Psychology, 123*(4), 737-753. doi:10.1037/a0037770

Stoeber, J. (2000). Frost multidimensional scale. In J. Maltby, C.A. Lewis, & A. Hill (Eds.). *Commissioned reviews of 250 psychological tests* (Vol. 1, pp. 310-314). Lampeter, UK: Edwin Mellen Press.

Stoeber, J. (2014). Perfectionism in sports and dance: A double-edged sword. *International Journal of Sport Psychology, 45,* 385-394.

Stoeber, J., & Crombie, R. (2010). Achievement goals and championship performance: Predicting absolute performance and qualification success. *Psychology of Sport and Exercise, 11,* 513-521. doi:10.1016/j.psychsport.2010.07.007

Thomas, A., Buboltz, W.C., Jr., Teague, S., & Seeman, E.A. (2011). The multidimensionality of the Desirability for Control Scale (Burger & Cooper, 1979). *Individual Differences Research, 9*(3), 173-182.

Valliant, P.M., Simpson-Housley, P., & McKelvie, S.J. (1981). Personality in athletic and non-athletic groups. *Perceptual and Motor Skills, 52*(3), 963-966. doi:10.2466/pms.1981.52.3.963

Vealey, R.S. (1989). Sport personology: A paradigmatic and methodological analysis. *Journal of Sport & Exercise Psychology, 11*(2), 216-235.

Vermillion, M., & Dodder, R.A. (2007). An examination of the Rosenberg Self-Esteem Scale using collegiate wheelchair basketball student athletes. *Perceptual and Motor Skills, 104*(2), 416-418. doi:10.2466/PMS.104.2.416-418

Wikman, J.M., Stelter, R., Melzer, M.L., Hague, L.T., & Elbe, A.M. (2014). Effects of goal setting on fear of failure in young elite athletes. *International Journal of Sport and Exercise Psychology, 12*(3). 185-205. doi:10.1080/1612197X.2014.881070

Chapter 7

Albrecht, R.R., & Feltz, D.L. (1987). Generality and specificity of attention related to competitive anxiety and sport performance. *Journal of Sport & Exercise Psychology, 9,* 231-248.

Bandura, A. (2006). Guide for constructing self-efficacy scales. In F. Pajares & T. Urdan (Eds.), *Self-efficacy beliefs of adolescents* (pp. 307-337). Greenwich, CT: Information Age.

Beauchamp, M.K., Harvey, R.H., & Beauchamp, P.H. (2012). An integrated biofeedback and psychological skills training program for Canada's Olympic short-track speedskating team. *Journal of Clinical Sport Psychology, 6,* 67-84.

Clough, P., Earle, K., & Sewell, D. (2002). Mental toughness: The concept and its measurement. In I. Cockerill (Ed.), *Solutions in sport psychology* (pp. 32-45). London: Thomson.

Conroy, D.E., Elliot, A.J., & Hofer, S.M. (2003). A 2 × 2 Achievement Goals Questionnaire for Sport: Evidence for factorial invariance, temporal stability, and external validity. *Journal of Sport & Exercise Psychology, 25,* 456-476.

Cox, R.H., Martens, M.P., & Russell, W.D. (2003). Measuring anxiety in athletics: The revised Competitive State Anxiety Inventory-2. *Journal of Sport and Exercise Psychology, 25*(4), 519-533.

Cox, R.H., Russell, W.D., & Robb, M. (1998). Development of a CSAI-2 short-form for assessing competitive state anxiety during and immediately prior to competition. *Journal of Sport Behavior, 21,* 30-40.

Deci, E.L., & Ryan, R.M. (2000). The "what" and "why" of goal pursuits: Human needs and the self-determination of behavior. *Psychological Inquiry, 11,* 227-268.

Doyle, J., & Parfitt, G. (1996). Performance profiling and predictive validity. *Journal of Applied Sport Psychology, 8,* 160-170.

Doyle, J., & Parfitt, G. (1997). Performance profiling and construct validity. *The Sport Psychologist, 11,* 411-425.

Duda, J.L. (1989). The relationship between task and ego orientation and the perceived purpose of sport among male and female high school athletes. *Journal of Sport & Exercise Psychology, 11,* 318-335.

Durand-Bush, N., Salmela, J.H., & Green-Demers, I. (2001). The Ottawa Mental Skills Assessment Tool (OMSAT-3*). *The Sport Psychologist, 15,* 1-19.

Elliot, A.J., & McGregor, H.A. (2001). A 2 × 2 Achievement Goal Framework. *Journal of Personality and Social Psychology, 80,* 501-519.

Etzel, E.F., Jr. (1979). Validation of a conceptual model characterizing attention among international rifle shooters. *Journal of Sport Psychology, 1,* 281-290.

Fisher, A.C., & Taylor, A.H. (1980). Attentional style of soccer players [Abstract]. *Proceedings of the annual conference of the American Alliance for Health, Physical Education, Recreation and Dance.* Detroit: AAHPERD.

Gardner, F.L., & Moore, Z.E. (2007). *The psychology of enhancing human performance: The Mindfulness-Acceptance-Commitment (MAC) approach.* New York: Springer.

Gleeson, N.P., Parfitt, G., Doyle, J., & Rees, D. (2005). Reproducibility and efficacy of the performance profile technique. *Journal of Exercise Science and Fitness, 3,* 66-73.

Grove, J.R., Norton, P.J., Van Raalte, J.L., & Brewer, B.W. (1999). Stages of change as an outcome measure in the evaluation of mental skills training programs. *The Sport Psychologist, 13,* 107-116.

Gucciardi, D.F., & Gordon, S. (2009). Revisiting the performance profile technique: Theoretical underpinnings and application. *The Sport Psychologist, 23,* 93-117.

Hall, C.R., Mack, D., Paivio, A., & Hausenblas, H.A. (1998). Imagery use by athletes: Development of the Sport Imagery Questionnaire. *International Journal of Sport Psychology, 29,* 73-89.

Hall, C.R., & Martin, K.A. (1997). Measuring movement imagery abilities: A revision of the Movement Imagery Questionnaire. *Journal of Mental Imagery, 21,* 143-154.

Hall, C.R., Munroe-Chandler, K.J., Fishburne, G.J., & Hall, N.D. (2009). The Sport Imagery Questionnaire for Children (SIQ-C). *Measurement in Physical Education and Exercise Science, 13,* 93-107.

Hall, C.R., Stevens, D.E., & Paivio, A. (2005). *Sport Imagery Questionnaire: Test manual.* Morgantown, WV: Fitness Information Technology.

Hardy, J., Hall, C.R., & Hardy, L. (2005). Quantifying athlete self-talk. *Journal of Sports Sciences, 23,* 905-917.

Hardy, L., Roberts, R., Thomas, P.R., & Murphy, S.M. (2010). Test of Performance Strategies (TOPS): Instrument refinement using confirmatory factor analysis. *Psychology of Sport and Exercise, 11,* 27-35.

Hayslip, B., Petrie, T.A., MacIntire, M.M., & Jones, G.M. (2010). The influences of skill level, anxiety, and psychological skills use on amateur golfers' performances. *Journal of Applied Sport Psychology, 22,* 123-133.

Jones, G., Hanton, S., & Connaughton, D. (2007). A framework of mental toughness in the world's best performers. *The Sport Psychologist, 21,* 243-264.

Kothari, C.R. (2004). *Research methodology: Methods and techniques* (2nd ed.). New Delhi: New Age International.

Krane, V. (1994). The Mental Readiness Form as a measure of competitive state anxiety. *The Sport Psychologist, 8,* 189-202.

Landers, D.M., & Arent, S.M. (2010). Arousal-performance relationships. In J.M. Williams (Ed.), *Applied sport psychology: Personal growth to peak performance* (pp. 221-246). New York: McGraw-Hill.

Leffingwell, T.R., Rider, S.P., & Williams, J.M. (2001). Application of the transtheoretical model to psychological skills training. *The Sport Psychologist, 15,* 168-187.

Lonsdale, C., Hodge, K., & Rose, E.A. (2008). The Behavioral Regulation in Sport Questionnaire (BRSQ): Instrument development and initial validity evidence. *Journal of Sport and Exercise Psychology, 30,* 323-355.

MacIntyre, T., Moran, A., Collet, C., Guillot, A., Campbell, M., Matthews, J., Mahoney, C., & Lowther, J. (2013). The BASES expert statement on the use of mental imagery in sport, exercise and rehabilitation contexts. *The Sport and Exercise Scientist, 38,* 10-11.

Mallett, C., Kawabata, M., Newcombe, P., Otero-Forero, A., & Jackson, S. (2007). Sport Motivation Scale-6 (SMS-6): A revised six-factor sport motivation scale. *Psychology of Sport and Exercise, 8,* 600-614.

Martens, R. (1977). *Sport competition anxiety test.* Champaign, IL: Human Kinetics.

Martens, R., Burton, D., Vealey, R.S., Bump, L.A., & Smith, D.E. (1990). Development and validation of the Competitive State Anxiety Inventory-2. In R. Martens, R.S. Vealey, & D. Burton (Eds.), *Competitive anxiety in sport* (pp. 117-190). Champaign, IL: Human Kinetics.

Martens, R., Vealey, R.S., & Burton, D. (1990). *Competitive anxiety in sport.* Champaign, IL: Human Kinetics.

Martin, K.A., Moritz, S.E., & Hall, C.R. (1999). Imagery use in sport: A literature review and applied model. *The Sport Psychologist, 13,* 245-268.

Martin, S.B, Kellman, M., Lavallee, D., & Page, S.J. (2002). Development and psychometric evaluation of the Sport Psychology Attitudes-Revised Form: A multiple group investigation. *The Sport Psychologist, 16,* 272-290.

Nideffer, R. (1976). Test of Attentional and Interpersonal Style. *Journal of Personality and Social Psychology, 34,* 394-404.

Norcross, J.C., Krebs, P.M., & Prochaska, J.O. (2011). Stages of change. In J.C. Norcross (Ed.), *Psychotherapy relationships that work* (2nd ed., pp. 279-300). New York: Oxford University Press. doi:10.1093/acprof:oso/9780199737208.003.0014

Pelletier, L.G., Fortier, M.S., Vallerand, R.J., Tuson, K.M., Brière, N.M., & Blais, M.R. (1995). Toward a new measure of intrinsic motivation, extrinsic motivation, and amotivation in sports: The Sport Motivation Scale (SMS). *Journal of Sport and Exercise Psychology, 17,* 35-53.

Prochaska, J.O., & DiClemente, C.C. (1983). Stages and processes of self-change of smoking: Toward an integrative model of change. *Journal of Consulting and Clinical Psychology, 51,* 390- 395. doi:10.1037/0022-006X.51.3.390

Raedeke, T.D., & Smith, A.L. (2001). Development and preliminary validation of an athlete burnout measure. *Journal of Sport & Exercise Psychology, 23,* 281-306.

Raedeke, T.D., & Smith, A.L. (2009). *The Athlete Burnout Questionnaire manual.* Morgantown, WV: Fitness Information Technology.

Roberts, G.C., Treasure, D.C., & Balague, G. (1998). Achievement goals in sport: The development and validation of the Perception of Success Questionnaire. *Journal of Sports Sciences, 16,* 337-347.

Roberts, G.C., Treasure, D.C., & Conroy, D.E. (2007). Understanding the dynamics of motivation in sport and physical activity. In G. Tenenbaum & R.C. Eklund (Eds.), *Handbook of sport psychology* (pp. 3-30). Hoboken, NJ: Wiley.

Roberts, R., Callow, N., Hardy, L., Markland, D., & Bringer, J. (2008). Movement imagery ability: Development and assessment of a revised version of the Vividness of Movement Imagery Questionnaire. *Journal of Sport & Exercise Psychology, 30,* 200-221.

Scanlan, T.K., Chow, G.M., Sousa, C., Scanlan, L.A., & Knifsend, C.A. (2016). The development of the Sport Commitment Questionnaire-2 (English Version). *Psychology of Sport and Exercise, 22,* 233-246.

Silva, J.M., Metzler, J.N., & Lerner, B. (2011). *Training professionals in the practice of sport psychology* (2nd ed.). Morgantown, WV: Fitness Information Technology.

Smith, R.E., & Christensen, D.S. (1995). Psychological skills as predictors of performance and survival in professional baseball. *Journal of Sport & Exercise Psychology, 17,* 399-415.

Smith, R.E., Schutz, R.W., Smoll, F.L., & Ptacek, J.T. (1995). Development and validation of a multidimensional measure of sport-specific psychological skills: The Athletic Coping Skills Inventory-28. *Journal of Sport & Exercise Psychology, 17,* 379-398.

Smith, R.E., Smoll, F.L., Cumming, S.P., & Grossbard, J.R. (2006). Measurement of multidimensional sport performance anxiety in children and adults: The Sport Anxiety Scale-2. *Journal of Sport & Exercise Psychology, 28,* 479-501.

Swift, J.K., & Greenberg, R.P. (2014). *Premature termination in psychotherapy: Strategies for engaging clients and improving outcomes.* Washington, DC: American Psychological Association.

Thienot, E., Dimmock, J., Jackson, B., Grove, R., Bernier, M., & Fournier, J. (2014). Development and validation of the Mindfulness Inventory for Sport. *Psychology of Sport and Exercise, 15,* 72-80.

Thomas, P.R., Hardy, L., & Murphy, S.M. (2007). Test of Performance Strategies (TOPS). Retrieved from: http://www.topsfirst.com/

Tod, D., Hardy, J., & Oliver, E. (2011). Effects of self-talk: A systematic review. *Journal of Sport & Exercise Psychology, 33,* 666-687.

Van Schoyck, S., & Grasha, A. (1981). Attentional style variations and athletic ability: The advantage of a sports-specific test. *Journal of Sport Psychology, 3,* 149-165.

Vealey, R.S. (1986). Conceptualization of sport-confidence and competitive orientation: Preliminary investigation and instrument development. *Journal of Sport Psychology, 8,* 221-246.

Vealey, R.S., Hayashi, S.W., Garner-Holman, M., & Giacobbi, P. (1998). Sources of sport-confidence: Conceptualization and instrument development. *Journal of Sport and Exercise Psychology, 20,* 54-80.

Weinberg, R.S., & Williams, J.M. (2010). Integrating and implementing a psychological skills training program. In J.M. Williams (Ed.), *Applied sport psychology: Personal growth to peak performance* (pp. 361-391). New York: McGraw-Hill.

Williams, S.E., Cooley, S.J., Newell, E., Weibull, F., & Cumming, J. (2013). Seeing the difference: Developing effective imagery scripts for athletes. *Journal of Sport Psychology in Action, 4,* 109-121.

Zourbanos, N., Hatzigeorgiadis, A., Chroni, S., Theodorakis, Y., & Papaioannou, A. (2009). Automatic Self-Talk Questionnaire for Sports (ASTQS): Development and preliminary validation of a measure identifying the structure of athletes' self-talk. *The Sport Psychologist, 23,* 233-251.

Chapter 8

Akiskal, H.S., & Akiskal, H. (1994). Mental status examination: The art and sciences of the clinical interview. In M. Hersen & S.M. Turner (Eds.), *Diagnostic interviewing* (2nd ed., pp. 25-50). New York: Plenum Press.

Association of Applied Sport Psychology (AASP). (n.d.). *Ethics code: AASP ethical principles and standards.* Retrieved from www.appliedsportpsych.org/about/ethics/ethics-code/.

Butcher, J.N., Mineka, S., & Hooley, J.M. (2010). *Abnormal psychology* (14th ed.). Boston: Allyn & Bacon.

Cleary, P.D., Mechanic, D., Weiss, N. (1981). The effects of interview characteristics on responses to a mental health interview. *Journal of Health & Social Behavior, 22,* 183-193.

Cormier, W.H., & Cormier, L.S. (1991). Interviewing strategies for helpers (3rd Ed.). Pacific Grove, CA: Brooks/Cole.

Crandall, S.J. (1998). Using interviews as a needs assessment tool. *Journal of Continuing Education in the Health Professions, 18*(3), 155-162.

Creswell, J.W., & Miller, D.L. (2000). Determining validity in qualitative inquiry. *Theory Into Practice, 39*(3), 124-130.

Hays, K., Maynard, I., Thomas, O., & Bawden, M. (2007). Sources and types of confidence identified by world-class sport performers. *Journal of Applied Sport Psychology, 19*, 434-456.

Holstein, J.A., & Gubrium, J.F. (2011). The constructionist analytics of interpretive practice. In J.A. Holstein & J.F. Gubrium (Eds.), *The SAGE handbook of qualitative research* (pp. 341-357). Thousand Oaks, CA: Sage.

Hylton, K. (2013). *Sports development: Policy, process and practice* (3rd ed.). New York: Routledge.

Kahneman, D., & Tversky, A. (1974). Judgment under uncertainty: Heuristics and biases. *Science, 185*, 1125-1131.

Kahneman, D., Lovallo, D., & Sibony, O. (2011). The big idea: Before you make that big decision . . . *Harvard Business Review.* Retrieved from https://hbr.org/2011/06/the-big-idea-before-you-make-that-big-decision.

Kvale, S., & Brinkmann, S. (2009). *Interviews: Learning the craft of qualitative research interviewing.* Thousand Oaks, CA: Sage.

McNaughton, D., Hamlin, D., McCarthy, J., Head-Reeves, D., & Schreiner, M. (2008). Learning to listen: Teaching an active listening strategy to preservice education professionals. *Topics in Early Childhood Special Education, 27*(4), 223-231.

Meyer, G.J., Finn S.E., Eyde, L.D., Kay, G.G., Moreland, K.L., Dies, R.R., . . . Reed, G.M. (2001). Psychological testing and psychological assessment. A review of evidence and issues. *American Psychologist, 56*(2), 128-165. doi.org/10.1037/0003-066X.56.2.128

Omi, M.A., & Winant, H. (2015, February 4). *Racial formation in the United States: Introduction to the 3rd edition talk given at the University of California Berkley campus.* Retrieved from www.youtube.com/watch?v=yawU5yhHGug&feature=youtu.be.

Pinel, J.P.J. (2011). *Biopsychology* (8th ed.). Boston: Pearson Education.

Pollio, H.R., Henley, T.B., & Thompson, C.J. (1997). *The phenomenology of everyday life.* Cambridge, UK: Cambridge University Press.

Potter, J., & Hepburn, A. (2005). Qualitative interviews in psychology: Problems and possibilities. *Qualitative Research in Psychology, 2*(4), 281-307.

Prout, T.A., & Wadkins, M.J. (2014). *Essential interviewing and counseling skills: An integrated approach to practice.* New York: Springer.

Rosqvist, J., Björgvinsson, T., & Davidson, J. (2007). Philosophical underpinnings of clinical interviewing. In M. Hersen & J.C. Thomas (Eds.), *Handbook of clinical interviewing with adults* (pp. 2-7). Thousand Oaks, CA: Sage.

Rubin, H.J., & Rubin, I.S. (2012). *Qualitative interviewing: The art of hearing data* (3rd ed.). Thousand Oaks, CA: Sage.

Schinke, R.J., & Hanrahan, S.J. (2009). *Cultural sport psychology.* Champaign, IL: Human Kinetics.

Silverman, D. (2001). *Interpreting qualitative data: Methods for analyzing talk, text and interaction.* London: Sage.

Shea, C.S. (1998). *Psychiatric interviewing: The art of understanding* (2nd ed.). Philadelphia: W.B. Saunders.

Steele, C.M. (2011). *Whistling Vivaldi: How stereotypes affect us and what we can do.* New York: Norton.

Taylor, J., & Schneider, B.A. (1992). The Sport-Clinical Intake Protocol: A comprehensive interviewing instrument for sport. *Professional Psychology: Research and Practice, 23*, 318-325.

Thomas, S.P., & Pollio, H.R. (2002). *Listening to patients: A phenomenological approach to nursing research and practice.* New York: Springer.

Voight, M. (2014). *The sports leadership playbook: Principles and techniques for coaches and captains.* Jefferson, NC: McFarland.

Chapter 9

Anderson, A.G., Miles, A., Mahoney, C., & Robinson, P. (2002). Evaluating the effectiveness of applied sport psychology practice: Making the case for a case study approach. *The Sport Psychologist, 16*, 432-453.

Austin, J., & Carr, J. (2000). *Handbook of applied behavior analysis.* Reno, NV: Context Press.

Beauchamp, P.H., Halliwell, W.R., Fournier, J.F., & Koestner, R. (1996). Effects of cognitive-behavioral psychological skills training on the motivation, preparation, and putting performance of novice golfers. *The Sport Psychologist, 10*, 157-170.

Beckmann, J., & Kellmann, M. (2003). Procedures and principles of sport psychological assessment. *The Sport Psychologist, 17*, 338-350.

Bowker, A., Boekhoven, B., Nolan, A., Bauhaus, S., Glover, P., Powell, T., & Taylor, S. (2009). Naturalistic observations of spectator behavior at youth hockey games. *The Sport Psychologist, 23*, 301-316.

Brown, C.H., Gould, D., & Foster, S. (2005). A framework for developing contextual intelligence (CI). *The Sport Psychologist, 19*, 51-62.

Brown, C.H., & McDaniel, S. (1995, Summer). Spam and bagels: Recipes for healthy consultations. *The Family Psychologist, 11*, 14-15.

Bull, S.J. (1995). Reflections on a 5-year consultancy program with the England Women's Cricket team. *The Sport Psychologist, 9*, 148-163.

Cohn, P.J., Rotella, R.J., & Lloyd, J.W. (1990). Effects of a cognitive-behavioral intervention on the preshot routine and performance in golf. *The Sport Psychologist, 4*, 33-47.

DeMarco, G.M., Mancini, V.H., Wuest, D.A., & Schempp, P.G. (1996). Becoming reacquainted with a once familiar and still valuable tool: Systematic observation methodology revisited. *International Journal of Physical Education, 32*, 17-26.

Ekman, P. (2003). *Emotions revealed.* New York: St. Martins Press.

Fletcher, D., & Wagstaff, C.R.D. (2009). Organizational psychology in elite sport: Its emergence, application and future. *Psychology of Sport and Exercise, 10*, 427-434. doi:10.1016/j.psychsport.2009.03.009

Gardner, F.L. (2009). Efficacy, mechanisms of change and the scientific development of sport psychology. *Journal of Clinical Sport Psychology, 3*, 139-155.

Gee, C.J. (2011). Aggression in competitive sports: Using direct observation to evaluate incidence and prevention focused intervention. In J.K. Luiselli & D.D. Reed (Eds.), *Behavioral sport psychology: Evidence-based approaches to performance enhancement* (pp. 199-210). New York: Springer.

Gillham, B. (2008). *Observation techniques: Structured to unstructured.* London: Continuum International.

Gresham, F.M. (2011). Social behavioral assessment and intervention: Observations and impressions. *School Psychology Review, 40*, 275-283.

Hargie, O. (2006). *The handbook of communication skills.* London: Routledge.

Hauer, K.E., Holmboe, E.S., & Kogan, J.R. (2011). Twelve tips for implementing tools for direct observation of medical trainees' clinical skills during patient encounters. *Medical Teacher, 33*, 27-33. doi:10.3109/0142159x.2010.507710

Hawkins, R.P. (1986). Selection of target behaviors. In R.O. Nelson & S.C. Hayes (Eds.), *Conceptual foundations of behavioral assessment* (pp. 331-345). London: The Guildford Press.

Hemmings, B., & Holder, T. (2009). *Applied sport psychology: A case-based approach.* Cornwall, UK: Wiley-Blackwell.

Katz, J., & Hemmings, B. (2009). *Counselling handbook for the sport psychologist.* Leicester, UK: British Psychological Society.

Leffingwell, T.R., Durand-Bush, N., Wurzberger, D., & Cada, P. (2005). Psychological assessment. In J. Taylor & G.S. Wilson (Eds.), *Applying sport psychology: Four perspectives* (pp. 85-100). Champaign, IL: Human Kinetics.

Lewis-Smithson, C., Mogge, N.L., & LePage, J.P. (2010). A comparison of the behavioral observation system with clinical ratings of psychosis and mania. *Journal of Clinical Psychology, 66*, 333-338.

Lines, J.B., Schwartzman, L., Tkachuk, G.A., Leslie-Toogood, S.A., & Martin, G.L. (1999). Behavioral assessment in sport psychology consulting: Applications to swimming and basketball. *Journal of Sport Behavior, 22*, 558-569.

Lloyd, R.J., & Trudel, P. (1999). Verbal interactions between an eminent mental training consultant and elite level athletes: A case study. *The Sport Psychologist, 13*, 418-443.

Markman, H.J., Leber, B.D., Cordova, A.D., & St. Peters, M. (1995). Behavioral observation and family psychology—strange bedfellows or happy marriage? Comment on Alexander et al. (1995). *Journal of Family Psychology, 9*, 371-379. doi:10.1037/0893-3200.9.4.371

Martin, G.L., Toogood, A., & Tkachuk, G.A. (1997). *Behavioral assessment forms for sport psychology consulting.* Winnipeg, MB: Sport Science Press.

McKenzie, T.L., & van der Mars, H. (2015). Top 10 research questions related to assessing physical activity and its contexts using systematic observation. *Research Quarterly for Exercise and Sport, 86*, 13-29. doi:10.1080/02701367.2015.991264

Murphy, S.M., & Murphy, A.I. (2010). Attending and listening. In S.J. Hanrahan & M.B. Anderson (Eds.), *Routledge handbook of sport psychology: A comprehensive guide for students and practitioners* (pp. 12-20). Abingdon, UK: Routledge.

Petitpas, A.J., Giges, B., & Danish, S.J. (1999). The sport psychologist-athlete relationship: Implications for training. *The Sport Psychologist, 13*, 344-357.

Poczwardowski, A., Sherman, C.P., & Ravizza, K. (2004). Professional philosophy in sport psychology service delivery: Building on theory and practice. *The Sport Psychologist, 18*, 445-463.

Ravizza, K. (1988). Gaining entry with athletic personnel for season-long consulting. *The Sport Psychologist, 2*, 243-254.

Rosenfeld, L., & Wilder, L. (1990). Active listening. *Sport Psychology Training Bulletin, 1*(5), 1-8.

Rushall, B. (1979). *Psyching in sport: The psychological preparation for serious competition in sport.* London: Pelham Books.

Sauter, D.A., Eisner, F., Ekman, P., & Scott, S.K. (2010). Cross-cultural recognition of basic emotions through nonverbal emotional vocalizations. *Proceedings of the National Academy of Sciences, 107*, 2408-2412. doi:10.1073/pnas.0908239106

Savelsbergh, G.J.P., Williams, A.M., van der Kamp, J., & Ward, P. (2002). Visual search, anticipation and expertise in soccer goalkeepers. *Journal of Sports Sciences, 20*, 279-287.

Smith, R.E., Smoll, F.L., & Hunt, E.B. (1977). A system for the behavioral assessment of athletic coaches. *Research Quarterly, 48*, 401-407.

Smith, N., Tessier, D., Tzioumakis, Y., Quested, E., Appleton, P., Sarrazin, P., Papaioannou, A., & Duda, J. (2015). Development and validation of the multidimensional motivational climate observation system. *Journal of Sport and Exercise Psychology, 37*, 4-22. https://doi.org/10.1123/jsep.2014-0059

Taylor, J. (1995). A conceptual model for integrating athletes' needs and sport demands in the development of competitive mental preparation strategies. *The Sport Psychologist, 9*, 339-357.

Tenenbaum, G., Ecklund, R., & Kamata, A. (2012). *Measurement in sport and exercise psychology*. Champaign, IL: Human Kinetics.

Tkachuk, G., Leslie-Toogood, A., & Martin, G.L. (2003). Behavioral assessment in sport psychology. *The Sport Psychologist, 17*, 104-117.

Tryon, W.W. (1998). Behavioral observation. In A.S. Bellack & M. Hersen (Eds.), *Behavioral assessment: A practical handbook* (pp. 79-103). Needham Heights, MA: Allyn and Bacon.

Van Raalte, J.L., Brewer, B.W., Rivera, P.M., & Petitpas, A.J. (1994). The relationship between observable self-talk and competitive junior tennis players' match performances. *Journal of Sport and Exercise Psychology, 16*, 400-415.

Wang, J., & Straub, W.F. (2012). An investigation into the coaching approach of a successful world-class soccer coach: Anson Dorrance. *International Journal of Sports Science and Coaching, 7*, 431-447.

Watson, J.C., II, & Shannon, V. (2010). Individual and group observation. Purposes and processes. In S.J. Hanrahan & M.B. Anderson (Eds.), *Routledge handbook of sport psychology: A comprehensive guide for students and practitioners* (pp. 90-100). Abingdon, UK: Routledge.

Winter, S., & Collins, D. (2015). Where is the evidence in our sport psychology practice? A UK perspective on the underpinnings of action. *Professional Psychology: Research and Practice, 46*, 175-182. doi:10/1037/pro0000014

Wood, J., Collins, J., Burnside, E.S., Albanese, M.A., Propeck, P.A., Kelcz, F., Splide, J.M., & Schmaltz, L.M. (2004). Patient and self-assessment of radiology resident performance: A 360-degree method of measuring professionalism and interpersonal/communication skills. *Academic Radiology, 11*, 931-939. doi:10.1016/j.acra.2004.04.016

Chapter 10

Abernathy, B., Baker, J., & Cote, J. (2005). Transfer of pattern recall skills as a contributor to the development of sport expertise. *Applied Cognitive Psychology, 19*, 705-718.

Appelhans, B.M., & Luecken, L.J. (2006). Heart rate variability as an index of regulated emotional responding. *Review of General Psychology, 10*, 229-240.

Arave, D.J. (2012). The golfer who couldn't pass the anxiety test! In W.A. Edmonds & G. Tenenbaum (Eds.), *Case studies in applied psychophysiology: Neurofeedback and biofeedback treatment for advances in human performance* (pp. 94-109). Oxford: Wiley-Blackwell.

Babiloni, C., Marzano, N., Iacoboni, M., Infarinato, F., Aschiere, P., Buffo, P., et al. (2010). Resting state cortical rhythms in athletes: A high resolution EEG Study. *Brain Research Bulletin, 81*, 149-156.

Beauchamp, M.K., Harvey, R.H., & Beauchamp, P.H. (2012). Integrated biofeedback and psychological skills training for Canada's Olympic speedskating team. *Journal of Clinical Sport Psychology, 6*, 67-84.

Bilalic, M., Langner, R., Erb, M., & Grodd, W. (2010). Mechanisms and neural basis of object and pattern recognition: A study with chess experts. *Journal of Experimental Psychology: General, 139*(4), 728-742.

Blumenstein, B. (2002). Biofeedback applications in sport and exercise: Research findings. In B. Blumenstein, M. Bar-Eli, & G. Tennenbaum (Eds.), *Brain and body in sport and exercise. Biofeedback applications in performance enhancement* (pp. 37-54). New York: Wiley.

Blumenstein, B., Bar-Eli, M., & Tenenbaum, G. (1997). A five-step approach to mental training incorporating biofeedback. *Sport Psychology, 11*, 440-453.

Braun, J., & Deco, G., (2013). B9: Attractor Networks and the Dynamics of Visual Perception. *Perception, 42*(ECVP Abstract Suppl.), 4.

Bridgeman, B. (2007). A test of the sensorimotor theory of visual calibration. *Journal of Vision, 7*(9), 83.

Caserta, R.J., & Abrams, L. (2007). The relevance of situational awareness in older adults' cognitive functioning: A review. *European Review of Aging and Physical Activity, 4*, 3-13.

Collins, D. (1995). Psychophysiology and sport performance. In S.J.H. Biddle (Ed.), *European perspective in exercise and sport* (pp. 154-178). Leeds, UK: Human Kinetics.

Cribbet, M.R., Williams, P.G., Gunn, H.E., & Rau, H.K. (2011). Effects of tonic and phasic respiratory sinus arrhythmia on affective stress responses. *Emotion, 11*, 188-193.

Crognier, L., & Fery, Y. (2005). Effect of tactical initiative on predicting passing shots in tennis. *Applied Cognitive Psychology, 19*, 1-13.

Dupee, M., & Werthner, P. (2011). Managing the stress response: The use of biofeedback and neurofeedback with Olympic athletes. *Biofeedback, 39*, 92-94.

Farrow, D., & Abernathy, B. (2002). Can anticipatory skills be learned through implicit video-based perceptual training? *Journal of Sport Sciences, 20*, 471-485.

Farrow, D., Abernathy, B., & Jackson, R.C. (2005). Probing expert anticipation with the temporal occlusion paradigm: Experimental investigations of some methodological issues. *Motor Control*, 9, 332-351.

Gegenfurtner, A., Lehtinen, E., & Säljö, R. (2011). Expertise differences in the comprehension of visualizations: A meta-analysis of eye-tracking research in professional domains. *Educational Psychology Review*, 23(4), 523-552. doi:10.1007/s10648-011-9174-7

Gerstenberg, F.X.R. (2012). Sensory-processing sensitivity predicts performance on a visual search task followed by an increase in perceived stress. *Personality and Individual Differences*, 53, 496-500.

Gyurak, A., & Ayduk, A. (2008). Resting respiratory sinus arrhythmia buffers against rejection sensitivity via emotion control. *Emotion*, 8, 458-467.

Hansen, A.L., Johnsen, B.H., & Thayer, J.F. (2003). Vagal influences on working memory and attention. *International Journal of Psychophysiology*, 48, 263-274.

Harvey, R., & Peper, E. (2012). Case 8—I thought I was relaxed: The use of SEMG biofeedback for training awareness and control. In W.A. Edmonds & G. Tenenbaum (Eds.), *Case studies in applied psychophysiology: Neurofeedback and biofeedback treatment for advances in human performance* (pp. 144-159). New York: Wiley.

Holmqvist, K., & Nystrom, M. (2011). *Eye tracking: A comprehensive guide to methods and measures.* New York: Oxford University Press.

Hunfalvay, M. (2004). Visual search strategies of expert able-bodied and wheelchair tennis players. *Dissertation Abstracts International*, 65(01), 79. (UMI No. 3118413)

Hunfalvay, M., Roberts, C.-M., Ryan, W., Murray, N.P., Tabano, J., & Martin, C. (in preparation). An exploration of dynamic shifts in visual fixation prior to the execution of baseball batting.

Jomier, J., Rault, E., & Aylward, S.R. (2004). Automatic quantification of pupil dilation under stress. *2nd IEEE International Symposium on Biomedical Imaging: Nano to Macro* (IEEE Cat No. 04EX821).

Karwowski, W. (2006). *International encyclopedia of ergonomics and human factors* (2nd ed.). Boca Raton, FL: Taylor and Francis.

Kim, J., Lee, H.M., Kim, W.J., Park, H.J., Kim, S.W., Moon, D.H., Woo, M., & Tennant, L.K. (2008). Neural correlates of pre-performance routines in expert and novice archers. *Neuroscience Letters*, 445, 236-241.

Klostermann, A., Kredel, R., Hossner, E.-J. (2013). The "Quiet Eye" and motor performance: Task demands matter! *Journal of Experimental Psychology*, 39(5), 1270-1278.

Lagos, L., Vaschillo, E., Vaschillo, B., Lehrer, P., Bates, M., & Pandina, R. (2011). Virtual reality-assisted heart rate variability biofeedback as a strategy to improve golf performance: A case study. *Biofeedback*, 39, 15-20.

Landers, D.M. (1985). Psychophysiological assessment and biofeedback—Applications for athletes in closed-skill sports. In J. Sandweiss & S. Wolf (Eds.), *Biofeedback and sport science* (pp. 63-105). New York: Plenum.

Lehrer, P.M., & Gevirtz, R. (2014). Heart rate variability feedback: How and why does it work? *Frontiers in Psychology* Hypothesis & Theory Article, July 21. doi:10.3389/fpsyg.2014.00756

Lehrer, P., Vaschillo, B., Zucker, T., Graves, J., Katsamanis, M., Aviles, M., & Wamboldt, F. (2013). Protocol for heart rate variability biofeedback training. *Biofeedback*, 41(3), 98-109.

Lubar, J.F. (2003). Neurofeedback for the management of attention deficit disorders. In M.S. Schwartz & F. Andrasik (Eds.), *Biofeedback: A practitioner's guide* (3rd ed., pp. 409-437). New York: Guilford Press.

Mann, D., Ward, P., Williams, A.M., & Janelle, C.M. (2007). Perceptual cognitive expertise in sport: A meta-analysis. *Journal of Sport Exercise Psychology*, 29, 457-478.

Marcovitch, S., Leigh, J., Calkins, S.D., Leerkes, E.M., O'Brien, M., & Nayena Blankson, A. (2010). Moderate vagal withdrawal in 3.5-year-old children is associated with optimal performance on executive function tasks. Developmental Psychobiology, 52, 603-608.

McPherson, S.L., & Kernodle, M.W. (2003). Tactics, the neglected attribute of expertise: Problem representations and performance skill in tennis. In J.L. Starkes & K.A. Ericsson (Eds.), *Expert performance in sports: Advances in research on sport expertise* (pp. 137-168). Champaign, IL: Human Kinetics.

Mets, T., Konttinen, N., & Lyytinen, H. (2007). Shot placement within cardiac cycle in junior elite rifle shooters. *Psychology of Sport and Exercise*, 8(2), 169-177.

Monastra, V.J. (2003). Clinical applications of electroencephalographic biofeedback. In M.S. Schwartz & F. Andrasik (Eds.), *Biofeedback: A practitioner's guide* (pp. 438-463). New York: The Guilford Press.

Monastra, V.J., Lynn, S., Linden, M., Lubar, J.F., Gruzelier, J., & LaVaque, T.J. (2005). Electroencephalographic biofeedback in the treatment of attention deficit/hyperactivity disorder. *Applied Psychophysiology and Biofeedback*, 30(2), 95-114.

Muller, S., & Abernathy, B. (2006). Batting with occluded vision: An in situ examination of the information pick up and interceptive skills of high- and low-skilled cricket batsman. *Journal of Science and Medicine in Sport*, 9, 446-458.

Murray, N.P., & Hunfalvay, M. (2016). A comparison of visual search strategies of elite and non-elite tennis players through cluster analysis. *Journal of Sport Sciences*, 23, 1-6. DOI:10.1080/02640414.2016.1161215.

North, J.S., & Williams, A.M. (2008). Identifying the critical time period for information extraction when recognizing sequences of play. *Research Quarterly for Exercise and Sport, 79*(2), 268-273.

Peper, E., & Schmid-Shapiro, A.B. (1997). Peak performance training with electrodermal biofeedback 1. *Electromyography: Applications in chronic pain, physical medicine & rehabilitation.* Biofeedback Federation of Europe. Retrieved from www.bfe.org/protocol/pro12eng1.htm.

Peper, E., & Tibbetts, V. (1997). Effortless diaphragmatic breathing. *Electromyography: Applications in chronic pain, physical medicine & rehabilitation.* Biofeedback Federation of Europe. Retrieved from www.bfe.org/protocol/pro10eng1.htm.

Porges, S.W. (1995). Orienting in a defensive world: Mammalian modifications of our evolutionary heritage. A polyvagal theory. *Psychophysiology, 32,* 301-318.

Pusenjak, A., Tusak, M., Leskovsek, M., & Schwarzlin, R. (2015). Can biofeedback training of psychophysiological responses enhance athletes' sport performance? A practitioner's perspective. *The Physician and Sportsmedicine,* Early Online, 1-13. DOI:10.1080/00913847.2015.1069169.

Savelsbergh, G.J.P., Williams, A.M., van der Kamp, J., & Ward, P. (2002). Visual search, anticipation and expertise in soccer goal keepers. *Journal of Sport Sciences, 20,* 279-287.

Schmitt, L., Regnard, J., Desmarets, M., Mauny, F., Mourot, L., et al. (2013). Fatigue shifts and scatters heart rate variability in elite endurance athletes. *PLoS ONE, 8*(8), e71588. doi:10.1371/journal.pone.0071588

Schwarz, M.S., & Andrasik, F.(2003). *Biofeedback: A practitioner guide.* New York: The Guilford Press.

Sime, W.E. (1985). Physiological perception: The key to peak performance in athletic competition. In J. Sandweiss & S. Wolf (Eds.), *Biofeedback and sport science* (pp. 33-62). New York: Plenum.

Sterman, M.B. (1996). Physiological origins and functional correlates of EEG rhythmic activities: Implications for self-regulation. *Biofeedback and Self-Regulation, 21*(1), 3-49.

Strack B. (2003). *The effect of heart rate variability biofeedback on batting performance in baseball* (Doctoral dissertation). Alienate International University, San Diego.

Takeuchi, T., & Inomata, K. (2009). Visual search strategies and decision making in baseball batting. *Perceptual and Motor Skills, 108,* 971-980.

Thayer, J.F., Ahs, F., Fredrickson, M., Sollers, J.J., III, & Wager, T.D. (2012). A meta-analysis of heart rate variability and neuroimaging studies: Implications for heart rate variability as a marker of stress and health. *Neuroscience and Biobehavioral Reviews, 36,* 747-756.

Thayer J.F., & Lane, R.D. (2000). A model of neurovisceral integration in emotion regulation and dysregulation. *Journal of Affective Disorders, 61*(3), 201-216.

Thayer, J.F., & Lane, R.D. (2009). Claude Bernard and the heart–brain connection: Further elaboration of a model of neurovisceral integration. *Neuroscience and Biobehavioral Reviews, 33,* 81-88.

Thompson, M., & Thompson, L. (2003). *The neurofeedback book: An introduction to basic concepts in applied psychophysiology.* Wheat Ridge, CO: Association for Applied Psychophysiology and Biofeedback.

Thompson, M., & Thompson, L. (2007). Neurofeedback for stress management. In P.M. Lehrer, R.L. Woolfork, & W.E. Sime (Eds.), *Principles and practice of stress management* (3rd ed., pp. 249-287).

Tuominen, S. (2007). Elite Finnish cross-country skiers trust Firstbeat's heart beat analysis technology. *Finnish Coach, 28,* 9.

Vaeyens, R., Lenoir, M., Williams, A.M., Mazyn, L., & Philippaerts, R.M. (2007). The effects of task constraints on visual search behavior and decision-making skill in youth soccer players. *Journal of Sport and Exercise Psychology, 29,* 156-175.

Van der Lei, H., & Tenenbaum, G. (2012). Performance processes within affect-related performance zones: A multi-modal investigation of golf performance. *Applied Psychophysiology and Biofeedback, 37,* 229-240.

Vernon, D.J. (2005). Can neurofeedback training enhance performance? An evaluation of the evidence with implications for future research. *Applied Psychophysiology and Biofeedback, 30,* 347-363.

Vickers, J.N. (2007). *Perception, cognition and decision training. The quiet eye in action.* Champaign, IL: Human Kinetics.

Vickers, J.N., & Lewinski, W. (2012). Performing under pressure: Gaze control, decision making and shooting performance of elite and rookie police officers. *Human Movement Science, 31,* 101-117.

Vine, S.J., Moore, L.J., & Wilson, M.R. (2011). Quiet eye training facilitates competitive performance in elite golfers. *Frontiers in Psychology,* January 28. http://dx.doi.org/10.3389/fpsyg.2011.00008

Vine, S.J., Moore, L.J., & Wilson, M.R. (2014). Quiet eye training: The acquisition, refinement and resilient performance of targeting skills. *European Journal of Sport Science, 14*(Suppl. 1), S235-S242.

Whatmore, G.B., & Kohli, D.R. (1968). Dysponesis: A neurophysiology factor in functional disorders. *Behavioral Science, 13*(2), 102-124.

Williams, A.M., & Davids, K. (1998). Visual search strategy, selective attention and expertise in soccer. *Research Quarterly for Exercise and Sport, 69,* 111-128.

Williams, A.M., & Ericsson, K.A. (2005). Some considerations when applying the expert performance approach in sport. *Human Movement Science, 24,* 283-307.

Williams, A.M., & Ericsson, K.A. (2007). Perception, cognition, action and skilled performance. *Journal of Motor Behavior, 39*(5), 238-307.

Williams, A.M., Hodges, N.J., North, J.S., & Barton, G. (2006). Perceiving patterns of play in dynamic sport tasks: Identifying the essential information underlying skilled performance. *Perception, 35*, 317-332.

Wilson, M.R., Vine, S.J., & Wood G. (2009). The influence of anxiety on visual attentional control in basketball free throw shooting. *Journal of Sport and Exercise Psychology, 2*, 152-168.

Wilson, V.E., Ainsworth, M., & Bird, E.I. (1985). Assessment of attentional abilities in male volleyball athletes. *International Journal of Sport Psychology, 16*, 296-306.

Wilson, V., & Peper, E. (2011). Athletes are different: Factors that differentiate biofeedback/neurofeedback for sport versus clinical practice. *Biofeedback, 9*, 27-30.

Wilson, V.E., & Peper, E. (2014). Clinical tip: Relax and relax more. *Biofeedback, 42*(4), 163-164.

Wilson, V.E., & Shaw, L. (2011). Clinical use of a one Hertz bin electroencephalography assessment to distinguish elite from less elite and typical from atypical athlete profiles. *Biofeedback, 39*, 78-84.

Wilson, V.E., & Shaw, L. (2012a). Bad shot, good shot: Neurofeedback for world champion or developing athlete. In W.A. Edmonds & G. Tenenbaum (Eds.), *Case studies in applied psychophysiology: Neurofeedback and biofeedback treatment for advances in human performance* (pp. 31-46). Oxford: Wiley-Blackwell.

Wilson, V.E., & Shaw, L. (2012b). Imagery assessment and training with QEEG. What you see is not all there is. In W.A. Edmonds & G. Tenenbaum (Eds.), *Case studies in applied psychophysiology: Neurofeedback and biofeedback treatment for advances in human performance* (pp. 47-70). Oxford: Wiley-Blackwell.

Wilson, V.E., & Somers, K.M. (2011). Psychophysiological assessment and training with athletes. Knowing and managing your mind and body. In B. Strack, M. Linden, & V.S. Wilson (Eds.), *Biofeedback and neurofeedback applications in sport psychology*. Wheat Ridge, CO: Association for Applied Psychophysiology and Biofeedback.

Wilson, V.E., Thompson, M., Thompson, L, Thompson, J., Fallahpour, K., & Linden, M.K. (2011). Introduction to EEG biofeedback (neurofeedback). In B. Strack, M. Linden, & V.S. Wilson (Eds.), *Biofeedback and neurofeedback applications in sport psychology* (p. 181). Wheat Ridge, CO: Association for Applied Psychophysiology and Biofeedback.

Zaichkowsky, L.D. (1982). Biofeedback for self-regulation of competitive stress. In L.D. Zaichkowsky (Ed.), *Stress management for sport* (pp. 55-64). Reston, VA: American Alliance for Health, Physical Education, Recreation and Dance (AAHPERD) and National Association for Sport and Physical Education (NASPE).

Chapter 11

American Academy of Pediatrics (AAP) Committee on Sports Medicine and Fitness (2000). Intensive training and sports specialization in young athletes. *Pediatrics, 106*, 154-157.

Anderson, J.C., Funk, J.B., Elliott, R., & Smith, P. (2003). Parental support and pressure and children's extracurricular activities: Relationships with amount of involvement and affective experience of participation. *Journal of Applied Developmental Psychology, 24*, 241-257.

Apache, R.R. (2006). The behavioral assessment of parents and coaches at youth sports: Validity and reliability. *The Physical Educator, 63*, 126-133.

Atkins, M.R., Johnson, D.M., Force, E.C., & Petrie, T.A. (2015). Peers, parents, and coaches, oh my! The relation of the motivational climate to boys' intention to continue in sport. *Psychology of Sport and Exercise, 16*, 170-180.

Avolio, B.J., & Bass, B.M. (2004). *Multifactor Leadership Questionnaire: Manual and sampler set* (3rd ed.). Redwood City, CA: Mind Garden.

Aoyogi, M.W., Cox, R.H., & McGuire, R. (2008). Organizational citizenship behavior in sport: Relationships with leadership, team cohesion, and athlete satisfaction. *Journal of Applied Sport Psychology, 20*, 25-41.

Babkes, M.L., & Weiss, M.R. (1999). Parental influence on children's cognitive and affective responses to competitive soccer participation. *Pediatric Exercise Science, 11*, 44-62.

Bass, J.R., Vermillion, M., & Putz, P. (2014). "Going viral": The impact of forced crowdsourcing on coaching evaluation procedures. *International Sport Coaching Journal, 1*, 103-108.

Bell, R.Q., & Chapman, M. (1986). Child effects in studies using experimental or brief longitudinal approaches to socialization. *Developmental Psychology, 22*, 595-603.

Bell, R.Q., & Harper, L.V. (1977). *Child effects on adults*. London: University of Nebraska Press.Bloom, G.A., Crumpton, R., & Anderson, J.E. (1999). A systematic observation study of the teaching behaviors of an expert basketball coach. *The Sport Psychologist, 13*, 157-170.

Bremer, K.L. (2012). Parental involvement, pressure, and support in youth sport: A narrative literature review. *Journal of Family Theory & Review, 4*, 235-248.

Brewer, C.J., & Jones, R.L. (2002). A five-stage process for establishing contextually valid systematic observation instruments: The case of rugby union. *The Sport Psychologist, 16*, 138-159.

Briggs-Myers, I., & Briggs, K.C. (1985). *Myers-Briggs Type Indicator* (MBTI). Palo Alto, CA: Consulting Psychologists Press.

Bronfenbrenner, U. (2005). *Making human beings human: Bioecological perspectives on human development.* Thousand Oaks, CA: Sage.

Brustad, R., Babkes, M., & Smith, A.L. (2001). Youth in sport: Psychological considerations. In R.N. Singer, H.A. Hausenblas, & C.M. Janelle (Eds.), *Handbook of sport psychology* (2nd ed., pp. 604-635). New York: Wiley.

Burton, D., & Gillham, A. (2012). Exploring the potential of assessment efficacy in sports coaching: A commentary. *International Journal of Sports Science & Coaching, 7,* 207-210.

Carron, A.V., Widmeyer, W.N., & Brawley, L.R. (1985). The development of an instrument to assess cohesion in sport teams: The group environment questionnaire. *Journal of Sport Psychology, 7,* 244-266.

Caughlin, J.P. (2010). A multiple goals theory of personal relationships: Conceptual integration and program overview. *Journal of Social and Personal Relationships, 27,* 824-848.

Chelladurai, P. (2007). Leadership in sports. In G. Tenenbaum & R.C. Eklund (Eds.), *Handbook of sport psychology* (3rd ed., pp. 113-135). Morgantown, WV: Fitness Information Technology.

Chelladurai, P., & Arnott, M. (1985). Decision styles in coaching: Preferences of basketball players. *Research Quarterly for Exercise and Sport, 56,* 15-24.

Chelladurai, P., & Quek, C.B. (1991). Decision style choices of high school basketball coaches: The effects of situational and coach characteristics. *Journal of Sport Behavior, 18,* 91-108.

Chelladurai, P., & Riemer, H.A. (1998). In J.L. Duda (Ed.), *Advances in sport and exercise psychology* (pp. 227-253). Morgantown, WV: Fitness Information Technology.

Chelladurai, P., & Saleh, S. (1980). Dimensions of leader behavior in sports: Development of a leadership scale. *Journal of Sport Psychology, 2,* 34-45.

Coatsworth, J.D., & Conroy, D.E. (2006). Enhancing the self-esteem of youth swimmers through coach training: Gender and age effects. *Psychology of Sport and Exercise, 7,* 173-192.

Coatsworth, J.D., & Conroy, D.E. (2009). The effects of autonomy-supportive coaching, need satisfaction, and self-perceptions on initiative and identity in youth swimmers. *Developmental Psychology, 45,* 320-328.

Conroy, D.E., & Coatsworth, J.D. (2006). Coach training as a strategy for promoting youth social development. *The Sport Psychologist, 20,* 128-144.

Côté, J., & Gilbert, W. (2009). An integrative definition of coaching effectiveness and expertise. *International Journal of Sport Science & Coaching, 4,* 307-323.

Côté, J., Yardley, J., Hay, J., Sedgwick, W., & Baker, J. (1999). An exploratory examination of the Coaching Behavior Scale for Sport. *Avanté, 5,* 82-92.

Cushion, C.J., & Jones, R.L. (2001). A systematic observation of professional top-level youth soccer coaches. *Journal of Sport Behavior, 24,* 354-377.

Darling, N., & Steinberg, L. (1993). Parenting style as context: An integrative model. *Psychological Bulletin, 113,* 487-496.

Darst, P.W., Zakrajsek, D.B., & Mancini, V.H. (Eds.). (1989). *Analyzing physical education and sport instruction* (2nd ed.). Champaign, IL: Human Kinetics.

Dirks, K.T. (2000). Trust in leadership and team performance: Evidence from NCAA basketball. *Journal of Applied Psychology, 85,* 1004-1012.

Dix, T., Ruble, D.N., Grusec, J.E., & Nixon, S. (1986). Social cognition in parents: Inferential and affective reactions to children of three age levels. *Child Development, 57,* 879-894.

Dorsch, T.E., Smith, A.L., & Dotterer, A.M. (2016). Individual, relationship, and context factors associated with parent support and pressure in organized youth sport. *Psychology of Sport and Exercise, 23,* 132-141.

Dorsch, T.E., Smith, A.L., & McDonough, M.H. (2009). Parents' perceptions of child-to-parent socialization in organized youth sport. *Journal of Sport & Exercise Psychology, 31,* 444-468.

Dorsch, T.E., Smith, A.L., & McDonough, M.H. (2015). Parent goals and verbal sideline behavior in organized youth sport. *Sport, Exercise, and Performance Psychology, 4,* 19-35.

Dorsch, T.E., Smith, A.L., Wilson, S.R., & McDonough, M.H. (2015). Early socialization of parents through organized youth sport. *Sport, Exercise, and Performance Psychology, 4,* 3-18.

Duda, J.L., & Whitehead, J. (1998). Measurement of goal perspectives in the physical domain. In J.L. Duda (Ed.), *Advances in sport and exercise psychology measurement* (pp. 21-48). Morgantown, WV: Fitness Information Technology.

Dunn, C.R., Dorsch, T.E., King, M., & Rothlisberger, K. (2016). The impact of family financial investment on parent pressure, child enjoyment, and commitment to participation in organized youth sport. *Family Relations, 65,* 287-299.

Feltz, D.L., Chase, M.A., Moritz, S.E., & Sullivan, P.J. (1999). A conceptual model of coaching efficacy: Preliminary investigation and instrument development. *Journal of Educational Psychology, 91,* 765-776.

Franks, I.M., Johnson, R.B., & Sinclair, G.D. (1988). The development of a computerized coaching analysis system for recording behavior in sporting environments. *Journal of Teaching in Physical Education, 8*, 23-32.

Fraser-Thomas, J., Côté, J., & Deakin, J. (2005). Youth sport programs: An avenue to foster positive youth development. *Physical Education and Sport Pedagogy, 10*, 19-40.

Fraser-Thomas, J., Côté, J., & Deakin, J. (2008). Examining adolescent sport dropout and prolonged engagement from a developmental perspective. *Journal of Applied Sport Psychology, 20*, 318-333.

Fredricks, J.A., & Eccles, J.S. (2004). Parental influences on youth involvement in sports. In M.R. Weiss (Ed.), *Developmental sport and exercise psychology: A lifespan perspective* (pp. 145-164). Morgantown, WV: Fitness Information Technology.

Gallimore, R., & Tharp, P. (2004). What a coach can teach a teacher, 1975-2004: Reflections and reanalysis of John Wooden's teaching practices. *The Sport Psychologist, 18*, 119-137.

Gershgoren, L., Tenenbaum, G., Gershgoren, A., & Eklund, R.C. (2011). The effect of parental feedback on young athletes' perceived motivational climate, goal involvement, goal orientation, and performance. *Psychology of Sport and Exercise, 12*, 481-489.

Gilbert, W. (2017). *Coaching better ever season: A year-round process for athlete development and program success.* Champaign, IL: Human Kinetics.

Gilbert, W., & Baldis, M.W. (2014). Becoming an effective strength and conditioning coach. *Strength and Conditioning Journal, 36*, 28-34.

Gillham, A. (2015). Relationships between organizational justice and coaches' attitudinal outcomes in intercollegiate sports: A commentary. *International Journal of Sports Science & Coaching, 10*, 327-331.

Gillham, A., Burton, D., & Gillham, E. (2013). Going beyond won-loss record to identify successful coaches: Development and preliminary validation of the Coaching Success Questionnaire-2. *International Journal of Sports Science & Coaching, 8*, 115-138.

Gillham, A., Doscher, M., Schofield, G., Dalrymple, D., & Bird, S. (2015). Strength and conditioning roundtable: Working with novice coaches. *International Journal of Sports Science & Coaching, 10*(5), 985-1000.

Gillham, A., Gillham, E., & Hansen, K. (2015). Relationships among coaching success, servant leadership, cohesion, resilience and social behaviors. *International Sport Coaching Journal, 2*, 233-247.

Gillham, A., Hansen, K., & Brady, C. (2015). Coach evaluation from three perspectives: An athletic director, a coach and a consultant. *International Sport Coaching Journal, 2*, 192-200.

Gillham, A., Schofield, G., Doscher, M., Dalrymple, D., & Kenn, J. (2016). Developing and implementing a coaching philosophy: Guidance from award-winning strength and conditioning coaches. *International Sport Coaching Journal, 3*, 54-64.

Greendorfer, S.L. (2002). Socialization processes and sport behavior. In T. Horn (Ed.), *Advances in sport psychology* (2nd ed., 377-401). Champaign, IL: Human Kinetics.

Grolnick, W.S. (2003). *The psychology of parental control: How well-meant parenting backfires.* Mahwah, NJ: Erlbaum.

Grolnick, W.S., Deci, E.L., & Ryan, R.M. (1997). Internalization within the family: The self-determination theory perspective. In J.E. Grusec & L. Kuczynski (Eds.), *Parenting and children's internalization of values: A handbook of contemporary theory* (pp. 135-161). Hoboken, NJ: Wiley.

Hammermeister, J., Chase, M., Burton, D., Westre, K., Pickering, M., & Baldwin, N. (2008). Servant leadership in sport: A concept whose time has arrived. *Journal of Servant Leadership, 4*, 185-215.

Harter, S. (1999). *The construction of the self: A developmental perspective.* New York: Guilford Press.

Harwood, C.G., Keegan, R.J., Smith, J.M.J., & Raine, A.S. (2015). A systematic review of the intrapersonal correlates of motivational climate perceptions in sport ad physical activity. *Psychology of Sport and Exercise, 18*, 9-25.

Hellstedt, J.C. (1987). The coach/parent/athlete relationship. *The Sport Psychologist, 1*, 151-160.

Holt, N.L., Tamminen, K.A., Black, D.E., Sehn, Z.L., & Wall, M.P. (2008). Parental involvement in competitive youth sport settings. *Psychology of Sport and Exercise, 9*, 663-685.

Horn, T.S. (1984). Expectancy effects in the interscholastic athletic setting: Methodological considerations. *Journal of Sport Psychology, 7*, 60-76.

Horn, T.S. (1985). Coaches' feedback and changes in children's perceptions of their physical competence. *Journal of Educational Psychology, 77*, 174-186.

Horn, T.S. (2008). Coaching effectiveness in the sport domain. In T.S. Horn (Ed.), *Advances in sport psychology* (3rd ed., pp. 240-267). Champaign, IL: Human Kinetics.

Horn, T.S., & Horn, J.L. (2007). Family influences on children's sport and physical activity participation, behavior and psychosocial responses. In G. Tenenbaum & R.C. Eklund (Eds.), *Handbook of Sport Psychology* (3rd ed., pp. 685-711). Hoboken, NJ: Wiley.

Jellineck, M., & Durant, S. (2004). Parents and sports: Too much of a good thing? *Contemporary Pediatrics, 21*, 17-20.

Jowett, S., & Ntoumanis, N. (2004). The Coach–Athlete Relationship Questionnaire (CART-Q): Development and initial validation. *Scandinavian Journal of Medicine and Science in Sports, 14*, 245-257.

Kanters, M.A., Bocarro, J., & Casper, J. (2008). Supported or pressured? An examination of agreement among parents and children on parents' role in youth sports. *Journal of Sport Behavior, 31,* 64-80.

Kenow, L.J., & Williams, J.M. (1992). Relationship between anxiety, self-confidence, and evaluation of coaching behaviors. *The Sport Psychologist, 6,* 344-357.

Kenow, L.J., & Williams, J.M. (1999). Coach-athlete compatibility and athletes' perceptions of coaching behaviors. *Journal of Sport Behavior, 22,* 251-259.

Kidman, L., McKenzie, A., & McKenzie, B. (1999). The nature and target of parents' comments during youth sport competitions. *Journal of Sport Behavior, 22,* 54-68.

Kleinert, J., Ohlert, J., Carron, B., Eyes, M., Feltz, D., Harwood, C., Linz, L., Seiler, R., & Sulpriio, M. (2012). Group dynamics in sports: An overview and recommendations on diagnostic and intervention. *The Sport Psychologist, 26,* 412-434.

Knafo, A., & Schwartz, S.H. (2003). Parenting and adolescents' accuracy in perceiving parental values. *Child Development, 74,* 595-611.

Lacy, A.C., & Darst, P.W. (1984). Evolution of a systematic observation instrument: The ASU Observation Instrument. *Journal of Teaching in Physical Education, 3,* 59-66.

La Guardia, J.G., Ryan, R.M., Couchman, C.E., & Deci, E.L. (2000). Within-person variation in security of attachment: A self-determination theory perspective on attachment, need fulfillment, and well-being. *Journal of Personality and Social Psychology, 79,* 367-384.

Laursen, B., & Collins, W.A. (2009). Parent-child relationships during adolescence. In R.M. Lerner & L. Steinberg (Eds.), *Handbook of adolescent psychology* (3rd ed., pp. 3-42). Hoboken, NJ: Wiley.

Leff, S.S., & Hoyle, R.H. (1995). Young athletes' perceptions of parental support and pressure. *Journal of Youth and Adolescence, 24,* 187-203.

MacLean, J.C., & Chelladurai, P. (1995). Dimensions of coaching performance: Development of a scale. *Journal of Sport Management, 9,* 194-207.

Mallet, C., & Côté, J. (2006). Beyond winning and losing: Guidelines for evaluating high performance coaches. *The Sport Psychologist, 20,* 213-221.

Martin, K. (2002). Development and validation of the Coaching Staff Cohesion Scale. *Measurement in Physical Education and Exercise Science, 6,* 23-42.

McAuley, E., Duncan, T.E., & Russell, D.W. (1992). Measuring causal attributions: The revised Causal Dimension Scale (CDSII). *Personality and Social Psychology Bulletin, 18,* 566-573.

McHale, S.M., Amato, P., & Booth, A. (2014). *Emerging methods in family research.* Imprint: Springer.

More, K.G., & Franks, I.M. (1996). Analysis and modification of verbal coaching behaviors. The usefulness of a data-driven intervention strategy. *Journal of Sports Sciences, 14,* 523-543.

Myers, N.D., Feltz, D.L., Chase, M.A., Reckase, M.D., & Hancock, G.R. (2008). The Coaching Efficacy Scale-II: High school teams. *Educational and Psychological Measurement, 68,* 1059-1076.

Newton, M.L., Duda, J.L., & Yin, Z. (2000). Examination of the psychometric properties of the Perceived Motivational Climate in Sport Questionnaire-2 in a sample of female athletes. *Journal of Sport Sciences, 18,* 275-290.

Nicholls, J.G. (1984). Achievement motivation: Conceptions of ability, subjective experience, task choice, and performance. *Psychological Review, 91,* 328-346.

O'Rourke, D.J., Smith, R.E., Smoll, F.L., & Cumming, S.P. (2011). Trait anxiety in young athletes as a function of parental pressure and motivational climate: Is parental pressure always harmful? Journal of Applied Sport Psychology, 23, 398-412.

Page, D., & Wong, P.T.P. (2000). A conceptual framework for measuring servant leadership. In S. Adjiboloos (Ed.), *The human factor in shaping the course of history and development* (pp. 1-28). Lanham, MD: American University Press.

Parke, R.D., & Buriel, R. (2006). Socialization in the family: Ethnic and ecological perspectives. In N. Eisenberg, W. Damon, & R.M. Lerner (Eds.), *Handbook of child psychology: Social, emotional, and personality development* (6th ed., pp. 429-504). Hoboken, NJ: Wiley.

Pelletier, L.G., Fortier, M.S., Vallerand, R.J., & Briere, N.M. (2002). Associations among perceived autonomy support, forms of self-regulation, and persistence: A prospective study. *Motivation and Emotion, 25,* 279-306.

Pelletier, L.G., Tuson, K.M., & Haddad, N.K. (1997). The Client Motivation for Therapy Scale (CMOTS): A measure of intrinsic motivation, forms of extrinsic motivation, and amotivation for therapy. *Journal of Personality Assessment, 68,* 414-435.

Pelletier, L.G., & Vallerand, R.J. (1996). Supervisors' beliefs and subordinates' intrinsic motivation: A behavioral confirmation analysis. *Journal of Personality and Social Psychology, 71,* 331-341.

Peters, J.F. (1985). Adolescents as socialization agents to parents. *Adolescence, 20,* 921-933.

Riemer, H.A., & Chelladurai, P. (1998). Development of the Athlete Satisfaction Questionnaire (ASQ). *Journal of Sport & Exercise Psychology, 20,* 127-156.

Rowold, J. (2006). Transformational and transactional leadership in martial arts. *Journal of Applied Sport Psychology, 18,* 312-325.

Rushall, B.S., & Wiznuk, K. (1985). Athletes' assessment of the coach: The Coach Evaluation Questionnaire. *Canadian Journal of Applied Sport Sciences, 10,* 157-161.

Schmidt, S.J. (2007). *Histories & discourses: Rewriting constructivism.* Exeter, UK: Imprint-Academic.

Schwarz, J.C., Barton-Henry, M.L., & Pruzinsky, T. (1985). Assessing child-rearing behavior: A comparison of ratings made by mother, father, child, and sibling on the CRPBI. *Child Development, 56,* 462-479.

Schweizer, T. (1998). Epistemology: The nature and validation of anthropological knowledge. In H.R. Bernard (Ed.), *Handbook of methods in cultural anthropology* (pp. 39-59). Walnut Creek, CA: Alta Mira.

Shields, D.L., Bredemeier, B.L., LaVoi, N.M., & Power, F.C. (2005). The sport behavior of youth, parents, and coaches: The good, the bad, and the ugly. *Journal of Research in Character Education, 3,* 43-59.

Short, S.E., Sullivan, O., & Feltz, D.L. (2005). Development and preliminary validation of the collective efficacy questionnaire for sports. *Measurement in Physical Education and Exercise Science, 9,* 181-202.

Smith, R.E., Cumming, S.P., & Smoll, F.L. (2008). Development and validation of the Motivational Climate Scale for Youth Sports. *Journal of Applied Sport Psychology, 20,* 116-136.

Smith, R.E., & Smoll, F.L. (1990). Self-esteem and children's reactions to youth sport coaching behaviors: A field study of self-enhancement processes. *Developmental Psychology, 26,* 987-993.

Smith, R.E., Smoll, F.L., & Christensen, D.S. (1996). Behavioral assessment and interventions in youth sports. *Behavior Modification, 20,* 3-44.

Smith, R.E., Smoll, F.L., & Hunt, E. (1977). A system for the behavioral assessment of athlete coaches. *Research Quarterly, 48,* 401-407.

Stein, G.L., Raedeke, T.D., & Glenn, S.D. (1999). Children's perceptions of parent sports involvement: It's not how much, but to what degree that's important. *Journal of Sport Behavior, 22,* 591-601.

Tharp, R.G., & Gallimore, R. (1976). What a coach can teach a teacher. *Psychology Today,* January, 75-78.

Thelwell, R.C., Weston, N.J.V., Greenlees, I.A., & Hutchings, N.V. (2008). A qualitative exploration of psychological-skills use in coaches. *The Sport Psychologist, 22,* 38-53.

Ullrich-French, S., & Smith, A.L. (2006). Perceptions of relationships with parents and peers in youth sport: Independent and combined prediction of motivational outcomes. *Psychology of Sport and Exercise, 7,* 193-214.

Vallerand, R.J., & Blanchard, C.M. (2000). The study of emotion in sport and exercise. In Y.L. Hanin (Ed.), *Emotions in sport* (pp. 3-37). Champaign, IL: Human Kinetics.

Vella, S.A., Oades, L.G., & Crowe, T.P. (2012). Validation of the differentiated transformational leadership inventory as a measure of coach leadership in youth soccer. *Sport Psychologist, 26,* 207-223.

Vidic, Z., & Burton, D. (2011). Developing effective leaders: Motivational correlates of leadership styles. *Journal of Applied Sport Psychology, 23,* 277-291.

Viswanathan, M. (2005). *Measurement error and research design.* Los Angeles: Sage.

Watson, D., & Clark, L.A. (1994). *Manual for the Positive and Negative Affect Schedule (expanded form).* Iowa City, IA: University of Iowa.

Weiss, M.R., & Hayashi, C.T. (1995). All in the family: Parent-child influences in competitive youth gymnastics. *Pediatric Exercise Science, 7,* 36-48.

Weiss, M.R., & Smith, A.L. (1999). Quality of youth sport friendships: Measurement development and validation. *Journal of Sport & Exercise Psychology, 21,* 145-166.

Williams, J.M., Jerome, G.J., Kenow, L.J., Rogers, T., Sartain, T.A., & Darland, G. (2003). Factor structure of the Coaching Behavior Questionnaire and its relationship to athlete variables. *The Sport Psychologist, 17,* 16-34.

Chapter 12

Abbott, A., & Collins, D. (2004). Eliminating the dichotomy between theory and practice in talent identification and development: Considering the role of psychology. *Journal of Sports Sciences, 22,* 395-408.

Andersen, M.B. (2000). Beginnings: Intakes and the initiation of relationships. In M.B. Andersen (Ed.), *Doing sport psychology* (pp. 3-16). Champaign, IL: Human Kinetics.

Anshel, M.H., & Lidor, R. (2012). Talent detection programs in sport: The questionable use of psychological measures. *Journal of Sport Behavior, 35,* 239-266.

Barker, J., McCarthy, P., Jones, M., & Moran, A. (2011). *Single-case research methods in sport and exercise psychology.* Abingdon, UK: Routledge.

Bar-Or, O. (1975). Predicting athlete performance. *Physician and Sports Medicine, 3,* 81-85.

Beedie, C.J., Terry, P.C., & Lane, A.M. (2000). The Profile of Mood States and athletic performance: Two meta-analyses. *Journal of Applied Sport Psychology, 12,* 49-68.

Bloom, B.S. (1985). *Developing talent in young people.* New York: Ballantine.

Bresciani, G., Cuevas, M.J., Molinero, O., Almar, M., Suay, F., Salvador, A.,... & González-Gallego, J. (2011). Signs of overload after an intensified training. *International Journal of Sports Medicine, 32,* 338-343.

Butler, R.J., & Hardy, L. (1992). The performance profile: Theory and application. *The Sport Psychologist, 6,* 253-264.

Cattell, H.E.P. (1996). The original big five: A historical perspective. *European Review of Applied Psychology, 46,* 5-14.

Cattell, H.E.P., & Mead, A.D. (2008). The Sixteen Personality Factor questionnaire (16PF). In G.J. Boyle, G. Matthews, & D.H. Saklofske (Eds.), *The SAGE handbook of personality theory and assessment, personality theories and models* (Vol. 1, pp. 295-312). Los Angeles: Sage.

Cattell, R.B., Cattell, A.K., & Cattell, H.E.P. (1993). *16PF Fifth Edition questionnaire.* Champaign, IL: Institute for Personality and Ability Testing.

Chapman, D.S., & Zweig, D.I. (2005). Developing a nomological network for interview structure: Antecedents and consequences of the structured selection interview. *Personnel Psychology, 58,* 673-702.

Collins, D., & MacNamara, Á. (2011). Comments on 'Expert performance in sport and the dynamics of talent development'. *Sports Medicine, 41,* 609-610.

Côté, J. (1999). The influence of the family in the development of talent in sports. *The Sport Psychologist, 13,* 395-417.

Côté, J., Baker, J., & Abernethy, B. (2003). From play to practice: A developmental framework for the acquisition of expertise in team sport. In J. Starkes & K.A. Ericsson (Eds.), *Expert performance in sports: Advances in research on sport expertise* (pp. 89-114). Champaign, IL: Human Kinetics.

Côté, J., Ericsson, K.A., & Law, M.P. (2005). Tracing the development of athletes using retrospective interview methods: A proposed interview and validation procedure for reported information. *Journal of Applied Sport Psychology, 17,* 1-19.

Craft, L.L., Magyar, M., Becker, B.J., & Feltz, D.L. (2003). The relationship between the Competitive State Anxiety Inventory-2 and sport performance: A meta-analysis. *Journal of Sport & Exercise Psychology, 25,* 44-65.

Crowne, D.P., & Marlowe, D. (1960). A new scale of social desirability independent of psychopathology. *Journal of Consulting Psychology, 24,* 349-354.

Crust, L., & Clough, P.J. (2005). Relationship between mental toughness and physical endurance. *Perceptual and Motor Skills, 100,* 192-194.

Crust, L., & Swann, C. (2011). Comparing two measures of mental toughness. *Personality and Individual Differences, 50,* 217-221.

Driediger, M., Hall, C., & Callow, N. (2006). Imagery use by injured athletes: A qualitative analysis. *Journal of Sports Sciences, 24,* 261-272.

Duda, J.L. (1989). The relationship between task and ego orientation and the perceived purpose of sport among male and female high school athletes. *Journal of Sport and Exercise Psychology, 11,* 318-335.

Duda, J.L. (2005). Motivation in sport: The relevance of competence and achievement goals. In A.J. Elliot, & C.S. Dweck (Eds.), *Handbook of competence motivation* (pp. 318-335). New York: The Guilford Press.

Durand-Bush, N., & Salmela, J.H. (2001). The development of talent in sport. In R. Singer, H. Hausenblas, & C. Janelle (Eds.), *Handbook of sport psychology* (2nd ed., pp. 269-289). New York: Wiley.

Durand-Bush, N., Salmela, J.H., & Greens-Demers, I. (2001). The Ottawa Mental Skills Assessment Tool (OMSAT-3*). *The Sport Psychologist, 15,* 1-19.

Ericsson, K.A., & Smith, J. (1991). Prospects and limits of the empirical study of expertise: An introduction. In K.A. Ericsson & J. Smith (Eds.), *Towards a general theory of expertise: Prospects and limits* (pp. 1-29). Cambridge, UK: Cambridge University.

Fletcher, D., & Sarkar, M. (2012). A grounded theory of psychological resilience in Olympic champions. *Psychology of Sport and Exercise, 13,* 669-678.

Gardner, F., & Moore, Z. (2005). *Clinical sport psychology.* Champaign, IL: Human Kinetics.

Gimbel, B. (1976). Possibilities and problems in sports talent detection research. *Leistungssport, 6,* 159-167.

Goho, J., & Blackman, A. (2006). The effectiveness of academic admission interviews: An exploratory meta-analysis. *Medical Teacher, 28,* 335-340.

Grös, D.F., Antony, M.M., Simms, L.J., & McCabe, R.E. (2007). Psychometric properties of the State-Trait Inventory for Cognitive and Somatic Anxiety (STICSA): Comparison to the State-Trait Anxiety Inventory (STAI). *Psychological Assessment, 19,* 369-381.

Gucciardi, D.F., Mallet, C.J., Hanrahan, S.J., & Gordon, S. (2011). Measuring mental toughness in sport: Status and future directions. In D.F. Gucciardi & S. Gordon (Eds.), *Mental toughness in sport: Development in theory and research* (pp. 108-132). Oxford, UK: Routledge.

Gulbin, J.P., Croser, M.J., Morley, E.J., & Weissensteiner, J.R. (2013). An integrated framework for the optimisation of sport and athlete development: A practitioner approach. *Journal of Sports Sciences, 31,* 1319-1331.

Hardy, L., Roberts, R., Thomas, P.R., & Murphy, S.M. (2010). Test of Performance Strategies (TOPS): Instrument refinement using confirmatory factor analysis. *Psychology of Sport and Exercise, 11,* 27-35.

Harmison, R.J. (2011). Peak performance in sport: Identifying ideal performance states and developing athletes' psychological skills. *Sport, Exercise, and Performance Psychology, 1*(S), 3-18.

Hayslip, B., Petrie, T.A., MacIntire, M.M., & Jones, G.M. (2010). The influences of skill level, anxiety, and psychological skills use on amateur golfers' performances. *Journal of Applied Sport Psychology, 22,* 123-133.

Hill, D.M., & Shaw, G. (2013). A qualitative examination of choking under pressure in team sport. *Psychology of Sport and Exercise, 14*, 103-110.

Holt, N.L., & Dunn, J.G.H. (2004). Toward a grounded theory of psychosocial competencies and environmental conditions associated with soccer success. *Journal of Applied Sport Psychology, 16*, 199-219.

Holt, N.L., & Tamminen, K.A. (2010). Moving forward with grounded theory in sport and exercise psychology. *Psychology of Sport and Exercise, 11*, 419-422.

Huffcutt, A.I. (2010). From science to practice: Seven principles for conducting employment interviews. *Applied H.R.M. Research, 12*, 121-136.

Jones, G., Hanton, S., & Connaughton, D. (2002). What is this thing called mental toughness? An investigation of elite sport performers. *Journal of Applied Sport Psychology, 14*, 205-218.

Kenow, L., & Williams, J.M. (1999). Coach-athlete compatibility and athlete's perception of coaching behaviors. *Journal of Sport Behavior, 22*, 251-259.

Lane, A.M., & Lane, H.J. (2002). Predictive effectiveness of mood measures. *Perceptual and Motor Skills, 94*, 785-791.

Loehr, J.E. (1986). *Mental toughness training for sports: Achieving athletic excellence.* Lexington, MA: S. Greene Press.

MacNamara, Á., Button, A., & Collins, D. (2010). The role of psychological characteristics in facilitating the pathway to elite performance. Part 1: Identifying mental skills and behaviours. *The Sport Psychologist, 24*, 52-73.

MacNamara, Á., & Collins, D. (2011). Development and initial validation of the Psychological Characteristics of Developing Excellence Questionnaire. *Journal of Sport Sciences, 29*, 1273-1286.

MacNamara, Á., & Collins, D. (2014). More of the same? Comment on "An integrated framework for the optimization of sport and athlete development: A practitioner approach." *Journal of Sports Sciences, 32*, 793-795.

MacNamara, Á., & Collins, D. (2015). Profiling, exploiting, and countering psychological characteristics in talent identification and development. *The Sport Psychologist, 29*, 73-81.

Martens, R. (1977). *Sport Competition Anxiety Test.* Champaign, IL: Human Kinetics.

Martens, R., Burton, D., Vealey, R.S., Bump, L.A., & Smith, D.E. (1990). Competitive State Anxiety Inventory-2. In R. Martens, R.S. Vealey, & D. Burton (Eds.), *Competitive anxiety in sport* (pp. 117-213). Champaign, IL: Human Kinetics.

Martens, R., Burton, D., Vealey, R.S., Bump, L.A., & Smith, D.E. (2002). Competitive State Anxiety Inventory-2 (CSAI-2). In A.C. Ostrow (Ed.), *Directory of psychological tests in the sport and exercise sciences*

(2nd ed., pp. 61-67). Morgantown, WV: Fitness Information Technology.

Martens, R., Gill, D., Scanlan, T., & Simon, J. (2002). Sport Competition Anxiety Test (SCAT). In A.C. Ostrow (Ed.), *Directory of psychological tests in the sport and exercise sciences* (2nd ed., pp. 61-67). Morgantown, WV: Fitness Information Technology.

Martin, B.A., Bowen, C.-C., & Hunt, S.T. (2002). How effective are people at faking on personality questionnaires. *Personality and Individual Differences, 32*, 247-256.

McNair, D.M., Lorr, M., & Droppleman, L.F. (1971). *ETIS manual for the Profile of Mood States.* San Diego: Educational and Industrial Testing Service.

Palmer, J.K., & Loveland, J.M. (2004). Further investigation of the psychometric properties of Saucier's big five "mini-markers": Evidence for criterion and construct validity. *Individual Differences Research, 2*, 231-238.

Perry, J.L., Clough, P.J., Crust, L., Earle, K., & Nicholls, A.R. (2013). Factorial validity of the Mental Toughness Questionnaire 48. *Personality and Individual Differences, 54*, 587-592.

Pinder, R.A., Renshaw, I., & Davids, K. (2013). The role of representative design in talent development: A comment on "Talent identification and promotion programmes of Olympic athletes." *Journal of Sports Sciences, 31*, 803-806.

Ree, M.J., French, D., MacLeod, C., & Locke, V. (2008). Distinguishing cognitive and somatic dimensions of state and trait anxiety: Development and validation of the State-Trait Inventory for Cognitive and Somatic Anxiety (STICSA). *Behavioral and Cognitive Psychotherapy, 36*, 313-332. http://dx.doi.org/10.1017/S1352465808004232

Régnier, G., Salmela, J.H., & Russell, S.J. (1993). Talent detection and development in sport. In R.N. Singer, M. Murphey, & L.K. Tennant (Eds.), *Handbook of research on sport psychology* (pp. 290-313). New York: Macmillan.

Roberts, K.E., Hart, T.A., & Eastwood, J.D. (2015). Factor structure and validity of the State-Trait Inventory for Cognitive and Somatic Anxiety. *Psychological Assessment.* Advance online publication.

Roulin, N., Bangerter, A., & Yerly, E. (2011). The uniqueness effects in selection interviews. *Journal of Personnel Psychology, 10*, 43-47.

Rowley, A., Landers, D., Kyllo, L., & Etnier, J. (1995). Does the iceberg profile discriminate between successful and less successful athletes? A meta-analysis. *Journal of Sport and Exercise Psychology, 17*, 185-199.

Saucier, G. (1994). Mini-Markers: A brief version of Goldberg's unipolar big-five markers. *Journal of Personality Assessment, 63*, 506-516.

Sheard, M., Golby, J., & van Wersch, A. (2009). Progress toward construct validation of the Sports Mental

Toughness Questionnaire (SMTQ). *European Journal of Psychological Assessment, 25*, 186-193.

Simonsohn, U., & Gino, F. (2013). Daily horizons: Evidence of narrow bracketing in judgment from 10 years of M.B.A. admissions interviews. *Psychological Science, 24*, 219-224.

Smith, B., & Caddick, N. (2012). Qualitative methods in sport: A concise overview for guiding social scientific sport research. *Asia Pacific Journal of Sport and Social Science, 1*, 60-73.

Smith, R.E., Schultz, R.W., Smoll, F.L., & Ptacek, J.T. (1995). Development and validation of a multidimensional measure of sport-specific psychological skills: The Athletic Coping Skills Inventory-28. *Journal of Sport & Exercise Psychology, 17*, 379-398.

Sparks, A.C., & Smith, B. (2014). *Qualitative research methods in sport, exercise, and health: From process to product.* Abingdon, UK: Routledge.

Spielberger, C.D. (1983). *State-Trait Anxiety Inventory for Adults.* Palo Alto, CA: Consulting Psychologists Press.

Spielberger, C.D., Gorsuch, R.L., & Lushene, R. (1970). *STAI manual.* Palo Alto, CA: Consulting Psychologists Press.

Taylor, J., & Schneider, B.A. (1992). The Sport-Clinical Intake Protocol: A comprehensive interviewing instrument for applied sport psychology. *Professional Psychology: Research and Practice, 23*, 318-325.

Taylor, M.K., Gould, D., & Rolo, C. (2008). Performance strategies of US Olympians in practice and competition. *High Ability Studies, 19*, 19-36.

Terry, P.C. (1995). The efficacy of mood state profiling among elite competitors: A review and synthesis. *The Sport Psychologist, 9*, 309-324.

Terry, P.C., Lane, A.M., Lane, H.J., & Keohane, L. (1999). Development and validation of a mood measure for adolescents: POMS-A. *Journal of Sports Sciences, 17*, 861-872.

Vaeyens, R., Güllich, A., Warr, C.W., & Philippaerts, R. (2009). Talent identification and promotion programmes of Olympic athletes. *Journal of Sports Sciences, 27*, 1367-1380.

Van Iddekinge, C.H., Raymark, P.H., Eidson, C.E., Jr., & Attenweiler, W.J. (2004). What do structured selection interviews really measure? The construct validity of behavior description interviews. *Human Performance, 17*, 71-93.

Vealey, R.S. (1986). Conceptualization of sport-confidence and competitive orientation: Preliminary investigation and instrument development. *Journal of Sport Psychology, 8*, 221-246.

Vealey, R.S. (2002). State Sport-Confidence Inventory (SSCI). In A.C. Ostrow (Ed.), *Directory of psychological tests in the sport and exercise sciences* (2nd ed., pp. 297-299). Morgantown, WV: Fitness Information Technology.

Williams, L. (1998). Contextual influences and goal perspectives among female youth participants. *Research Quarterly for Exercise and Sport, 69*, 47-57.

Woodman, T., & Hardy, L. (2003). The relative impact of cognitive anxiety and self-confidence upon sport performance: A meta-analysis. *Journal of Sport Sciences, 21*, 443-457.

Woodman, T., Zourbanos, N., Hardy, L., Beattie, S., McQuillan, A. (2010). Do performance strategies moderate the relationship between personality and training behaviors? An exploratory study. *Journal of Applied Sport Psychology, 22*, 183-197.

Chapter 13

Andersen, M.B. (2004). Recognizing psychopathology. In G.S. Kolt & M.B. Andersen (Eds.), *Psychology in the physical and manual therapies* (pp. 81-92). Philadelphia: Churchill Livingstone.

Arvinen-Barrow, M., & Clement, D. (2015). A preliminary investigation into athletic trainers' views and experiences of multidisciplinary team approach to sport injury rehabilitation. *Athletic Training and Sports Health Care, 7*(3), 97-107.

Arvinen-Barrow, M., & Clement, D. (2017). Preliminary investigation into sport/exercise psychology consultants' views and experiences of a multidisciplinary approach to sport injury rehabilitation. *Journal of Interprofessional Care, 31*(1), 66-74. doi:10.1080/13561820.2016.1235019

Arvinen-Barrow, M., Clement, D., & Bayes, N. (2012). Athletes' attitudes toward physiotherapist. *International Journal of Multi-Disciplinary Studies and Sports Research, 2*(July), 324-334.

Arvinen-Barrow, M., Clement, D., Hamson-Utley, J.J., Zakrajsek, R., Kamphoff, C., Lee, S.-M., . . . Martin, S.B. (2015). Athletes' expectations about sport injury rehabilitation: A cross-cultural study. *Journal of Sport Rehabilitation, 25*(4), 338-347. doi: 10.1123/jsr.2015-0018

Arvinen-Barrow, M., & Hemmings, B. (2013). Goal setting in sport injury rehabilitation. In M. Arvinen-Barrow & N. Walker (Eds.), *Psychology of sport injury and rehabilitation* (pp. 56-70). Abingdon, UK: Routledge.

Arvinen-Barrow, M., Hemmings, B., Weigand, D.A., Becker, C.A., & Booth, L. (2007). Views of chartered physiotherapists on the psychological content of their practice: A national follow-up survey in the United Kingdom. *Journal of Sport Rehabilitation, 16*(2), 111-121. doi:10.1123/jsr.16.2.111

Bandura, A. (1977). Self-efficacy: Towards a unifying theory of behavior change. *Psychological Reviews, 84(2)*, 191-215. doi: 10.1037/0033-295X.84.2.191

Beck, A.T., Ward, C.H., Mendelson, M., Mock, J., & Erbaugh, J. (1961). An inventory for measuring depression.

Archives of General Psychiatry, 4(6), 561-571. doi:10.1001/archpsyc.1961.01710120031004

Brewer, B.W., Andersen, M.B., & Van Raalte, J.L. (2002). Psychological aspects of sport injury rehabilitation: Toward a biopsychological approach. In D.I. Mostofsky & L.D. Zaichkowsky (Eds.), *Medical aspects of sport and exercise* (pp. 41-54). Morgantown, WV: Fitness Information Technology.

Brewer, B.W., Van Raalte, J.L., Cornelius, A.E., Petitpas, A.J., Sklar, J.H., Pohlman, M.H., . . . Ditmar, T.D. (2000). Psychological factors, rehabilitation adherence, and rehabilitation outcome after anterior cruciate ligament reconstruction. *Rehabilitation Psychology, 45*(1), 20-37. doi:10.1037/0090-5550.45.1.20

Carver, C.S. (1997). You want to measure coping but your protocol's too long: Consider the Brief COPE. *International Journal of Behavioral Medicine, 4*(1), 92-100. doi:10.1207/s15327558ijbm0401_6

Clement, D. (2008). The transtheoretical model: An exploratory look at its applicability to injury rehabilitation. *Journal of Sport Rehabilitation, 17*(3), 269-282. doi: 10.1123/jsr.17.3.269

Clement, D., & Arvinen-Barrow, M. (2013). Sport medicine team influences in psychological rehabilitation: A multidisciplinary approach. In M. Arvinen-Barrow & N. Walker (Eds.), *The psychology of sport injury and rehabilitation* (pp. 156-170). Abingdon, UK: Routledge.

Clement, D., Arvinen-Barrow, M., & Fetty, T. (2015). Psychosocial responses during different phases of sport injury rehabilitation: A qualitative study. *Journal of Athletic Training, 50*(1), 95-104. doi:10.4085/1062-6050-49.3.52

Clement, D., Granquist, M.D., & Arvinen-Barrow, M. (2013). Psychosocial aspects of athletic injuries as perceived by athletic trainers. *Journal of Athletic Training, 48*(4), 512-521. doi:10.4085/1062-6050-49.3.52

Clement, D., Hamson-Utley, J.J., Arvinen-Barrow, M., Kamphoff, C., Zakrajsek, R.A., & Martin, S.B. (2012). College athletes' expectations about injury rehabilitation with an athletic trainer. *International Journal of Athletic Therapy & Training, 17*(4), 18-27. doi: 10.1123/ijatt.17.4.18

Deroche, T., Yannick, S., Brewer, B.W., & Le Scanff, C. (2007). Predictors of perceived susceptibility to sport-related injury. *Personality and Individual Differences, 43*(8), 2218-2228. doi:10.1016/j.paid.2007.06.031

DiMatteo, M.R., Lepper, H.S., & Croghan, T.W. (2000). Depression is a risk factor for noncompliance with medical treatment: Meta-analysis of the effects of anxiety and depression on patient adherence. *Archives of Internal Medicine, 160*(14), 2101-2107. doi:10.1001/archinte.160.14.2101

Glazer, D.D. (2009). Development and preliminary validation and the injury-psychological readiness to return

to sport scale (I-PRRS). *Journal of Athletic Training, 44*(2), 185-189. doi:10.4085/1062-6050-44.2.185

Gnasinski, S.L., Arvinen-Barrow, M., Brewer, B.W., & Meyer, B.B. (2016). Factorial validity and measurement invariance of the Perceived Susceptibility to Sport Injury scale. *Scandinavian Journal of Sports Medicine.* Advanced online publication. doi:10.1111/sms.12681

Granquist, M.D., & Brewer, B.W. (2013). Psychological aspects of rehabilitation adherence. In M. Arvinen-Barrow & N. Walker (Eds.), *Psychology of sport injury and rehabilitation* (pp. 40-53). Abingdon, UK: Routledge.

Granquist, M.D., Gill, D.L., & Appaneal, R.N. (2010). Development of a measure of rehabilitation adherence for athletic training. *Journal of Sport Rehabilitation, 19*(3), 249-267. doi:10.1123/jsr.19.3.249

Granquist, M.D., & Stadden, S.A. (2015). Social support and the athletic trainer. In M.D. Granquist, J.J. Hamson-Utley, L.J. Kenow, & J. Stiller-Ostrowski (Eds.), *Psychosocial strategies for athletic training* (pp. 209-229). Philadelphia: FA Davis.

Granquist, M.D., & Stiller-Ostrowski, J. (2014). Introduction and overview to pain. In M.D. Granquist, J.J. Hamson-Utley, L. Kenow, & J. Stiller-Ostrowski (Eds.), *Psychosocial strategies for athletic training* (pp. 209-229). Philadelphia: FA Davis.

Hamilton, M. (1960). A rating scale for depression. *Journal of Neurological Neurosurgical Psychiatry, 23*(1), 56-62. doi:10.1136/jnnp.23.1.56

Hamson-Utley, J.J., Arvinen-Barrow, M., & Granquist, M.D. (2014). Psychosocial strategies: Effectiveness and application. In M.D. Granquist, J.J. Hamson-Utley, L. Kenow, & J. Stiller-Ostrowski (Eds.), *Psychosocial strategies for athletic trainers: An applied and integrated approach* (pp. 231-268). Philadelphia: FA Davis.

Kamphoff, C., Thomae, J., & Hamson-Utley, J.J. (2013). Integrating the psychological and physiological aspects of sport injury rehabilitation: Rehabilitation profiling and phases of rehabilitation. In M. Arvinen-Barrow & N. Walker (Eds.), *Psychology of sport injury and rehabilitation* (pp. 134-155). Abingdon, UK: Routledge.

Kolt, G.S., Brewer, B.W., Pizzari, T., Schoo, A.M.M., & Garrett, N. (2007). The Sport Injury Rehabilitation Adherence Scale: A reliable scale for use in clinical physiotherapy. *Physiotherapy, 93*(1), 17-22. doi:10.1016/j.physio.2006.07.002

Kontos, A.P. (2004). Perceived risk, risk taking, estimation of ability and injury among adolescent sport participants. *Journal of Pediatric Psychology, 29*(6), 447-455. doi:10.1093/jpepsy/jsh048

Lane, A.M., & Lane, H.J. (2002). Predictive effectiveness of mood measures. *Perceptual and Motor Skills, 94*(3), 785-791. doi:10.2466/pms.2002.94.3.785

Lavallee, D., & Flint, F. (1996). The relationship of stress, competitive anxiety, mood state, and social support to athletic injury. *Journal of Athletic Training, 31*(4), 296-299.

Levy, A.R., Polman, R.C.J., & Clough, P.J. (2008). Adherence to sport injury rehabilitation programmes: An integrated psycho-social approach. *Scandanavian Journal of Medicine and Science in Sports, 18*(6), 798-809. doi:10.1111/j.1600-0838.2007.00704

McNair, D.M., Lorr, M., & Droppleman, L.F. (1971). *ETIS manual for the Profile of Mood States.* San Diego: Educational and Industrial Testing Services.

Meyers, M.C., Bourgeois, A.E., Stewart, S., & LeUnes, A. (1992). Predicting pain response in athletes: Development and assessment of the sports inventory for pain. *Journal of Sport & Exercise Psychology, 14*(3), 249-261. doi:10.1123/jsep.14.3.249

Miller, R.P., Kori, S.H., & Todd, D.D. (1991). The Tampa Scale: A measure of kinesiophobia. *Clinical Journal of Pain, 7*(1), 51-52. doi:10.1097/00002508-199103000-00053

Murphy, G.C., Foreman, P.E, Simpson, C.A., Molloy, G.N., & Molley, E.K. (1999). The development of a locus of control measure predictive of injured athletes' adherence to treatment. *Journal of Science and Medicine in Sport, 2*(2), 145-152. doi:10.1016/S1440-2440(99)80194-7

Nyland, J., Cottell, B., Harreld, K., & Caborn, N.M. (2013). Self-reported outcomes after anterior cruciate ligament reconstruction: An internal locus of control score comparison. *Arthrospcopy, 22*(11), 1225-1232. doi:/10.1016/j.arthro.2006.05.034

Pelletier, L., Rocchi, M., Vallerand, R.J., Deci, E.L., & Ryan, R.E. (2013). Validation of the revised Sport Motivation Scale (SMS-II). *Psychology of Sport & Exercise, 14*(3), 329-341. doi:10.1016/j.psychsport.2012.12.002

Podlog, L., & Eklund, R.C. (2005). Return to sport after serious injury: A retrospective examination of motivation and psychological outcomes. *Journal of Sport Rehabilitation, 14*(1), 20-34. doi:10.1123/jsr.14.1.20

Podlog, L., & Eklund, R.C. (2006). A longitudinal investigation of competitive athletes' return to sport following serious injury. *Journal of Applied Sport Psychology, 18*(1), 44-68. doi:10.1080/10413200500471319

Sarason, I.G., Sarason, B.R., Shearin, E.N., & Pierce, G.R. (1987). A brief measure of social support: Practical and theoretical implications. *Journal of Social and Personal Relationships, 4*(4), 497-510. doi:10.1177/0265407587044007

Smith, R.E., Schutz, R.W., Smoll, F.L., & Ptacek, J.T. (1995). Sport psychology development and validation of a multidimensional measure of sport-specific psychological skills: The Athletic Coping Skills Inventory-28. *Journal of Sport & Exercise Psychology, 17*(4), 379-398. doi:10.1123/jsep.17.4.379

Sordoni, C., Hall, C., & Forwell, L. (2002). The use of imagery in athletic injury rehabilitation and its relationship to self-efficacy. *Physiology Canada, 54,* 177-185.

Spielberger, C.D. (1983). *Manual for the State-Trait Anxiety Inventory (STAI).* Palo Alto, CA: Consulting Psychologist Press.

Spielberger, C.D. (1988). Stress and anxiety in sports. In D. Hackford & C. Spielberger (Eds.), *Anxiety in sport: An international perspective* (pp. 3-17). Washington, DC: Hemisphere/Harper & Row.

Spielberger, C.D. (1999). *State-Trait Anger Expression Inventory-2 (STAXI-2): Professional manual.* Tampa, FL: Psychological Assessment Resources.

Spielberger, C.D., Gorsuch, R.L., & Lushene, R. (1970). *STAI manual.* Palo Alto, CA: Consulting Psychologists Press

Taylor, A.H., & May, S. (1996). Threat and coping appraisal as determinants of compliance with sports injury rehabilitation: An application of protection motivation theory. *Journal of Sports Sciences, 14*(6), 471-482. doi:10.1080/02640419608727734

Taylor, J., & Taylor, S. (1997). *Psychological approaches to sports injury rehabilitation.* Gaithersburg, MD: Aspen.

Terry, P.C., Lane, A.M., Lane, H.J., & Keohane, L. (1999). Development and validation of a mood measure for adolescents. *Journal of Sports Sciences, 17*(11), 861-872. doi:10.1080/026404199365425

Thomeé, P., Währberg, P., Börjesson, M., Thomeé, R., Eriksson, B.I., & Karlsson, J. (2007). Self-efficacy, symptoms and physical activity in patients with an anterior cruciate injury: A prospective study. *Scandinavian Journal of Medicine & Science in Sports, 17*(3), 238-245. doi:10.1111/j.1600-0838.2006.00557.x

Udry, E., Gould, D., Bridges, D., & Tuffey, S. (1997). People helping people? Examining the social ties of athletes coping with burnout and injury stress. *Journal of Sport & Exercise Psychology, 19*(4), 368-395. doi:10.1123/jsep.19.4.368

Walker, N., Thatcher, J., & Lavallee, D. (2010). A preliminary development of the Re-Injury Anxiety Inventory (RIAI). *Physical Therapy in Sport, 11*(1), 23-29. doi:10.1016/j.ptsp.2009.09.003

Wallston, K.A., Stein, M.J., & Smith, C.A. (1994). Form C of the MHLC scales: A condition-specific measure of locus of control. *Journal of Personality Assessment, 63*(3), 534-553. doi:10.1207/s15327752jpa6303_10

Weiner, B. (1985). An attributional theory of achievement motivation and emotion. *Psychological Reviews, 92*(4), 548-573. doi:10.1037/0033-295X.92.4.548

Wiese-Bjornstal, D.M., Smith, A.M., Shaffer, S.M., & Morrey, M.A. (1998). An integrated model of response to sport injury: Psychological and sociological dynamics. *Journal of Applied Sport Psychology, 10*(1), 46-69. doi:10.1080/10413209808406377

Wong, I. (1998). *Injury rehabilitation behavior: An investigation of stages and processes of change in the athletic-therapist relationship.* (Unpublished master's thesis). University of Oregon, Eugene, OR.

Yang, J.Z., Shaefer, J.T., Zhang, N., Covassin, T., Ding, K., & Heiden, E. (2014). Social support from the athletic trainer and symptoms of depression and anxiety at return to play. *Journal of Athletic Training, 49*(6), 773-779. doi:10.4085/1062-6050-49.3.65

Chapter 14

Allen, L.M., Conder, R.L., Green, P., & Cox, D.R. (1997). *CARB 97 manual for the Computerized Assessment of Response Bias.* Durham, NC: CogniSyst.

Alsalaheen, B., Stockdale, K., Pechumer, D., & Broglio, S. (2015). Measurement error in the Immediate Postconcussion Assessment and Cognitive Testing (ImPACT): Systematic review. *Journal of Head Trauma Rehabilitation, 31,* 242-251.

Beck, A.T., Ward, C.H., Mendelson, M., Mock, J., & Erbaugh, J. (1961). An inventory for measuring depression. *Archives of General Psychiatry, 4,* 561-571.

Benedict, R.H., Schretlen, D., Groninger, L., Dobraski, M., & Shpritz, B. (1996). Revision of the Brief Visuospatial Memory Test: Studies of normal performance, reliability, and validity. *Psychological Assessment, 8*(2), 145.

Benton, A.L., Hamsher, S.K., & Sivan, A.B. (1983). *Multilingual aplasia examination* (2nd ed.). Iowa City, IA: AJA Associates.

Boone, K.B., Lu, P., & Hertzberg, D.S. (2002). *The Dot Counting Test manual.* Los Angeles: Western Psychological Services.

Brandt, J., & Benedict, R.H. (2001). *Hopkins Verbal Learning Test–Revised: Professional manual.* Baltimore: Psychological Assessment Resources.

Broglio, S.P., Cantu, R., Gioia, G., Guskiewicz, K.M., Kutcher, J., Palm, M., & McLeod, T.C. (2014). National Athletic Trainers' Association position statement: Management of sport concussion. *Journal of Athletic Training, 49*(2), 245-265.

Broshek, D.K., DeMarco, A.P., & Freeman, J.R. (2015). A review of post-concussion syndrome and psychological factors associated with concussion. *Brain Injury, 29*(2), 228-237.

Butcher, J.N., Dahlstrom, W.G., Graham, J.R., Tellegen, A., & Kaemmer, B. (1989). The Minnesota Multiphasic Personality Inventory-2 (MMPI-2): Manual for administration and scoring. Minneapolis: University of Minnesota Press.

Centers for Disease Control and Prevention (CDC). (2013). Injury prevention and control: Traumatic brain injury: Mild traumatic brain injury/concussion. Retrieved from www.cdc.gov/concussion/signs_symptoms.html.

Cogstate CCAT (2016). Manual for Cogstate Computerized Cognitive Assessment Tool. Melbourne, Australia: Cogstate.

Conder, A. (2013). *Academic accommodations for the concussed student athlete.* Paper presented at the Second Matthew Gfeller Sport-Related Neurotrauma Symposium, Chapel Hill, NC.

Conder, R., Allen, L., & Cox, D. (1992). *Manual for the computerized assessment of response bias.* Durham, NC: CogniSyst.

Conder, R., & Conder, A. (2014). Heart rate variability interventions for concussion and rehabilitation. *Frontiers in Psychology, 5,* 1-7.

Conder, R., & Conder, A. (2015a). Sports-related concussions. *North Carolina Medical Journal, 76,* 89-95.

Conder, R., & Conder, A. (2015b). Neuropsychological and psychological rehabilitation interventions in refractory sport-related post-concussive syndrome. *Brain Injury, 29*(2), 249-262.

Conder, R., Conder, A., Register-Mihalik, J., Conder, L., & Newton, S. (2015). Preliminary normative data on the Penn State University symbol cancellation task with nonconcussed adolescents. *Applied Neuropsychology: Child, 4*(3), 141-147.

Covassin, T., Crutcher, B., Bleecker, A., Heiden, E.O., Daily, A., & Yang, J.Z. (2014). Postinjury anxiety and social support among collegiate athletes: A comparison between orthopedic injuries and concussions. *Journal of Athletic Training, 49*(4), 462-468.

Cox, R.H., Martens, M.P., & Russell, W.D. (2003). Measuring anxiety in athletics: The Revised Competitive State Anxiety Inventory-2. *Journal of Sport & Exercise Psychology, 25,* 519-533.

Cullum, K.G., & Mayo, A.M. (2015). A review of the Child and Adolescent Social Support Scale for Healthy Behaviors. *Clinical Nurse Specialist, 29*(4), 198-202.

Echemendia, R.J., Giza, C.C., & Kutcher, J.S. (2015). Developing guidelines for return to play: Consensus and evidence-based approaches. *Brain Injury, 29*(2), 185-194.

Echemendia, R.J., Iverson, G.L., McCrea, M., Macciocchi, S.N., Gioia, G.A., Putukian, M., & Comper, P. (2013). Advances in neuropsychological assessment in sport-related concussion. *British Journal of Sports Medicine, 47,* 294-298.

D'Elia, L., & Satz, P. (1996). *Color Trails Test.* Baltimore: Psychological Assessment Resources

Echemendia, R.J., Putukian, M., Mackin, R.S., Julian, L., & Shoss, N. (2001). Neuropsychological test performance prior to and following sports related mild traumatic brain injury. *Clinical Journal of Sports Medicine, 11,* 23-31.

Gilchrist, J., Thomas, K.E., Xu, L., McGuire, L.C., & Coronado, V.G. (2011). Nonfatal sports and recreation related traumatic brain injuries among children and adolescents treated in emergency departments in the United States, 2001–2009. *Morbidity and Mortality Weekly Review, 60,* 1337-1342.

Guskiewicz, K.M. (2015). Sport-related concussions: Paranoia or legitimate concerns? *North Carolina Medical Journal, 76*(2), 93-94.

Halstead, M.E., McAvoy, K., Devorc, C.D., Carl, R., Lee, M., & Logan, K. (2013). Returning to learning following a concussion. *Pediatrics, 132*(5), 948-957.

Hamilton, M. (1960). A rating scale for depression. *Journal of Neurological Neurosurgical Psychiatry, 23,* 56-62. Henry, L.C., Elbin, R.J., Collins, M.W., Marchetti, G., & Kontos, A.P. (2015). Examining recovery trajectories after sport-related concussion with a multimodal clinical assessment approach. *Neurosurgery, 78*(2), 232-241.

ImPACT Applications. (2015). *Immediate Post-Concussion Assessment and Cognitive Testing (ImPACT).* Pittsburgh: ImPACT Applications. Retrieved from www.impacttest.com.

Iverson, G.L., Brooks, B.L., White, T., & Stern, R.A. (2008). Neuropsychological Assessment Battery (NAB): Introduction and advanced interpretation. In A.M. Horton Jr. & D. Wedding (Eds.), *The neuropsychology handbook* (pp. 279-343). New York: Springer.

Jenkinson, C., Layte, R., Jenkinson, D., Lawrence, K., Petersen, S., Paice, C., & Stradling, J. (1997). A shorter form health survey: Can the SF-12 replicate results from the SF-36 in longitudinal studies? *Journal of Public Health Medicine, 19*(2), 179-186.

Kontos, A.P., Covassin, T., Elbin, R.J., & Parker, T. (2012). Depression and neurocognitive performance after concussion among male and female high school and college athletes. *Archives of Physical Medicine and Rehabilitation, 93,* 1751-1756.

Lam, K.C., Valier, A.R., Bay, R.C., & McLeod, T.C. (2013). A unique patient population? Health-related quality of life in adolescent athletes versus general, health adolescent individuals. *Journal of Athletic Training, 48*(2), 233-241.

Leong, D.F., Balcer, L.J., Galetta, S.L, Evans, G., Gimre, M., & Watt, D. (2015). The King–Devick test for sideline concussion screening in collegiate football. *Journal of Optometry, 8*(2), 131-139.

Lovell, M.R. (2006). Neuropsychological assessment of the professional athlete. In R.J. Echemendia (Ed.), *Sports neuropsychology: Assessment and management of traumatic brain injury* (pp. 176-192). New York: Guilford.

Mainwaring, L.M., Hutchison, M., Bisschop, S.M., Comper, P., & Richards, D.W. (2010). Emotional response to sport concussion compared to ACL injury. *Brain Injury, 24*(4), 589-597.

McCrory, P., Meeuwisse, W., Aubry, M., Cantu, B., Dvorak, J., Echemendia, R.J., . . . Turner, M. (2013). Consensus statement on concussion in sport: The 4th International Conference on Concussion in Sport held in Zurich, November 2012. *Clinical Journal of Sport Medicine, 23*(2), 89-117.

McNair, D., Lorr, M., & Dropplemen, L. (1971). *Profile of Mood States.* San Diego: Educational and Industrial Testing Services.

Meehan, W., Mannix, R., Straccioloni, A., Elbin, R., & Collins, M. (2013). Symptom severity predicts prolonged recovery after sport-related concussion, but age and amnesia do not. *Journal of Pediatrics, 163*(3), 721-725. doi:10.1016/j.jpeds.2013.03.012

Millis, S. (2015). What clinicians really need to know about symptom exaggeration, insufficient effort and malingering: Statistical and measurement matters. In J.E. Morgan & J.J. Sweet (Eds.), *Neuropsychology of malingering casebook* (pp. 21-38). New York: Psychology Press.

National Collegiate Athletic Association (NCAA). (2014). Concussion: Return-to-learn guidelines. Retrieved from http://www.ncaa.org/sport-science-institute/concussion-diagnosis-and-management-best-practices.

Nelson, L.D., Janecek, J.K., & McCrea, M.A. (2013). Acute clinical recovery from sport-related concussion. *Neuropsychology Review, 23*(4), 285-299.

Nelson, L.D., LaRoche, A.A., Pfaller, A.Y., Lerner, E.B., Hammeke, T.A., Randolph, C., Barr, W.B., Guskiewicz, K., & McCrae, M. (2016). Prospective, head-to-head study of three computerized neurocognitive assessment tools (CNTs): Reliability and validity for the assessment of sport-related concussions. *Journal of the International Neuropsychological Society, 22,* 24-37.

Newlin, L., & Hooper, S.R. (2015). Return-to-school protocols following a concussion. *North Carolina Medical Journal, 76*(2), 107-108.

North Carolina State Board of Education (2016). *Return to learn after concussion: Implementation guide.* Retrieved from http://www.nchealthyschools.org/docs/legislation/stateboard/implementation-guide.pdf.

Ontario Neurotrauma Foundation. *Guidelines for mild traumatic brain injury and persistent symptoms.* Retrieved from http://onf.org/system/attachments/60/original/Guidelines_for_Mild_Traumatic_Brain_Injury_and_Persistent_Symptoms.pdf.

Pardini, D., Stump, J.E., Lovell, M.R., Collins, M.W., Moritz, K., & Fu, F.H. (2004). The Post-Concussion Symptom Scale (PCSS): A factor analysis. *British Journal of Sports Medicine, 38,* 661-662.

Radloff, L.S. (1991). The use of the Center for Epidemiologic Studies Depression Scale in adolescents and young adults. *Journal of Youth and Adolescence, 20*(2), 149-166.

Randolph, C. (2011). Baseline neuropsychological testing in managing sport-related concussion: Does it modify risk? *Current Sports Medicine Reports, 10*(1), 21-26.

Reznek, L.I. (2005). The Rey 15-item measure for malingering: A meta-analysis. *Brain Injury, 19*(7), 539-543.

Schneider, K.J., Iverson, G.I., Emery, C.A., McCrory, P., Herring, S.A., & Meeuwise, W.H. (2013). The effects of rest and treatment following sport-related concussion: A systematic review of the literature. *British Journal of Sports Medicine, 47*, 304-307.

Schretlen, D. (1989). *Brief Test of Attention.* Baltimore: Psychological Assessment Resources.

Schroeder, R.W., Twumasi-Ankrah, P, Baade, L.E., & Marshall, P. (2011). Reliable digit span: A systemic review and cross-validation study. *Assessment, 19*(1), 21-30.

Smith, A. (2002). *Symbol Digit Modalities Test.* Torrance, CA: Western Psychological Services.

Smith, R.E., Smoll, F.L., & Cumming, S.P. (2007). Effects of a motivational climate intervention for coaches on young athletes' sport performance anxiety. *Journal of Sport & Exercise Psychology, 29*, 39-59.

Smith, R.E., Smoll, F.L., Cumming, S.P., & Grossbard, J.R. (2006). Measurement of multidimensional sport performance anxiety in children and adults: The Sport Anxiety Scale-2. *Journal of Sport & Exercise Psychology, 28*, 479-501.

Spielberger, C.D. (1988). Stress and anxiety in sports. In D. Hackford & C.D. Spielberger, (Eds.), *Anxiety in sport: An international perspective* (pp. 3-17). Washington, DC: Hemisphere/Harper & Row.

Spielberger, C.D., Gorsuch, R.L., & Lushene, R. (1970). *STAI manual.* Palo Alto, CA: Consulting Psychologists Press.

Turner & Wooden v. National Football League & NFL Properties, No. 2 (LLC United States District Court of the Eastern District of Pennsylvania April, 2015).

Vargas, G., Rabinowitz, A., Meyer, J., & Arnett, P.A. (2015). Predictors and prevalence of postconcussion depression symptoms in collegiate athletes. *Journal of Athletic Training, 50*(3), 250-255.

Varni, J.W., & Limbers, C.A. (2009). The Pediatric Quality of Life Inventory: Measuring pediatric health-related quality of life from the perspective of children and their parents. *Pediatric Clinics, 56*(4), 843-863.

Ware, J.E., Snow, K.K., Kosinski, M., & Gandek, B. (1993). *SF-36 Health Survey manual and interpretation guide.* Boston: The Health Institute.

Wechsler, D. (2009). *Advanced clinical solutions for the WAIS-IV and WMS-IV.* San Antonio: Pearson.

Weiss, M.R., Kipp, L.E., & Bolter, N.D. (2012). Training for life: Optimizing positive youth development through sport and physical activity. In S.M. Murphy (Ed.), *The Oxford handbook of sport and performance psychology* (pp. 448-475). New York: Oxford.

Chapter 15

Alfermann, D., & Stambulova, N. (2007). Career transitions and career termination. In G. Tenenbaum & R.C. Eklund (Eds.), *Handbook of Sport Psychology* (3rd ed., pp. 712-736). New York: Wiley.

Betz, N.E., Klein, K.L., & Taylor, K.M. (1996). Evaluation of a short form of the Career Decision-Making Self-Efficacy Scale. *Journal of Career Assessment, 4*, 47–57.

Blann, F.W., & Zaichkowsky, L. (1989). *National Hockey League and Major League Baseball players' post-sport career transition surveys.* Final report prepared for the National Hockey League Players' Association, USA.

Bloom, B.S. (1985). *Developing talent in young people.* New York: Ballantine.

Brewer, B.W., & Cornelius, A.E. (2001). Norms and factorial invariance of the Athletic Identity Measurement Scale. Academic Athletic Journal, 16, 103–113.

Brewer, B.W., Van Raalte, J.L., & Linder, D.E. (1990). *Development and preliminary validation of the athletic identity measurement scale.* Paper presented at the North American Society of Sport and Physical Activity Conference, Houston, TX.

Brewer, B.W., Van Raalte, J.L., & Linder, D.E. (1993). Athletic identity: Hercules' muscles or Achilles heel? *International Journal of Sport Psychology, 24*, 237-254.

Briggs-Myers, I., & Briggs, K.C. (1985). *Myers-Briggs Type Indicator (MBTI).* Palo Alto, CA: Consulting Psychologists Press.

Burke, P.J. (1991). Identity processes and social stress. *American Sociological Review, 56*, 836-849.

Campbell, D.P. (1995). The Campbell Interest and Skill Survey (CISS): A product of ninety years of psychometric evolution. *Journal of Career Assessment, 3*, 391-410.

Carver, C.S. (1997). You want to measure coping but your protocol's too long: Consider the Brief COPE. *International Journal of Behavioral Medicine, 4*, 92-100.

Carver, C.S., Scheier, M.F., & Weintraub, J.K. (1989). Assessing coping strategies: A theoretically based approach. *Journal of Personality and Social Psychology, 56*, 267-283.

Cieslak, T. (2004). *Describing and measuring the athletic identity construct: Scale development and validation.* (Unpublished doctoral dissertation). Ohio State University, Columbus, OH.

Clifton, D.O., & Anderson, E. (2001). *StrengthsQuest: Discover and develop your strengths in academics, career, and beyond.* Washington, DC: Gallup Organization.

Cosh, S., Crabb, S., & LeCouteur, A. (2013). Elite athletes and retirement: Identity, choice and agency. *Australian Journal of Psychology, 65*, 89-97.

Côté, J. (1999). The influence of the family in the development of talent in sports. *The Sport Psychologist, 13*, 395-417.

Crites, J.O. (1978). *Administration and use manual for the career maturity inventory* (2nd ed.). Monterey, CA: McGraw-Hill.

Curry, T.J., & Weaner, J.S. (1987). Sport identity salience, commitment, and the involvement of self in role: Measurement issues. *Sociology of Sport Journal, 4*, 280-288.

Durand-Bush, N., & Salmela, J.H. (2002). The development and maintenance of expert athletic performance: Perceptions of world and Olympic champions. *Journal of Applied Sport Psychology, 14*, 154-171.

Fernandez, A., Stephan, Y., & Fouquereau, E. (2006). Assessing reasons for sport career termination: Development of Athletes Retirement Decision Inventory (ARDI). *Psychology of Sport and Exercise, 7*, 407-421.

Folkman, S., & Lazarus, R.S. (1988). *Manual for the Ways of Coping Questionnaire*. Palo Alto, CA: Consulting Psychologists Press.

Freeman, P., Coffee, P., & Rees, T. (2011). The PASS-Q: The Perceived Available Support in Sport Questionnaire. *Journal of Sport & Exercise Psychology, 33*, 54-74.

Grove, J.R., Lavallee, D., & Gordon, S. (1997). Coping with retirement from sport: The influence of athletic identity. *Journal of Applied Sport Psychology, 9*(2), 191-203.

Gysbers, N.C., & Moore, E.J. (1975). Beyond career development—Life career development. *Personal and Guidance Journal, 53*, 647-652.

Heppner, M.J. (1998). The Career Transitions Inventory measuring internal resources in adulthood. *Journal of Career Assessment, 6*, 135-145.

Holland, J.L. (1985). *Making vocational choices: A theory of vocational personalities and work environments*. Englewood Cliffs, NJ: Prentice Hall.

Holland, J.L. (1997). *Making vocational choices: A theory of vocational personalities and work environments* (3rd ed.). Odessa, FL: Psychological Assessment Resources.

Holland, J.L., Daiger, D.C., & Power, P.G. (1980). *My Vocational Situation*. Palo Alto, CA: Consulting Psychologists Press.

House, J.S. (1981). *Work stress and social support*. Reading, MA: Addison-Wesley.

Jones, R.A., Mahoney, J.W., & Gucciardi, D.F. (2014). On the transition into elite rugby league: Perceptions of players and coaching staff. *Sport, Exercise and Performance Psychology, 3*, 28-45.

Kowalski, K.C., & Crocker, P.R.E. (2001). Development and validation of the Coping Function Questionnaire for adolescents in sport. *Journal of Sport and Exercise Psychology, 23*, 136-155.

Krumboltz, J.D. (2009). The happenstance learning theory. *Journal of Career Assessment, 17*, 135-154.

Krumboltz, J.D., & Vosvick, M.A. (1996). Career assessment and the career beliefs inventor. *Journal of Career Assessment, 4*, 345-361.

Lavallee, D., & Wylleman, P. (1999). Toward an instrument to assess the quality of adjustment to career transitions in sport: The British Athlete Lifestyle Assessment Needs in Career and Education (BALANCE) Scale. In V. Hosek, P. Tilinger, & L. Bilek (Eds.), *Psychology of sport and exercise: Enhancing the quality of life: Proceedings of the 10th European Congress of Sport Psychology, Prague: Charles University* (pp. 322-324). Prague: The 10th European Congress of Sport Psychology.

Lent, R.W., & Brown, S.D., (2013). Social cognitive model of career self-management: Toward a unifying view of adaptive career behavior across the life span. *Journal of Counseling Psychology, 60*, 557-568.

Lent, R.W., Brown, S.D., & Hackett, G. (1994). Toward a unifying social cognitive theory of career and academic interest, choice, and performance. *Journal of Vocational Behavior, 45*, 79-122.

Markus, H., & Nurius, P. (1986). Possible selves. *American Psychologist, 41*, 954-969.

McAuley, E., Duncan, T., & Russell, D. (1992). Measuring causal attributions: The revised Causal Dimension Scale (CDSII). *Personality and Social Psychology Bulletin, 18*, 566-573.

McKnight, K., Bernes, K., Gunn, T., Chorney, D., Orr, D. & Bardick, A. (2009). Life After Sport: Athletic career transition and transferable skills. Journal of Excellence, 13, 63-77.

Nasco, S.A., & Webb. W.M. (2006). Towards an expanded measure of athletic identity: The inclusion of public and private dimensions. *Journal of Sport and Exercise Psychology, 28*, 434-453.

National Center for O*NET Development. (n.d.). *My Next Move: Interest Profiler*. Retrieved from www.mynextmove.org.

National Center for O*NET Development. (n.d.). *Work Importance Profiler (WIP)*. O*NET Resource Center. Retrieved from www.onetcenter.org/WIP.html.

Nicholls, A.R. (2010). Effective versus ineffective coping in sport. In A.R. Nicholls (Ed.), *Coping in sport: Theory, methods, and related constructs* (pp. 263-276). Hauppauge, NY: Nova Science.

Nideffer, R.M., & Sagal, M.S. (2001). *Assessment in sport psychology*. Morgantown, WV: Fitness Information Technology.

Peterson, C., & Seligman, M.E.P. (2004). *Character strengths and virtues: A handbook and classification*. New York and Washington, DC: Oxford University Press and American Psychological Association.

Petitpas, A., Champagne, D., Chartrand, J., Danish, S., & Murphy, S. (1997). *Athlete's guide to career planning: Keys to success from the playing field to professional life.* Champaign, IL: Human Kinetics.

Pittenger, D.J. (1993). Measuring the MBTI . . . and coming up short. *Journal of Career Planning and Employment, 54,* 48-53.

Quenk, N.L., Hammer, A.L., & Majors, M.S. (2001). *MBTI Step II manual: Exploring the next level of type with the Myers-Briggs Type Indicator Form Q.* Palo Alto, CA: Consulting Psychologists Press.

Roberts, C.-M., Mullen, R., Evans, L., & Hall, R.J. (2015). An in-depth appraisal of career termination experiences in elite cricket. *Journal of Sport Science, 33,* 935-944. doi:10.1080/02640414.2014.977936

Salmela, J.H. (1994). Stages and transitions across sports careers. In D. Hackfort (Ed.), *Psycho-social issues and interventions in elite sports* (pp. 11-28). Frankfurt am Main: Lang.

Savickas, M.L., & Porfeli, E.J. (2012). Career adapt-abilities scale: Construction, reliability, and measurement equivalence across 13 countries. *Journal of Vocational Behavior, 80,* 661-673. http://dx.doi.org/10.1016/j.jvb.2012.01.011

Schlossberg, N.K. (1981). A model for analyzing human adaptation to transition. *The Counseling Psychologist, 9,* 2-18. doi:10.1177/001100008100900202

Schwarzer, R., & Schwarzer, C. (1996). A critical survey of coping instruments. In M. Zeidner & N.S. Endler (Eds.), *Handbook of coping* (pp. 107-132). New York: Wiley.

Sinclair, D.A., & Orlick, T. (1993). Positive transitions from high-performance sport. *The Sport Psychologist, 7,* 138-150.

Stambulova, N. (1994). Developmental sports career investigations in Russia: A post-Perestroika analysis. *The Sport Psychologist, 8,* 221-237.

Stambulova, N. (2003). Symptoms of a crisis-transition: A grounded theory study. In N. Hassmén (Ed.), *SIPF Yearbook 2003* (pp. 97-109). Örebro, Sweden: Örebro University Press.

Stambulova, N. (2012). Assistance in career transitions. In S. Hanton & S.D. Mellalieu (Eds.), *Professional practice in sport psychology: A review* (pp. 165-194). Oxford, UK: Routledge.

Stambulova, N. (2014). Career transitions. In R. Eklund & G. Tenenbaum (Eds.), *Encyclopaedia of sport and exercise psychology* (Vol. 3, pp. 111-116). Thousand Oaks, CA: Sage. http://dx.doi.org/10.4135/9781483332222.n44

Stambulova, N., Alfermann, D., Statler, T., & Côté, J. (2009). ISSP position stand: Career development and transitions of athletes. *International Journal of Sport and Exercise Psychology, 7,* 395-412.

Stambulova, N.B., & Ryba, T.V. (2013). Setting the bar: Towards cultural praxis of athletes' careers. In N. Stambulova & T.V. Ryba (Eds.), *Athletes' careers across cultures* (pp. 235-254). London: Routledge.

Stryker, S. (1980). *Symbolic interactionism: A social structural version.* Menlo Park, CA: Benjamin/Cummings.

Taylor, J., & Ogilvie, B.C. (1994). A conceptual model of adaptation to retirement among athletes. *Journal of Applied Sport Psychology, 6,* 1-20.

Taylor, K.M., & Betz, N.E. (1983). Applications of self-efficacy theory to the understanding and treatment of career indecision. *Journal of Vocational Behavior, 22,* 63-81.

Wethington, E., & Kessler, R. (1986). Perceived support, received support and adjustment to stressful life events. *Journal of Health and Social Behavior, 27,* 78-89.

Wylleman, P., De Knop, P., Vanden Auweele, Y., Sloore, H., & De Martelaer, K. (1996). Sport Interpersonal Relationships Questionnaires (SIRQ). In A. Ostrow (Ed.), *Directory of psychological tests in the sport and exercise sciences* (pp. 162-164). Morgantown, WV: Fitness Information Technology.

Wylleman, P., & Lavallee, D. (2004). A developmental perspective on transitions faced by athletes. In M. Weiss (Ed.), *Developmental sport and exercise psychology: A lifespan perspective* (pp. 507-527). Morgantown, WV: Fitness Information Technology.

Wylleman, P., Lavallee, D., & Alfermann, D. (Eds.). (1999). *FEPSAC Monograph Series. Career transitions in competitive sports.* Lund, Sweden: European Federation of Sport Psychology FEPSAC.

Wylleman, P., Reints, A., & De Knop, P. (2013). Athletes' careers in Belgium. A holistic perspective to understand and alleviate challenges occurring throughout the athletic and post- athletic career. In N. Stambulova & T. Ryba (Eds.), *Careers across cultures* (pp. 31-42). London: Routledge.

Wylleman, P., Vanden Auweele, Y., De Knop, P., Sloore, H., & De Martelaer, K. (1995). Elite young athletes, parents and coaches: relationships in competitive sports. In F.J. Ring (Ed.), *The 1st Bath Sports Medicine Conference* (pp. 124-133). Bath, UK: Centre for Continuing Education and contributors.

Chapter 16

American Educational Research Association (AERA), American Psychological Association (APA), National Council on Measurement in Education (NCME), & Joint Committee on Standards for Educational and Psychological Testing (JCSEPT). (2014). *Standards for educational and psychological testing.* Washington, DC: Authors.

Boehm-Davis, D., Durso, F., and Lee, J.D. (Eds.). (2014). *APA handbook of human services integration.* Washington, DC: American Psychological Association.

Groth-Marnat, G. (2009). *Handbook of psychological assessment* (5th ed.). Hoboken, NJ: Wiley.

Hoymand, P.S., & Gillespie, P. (2010). Implementation of evidence-based practice and organizational performance. *Journal of Behavioral Health Services Research*, 37(1), 79-94.

Kaufman, R. (2000). *Mega planning: Practical tools for organizational success.* Thousand Oaks, CA: Sage.

Kilbourne, A.M., Neumann, M., Pincus, H.A., Bauer, M.S., and Stall, R. (2007). Implementing evidence-based interventions in health care: Applications of the replicating effective programs framework. *Implementation Science*, 2(1), 22-42.

Maher, C.A. (2012). *Planning and evaluating human services programs: A resource guide for practitioners.* Bloomington, IN: Authorhouse.

Mertens, D.M. (2005). *Research and evaluation in education and psychology* (2nd ed.). Thousand Oaks, CA: Sage.

Miller, G.A. (1978). *Living systems.* New York: Macmillan.

Salmon, P.M., Stanton, N.A., Gibbon, A.C., Jenkins, D.P., & Walker, G.H. (2012). *Human factors methods and sport sciences: A practical guide.* Boca Raton, FL: CRC Press.

Tennenbaum, G.T. Eklund, R.C., & Kamata, A. (Eds.). (2012). *Measurement and evacuation in sport and exercise psychology.* Champaign, IL: Human Kinetics.

Weiner, B.J., (2009). A theory of organizational readiness for change. *Implementation Science*, 4(1), 44-67.

Wright, A.J. (2010). *Conducting psychological assessment: A guide for practitioners.* Hoboken, NJ: Wiley.

Chapter 17

Andersen, M.B., 2000. Beginnings: Intakes and the initiation of relationships. In M.B. Andersen (Ed.), *Doing sport psychology* (pp. 3-16). Champaign, IL: Human Kinetics.

Anderson, A.G., Knowles, Z., & Gilbourne, D. (2004). Reflective practice for sport psychologists: Concepts, models, practical implications, and thoughts on dissemination. *Sport Psychologist*, 18(2), 188-203. doi.org: 10.1123/tsp.18.2.188

Anderson, A.G., Miles, A., Mahoney, C., & Robinson, P. (2002). Evaluating the effectiveness of applied sport psychology practice: Making the case for a case study approach. *The Sport Psychologist*, 16(4), 432-453. doi:10.1016/S1469-0292(03)00005-0

Anderson, A., Miles, A., Robinson, P., & Mahoney, C. (2004). Evaluating the athlete's perception of the sport psychologist's effectiveness: What should we be assessing? *Psychology of Sport and Exercise*, 5(3), 255-277. doi.org: 10.1016/s1469-0292(03)00005-0

Costa, A.L., & Kallick, B. (2008). Learning through reflection. In A.L. Costa & B. Kallick (Eds.), *Learning and leading with habits of the mind: 16 essential characteristics for success* (pp. 221-235). Alexandria, VA: Association for Supervision and Curriculum Development (ASCD).

Cropley, B., & Hanton, S. (2011). The role of reflective practice in applied sport psychology: Contemporary issues for professional practice. In S. Hanton & S.D. Mellalieu (Eds.), *Professional practice in sport psychology: A review* (pp. 307-336). London: Routledge.

Cropley, B., Hanton, S., Miles, A., & Niven, A. (2002). The value of reflective practice in professional development: An applied sport psychology review. *Sport Science Review*, 19(3-4), 179-208. doi:10.2478/v10237-011-0025-8

Cropley, B., Miles, A., Hanton, S., & Anderson, A. (2007). Improving the delivery of applied sport psychology support through reflective practice. *The Sport Psychologist*, 21(4), 475-494. doi: 10.1123/tsp.21.4.475

Dunn, J.H., & Holt, N.L. (2003). Collegiate ice hockey players' perceptions of the delivery of an applied sport psychology program. *Sport Psychologist*, 17(3), 351-368. doi: 10.1123/tsp.17.3.351

Fukkink, R.G., Trienekens, N., & Kramer, L.J. (2011). Video feedback in education and training: Putting learning in the picture. *Educational Psychology Review*, 23(1), 45-63. doi:10.1007/s10648-010-9144-5

Gibbs, G. (1988). *Learning by doing: A guide to teaching and learning methods.* Oxford, UK: Oxford Brookes University, Further Education Unit.

Goldman, R., Pea, R., Barron, B., & Derry, S.J. (2014). *Video research in the learning sciences.* New York: Routledge.

Gould, D., Murphy, S., Tammen, V., & May, J. (1991). An evaluation of U.S. Olympic consultant effectiveness. *The Sport Psychologist*, 5(2), 111-127. doi: 10.1123/tsp.5.2.111

Grove, J.R., Norton, P.J., Van Raalte, J.L., & Brewer, B.W. (1999). Stages of change as an outcome measure in the evaluation of mental skills training programs. *The Sport Psychologist*, 13(1), 107-116.

Haberl, P., & McCann, S. (2012). Evaluating USOC consultant effectiveness: A philosophical and practical imperative at the Olympic Games. *Journal of Sport Psychology in Action*, 3(2), 65-76. doi:10.1080/21520704.2012.683095

Halliwell, W. (1990). Providing sport psychology consulting services in professional hockey. *The Sport Psychologist*, 4(4), 369-377.

Hankes, D.M. (1996). *Applied sport psychology consultation: Effects of academic training, past athletics experience, and interpersonal skill on female athletes' ratings.* (Unpublished doctoral dissertation). University of North Texas, Denton, TX.

Knowles, Z., Gilbourne, D., Tomlinson, V., & Anderson, A.G. (2007). Reflections on the application of reflective practice for supervision in applied sport psychology. *Sport Psychologist*, 21(1), 109. doi: 10.1123/tsp.21.1.109

Kolb, D.A. (1984). *Experiential learning: Experience as the source of learning and development.* Englewood Cliffs, NJ: Prentice-Hall.

Lubker, J.R., Visek, A.J., Watson, J.C., & Singpurwalla, D. (2012). Athletes' preferred characteristics and qualifications of sport psychology practitioners: A consumer market analysis. *Journal of Applied Sport Psychology, 24*(4), 465-480. doi:10.1080/10413200.2012.694968

Martindale, A., & Collins, D. (2007). Enhancing the evaluation of effectiveness with professional judgment and decision making. *Sport Psychologist, 21*(4), 458-474. doi: 10.1123/tsp.21.4.458

McNair, D.M., Lorr, M., & Droppleman, L.F. (1971). Profile of Mood States. San Diego: Educational and Industrial Testing Service.

Mugford, A., Hesse, D., & Morgan, T. (2014). Developing the total consultant. In J.G. Cremedes & L. Tashman (Eds.), *Becoming a sport, exercise, and performance psychology professional: A global perspective* (pp. 268-275). New York: Psychology Press.

Orlick, T., & Partington, J. (1987a). The consultant: Analysis of critical components as viewed by Canadian Olympic athletes. *The Sport Psychologist, 1*(1), 4-17. doi: 10.1123/tsp.1.1.4

Orlick, T, & Partington, J. (1987b). The consultant: Olympic coaches' views. *The Sport Psychologist, 1*(2), 95-102.

Parker, R.M., & Thomas, K.R. (1980). Fads, flaws, fallacies, and foolishness in the evaluation of rehabilitation programs. *Journal of Rehabilitation, 46*, 32-34. doi: 10.1142/9789812708434

Partington, J., & Orlick, T. (1987). The consultant evaluation form. *The Sport Psychologist, 1*(4), 309-317. doi: 10.1123/tsp.1.4.309

Rowell, S. (1998). Sport science education program report. In *Final report 1988-1998: Sport science support programmes* (pp. 3-5). Leeds, UK: Sports Council/The National Coaching Foundation.

Schön, D.A. (1983). *The reflective practitioner.* New York: Basic Books.

Sharpe, L., & Hodge, K. (2011). Sport psychology consulting effectiveness: The consultant's perspective. *Journal of Applied Sport Psychology, 23*, 360-376. doi:10.1080/10413200.2011.583619

Smith, R.E. (1989). Applied sport psychology in an age of accountability. *Journal of Applied Sport Psychology, 1*(2), 166-180. doi:10.1080/10413208908406413

Smith, R.E., Schutz, R.W., Smoll, F.L., & Ptacek, J.T. (1995). Development and validation of a multidimensional measure of sport-specific psychological skills: The Athletic Coping Skills Inventory-28. *Journal of Sport and Exercise Psychology, 17*(4), 379-398. doi: 10.1123/jsep.17.4.379

Strean, W. (1998). Possibilities for qualitative research in sport psychology. *The Sport Psychologist, 12*(3), 333-345. doi: 10.1123/tsp.12.3.333

Thomas, P.R., Murphy, S.M., & Hardy, L. (1999). Test of performance strategies: Development and preliminary validation of a comprehensive measure of athletes' psychological skills. *Journal of sports sciences, 17*(9), 697-711. doi:10.1080/026404199365560

Woodcock, C., Richards, H., & Mugford, A. (2008). Quality counts: Critical features for neophyte professional development. *The Sport Psychologist, 22*(4), 491-506. doi: 10.1123/tsp.22.4.491

ADDITIONAL RESOURCES

Chapter 2

McCann, S.C., Jowdy, D.P., & Van Raalte, J.L. (2002). Assessment in sport and exercise psychology. In J.L. Van Raalt & B.W. Brewer (Eds.), *Exploring sport and exercise psychology* (2nd ed., pp. 291-305). Washington, DC: American Psychological Association.

Ostrow, A. (Ed.). (2002). *Directory of psychological test in the sport and exercise sciences* (2nd ed.). Morgantown, WV: Fitness Information Technology.

Razon, S., & Tenenbaum, G. (2014). Measurement in sport and exercise psychology. In J.L. Van Raalte & B.W. Brewer (Eds.), *Exploring sport and exercise psychology* (3rd ed., pp. 279-309). Washington, DC: American Psychological Association.

Smith, R.E., & Smoll, F.L. (2005). Assessing psychosocial outcomes in coach training programs. In D. Hackfort, J.L. Duda, & R. Lidor (Eds.), *Handbook of research in applied sport and exercise psychology: International perspective* (pp. 293-316). Morgantown, WV: Fitness Information Technology.

Chapter 4

Books

Allison, L. (2005). *The global politics of sport: The role of global institutions in sport.*

New York: Psychology Press.

Cunningham, G.B. (2015). *Diversity & inclusion in sport organizations* (3rd ed.). Scottsdale, AZ: Holcomb Hathaway.

Helmeke, K.B., & Sori, C.F. (Eds.). (2006). *The therapist's notebook for integrating spirituality in counseling: Homework, handouts, and activities for use in psychotherapy.* New York: Routledge.

Miller, T., Lawrence, G.A., McKay, J., & Rowe, D. (2001). *Globalization and sport: Playing the world.* London: Sage.

Parry, J., Robinson, S., Watson, N.J., & Nesti, M. (2007). *Sport and spirituality: An introduction.* New York: Routledge.

Roper, E.A. (2013). *Gender relations in sport.* Rotterdam, The Netherlands: Sense.

Sugden, J.P., & Tomlinson, A. (2002). *Power games: A critical sociology of sport.* New York: Psychology Press.

Electronic Resources

Women in Sport and Physical Activity Journal: http://journals.humankinetics.com/wspaj

Organizations

Women's Sports Foundation: www.womenssports foundation.org

Tucker Center for Research on Girls and Women in Sport: www.tuckercenter.org

Websites

International Classification of Functioning, Disability and Health (ICF) illustration library: www.icfillustration.com/icfil_eng/

Neumann University Institute for Sport, Spirituality and Character Development (ISSCD): http://isscd.org

The Spiritual Life of College Students: A National Study of College Students' Search for Meaning and Purpose: http://spirituality.ucla.edu

The Institute for Diversity and Ethics in Sport (TIDES): www.tidesport.org

World Health Organization (WHO) ICF application and training tools: www.who.int/classifications/icf/icfapptraining/en/

Chapter 5

Anxiety

Anxiety and Depression Association of America: www.adaa.org

Teens Health: http://kidshealth.org/teen/school_jobs/school/test_anxiety.html

Attention-Deficit/Hyperactivity Disorder (ADHD)

Children and Adults with Attention-Deficit/Hyperactivity Disorder (CHADD): www.chadd.org

Depression and Suicide

American Foundation for Suicide Prevention: www.afsp.org

Anxiety and Depression Association of America: www.adaa.org

National Suicide Prevention Hotline: 1-800-273-TALK

National Suicide Prevention Lifeline Crisis Chat: http://suicidepreventionlifeline.org/GetHelp/LifelineChat.aspx

The Trevor Lifeline (Suicide Prevention for LGBTQ Youth): 1-866-4-U-TREVOR

Eating Disorders

Academy for Eating Disorders: www.aedweb.org

Eating Disorders Special Interest Group (SIG), Association for Applied Sport Psychology (AASP): www .appliedsportpsych.org/about/special-interest-groups/ eating-disorders/

International Association of Eating Disorder Professionals (IAEDP) Foundation: www.iaedp.com

National Eating Disorders Association (NEDA): www .nationaleatingdisorders.org and 1-800-931-2237 (confidential helpline)

General Mental Health

Active Minds: www.activeminds.org

American Psychological Association (APA): www.apa .org/topics/index.aspx

National Institute of Mental Health (NIMH): www .nimh.nih.gov

U.S. Department of Health and Human Services (HHS): www.mentalhealth.gov

Mental Health in Athletes

Athletes Connected, University of Michigan: http:// athletesconnected.umich.edu

International Society for Sport Psychiatry (ISSP): http:// sportspsychiatry.org

NCAA Sport Science Institute: www.ncaa.org/health-and-safety/medical-conditions/mental-health

Play Like a Champion (ADHD): https://www.play likeachampion.org/exceptionalities

Student-Athlete Mental Health Initiative: www.samhi.ca

Support for Sport: www.supportforsport.org/index-mental-health.html

Stress

American Institute of Stress: www.stress.org

Substance Use

Alcohol and Drug Abuse Hotline: 1-800-729-6686

American Public Health Association and Education Development Center, Inc. (2008). *Alcohol screening and brief intervention: A guide for public health practitioners.* Washington DC: National Highway Traffic Safety Administration, U.S. Department of Transportation.

Babor, T.F., Higgins-Biddle, J.C., Saunders, J.B., & Monteiro, M.G. (2001). *The Alcohol Use Disorders Identification Test: Guidelines for use in primary care* (2nd Ed.). World Health Organization. Retrieved from http://www.talkingalcohol.com/files/pdfs/ WHO_audit.pdf

National Institute on Alcohol and Alcoholism (NIAA): http://pubs.niaaa.nih.gov/publications/practitioner/ cliniciansguide2005/guide.pdf

National Institute on Drug Abuse (NIDA): www.drug abuse.gov

Quinn-Zobeck, A. (March, 2007). *Screening and brief intervention tool kit for college and university campuses.* National Highway Traffic Safety Administration. Retrieved from http://www.integration.samhsa. gov/clinical-practice/sbirt/NHTSA_SBIRT_for_ Colleges_and_Universities.pdf

Substance Use and Mental Health Services Administration (SAMHSA): www.samhsa.gov/disorders/substance-use

INDEX

Note: The italicized *f* and *t* following page numbers refer to figures and tables, respectively.

ABOUT THE EDITOR

Jim Taylor, PhD, CC-AASP, is an internationally recognized consultant and presenter on the psychology of sport and parenting. He has served as a consultant for the U.S. and Japanese ski teams, the United States Tennis Association, and USA Triathlon. He has worked with professional and world-class athletes in tennis, skiing, cycling, triathlon, track and field, swimming, golf, and many other sports. He has been invited to lecture by the Olympic Committees of Spain, France, Poland, and the United States, and he has been a consultant to the athletic departments at Stanford University and the University of California, Berkeley. Taylor has authored or edited 18 books, published more than 800 articles, and given more than 1,000 workshops and presentations throughout North and South America, Europe, and the Middle East.

Courtesy of Kane Minkus.

A former world-ranked alpine ski racer, Taylor is a second-degree black belt and certified instructor in karate, a marathon runner, and an Ironman triathlete. He earned his PhD in psychology from the University of Colorado. He is a former associate professor in the school of psychology at Nova University and a former clinical associate professor in the sport and performance psychology graduate program at the University of Denver. Taylor is currently an adjunct faculty member at the University of San Francisco.

CONTRIBUTORS

Monna Arvinen-Barrow, PhD, CPsychol AFBPsS, UPV Sert.
University of Wisconsin-Milwaukee

Angel L. Brutus, PsyD, LPC, CRC, DCC
Private Practice

Pierre Beauchamp, PhD, CC-CSPA
MindroomPSP

Graig M. Chow, PhD
Florida State University

Alanna Adler Conder, PsyD
Carolina Neuropsychological Service

Robert Conder, PsyD, ABPP
Carolina Neuropsychological Service

Ian Connole, PhD, CC-AASP
Kansas State University Athletics

Marisa O. Davis, MEd
University of Missouri

J.D. DeFreese, PhD
University of North Carolina at Chapel Hill

Travis Dorsch, PhD
Utah State University

Teresa B. Fletcher, PhD, LPC
Adler University

Latisha Forster Scott, PhD
Rutgers University

Andy Gillham, PhD, CC-AASP, CSCS
Ludus Consulting, LLC

Todd A. Gilson, PhD
Northern Illinois University

Stacy L. Gnacinski, PhD
Drake University

Stephen P. Gonzalez, PhD, CC-AASP
The College at Brockport, State University of New York

Jordan Hamson-Utley, PhD, LAT, ATC
University of St. Augustine

Erin N. J. Haugen, PhD, LP, CC-AASP
Assessment and Therapy Associates of Grand Forks, PLLC

Tim Herzog, EdD, CC-AASP
Reaching Ahead, LLC

Tim Holder, PhD
University of Central Lancashire

Melissa Hunfalvay, PhD, CC-AASP
RightEye, LLC.

Anita N. Lee, DPE
Eastern Connecticut State University

M. Penny Levin, PhD
Aeropsych and Temple University

Charles A. Maher, PsyD, CC-AASP
Rutgers University and Cleveland Indians

Claire-Marie Roberts, PhD
University of Worcester, UK

Barbara B. Meyer, PhD, CC-AASP
University of Wisconsin-Milwaukee

Marshall L. Mintz, PsyD
Springfield Psychological Associates, LLP

Angus Mugford, PhD, CC-AASP
The Toronto Blue Jays, Major League Baseball

Kwok Ng, PhD
University of Jyväskylä

Brandon Orr, PhD
University of Missouri

Megan E. Pietrucha, PsyD
The Chicago School of Professional Psychology

Steve Portenga

Melanie Poudevigne, PhD, FACSM, CC-AASP
Clayton State University

Duncan Simpson, PhD
Barry University

Sheryl Smith, PhD, BCB, CC-AASP
Clinical & Sport Psychology

James G. Tabano, EdD
The George Washington University

Jenni Thome, PhD
Illinois State University

Taunya Marie Tinsley, PhD
Waynesburg University

Barbara J. Walker, PhD, CC-AASP
Center for Human Performance

Stacy Winter, DProf
St. Mary's University

Jenny Lind Withycombe, PhD, CC-AASP
Withycombe Consulting

Michael D. Zito, PhD
Morristown Clinical and Sport Psychology

Assessment in applied sport
psychology